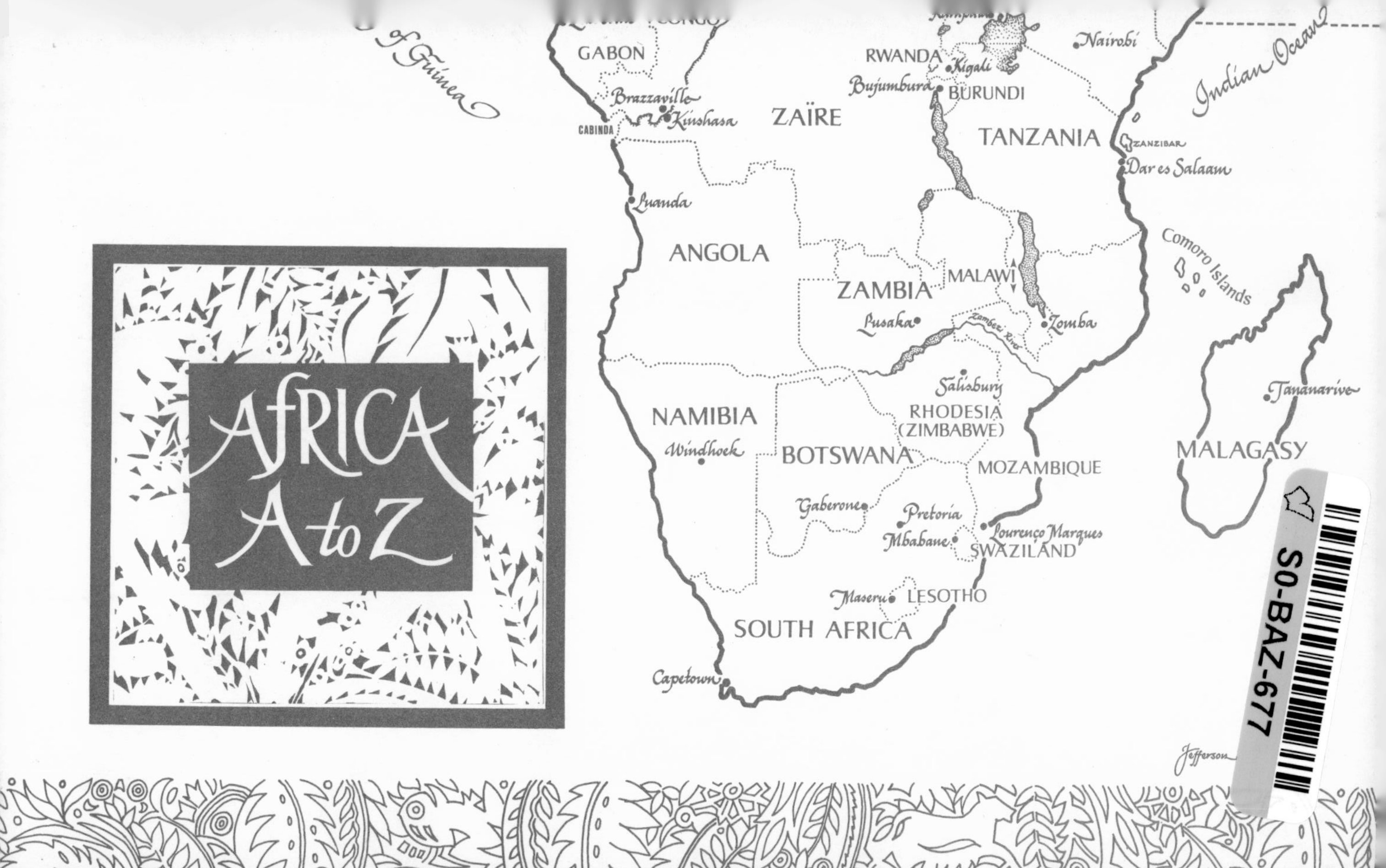
AfRICA
A to Z
of Guinea
GABON
Brazzaville
Kinshasa
CABINDA
Luanda
ZAÏRE
ANGOLA
RWANDA
Kigali
Bujumbura
BURUNDI
TANZANIA
Nairobi
ZANZIBAR
Dar es Salaam
Indian Ocean
Comoro Islands
ZAMBIA
Lusaka
MALAWI
Zomba
Zambezi River
Salisbury
RHODESIA
(ZIMBABWE)
NAMIBIA
Windhoek
BOTSWANA
Gaberone
Pretoria
Mbabane
SWAZILAND
Lourenço Marques
MOZAMBIQUE
Tananarive
MALAGASY
Maseru
LESOTHO
SOUTH AFRICA
Capetown
Jefferson

Books by Robert S. Kane

AFRICA A TO Z

SOUTH AMERICA A TO Z

ASIA A TO Z

CANADA A TO Z

SOUTH PACIFIC A TO Z

EASTERN EUROPE A TO Z

AFRICA A to Z

AFRICA A to Z

Revised Edition

ROBERT S. KANE

Doubleday & Company, Inc., Garden City, New York

Endpaper map by Louise E. Jefferson

ISBN: 0-385-02679-x
LIBRARY OF CONGRESS CATALOG CARD NUMBER 75–175386

PRINTED IN THE UNITED STATES OF AMERICA

For Clara Claasen

CONTENTS

INTRODUCTION

Africa is no more a conventional continent today than it was when the first edition of this book was published in the early sixties—when the continent of colonies was largely transforming itself into a continent of independent states. The Africa of the seventies is prouder and more secure to be sure, but no more conventional a segment of the planet than it has ever been.

And this new edition of this book is no more conventional than the original. Negative opinions are expressed, and there are most certainly allusions to political situations, a subject more travel writers than not enjoy steering clear of. These are coupled with personal reactions, as well as historical and cultural background—all of which complement the core of the book; factual material which, it is hoped, will help the prospective visitor, as well as the armchair traveler, whose curiosity may be whetted, at least in part, by a concise, nutshell picture of contemporary Africa—from the Mediterranean to the Cape of Good Hope, from the Atlantic beaches in the west to the Indian Ocean shores of the east.

The visitor with even a modicum of sensitivity cannot help but be excited by the flux of today's Africa, by the vitality that sovereignty has engendered in the new states, of which there are two-score plus. He cannot close his eyes or ears to the dynamism of the human side of the African scene. He cannot isolate himself—or his opinions, whatever they may be—from the activity that surrounds him. And if he is an American, he will inevitably think of the early struggles of his own country, and of the millions of his own countrymen whose ancestors crossed the Atlantic from Africa—against their will—many generations ago.

Still, at the same time, he can savor the fantastic diversity of the Tourist Africa—eternally snow-covered peaks in the tropics, armies of magnificent wild game on the great plains, geography-book villages in the emerald forests, skyscraper cities often as luxury-equipped as his own. He will find that travel in Africa is considerably more comfortable than he may have imagined, and that happily, the group and excursion fares of the airlines have brought the cost of it down to the reach of the moderate-income vacationer.

Wherever he goes, the traveler encounters the people of Africa and the objects of their cultures—cultures that archaeologists are now discovering to be considerably richer and more advanced than the European colonials of recent centuries wanted the outer world to believe. If he will look and listen, the visitor will hear the music from which derived Western jazz, see the culture that inspired so much of contemporary art, witness dance forms quite as rhythmic and subtle as his own, observe African architecture, religions, modes of dress, family and village life—and hospitality. At the same time, he will encounter the European and his way of life. On occasion, depending upon the imagination and flexibility of the European, it has been adapted to blend well with that of Africa. At other times, it clashes. At all times, it is absorbing to witness—to some gladdening, to others, saddening.

The traveler who can have a look for himself will not like all that he sees; much of southern Africa, after all, remains the most immorally governed area of the planet. But by the time he returns home, he will have had a first-hand impression, and his journey will have seemed more an adventure than it might in more traveled parts of the world.

He will find, very often, that he is regarded with as much curiosity as he may regard his hosts with. Very rarely will he be considered an item in a package, as might be the case with the tightly packed rubberneckers on a bus tour of Paris, Tokyo, or Rio de Janeiro. The tourist in most of Africa is still an individual; he is treated like one and he *feels* like one.

The Africa of today versus the Africa of a decade ago? Modern ways and methods, presidents and premiers where there were governors and prefects, new programs and enthusiasms, new faces, new hotels, new national parks. Gone from the scene are Tubman of Liberia, the beloved "Zik" of Nigeria, Nasser of Egypt, Buganda's King Freddie, the Nkrumah in which Ghana understandably but tragically misplaced its faith; brilliant, still-young Tom Mboya, Kenyan by nationality, but surely the first major symbol and the major exponent of the new Africa.

Still, some familiar figures remain. Ethiopia's remarkable Haile Selassie may well go into the twenty-first century, so astonishing is his staying power and energy. Guinea's ever-idealistic Sékou Touré remains at his now unhappy country's helm. Kenya's Grand Old Man, Jomo Kenyatta—a prisoner of the British when this book's first edition appeared—is now his country's President. Tanzania's Julius Nyerere, elected a youthful Chief Minister under the British in 1960, continues to lead his nation. And so, in Zambia, does Kenneth Kaunda, who first came to America in the late nineteen-fifties to plead the cause of freedom for what was then the British Protectorate of Northern Rhodesia. The Ivory Coast's Houphouët-Boigny remains at his booming country's helm, as does poet Leopold Senghor, in Senegal. The cast of characters is not, in other words, all that changed, nor for that matter, is the continent's dual appeal. I wrote, in the first edition of this book, that it is quite as thrilling to see a new state emerge as it is to spot a lion in the bush. That is, happily, still the case.

Robert S. Kane

AFRICA ALPHABETICALLY

Country	*Government*	*Capital*	*Area (Sq. Miles)*	*Population*
Afars and Issas, Territory of	French Overseas Territory	Djibouti	9000	125,000
Algeria	Republic	Algiers	919,590	14,000,000
Angola	Portuguese "Autonomous Region"	Luanda	48,351	5,362,000
Botswana	Republic	Gaberone	275,000	648,000
Burundi	Republic	Bujumbura	10,747	4,380,000
Cameroon	Republic	Yaoundé	183,581	5,800,000
Cape Verde Islands	Portuguese "Autonomous Region"	Praia	1557	245,000
Central African Republic	Republic	Bangui	240,534	1,500,000
Chad	Republic	Fort-Lamy	495,752	4,000,000
Comoro Islands	French Overseas Territory	Moroni	863	260,000
Congo	Republic	Brazzaville	132,046	915,000
Dahomey	Republic	Porto Novo	43,483	2,700,000
Egypt	Republic	Cairo	386,100	33,900,000
Equatorial Guinea	Republic	Santa Isabel	10,830	300,000
Ethiopia	Empire	Addis Ababa	457,256	25,000,000
Gabon	Republic	Libreville	102,089	500 000

Gambia, The	Republic	Bathurst	4361	400,000
Ghana	Republic	Accra	91,843	9,000,000
Guinea	Republic	Conakry	94,925	3,900,000
Guinea-Bissau	Portuguese "Autonomous Region"	Bissau	13,948	529,000
Ivory Coast	Republic	Abidjan	127,520	4,300,000
Kenya	Republic	Nairobi	224,959	10,900,000
Lesotho	Kingdom	Maseru	11,720	1,000,000
Liberia	Republic	Monrovia	43,000	1,200,000
Libya	Republic	Tripoli	679,362	1,900,000
Malagasy (Madagascar)	Republic	Tananarive	226,657	6,900,000
Malawi	Republic	Zomba/Lilongwe	36,100	4,400,000
Mali	Republic	Bamako	464,000	5,100,000
Mauritania	Republic	Nouakchott	419,231	1,200,000
Mauritius	Independent member of British Commonwealth	Port Louis	720	825,000
Morocco	Kingdom	Rabat	171,834	15,310,000
Mozambique	Portuguese "Autonomous Region"	Lourenço Marques	300,000	7,274,000
Namibia (South West Africa)	in dispute, administered by South Africa	Windhoek	318,261	605,000
Nigeria	Republic	Lagos	356,669	66,174,000
Niger	Republic	Niamey	481,191	3,800,000

Country	Government	Capital	Area (Sq. Miles)	Population
Réunion Island	French Overseas Department	St.-Denis	969	426,000
Rhodesia (Zimbabwe)	Republic	Salisbury	150,333	5,400,000
Rwanda	Republic	Kigali	10,169	3,600,000
São Tomé and Príncipe	Portuguese "Autonomous Region"	São Tomé	372	65,000
Senegal	Republic	Dakar	75,750	3,900,000
Seychelles Islands	British Colony	Victoria	91	49,000
Sierra Leone	Republic	Freetown	27,699	2,600,000
Somalia	Republic	Mogadiscio	246,199	2,800,000
South Africa	Republic	Pretoria and Cape Town	472,359	20,100,000
Spanish Sahara	Spanish Overseas Province	El Aaiún	102,700	48,000
Sudan	Republic	Khartoum	967,500	15,800,000
Swaziland	Kingdom	Mbabane	6704	420,700
Tanzania	Republic	Dar es Salaam	363,708	13,200,000
Togo	Republic	Lomé	21,850	1,900,000
Tunisia	Republic	Tunis	63,378	5,100,000
Uganda	Republic	Kampala	93,981	9,760,000
Upper Volta	Republic	Ouagadougou	105,869	5,400,000
Zaïre	Republic	Kinshasa	905,568	21,637,000
Zambia	Republic	Lusaka	290,584	4,300,000

AFRICA: THE BACKGROUND

"The darkest thing about Africa has always been our ignorance of it."
—George H. T. Kimble

AFRICA AND AFRICANS

"The less intelligent the white man is, the more stupid he thinks the African."
—André Gide

There are three points worth considering in any generalizations made about Africa: it is very big, it is at once as old as time and as new as tomorrow—and it is dark only at night. The European colonials who found it expedient to dub it "the Dark Continent" must certainly rank amongst the most successful hucksters of all time. The whole world bought their two-word description of Africa, including the writers of geography books, travel folders, adventure-movie scenarios and Foreign Office press releases. They should all be ashamed of themselves, and so should we—for having gone along with them for so long.

We have chosen to ignore—at least until relatively recently—the records of early foreign visitors to Africa—Arabs and Portuguese, mainly. We have chosen arbitrarily to divorce the history of North Africa from that of the continent below the Sahara—when the two are very much related. We have chosen to believe only the most hair-raising tales of the slave traders, merchant captains, missionaries, settlers, journalists, explorers, and civil servants.

We have called Africans savages, when the warfare Westerners have engaged in—as recently as four decades ago, when millions of people were burned alive in gas chambers—is nothing in which we can take pride. We have called Africans "pagans," although they are generally a profoundly spiritual people who believe in a Supreme Being who motivates much of their life. We have called them "primitive," while at the same time basing the "modern" art of this century on their traditional art and adapting their rhythms into a form of music which has become a common denominator of Western culture and even made inroads in the Far East. We seem to forget that the civilization generally recognized as the world's oldest—and one of its greatest—is African, born along the banks of the Nile River. We virtually ignore the richness of the Black African cultures which thrived during the greatness of empires such as Mali, Ghana, and Songhai—when Timbuktu and Gao were truly international centers of learning, ambassadors were exchanged with foreign courts, and comparisons were in many ways favorable with those of medieval Europe.

We have incorrectly tended to attribute foreign origins to brilliant remnants of Africa's past—for example, the ruins of Zimbabwe, the art of Ife and Benin, the flourishing old cities of the Indian Ocean coast, and even Swahili, the lingua franca of many millions of Africans, which is primarily an African language with Arabic influence, and not the reverse. We have gone along with guilt-ridden European exploiters, who have had fantastic success in accentuating the negative aspects of Africa, at the expense of emphasizing the positive.

There is no doubt that Black Africa's greatness had subsided by the time Europeans in any number began to visit Africa; the slave traders—Arab as well as European—had seen to that by decimating and demoralizing great populations in their lust for "black ivory." And so had invading armies from countries north of the Sahara. It may be true that there were no known indigenous written languages below the Sahara—while Europe developed the written word, Black Africa cultivated the spoken word—but it is also true that Arabic had been adapted—both in writing and verbally—by African peoples in many areas, just as had Latin in early England. It is true that Europe outranked Africa technologically, but at the same time African societies had worked in iron and gold and brass and copper; practiced terraced farming; levied taxes systematically; organized peoples into viable units, ranging from great cities of elaborate houses and palaces to small, simple villages; developed exquisite art forms, gracious social customs (including that of hospitality, which remains to this day), religious philosophies, and—not unlike the white Christians who were to conquer them, often by force of arms—the practice of warfare. Cannibalism? Savagery? These were no more widespread in Africa than are the practices of Jehovah's Witnesses in America, which discourage the amputation of a limb even if there is no other way to save an injured person's life. Atrocities? They were unheard of in the old Congo before the white agents of King Leopold II severed untold thousands of hands and feet from Africans who did not produce their quotas of ivory and rubber. Caste systems? What class distinctions there are pale in contrast to those of pre-independence India, the apartheid of South Africa, the Jim Crow of the old pre-independence Kenya and of still-white-ruled Rhodesia.

Africans, in short, are human beings—warm and gentle, cold and hostile, brilliant and articulate, dull and dreary, exciting and talented, clumsy and inept. They have, in other words, all the characteristics of peoples all over the face of the globe. The visitor cannot be expected to like every African he comes in contact with, any more than he would like every Frenchman or Japanese or Uruguayan that he meets. That, of course, would be snobbism in reverse.

GEOGRAPHY CAPSULIZED

So geographers, in Afric maps,
With savage pictures fill their gaps,
And o'er uninhabitable downs
Place elephants for want of towns.
—Jonathan Swift (1667–1745)

The immensity of Africa is sometimes difficult to comprehend, particularly for the American, who himself comes from a big continent. Still, Africa is four times the area of the United States. It embraces a full fifth of the land area of the globe, and it constitutes the second largest land mass in the world, with an area of 11,860,000 square miles. It is more than 4900 miles long, and some 4700 miles wide. It contains more than half a hundred countries. Just one of these—Nigeria—would, if superimposed on a map of the eastern United States, extend west to Illinois, and south to the Carolinas. Another—Tanzania—is the size of France and Germany combined.

So much for Africa's vastness. What about its topography? It is entirely surrounded by water, except for its northeast corner, where the Sinai Peninsula of Egypt borders the Negev of Israel. It is bounded on the north by the Mediterranean Sea, on the west by the Atlantic Ocean (including the Gulf of Guinea), and on the east by the Indian Ocean, the Gulf of Aden, and the Red Sea. The coastline is one of the smoothest of any continent—a handicap, for it means that there are relatively few natural harbors. The interior is mostly plateau, rising 2000 feet and upward; it recedes—almost everywhere—in the direction of the low, flat coast. The major mountains are those of the Atlas ranges of the northeast, the Drakensberg of the southwest, and the eternally snow-covered peaks of east-central Africa, including the legendary Mountains of the Moon (Ruwenzori) and Kilimanjaro—the continent's highest, with a height exceeding 19,000 feet. The great lakes are also concentrated in east-central Africa, and include immense Tanganyika, Malawi, and Kivu—the only ones with African names, as well as Victoria, Albert, Edward, and Rudolf, reading like a roster of nineteenth-century European royalty. These feed rivers such as the Nile, the Congo, and the Zambezi, but the continent is not without other major waterways, including the Niger, Volta and Senegal rivers of the west.

Though mainly tropical, Africa runs the gamut of climates. Much of the north (which of course includes the mammoth Sahara as well as the Libyan Desert and part of the Arabian

Desert) is arid, and so is that portion of the south which embraces the Kalahari Desert. Open, sparsely foliaged savannas—known collectively as the Sudan, and the origin of the name of an African republic—form the southern borders of the Sahara and divide it from the verdant equatorial forests which cover much of the bulge of western and central Africa. Below the equator, as one approaches the southern reaches of the continent, the climate becomes mildly temperate, with the seasons the reverse of those in Europe and North America. The population of Africa—though it seems dense if one visits only the teeming coastal cities—is relatively sparse: about 350,000,000. Much of the area is uninhabitable: the great desert wastes, immense regions where the tsetse fly reigns, and the dense forests, where not many people live. There are physical problems in today's Africa: erosion is increasing, the desert is advancing, the forests are diminishing, and the water level is receding. Certain species of the great wildlife wealth—unique in the world—are endangered by still-widespread poaching. But there is also great natural potential in Africa. It is a treasure chest of gold, copper, diamonds, uranium, tin, phosphates, lumber, as well as peanuts, oils, perfumes, spices, rubber, cotton, and a great deal else. Africa's riches have only begun to be tapped.

A SOUPÇON OF HISTORY

> "*I hold thee fast, Africa.*"
> —JULIUS CAESAR

Africa is, of course, the seat of the world's oldest settled culture—that of ancient Egypt, whose Pharaonic civilization, dating back many millennia, was one of the greatest in the history of man. Of importance, too, are the lesser-known contemporaries of Egypt—Cush and Meroë, to the south, in what is now the Republic of the Sudan and Ethiopia. The latter land's three-thousand-year history includes the Empire of Axum, whose tall obelisks still stand in the easily visited city of that name. All of these cultures played a part in the evolution of society in sub-Sahara Africa. And at the same time the peoples of the northeast corner of the continent gained from interchanges with their neighbors south of the Sahara.

But the people below the desert had the handicap of the great sands. As early as five centuries before Christ, the Sahara had become a massive geographical barrier, isolating those south of it from those on the shores of the Mediterranean, who were able to associate more freely with peoples of adjoining areas, and so develop more rapidly. Progress was slower in sub-Sahara Africa because of an isolated environment, with a climate that precluded the need for the kind of shelter required in colder areas, and a setting where there was never a shortage of food, or a need to store it; game was everywhere, and people simply moved about to find it. Eventually, though, these peoples organized themselves—from family clans to tribes to kingdoms, they began to till and irrigate the soil on terraced hillsides, work with iron, develop effective medicinal techniques and formulas, acquire their own religions, art forms, and social philosophies, which culminated very often in highly advanced empires, the details of which archaeology is only just beginning to discover. There is no doubt that these African civilizations were influenced from the outside; there had been sailors and traders and explorers along the coast for many centuries—the Phoenicians, the Greeks, the Arabs, the Chinese, among them. But most of sub-Sahara African culture, it is now believed, was substantially African. Some of its manifestations are briefly mentioned later on in this book. And the rich background of the northern countries—Morocco, Tunisia, Libya, Algeria, Egypt—is touched upon in the chapters on those nations, from the early migrations of Berbers of the East, who still form the bulk of the population, through the invasions of the Romans, Greeks, Vandals, Arabs, Turks, and Western Europeans, almost all of whom left vestiges of their cultures, particularly the militant Arabs, who brought their language and Islamic religion not only to the north but to a surprisingly large area of sub-Sahara Africa.

Modern African history began with the earliest journeys of the Portuguese, intent on finding a safe trade route to India. Bartholomeu Dias was the first to round the Cape of Good Hope, in 1488, and a decade later he was followed by Vasco da Gama, who not only reached India but set up forts along the Indian Ocean coast. Other Europeans—French, Dutch, British—followed the Portuguese to Africa, and provided stiff competition for them. In the beginning, the trade was in spices, ivory and gold, and during this period Portuguese accounts—those few that remain—portray Africa and Africans favorably. Portuguese traders, for example, lived with ancestors of contemporary Nigerians in the old Kingdom of Benin, and sent back to their king glowing accounts of their host-sovereign's glittering court. But with the advent of the slave trade, the reporting slant changed. Europeans assuaged their guilt by picturing the Africans as primitive savages, good for little else except to serve as slaves. It was not until the mid-nineteenth century, when the slave trade—a largely coastal operation—was finally suppressed, that some Europeans decided to have a look at Africa's interior. James Bruce and Mungo Park—two Scotsmen—had served as an earlier vanguard, paving the way for the later explorers, such as Britons John Speke, David Livingstone, and Henry M. Stanley, as well as Savorgnan de Brazza, an Italian-born naturalized Frenchman, and others from France—Binger, Foureau, Caillié, and Marchand. In 1885 the major powers, at the Berlin Conference, chopped up Africa between them, and by 1912 they had accomplished its partition, leaving only Liberia (founded by Americans as a haven for freed United States slaves), Ethiopia, and Egypt independent. After World War I, Germany's possessions became League of Nations mandates, and were divided up among Britain, Belgium, France, and South Africa. Following World War II, Ethiopia—which Italy had invaded a few years previously—again became free, Italy lost Libya, and Italian Somalia became a United Nations Trust Territory, along with all the former League of Nations mandates, except for Namibia (South West Africa). That unhappy country, administered by South Africa (by then a completely sovereign dominion of the British Commonwealth) has still not been relinquished by its occupiers to the UN.

The French, after World War II, began to give their Black African colonies more freedom, and their African peoples more privileges. They (along with the Spaniards) granted independence to Morocco, and to Tunisia. The British, at least in West Africa, did likewise, and in 1957 the Gold Coast Colony, as Ghana, became completely sovereign, and a member of the British Commonwealth—the first sub-Saharan African colony to gain freedom. Though a small country, its impact on the course of African nationalism was immense. It triggered the independence movement that swept Africa—more often than not, with success. In 1959 General De Gaulle established the French Community, and all but one of the provinces (Guinea) of French West Africa and French Equatorial Africa (as well as Madagascar) chose to enter it voluntarily, as semi-independent states. But by 1960 they all opted to become completely sovereign. That same year saw the emergence of the Republics of Togo and Cameroon (ex-French UN Trust Territories) as well as the Republic of Zaïre (ex-Congo), immense Nigeria (Africa's most populous country, and the biggest Negro state in the world), and the Republic of Somalia, a liaison of the former Italian and Somali regions. All told there were twenty-two African states at the end of 1960; sixteen of them were born that year. And a decade later, as Africa entered the seventies, it had become a predominantly independent continent, with more than two-score fully sovereign nations.

African influence had begun to make itself known in the United Nations, so much so that in late 1971, a group of African delegations began to promote the idea of a United Nations Security Council meeting in Africa. There were objections from some states—the larger ones that pay most of the UN's bills—that such a session would be excessively costly at a time when the UN was strapped for funds. But the meeting was voted. It was, of course, the first on the continent of Africa, and the first away from New York, in two decades. The site was Africa Hall—home of the Organization of African Unity in Addis Ababa, and between January 28 and February 4, 1972, the Council heard the then new Secretary General, Kurt Waldheim of Austria, urge action on Africa's problems; saw Britain veto a strong resolution condemning the terms of the British-white Rhodesian settlement, and listened to pleas for help from representatives of a number of nationalist groups waging guerrilla war against the Portuguese in Guinea-Bissau, Angola, and Mozambique, and in South Africa, Namibia, and Rhodesia.

Portugal remains the only colonial power of consequence. There are a few tiny Spanish possessions, as well, and but a single bit of French territory on the continent proper—the small but long-named Territory of the Afars and Issas, formerly French Somaliland.

It is difficult to generalize about the contributions of the Europeans in Africa. They vary, country by country, occupier by occupier. But, broadly speaking: 1. The Europeans brought Africa—and that portion of the African community that it chose to educate—into contact with the outer world, and acquainted it with non-African cultures, Western technology, and Western forms of government; by so doing, they sowed the seeds—however unintentionally—of African nationalism. 2. Invariably, Africans received no benefits—salary increases, schools, or grants of self-government and independence—without asking for them, or, indeed, agitating for them. Even with the British, whose professed aim in Africa was "eventual independence" for its territories, relentless and intense prodding was necessary. 3. A good deal, but by no means all, of the modern façade of Africa, created by the Europeans, was intended for the comfort of resident colonists, not Africans. There are exceptions to the rule, though: schools, a handful of universities, hospitals and housing developments, many of them segregated when established. Reactions toward Africans vary, often by nationality. Most bigoted, racially, are the British, with the Belgians not far behind. Least prejudiced, in this respect, are the Latin peoples—Portuguese, French, Italians, Spaniards, irrespective of their official policies and programs in Africa. Most curious about, and appreciative, of African cultures are the French; least, the British.

Independence was not, of course, a panacea. Not even the colonies Britain has administered—and presumably prepared for sovereignty—emerged with really substantial educated classes. The former French colonies had even smaller leadership elites. Although virtually every one of the new states has aspired toward a kind of democracy, sometimes termed "African socialism," success has been difficult. In terms of history, these new states are still infants. Still, over a period of a decade and a half, leading into the seventies, the continent saw bloody civil wars in Nigeria and Zaïre, then the Congo, and has seen more than a score of military *coups d'état*. There appears to be some sort of pattern in this respect, with independence for a starter, Africanization of the officers corps of the army following, and then a military coup, not infrequently when the top man was out of the country; Uganda, Ghana, and Libya are examples. Besides these countries, and others including the Sudan, Sierra Leone, and Nigeria, the French-speaking nations have had upsets, too—with military upsets in such lands as Dahomey, Togo, Upper Volta, the Central African Republic, and Mali. There are, additionally, guerrilla movements of considerable strength in the Portuguese colonies, a strong independence movement among the majority blacks in Rhodesia—who look to the day when they shall control their country after they have redesignated it Zimbabwe, after the ancient African state so named; and a situation fluid enough in South Africa to have elicited government admissions, at the end of 1971, to the effect that the lot of the South African nonwhite is vastly inferior to that of the excessively privileged South African white, and that unless moves are made toward appreciably improving the status of the black, trouble can be expected.

The new states' principal problems are economic. As colonies, their chief function had been to serve as adjuncts to the economies of the mother countries, who took out—mainly in the form of raw materials—much more than they put in. Many more Africans than not, as a result, remain subsistence farmers who continue to rely on the traditional tribalism of the continent to provide not only economic sustenance through the sharing of incomes, but as a kind of identity for the impoverished and semiliterate, or illiterate. Tribalism, at the same time, remains a major impediment to progress. It impedes political development, sustaining a kind of ancient factionalism and separatism that encourages corruption in office and a status-quo kind of lethargy.

This is hardly to say that the new nations are simply resigned to their lot. On the contrary. Substantial efforts are being made toward self-betterment. The Organization of African Unity, with headquarters at the modern Africa Hall at Addis Ababa, emerged a dynamic force with a dynamic policy, political and otherwise, under the Secretary Generalship of Diallo Telli, a ball-of-fire Guinean. Telli was succeeded in 1972 by Nzo Ekangaki, a young (born 1934) albeit seasoned diplomat-politician from Cameroon. The African nations collaborate in nonpolitical matters through the United Nations Economic Commission for Africa (headquarters, like OAU, are at Africa Hall in Addis Ababa). At their 1971 meeting in Tunis, a majority of African nations pledged to strengthen cooperation among themselves as a way of hastening economic development. They agreed that they needed to make bigger contributions to each other's progress through mutually beneficial projects; and they agreed on the need to act jointly to better their commerce with the rich industrialized nations—for whom they depend for 90 percent of their export trade. Though apparently modest enough, such goals are not easy of achievement, for obstacles to cooperation prevail, ranging from rivalry between English-speaking and French-speaking countries to lack of really adequate communications and transport from one country or region to another.

Most of the continent's sub-Saharan, French-speaking countries are affiliated with the African-Malagasy-Mauritius Common Organization (O.C.A.M.), with headquarters in Yaoundé, Cameroon. It was founded in 1965 to promote development and cooperation, and its most noteworthy achievement was the establishment of the multinational Air Afrique. However, at its meeting in 1972, it agreed to concentrate on mutual cultural and economic problems, to promote closer contacts between its own members and the English-speaking countries of the continent, and to encourage the formation of regional economic liaisons of West, East, and Central African nations.

Africa has become culturally aware. In 1969, representatives from countries all over the continent gathered in Algiers for the first Pan-African Cultural Festival, an event sponsored by the Algerian government. Just a couple of years before that, the Senegalese capital of Dakar was the site of the first international Negro Arts Festival, with artists—singers, dancers, painters, sculptors, actors, writers—present from every area of the black world, including North and South America, and the West Indies, as well as both English-speaking and French-speaking Africa. There are fairly frequent conferences on specialized and/or regional matters—from a 1970 get-together chaired by Emperor Haile Selassie in Addis Ababa on the urgent subject of road-building, to a Nairobi-based meeting, the same year, of the East African lands who formed Animal Interpol, to eradicate the poaching of wild game. Three of the East African countries—Kenya, Tanzania, and Uganda—have made considerable progress in regional cooperation with a common market of their own, providing a number of important shared services, and called the East African Community; its headquarters are in Arusha, Tanzania.

Concurrently, the new countries are continuing relationships with their old occupiers, with foreign countries—a completely new experience for them, for they could not engage in foreign affairs as colonies; and with the international religious bodies. The religious scene is experiencing marked changes. The traditional missionary programs of the Protestant faiths are giving way, not only as regards staff, with increasing Africanization of clergy, but theologically, as well, with distinctive new African churches and sects, and a still-small but articulate group of African scholars studying, and writing about, theology at African universities. The Roman Catholic Church recognized the importance of its African communicants when Pope Paul VI visited Uganda in 1969—the first Pontiff ever to travel to the continent of Africa. In Kampala, coincidentally, attending the Church's first Pan African Conference were more than forty bishops and all seven of the Church's cardinals in Africa. They included the first black cardinal, English-speaking Laurian Cardinal Rugambwa of Tanzania, and the second, French-speaking Paul Cardinal Zoungrana, a member of Upper Volta's Mossi tribe, with a no-nonsense point of view on the dangers of an African neocolonialism, and a deep conviction that Africans must do things in their own way; Upper Volta Catholics employ traditional drums and dancing in Church liturgy.

Like the Protestants, the Catholics are growing in number in Africa. There are some thirty million of them, with something less than a third of the priests African. All told, there are approximately forty-five million Christians in Africa. Aside from the indigenous animist faiths, by far the most popular—and fastest-multiplying—religious group is that of the Moslems. They number about a hundred million, and that total increases rapidly; they have the advantage of being known as a non-European religion.

In the realm of foreign aid, Africa has surprised the world in the manner of its acceptance. It has indeed welcomed all the help it can get—as well it should. But, contrary to predictions of the experts, it is not to any appreciable extent allowing itself to be taken over by its benefactors. This is not to say that their influence is not discernible. But even a country like Tanzania, which is accepting a great deal of Chinese aid and Chinese manpower, as well—in the construction of the Tanzan Railway linking landlocked Zambia with the port of Dar es Salaam on the Indian Ocean—is going about its business in a peculiarly Tanzanian way, all along welcoming aid and technical expertise from the West, as well.

There is no doubt but that the former occupier with the most pervasive continuing influence in Black Africa is France. General De Gaulle devoted more effort and attention to Africa than any other single post-World War II leader; his successor, President Georges Pompidou, has visited a number of African lands to make clear that French interest remains strong. During the colonial period, France invested little financially in its African empire, and it educated relatively few people. But those it did teach, it turned into Francophiles, occasionally even intermarrying—something unheard of in British Africa—there being several African Presidents married to Frenchwomen. France implanted the French culture—from the language to the cheeses. (You will still find French-operated restaurants in Africa importing their vegetables from France.) And with independence, it found the new governments anxious for its continuing largesse and presence. France is the only ex-colonial power with troops stationed in the territory of ex-colonies. Aside from the military, it has exported civilians, to the point where there are now more metropolitan Frenchmen living in Black Africa than there were before independence—approximately a quarter of a million. They are there not only as technicians and business and industrial executives, but in lesser jobs, as well—carpenters and truck drivers, for example—the kind of jobs that in ex-British colonies are now held exclusively by Africans.

France is, of course, paying to maintain *la présence Française.* There are some ten thousand French technicians working with the various governments, not to mention advisers on the staffs of certain of the ministries. And there is considerable financial aid extended, an estimated two hundred million dollars a year. In consequence, France is the major trading partner of her ex-colonies, it has a slew of good friends, in places where friends are important—the United Nations General Assembly, for example; and it sees a lot of the money being made ending up in French coffers, not appreciably unlike the situation that prevailed in pre-independence days.

Still, there has been other foreign capital invested in ex-French Africa. The Chinese have discovered Mauritania, and Uncle Sam has discovered Niger, where it built a two-million-dollar bridge across the Niger River in the capital of Niamey. These last-mentioned countries are typical of what the experts in the aid field rather bluntly term "noncountries." These are lands with about as little development potential as a country can have, and still be viable. They include a lot of ex-French Africa—particularly the landlocked states of the interior. And they are in contrast to nations on the other side of the ledger—the lands with possibilities for the future—like the booming Ivory Coast, for example, Kenya in East Africa, and copper-rich Zambia. Every country, potential or no, wants aid. But Africa is not getting rich on it. China projects just enough of an image with its major programs in Tanzania and Zambia, and in certain other countries. The Soviet Union's interest in Africa has not been at all extraordinary. Britain is, of course, very much on the scene what with a dozen ex-Union Jack territories on the continent. But its own economy is such that its financial help must be limited. Other lands, including some of the Eastern European countries, Israel and Japan, are present either as traders or aiders or both.

There remains the United States.

AMERICA AND AFRICA

What with fully a tenth of its people the descendants of Africans—what other major power may make that statement?—the United States has had no choice but to show some interest in Africa. But it has, on the official level, rarely been anything other than token, either financially or otherwise. There were, to be sure, efforts made in the early sixties as the colonies were becoming sovereign. But they were not to come to a great deal, which should have been no surprise to any observer looking at America's background in the area.

Until as recently as World War II, Liberia—founded by Americans—was all but neglected by the United States. The biggest American investment—private, to be sure—even today, is in South Africa, with its universally despised apartheid government. There has been a minimal aid program—probably under two hundred million dollars a year, continent-wide—for Vietnam has been something of a preoccupation. President Kennedy's appointment of ex-Michigan Governor G. Mennen Williams as Assistant Secretary of State for African Affairs was sound. Mr. Williams traveled a good deal in Africa and immersed himself in his work in Washington, where he was well liked by African diplomats. But he was not in a position to see to it that any really major U.S. projects were undertaken in Africa. (The railroad linking Zambia with the Tanzanian coast was taken on by the Chinese only after the West turned it down.) And none of his successors has made any firm impact on the public mind. President Johnson paid minimal attention to Africa. President Nixon sent Secretary of State William P. Rogers on a fifteen-day 1970 visit to ten African nations. Mr. Rogers made some nice—if unconvincing—speeches in favor of freedom for the African peoples, but in 1971, the Administration remained stonily silent as the Congress violated the United Nations embargo on Rhodesia by voting to import its chrome. Without doubt, the most resilient nongovernmental group concerned with Africa is the American Committee on Africa (164 Madison Avenue, New York 10016). Its general goal is U.S. policy that will effectively help achieve a fully free Africa, through termination of the white-minority regimes in South Africa, Namibia, and the Portuguese colonies.

By the end of 1971, opposition to Washington policy was making itself known. A fourteen-member panel of distinguished citizens, set up by the United Nations Association of the United States, headed by William Roth, a former United States special trade representative, completed a two-year study of the question of U.S. government and private industry relationships with southern Africa. The panel recommended that the government give nonmilitary support to black liberation movements in southern Africa, and it was urged to tighten economic pressure on white-minority regimes, for social change. The panel also called on the government to discourage new American investment in South Africa and to halt financial guarantees to businessmen who exported there. Further, it was severely critical of the practices, as regards employment, of most U.S. companies operating in South Africa, and asked them to give equal pay for equal work to nonwhites to make better-grade jobs available to nonwhites and to end Jim Crow at company programs and functions.

Just before 1972 was born, a long-time-moderate black member of the United States Congress, Representative Charles C. Diggs, Jr., of Detroit, made Page One news. He resigned from the United States delegation to the United Nations General Assembly to protest what he termed the "stifling hypocrisy" of the government's African policy. What impelled him to make his decision, he explained, was Washington's announcement that it was concluding an agreement with Portugal whereby it would have air-base rights in the Portuguese Azores in exchange for a 435-million-dollar grant to Portugal, which Representative Diggs regarded as material aid to that country in its continuing African colonial wars, to be used to "wage war against the black peoples" of its colonies. Mr. Diggs said that the action also indicated "increasing NATO interest in buttressing the white minority-ruled areas of Africa." He was also critical of a number of votes in the UN General Assembly in which the U.S. either abstained from supporting resolutions critical of South African apartheid, or voted against them. And he listed other U.S. actions, or lack of same, the lot adding up to what he termed a "sub rosa alliance with the forces of racism and repression in southern Africa."

THE BLACK CONNECTION

What has kept alive American interest in Africa over the years, and what continues to spark American interest in Africa are America's African-descended citizens. Black intellectuals, beginning with the late W. E. B. Du Bois, grand old man of the NAACP and an internationally distinguished writer and educator, led the U.S. delegation to the first Congress of Persons of Black African Descent, which took place in 1900 in London. He was later joined by the late Walter White, for many years the NAACP's executive secretary, and historian Rayford W. Logan in sparking the Pan-African, or independence movements. Du Bois organized the first Pan-African Congress in Paris in 1919. In

1942, at a conference at the University of Pennsylvania, Kwame Nkrumah, then a graduate student and later to become the first president of Ghana, was among the speakers. He predicted that a World War II victory for the Allies would result in freedom for the Black African peoples; his crystal ball proved accurate and clear. Dr. John A. Davis put it this way to the late, lamented American Society of African Culture: "Pride in racial origins, similarity of caste status between African Negroes and American Negroes, and the desire for a free and respected homeland, a desire shared with other Americans in the past, have all made the American Negro an ardent advocate of Black Pan-Africanism as a springboard for African independence." And Roy Wilkins, executive director of the NAACP, commented at the time when one colony after another was becoming sovereign: "This whole African emergence has sharpened American Negroes' appreciation of their disadvantageous position in this country." All the while, American blacks were taking increasing pride in themselves and their backgrounds, as expressed by the late Langston Hughes in this stanza of his poem, *My People:*

The night is beautiful
So the faces of my people.
The stars are beautiful
So the eyes of my people.
Beautiful, also, is the sun.
Beautiful also are the souls of my people.

Black had indeed—and at long last—become beautiful: Afro haircuts on both men and women . . . African-style jewelry and clothing . . . an "African Lipstick Collection" featured in a two-page color ad in *Ebony* magazine, with such shades as Ghana Red, Nairobi Beige, Congo Coffee, and Tanzania Flamingo-Frost . . . books on Africa, multiplied to the point where the list of one publisher's books on Africa totaled more than ninety . . . and perhaps most interestingly, the African Studies movement, which has mushroomed in the universities, with the Africana Studies and Research Center at Cornell opening as the first complete black studies program conceived and run by black educators at a major (that is, dominantly white) U.S. college. Studies on Africa had their beginnings in the Negro colleges, including Howard University, whose Moorland Collection is one of the largest repositories in the country of books by Africans on Africa; Atlanta, Fisk, and Lincoln universities—the latter school having served as a training ground for a number of contemporary African leaders.

A TRIO OF ANCIENT WEST AFRICAN EMPIRES

To appreciate fully the new states of West Africa, reaching from the Sahara south through the grassy savannas to the forests, one should have at least a brief picture of three important ancient empires, which embraced much of the region: Mali, Ghana, and Songhai.

Old Ghana was an immense, cohesive, and intricately organized empire long before A.D. 1000. Mali's greatness spanned four centuries, beginning with the thirteenth, and Songhai was a leading power in the fifteenth and sixteenth centuries. Early travelers—at first Arab and then European—compared their splendors favorably with those of medieval Europe. It was only the later Europeans—those drawn to Africa in search of slaves, those who found African civilizations shattered by the trade in "black ivory"—who brought back tales of savagery and primitiveness and who encouraged their governments and historians either to ignore or distort the significance of the old empires, empires which were destroyed by invasions from the north, and which never gained the strength to revive, under the enervating pressures of the Arab and European slavers, and later, the imperial conquests of the great European powers.

Still, these old societies bear inspection. Early Ghana fought its battles with iron spears and swords, and it became rich as a result of its gold. Its cities were communities of substantial houses, elaborate mosques (for Islam had penetrated the area), strong fortresses, glittering costumes, brilliant crafts and art forms. Its capital, most archaeologists now believe, was in what is now the Republic of Mali, and is thought to have been home to more than 25,000 people—a large community almost a thousand years ago. Its coffers were made rich by a system of taxation not unlike that of today.

Invasions from the north, and then from neighboring peoples, destroyed Ghana in the thirteenth century. Its major successor was Mali, whose most famed cities were Timbuktu (now a part of the modern Mali) and Djenné, known in their time throughout the world of Islam as centers of culture and education as well as of trade and commerce. One of Mali's most famous kings, Kankan Musa, made a pilgrimage to Mecca via Cairo in the early fourteenth century, and Egyptian accounts of his entourage indicate the richness of his empire—long columns of opulently groomed camels carrying a bevy of wives, platoons of servants, chests full of gifts, amidst an aura of great glitter and pageantry. Mali, at the time, was about the size of Western Europe—and its civilization compared with it, in many ways. This was a wealthy realm of iron, gold, copper, salt, and, of course, food crops. And with it came a period of prosperity and learning. Timbuktu's flat-roofed houses and mosques sheltered writers, physicians, and lawyers. Arabic was the literary language, much as Latin was in the Europe of the time, but Mandingo was the principal spoken language. It heavily influenced the little-known brand of African-English spoken in the ports of the Guinea Coast starting four centuries ago. Mandingo remains widely spoken throughout West Africa, and was the language of many early black Americans, through whom linguistics specialists believe it has contributed a number of words to American English—including okay, jazz, jitterbug, hep, banjo, boogie-woogie, jive, tote, cocktail, guy, and bogus—not to mention dig, as in "Dig?" The city of Djenné thrived much like Timbuktu. Industry emerged throughout the empire. Weavers, goldsmiths, coppersmiths, silversmiths, blacksmiths, dyers, tanners, woodcarvers—every town had its artisans. And over it all was a skillful political organization which welded the great empire together.

Mali was still functioning, but had passed its peak period, when Songhai began to thrive, in the Niger River valley. Its great city, Gao, was the equivalent of Timbuktu as a center of learning. Its people and their successors were reading and writing in Arabic centuries before Columbus discovered America. Though not a great power until the fifteenth century, Songhai, through its people (Negroes who bear that name to this day), had thrived several hundred years earlier, beginning in Gao and gradually expanding throughout the Sudan regions. The people of Songhai accepted Islam, which helped to unify them more than did their earlier tribal religions, and thrived as farmers, shepherds, fishermen, craftsmen in the metal arts, and shrewd traders and businessmen. Moreover, they were clever administrators and governors, and great warriors; they not only held off their own territory from attack after attack, but expanded it so that, in the late fifteenth century, Songhai had grown from a small state in the neighborhood of Gao to a substantial empire. It was destroyed in about 1590 by the Moroccans, coming from the north, and only now is its territory once again sovereign.

AFRICA: TOURIST TERRITORY

"I speak of Africa and golden joys."
—William Shakespeare (*King Henry IV*)

TOURISM: THE BIG PICTURE

Africa was the last of the continents—to be discovered, that is, by Americans. But it has become surprisingly well equipped to receive them. Major airlines serve it, and within its borders domestic carriers offer comprehensive, and often luxurious, service. Accommodations are everywhere available—from simple but clean rest camps in the bush to opulent hotels in the capitals, major towns, and resorts. There is no community of even minimal importance where good multilingual guide service is not available, and in many places packaged tours are offered. Rent-a-car service is universal; the taxi driver who doubles as local tour conductor is ubiquitous; and hotel porters and concierges are invariably sightseeing experts. Most important, safaris are no longer exclusively for rich men. And the welcome for visitors is warm. The new countries are anxious to meet strangers from abroad. Tourism as an industry is playing a role in at least one ministry of every government, and it is being promoted, as well, by transportation companies, hotel owners, resort operators, chambers of commerce, and *syndicats d'initiative*. Specific sources of information, country by country, are listed in the chapters following.

With the coming of independence to so many countries, cities that were formerly seats of colonial governments became international capitals, frequented by diplomats, correspondents, government officials, technical specialists—and tourists—from abroad.

They are sprouting new hotels, and many have spruced themselves up, with pride in their new importance on the world scene.

AFRICA IN MUSEUMS

Outstanding exhibits of Black African art are on display at the following museums:

American Museum of Natural History, New York; *Museum of Primitive Art,* New York; *Metropolitan Museum of Art,* New York; *Brooklyn Museum,* Brooklyn; *Buffalo Museum of Science,* Buffalo, N.Y.; *Barnes Foundation,* Merion, Pa.; *Newark Museum,* Newark, N.J.; *Peabody Museum,* Harvard University, Cambridge, Mass.; *Chicago Natural History Museum,* Chicago; *Fisk University Museum,* Nashville, Tenn.; *Denver Art Museum,* Denver, Colo.; *Royal Ontario Museum,* Toronto, Ont.; *Alain Locke African Collection, Howard University Gallery of Art,* Washington, D.C.; *Museum of African Art of the Frederick Douglass Institute of Negro Arts and History,* Washington, D.C.; *Johnson Collection of African and Afro-Americn Art and Sculpture,* Johnson Publishing Company Building (*Ebony* and *Jet* magazines), 820 South Michigan Avenue, Chicago; *Dusable Museum of African-American History,* 3806 South Michigan Avenue, Chicago. Travelers bound for Africa, via Europe, might benefit from African art collections on that continent. Outstanding are those of the *Musée des Arts Africains et Océaniens,* Paris; *Musée Royale de l'Afrique Centrale,* Brussels; *British Museum,* London; and *National Museum,* Copenhagen.

The leading collections of *Egyptian art,* outside of the Cairo Museum, are to be found in the *Metropolitan Museum of Art,* New York, and the *British Museum,* London. Many other museums have Egyptian exhibits as well.

PASSPORTS, VISAS, AND OTHER DOCUMENTS

There are a handful of African countries which do not require tourist visas of American citizens, only a valid passport. One must hope that their neighbors will soon emulate them, but meanwhile visas *are* required everywhere else in Africa, and the visitor must leave himself plenty of time to obtain them. *Before applying,* he must have a valid *passport,* a *health certificate* indicating valid inoculations for smallpox and yellow fever, a *transportation ticket* to show the authorities that he has provided in advance for his departure from their country (travel agents issue letters certifying that the ticket is being prepared, in cases where it is not ready at the time of making application for visas); passport-size *photographs* (from one to four, depending on the country—it is well to have several dozen made up at once if the itinerary is at all extensive), and—in but one or two instances—an easily obtained *certificate of good conduct* from the local police department, which assures the consulate that the visitor is a law-abiding citizen. Visas may be obtained from consular sections of embassies in Washington and missions to the United Nations of the various individual countries, and/or their consulates in New York. Travel agents and airlines serving Africa are familiar with the procedures for making visa applications, and with the frequently changing regulations, such as the amounts of fees and the number of photos required. The important thing, if one is going to a number of countries, is to allow enough time—a good month—for the passport must inexplicably remain overnight at many consulates, and it can be in only one consulate at a time. Firms whose business is visa-procurement can be helpful to the traveler in a hurry to take off, with a whole slew of visas to obtain. One such that I can recommend is: Visa and Passport Service, Charles H. Schultze, president; 513 South 23rd Street, Arlington, Virginia 22202. *Tip:* The easiest type of visa to apply for is a *tourist visa.* A U.S. passport, formerly valid for three years, and renewable for two additional years, is now valid for *five* years, but cannot be renewed. Instead, a new passport must be applied for. The charge for a passport is twelve dollars. For your *first* passport, you will need, aside from the twelve bucks, a pair of passport pictures (head-on—no profiles, 2½ inches to three inches square, with a white background, and, yes, you may smile), a birth or baptismal certificate or a notarized affidavit of your birth vouched for by a relative or someone who has known you from way back. For *successive* passports—any after the first—the expired passport will take the place of the birth or baptismal certificate or notarized affidavit of your birth, and a personal appearance is not required when applying. Passports may be obtained at Department of State passport offices in New York, Miami, San Francisco, Washington, D.C., Boston, Seattle, Los Angeles, Chicago, New Orleans, Honolulu, Philadelphia, and San Diego, or, in other cities, at the office of the clerk of a federal court; and, if the government's experiment continues a success, at some 3000 state courts and many post offices throughout the nation. Allow two weeks, although your passport may arrive in the mail sooner than that. If you are in a whiz-bang of a hurry, say so when applying; frequently, the authorities will try to speed things up for you. It should go without saying that your passport is one hell of an important document. Upon receipt of it, fill in your name, full address, and next of kin on the inside front cover. And keep the passport with you—*not packed in a suitcase*—while you're traveling. In case of loss, theft, or destruction, perish the thought, notify, or have your hotel notify, local police, and immediately get in touch with the nearest United States embassy or consulate, or the Passport Office, Department of State, Washington, D.C. 20524.

INOCULATIONS AND HEALTH

For entry into every African country a valid smallpox vaccination is necessary; it must be not less than eight days nor more than three years old, and should be validated by the local Board of Health. Generally, the only other inoculation required is for yellow fever. Still, it is usually advisable to play it safe and have also such inoculations as typhoid (paratyphoid is no longer considered medically advisable), polio, measles, typhus, tetanus (now combined with diphtheria for single-shot administration), and, as a precaution—*not a guarantee*—a shot of gamma globulin, against infectious hepatitis. It is not sufficient to ask your physician for his counsel in this area. So relatively few American physicians appear to be sufficiently familiar with the diseases we may contact in developing areas of the world that it is also necessary to ask your physician—politely, so he won't belt you one—if he is up to date on these diseases, and offer inoculations for them. If he is not, and you are sufficiently fearless, you might also ask him to consult his medical library or his specialist colleagues for the latest literature on the subject, or at least refer to such books written primarily for laymen as *How to Travel the World and Stay Healthy* by Patrick J. Boyle, M.D., and James E. Banta, M.D. (Acropolis Books).

Malaria precautions: Although malaria remains as a disease in tropical Africa, few travelers contract it today, so long as they take antimalaria pills regularly, wear long sleeves in buggy areas, and use mosquito netting in such areas, when sleeping in nonscreened settings. The favored antimalaria drug is chloroquine; in the United States, this is marketed commercially as Aralen. You do not need to start taking it a week or two in advance of your arrival in tropical Africa, as used to be the case with antimalaria drugs. But while in Africa, you should take it on the same day every week, and upon leaving the malaria area, it should be taken once a week for four additional weeks.

To drink or not to drink? The tap water, that is. In major cities, it is usually potable. In smaller places, it is advisable to drink it boiled or to order bottled water (both at the table and for one's room). The important thing is not to panic if you've gulped a mouthful, without thinking—or in rinsing your teeth after brushing; chances are that that little bit won't hurt you.

Other precautions: Remember that because water is frozen when it appears in ice-cube form does not necessarily mean that it is bacteria-free. Consider the source of the cubes when accepting drinks with them. Likewise, be wary, in developing and/

or tropical areas, of creamy, custardy foods including pastries, raw salads, clams, and other uncooked foods. Best bets are well-cooked foods, although fruits protected by their own skins—bananas are particularly exemplary—are invariably okay, when peeled.

A note about yellow fever inoculations: Because yellow fever serum must, for some reason or other, be even fresher than tomorrow's milk, inoculations for yellow fever are mainly administered by United States Public Health Service stations across the country. Because many Africa-bound travelers go through New York en route to Africa, and because *finding* the appropriate Public Health Service office in New York can be a time-consuming mystery, I provide the specifics herewith. The place you want is the U. S. Public Health Service Out Patient Clinic; it is located in a building of the U. S. Department of Health, Education, and Welfare (of which the Public Health Service is a division) at 245 West Houston Street, in lower Manhattan. To get there by public transportation, you take the IRT West Side *local* subway to Houston Street Station and lo! you emerge to the surface and the building is on the corner. However, you may go for your shot only between 1:30 P.M. and 2:30 P.M., Monday through Friday. If you get lost, the telephone number of the yellow fever-shot-givers is (212) 620-3284. *In other cities,* to find out where you must go, look in the telephone directory under United States Government, Department of Health, Education, and Welfare subcategory, United States Public Health Service sub*sub* category.

Inoculations in a hurry: The Life Extension Institute, 11 East 44th Street, New York (third floor), gives all the major inoculations (except for yellow fever) from 9 A.M. to 4 P.M., Monday through Friday, at five dollars per shot, with no appointments necessary. And note: the institute is authorized to validate smallpox vaccinations, saving one the trouble of having this done by a municipal or federal health department.

The Medic Alert emblem: Travelers with hidden medical problems—diabetes, epilepsy, heart condition, allergies, glaucoma, for example—will find the Medic Alert plan worth knowing about. It is the project of a nonprofit foundation. On the front of the emblem—worn on necklace or bracelet—are engraved the words, "Medic Alert." On the reverse is engraved the wearer's problem, his identification number, and the phone number of Medic Alert headquarters in California. Physicians, nurses, and law-enforcement officers may call that number collect, from any place in the world, to learn necessary additional information about the emblem's wearer, should he become incapacitated. Lifetime membership costs seven dollars. For information write Medic Alert, Turlock, California.

CLIMATE

An awful fuss is sometimes made about the climate of Africa, often by Americans who have seen too many movies and who themselves live in some of the world's most uncomfortably humid cities. There are areas where, during the worst part of the rainy or hot seasons, travel is not recommended, but *generally* one can visit almost any area of Africa at any time. Rainy seasons, it must be remembered, are often periods of occasional—not constant—rain, with the countryside fresher, greener, and sometimes cooler. Dry seasons, on the other hand, can have the disadvantage of being cloudless, with the countryside not as verdant as it is when there is rain. Winters, even in the north and the south, are mild and moderate, with delightfully warm, sunny days. The American summer months—when most people take vacations—are good for traveling in all regions of Africa except the deep Sahara and its immediate fringes, and certain sections of the interior of West Africa where the rains are heavy. This time of year is perfect for Central Africa, southern Africa, East Africa, and pleasant for the northern parts of North Africa. The best times for a visit in each country are noted in this book, country by country. But don't let the weather keep you away from *any* country, if you're in the neighborhood.

PACKING SIMPLIFIED

The what-to-pack bugaboo need not be that at all. International air travelers, by now accustomed to forty-four-pound (economy) and sixty-six-pound (first-class) limitations have learned that the best rule is: Easy does it. Wash-and-wear garments, with percentages of such fibers as dacron that preclude frequent pressing, are, of course, the easiest to care for, and in Africa are particularly convenient, even though laundry in this part of the world is rarely if ever a problem—hotels do it quickly and expertly. Extra-speedy service—for which there is, of course, a surcharge (exception: Hilton Hotels International, and a doff of the hat to them!)—is generally available; if the laundry is turned in before breakfast, it is back in one's room at dinnertime, with luck.

The travel-light policy hinges on acceptance of the fact that it is not necessary to appear in a smashing new costume every day of the week. When moving about, one sees people for periods often so brief that they're not able to note the variety of one's dress, even if they're so inclined. And in the case of Africa, where the vacationer is in the bush on safari a good bit of the time, there is even less call for a variety of in-town changes. Quantities of each type of clothing depend, of course, on individual stubbornness, as well as baggage allowance for air travelers.

A basic *woman's wardrobe*—and here I am indebted to Africa expert Jane Chapin of Adventures Unlimited at Abercrombie & Fitch in New York—would include: one or two lightweight travel suits and wash-and-wear blouses to be worn with them; two summer dresses, both of wash-and-wear materials and both dressy enough for evening wear; two or three pairs of drip-dry slacks that can be worn in the cities and on safari, with blouses to accompany them, at least one or two of these long-sleeved and tailored, for wear in the bush; several changes of lingerie and stockings;

housecoat and slippers, both lightweight; two lightweight but warm sweaters, one of which might double as an evening wrap; a pair of suede, rubber-soled desert boots (for wear in the bush), a pair of low-heeled sport shoes and/or sandals, and a pair of dressy shoes; a lightweight (and preferably waterproof) topcoat that can double as a raincoat; a crushable hat with a brim; silk scarves for accessorizing; a swimsuit in its own plastic bag so that it can be packed when wet; cosmetic and toilet requisites, and if you like, a wig. Though not essential, a bush or safari jacket is recommended; blouses, slacks, and skirts are available in matching materials. These can be purchased in advance, in the United States (Abercrombie & Fitch, incidentally, has jacket/slack safari outfits, with matching dresses) or bought—ready- or tailor-made—in Africa, particularly if one's first destination is Nairobi, where safari outfitting is a major specialty of the shops. Desert boots are a particularly good buy in Africa; they are locally made in Kenya and a number of other African countries.

A *man's wardrobe*, based upon my own experience, should include a dark (gray or navy blue) summerweight dacron-and-wool suit; a dacron-and-cotton blue or gray-and-white cord sport jacket and/or a summerweight navy blue blazer; a pair of summerweight gray dacron-and-wool slacks for wear with the cord jacket and/or blazer; several short-sleeved, wash-and-wear shirts that may be worn with ties and as sport shirts; a few additional short-sleeved wash-and-wear sport shirts; at least one long-sleeved sport shirt for wear on safari; one or two pairs of wash-and-wear khaki or chino slacks, for wear both in cities and in the bush; a good choice of ties, there being no better or lighter-in-weight variety-adders for the suit and sport-jacket combinations; a pair of drip-dry pajamas (wash them before breakfast; they're dry in the evening); a raincoat, which can double as a bathrobe; socks, underwear, handkerchiefs, a hat, if you wear one (you may want to buy a wide-brimmed hunter-style hat upon arrival in Africa), a pair of shoes and a pair of loafers (these double as bedroom slippers), as well as a pair of suede, rubber-soled desert boots for use while on safari, and obtainable inexpensively in Africa;

a safari jacket and matching slacks (also obtainable inexpensively in Africa, in cotton or drip-dry materials); a swimsuit in its own plastic bag so that it may be packed when wet; a lightweight sweater or turtleneck; and, of course, a toilet kit, the contents of which is easily replenishable in every African city. Easily purchasable on the scene in Africa are short-sleeved safari suits of wash-and-wear materials, the top parts of which double as shirt and jacket; variations of these have been popularized by Presidents Kaunda of Zambia and Nyerere of Tanzania; they're neat, cool, and practical for hot spots, both urban and rural.

Both men and women will want to take sunglasses, an extra pair of eyeglasses, and a copy of the prescription; some Band-Aids, adhesive tape, and gauze; a roll of Scotch Tape (it has innumerable uses on a trip), an envelope of rubber bands and paper clips—also valuable at the most unexpected times; Chiclets and Life Savers, both for yourself (particularly on flights when they're not served) and for kids encountered along the way; a supply of Wash'n Dris or similar premoistened disposable washcloths; a half-dozen of the cheapest ball-point pens—they are occasionally lost when filling out landing cards and customs forms; a tiny scissors, several plastic bags—of inestimable convenience; a pocket-size flashlight—handy in the bush and in towns, as well, when electric current may go out temporarily; a pocket French dictionary, for French-speaking areas, and a Swahili dictionary, for East Africa; printed or engraved personal or business cards; a plastic bottle of aspirin; an antidiarrhea preparation (paregoric is effective, although some physicians prescribe codeine, which doubles as an emergency pain-killer). Also worth packing are an antihistamine (for allergies or rashes that may develop), antibiotics, sleeping pills for overnight flights, and antimalaria preparation (see Inoculations and Health, page 43). Photographers will want, aside from their cameras and equipment, as much film as they think they will use; most common types can be replenished en route. Remember, too, to take along names and addresses of friends and friends of friends to contact; and it goes without saying, this book! Soap? A single small cake will suffice; hotels and safari lodges provide it, and it can be purchased everywhere.

CUSTOMS

In Africa: Travelers who are not returning residents rarely have any difficulty with customs inspectors. There are, as with countries on every continent, lists a mile or so long as to what one may or may not import, duty-free. But the ordinary tourist is not going to have problems in this respect, so long as he makes clear that whatever film he has is for his own use, that his cameras (two should be the maximum), tape recorder, and typewriter are his own and for his own use, and that he has only a reasonable quantity of cigarettes—say a carton or two, and of alcohol—say a fifth or a quart. It should go without saying that customs and immigration officers like to be regarded as officials of their governments—which they are. As on other continents, the best rule is: Speak politely, when spoken to; let *them* initiate the conversation.

Returning to America: The limit on duty-free purchases is one hundred dollars, allowable once every thirty days, providing you have been out of the country at least forty-eight hours (if you haven't, you're allowed a big, fat ten-dollar exemption). Worth noting: you may ship, *duty-free,* without having to declare them, and *not* counting as part of your hundred-dollar allowance, gifts or parcels not exceeding a total value of ten dollars, so long as they are not liquor, perfume, or tobacco. Send *as many as you like* from wherever you like, but not more than one parcel per day *to the same recipient.* Mark each such package "GIFT—TOURIST PURCHASE—VALUE UNDER TEN DOLLARS." Remember, too, that *antiques,* duly certified to be at least one hundred years old, are admitted duty-free, and do not count as part of the hundred-dollar quota; neither do *paintings, sculptures,* and other *works of art,* of any date, if certified as original; it is advisable that certification from the seller or other authority as to their authenticity accompany them. (Exceptionally fine, one-of-a-kind, museum-caliber African masks, carved and sculpted objects can fall within the original-works-of-art category, as can, of course, paintings and antiques. But I do not suggest you try and fob off mass-produced run-of-the-mill junk as works of art, at U.S. customs; our customs officers know their business. The best rule is that when you're purchasing something good, ask the seller to certify in writing—just a sentence on the bill of sale will do—the article's authenticity. In some countries, articles of certain materials—ivory pieces of appreciable size, in Uganda for instance—need a government permit for export; most shopkeepers have supplies of these and will issue them to you when you make your purchase.) Also exempt from U.S. duty, but as a part of the hundred-dollar quota; one quart of liquor. And—this is important—there is no restriction on how much one may bring in above the hundred-dollar limit so long as the duty is paid; on many articles the duty is surprisingly moderate.

YOUR AFRICAN HOSTS

The visitor will find his welcome warmer if he regards his hosts with dignity, addresses waiters as "waiter," and stewards as "steward"—never *ever* the now happily obsolete and odious "boy"; calls Africans "Africans" (or Senegalese or Ivorian or Nigerian or Kenyan or Zambian or Tunisian) rather than "natives"; terms non-Christians, non-Moslems, non-Jews, and non-Hindus as animists, rather than "pagans"; hesitates to use the word "primitive" unless it really applies (as it would, for example, with the culture of the Pygmies, but not with most others). In Moslem countries, particularly those above the Sahara, visitors in many private homes and public places should not be surprised to find women absent. In any instance where hospitality is offered—very often it will be coffee or a chilled soft drink—it is considered rude to refuse. The exception to this rule is cigarettes; people in Africa often offer them as a matter of course, but are not offended when they are turned down. In certain areas, African women—sometimes men as well—do not like their photographs taken, for religious or other reasons, and in some places military installations cannot be photographed. Where there is any doubt, ask before snapping, or if accompanied by a guide or local resident, request that he break the ice, if necessary. Some people—understandably enough—like to be remunerated in a small way, for serving as models. The only other suggestion to be made here obtains in every foreign country: Comparisons, especially when made by citizens of a rich country like the United States, can be odious. And so can obsequiousness.

SHOPPING AND THE ART OF BARGAINING

Interesting buys, country by country, are discussed in later chapters. Purchases can be shipped home to avoid overweight when flying. Bargaining is the rule everywhere except in department stores and certain stores in larger towns, particularly government-operated handicraft shops. It can be time-consuming, but it is often fun, always challenging, and a pleasant experience if undertaken with the right spirit. The prospective customer simply asks the price, offers at least one hundred per cent less, and eventually agrees upon a compromise price. It is wise not to appear overeager; the art of One-up-manship is always in order. Start to leave, if you wish to emphasize that the amount asked is too steep for you, or amble over and have a look at something else, rather casually. There is no place for guilt feelings in bargaining; the merchant is a good businessman, and he never loses!

CURRENCY

Travelers checks are recommended for the great bulk of one's funds. Take a good many in ten-dollar denominations—these are the most convenient, with most of the rest in twenties, and a few fifties in reserve. Carry along, too, about twenty or twenty-five one-dollar bills. These are negotiable for purchases of drinks and cigarettes on many international flights, and also come in handy for last-minute use just before leaving a country when it would be inconvenient to cash a travelers check. Credit cards—that of the Diners' Club appears to be the most acceptable in Africa—are most useful in charging at hotels, restaurants, and many shops.

TIPPING

Tip when service is good. The wages of waiters, porters, and chambermaids are low. Except where service charges are added to bills, tip 10 percent; up this to 15 percent if service has been particularly elaborate or outstanding. And when service is included in the bill, tip 5 percent. Allow the equivalent of about fifteen or twenty American cents per suitcase, in the case of baggage porters (a shilling per bag is the norm in East Africa), and the equivalent of thirty or forty U.S. cents per night for room servants or chambermaids. When arriving in a new country, exchange money either at the airport (most have branches of banks) or at the hotel, upon checking in. African bank tellers and hotel cashiers are like their counterparts the world over; they invariably loathe giving small change for tips; you must *insist*, as you do everywhere else.

MAIL

If your itinerary is planned in advance, have letters addressed to you in care of your hotels along the way. American embassies and consulates (where they exist) will also hold mail for you, but remember that they are closed evenings, Saturday afternoons, and Sundays. Correspondents should allow a week for delivery, via air mail. The regular air-mail-letter rate is twenty-one cents per one *half* ounce. Cheaper are international air letters, obtainable in any U.S. post office at fifteen cents. Air letters (*Aérogrammes* in French) are also available at the post offices of most foreign countries.

EMBASSIES, CONSULATES, AND RELIGIOUS MISSIONS

American embassies are found in the capital cities of independent states. American consulates-general or consulates are situated in the capital cities of most colonies, for ambassadors can be accredited only to sovereign nations; there are, as well, U.S. consulates in certain important commercial and port towns. In addition, there are, in certain capitals, offices of the United States Information Service and the American libraries connected with them, and primarily for local residents. Generally, these American outposts, particularly in the less-traveled countries, welcome visiting compatriots. Religious missions, frequently American-operated (both Protestant and Roman Catholic) usually welcome visitors, too, as do missions operated by Europeans.

LANGUAGE

English—and whatever French you can master—will see you through, all over Africa. Arabic is, of course, the principal language of the North African countries, and is also spoken in parts of East Africa, and Swahili is the lingua franca for millions of Africans—and many Europeans as well—in East Africa and Zaïre. (It is good, in this region, to know at least these two Swahili words: *jambo*—hello/goodbye and *asante sana*—thank you.) But never underestimate the language spadework done by the British. The English-speaking traveler invariably finds someone who speaks his language.

LOCAL GUIDES

In North Africa, guides are generally licensed or accredited by the local tourism authorities. Some Moroccan guides speak only enough English to say they speak English, and the non-French-speaking visitor should test them in advance. In Egypt, only guides (known as dragomen) licensed by the government Tourist Administration should be hired. All over Africa, local tourist offices, *syndicats d'initiative*, and airlines offices can arrange for guides, and so, of course, can hotel porters and concierges. Rates are invariably nominal—a few dollars per half day is average—but should be established in advance after consultation with the authority through whom they are engaged. Taxi drivers—provided they speak your language—often double as guides, and have been excellent, wherever I have used them; set prices in advance. Self-drive and chauffeur-driven cars may be hired everywhere, again through hotel porters and concierges; rates are cheaper for European than for American cars. Excursions from cities into nearby rural areas are often tailor-made, upon request of the individual traveler, in many sub-Saharan countries. The more passengers per car—or per jeep or per Land-Rover—the cheaper the rate for each person. Here one is advised to inquire of porters, concierges, airline and tourist offices, with a view to teaming up with strangers and thereby lowering costs.

YOUR TRIP TO AFRICA: THE NITTY-GRITTY

Chances are, you will fly to Africa. That is, unless you select one of the very occasional cruises out of New York that call at some African ports in the course of a long and elaborate itinerary, or unless you choose to go by freighter.

Air service is very good; recent years have seen a considerable increase in direct flights to Black Africa from the United States, with a multinational Black African carrier now flying its own aircraft across the Atlantic. Still other airlines fly one to Africa via European points. To give you an idea, here is a selective breakdown.

Airlines flying directly from New York to Black Africa include Air Afrique, Pan American World Airways, and Trans World Airlines. Air Afrique is the unique multinational airline of a number of French-speaking West African nations. With headquarters in Abidjan, Ivory Coast. Air France advised it technically during its formative years in the sixties, just after its owner-nations became sovereign republics, so that the *ambiance* on board is happily Franco-African. Flight crews are mostly European, with the stewards and stewardesses of the cabin staff representing all of the member countries. Cuisine and wines are sublimely French. Air Afrique is particularly proud of its North Atlantic route, between New York's Kennedy International Airport and Dakar, with intermediate stops at a number of West African points, and the terminus at Kinshasa. Air Afrique also flies to points throughout the territory of its member countries, to neighboring nonmember West African countries, and to Paris and other European cities, as well.

Pan American World Airways pioneered U.S. air routes to Black Africa, just as it has to so many other areas of the planet. (It flies to some eighty-five lands on all six continents.) It has routes to West Africa, East Africa, and southern Africa, and it touches down in North Africa, as well. The western–southern route goes from New York to Dakar, with intermediate stops along the West African coast, continuing on to Kinshasa and terminating in Johannesburg. Pan Am's East African route goes from New York to Casablanca, Morocco's major city, and thence across Africa nonstop to Entebbe, Nairobi, and Dar es Salaam.

Trans World Airlines is unique in that it has extensive U.S routes and flies, as well, to and through Europe, the Middle East, Asia, and the Pacific, not to mention Africa. TWA serves both North Africa—flying to Cairo from San Francisco, Chicago, and New York via Rome and Athens; and East Africa, serving Entebbe, Nairobi, and Dar es Salaam from San Francisco, Chicago, and New York, also via Rome and Athens.

European airlines serving Africa via their home countries include *Air France* (to North, West and East Africa, as well as Madagascar and Mauritius, via Paris; *Alitalia* (to North, East, West, and southern Africa, and Madagascar, via Rome); *BEA*, to North Africa, via London; *BUA*, to southern Africa, via London; *BOAC*, to North, East, West, and southern Africa, via

London; *Iberia,* to southern Africa, via Madrid; *KLM,* to North, East, West, and southern Africa, via Amsterdam; *Lufthansa,* to North, West, East, and southern Africa, via Frankfurt; *Olympic,* to North, East, and southern Africa, via Athens; *Sabena,* to North, West, East, and southern Africa, via Brussels; *SAS,* to North, West, East, and southern Africa, via Copenhagen; *Swissair,* to North, West, East, and southern Africa, via Zurich; and *TAP,* to the Portuguese colonies from Lisbon.

African airlines serving Africa from Europe include Ethiopian Airlines, East African Airlines, Zambia Airways, and the earlier-described Air Afrique, among others. *Ethiopian Airlines,* which has been operating under TWA management and assistance since it was established after World War II by Emperor Haile Selassie, has led all African airlines in the Africanization of staff and crews, and made history in 1971 when the emperor appointed an Ethiopian as president—flies from Addis Ababa north to Athens (via Asmara and Cairo) and also to Rome, Frankfurt, Paris, and Madrid. It also maintains a trans-Africa route, from Addis Ababa to West Coast capitals, and flies to Asia, as well. *East African Airways* is a multinational airline, a kind of African SAS, with the governments of Kenya, Uganda, and Tanzania its joint proprietors. It is one of the oldest and very best of the African carriers—service aloft is invariably delightful—with excellent routes linking East Africa with London and Paris, and to points as far east as Hong Kong, not to mention routes within Africa to destinations throughout the territory of the trio of owner-countries, and to a number of other African destinations, as well.

Zambia Airways is one of the newer African carriers. It operates with management assistance from Alitalia, which means that it has a pleasant, perky *ambiance,* with good Italian-accented food and wines. On-board service is very pleasant, and aside from the domestic routes within Zambia, and to neighboring Malawi, Zambia Airways flies all the way north to London via Nairobi and Rome, and has a convenient route to the island-state of Mauritius, in the Indian Ocean.

The Africa aviation picture: The most encouraging development of the African air-transport scene in recent years has been the introduction of inexpensive excursion and group fares. They have made African holidays possible for an immense new segment of travelers.

Air fares for Africa, as for the rest of the planet, break down into four general categories:

1. First class: First-class tickets are valid for a year, and are usable any day of the year. They are valid for passage in the first-class cabins of aircraft, with extra-wide, two-abreast seating, more legroom between seats than in economy class, more elaborate meals with complimentary cocktails, wines and after-meal liqueurs, and smaller passenger-complements allowing for considerably more personal attention and service than is possible in economy class. *Bonus:* a good many stopovers allowed en route.

2. Economy class: Economy-class tickets are also valid for a year, and are good at any time of the year, with no restrictions whatsoever on departure dates or times. They are valid for the economy section of aircraft. Configurations vary, of course, from the wide-bodied Boeing 747 with two aisles and nine-abreast seating to the conventional-size single-aisle jets—both Boeing and Douglas—with six-abreast seating. Meals can be very good indeed, if less elaborately and more simply served than in first class, and alcoholic beverages are charged for. *Bonus:* As in first class, a good many stopovers are allowed en route.

3. Excursion fare: This is for passage in the economy-class cabins of aircraft, but is cheaper than an ordinary economy-class ticket because there are conditions. One's minimum stay must be fourteen days, and the maximum stay is forty-five days. Additionally, there is a limitation of stopovers, with six being the maximum.

4. Group-inclusive tour fare (GIT): This is an even cheaper fare, because the passenger is incorporated—by his travel agent or the airline—into a group of travelers, all undertaking the same trip. The minimum stay is fourteen days, but the maximum is only twenty-one days (this may be lengthened, however). Seven stopovers are allowed, in contrast to the six of the excursion fare. However, in addition to the air-fare proper, the passenger must prepay a minimum of one hundred dollars in land arrangements, for hotels, sightseeing, and the like.

Sample air fares to selected cities: To give you an idea of how these four types of fares vary, here they are, round-trip, for several African cities, *subject, of course, to change:*

New York–Dakar	First class	$1120
	Economy	710
	Excursion	492
	GIT	377
New York–Abidjan	First class	$1306
	Economy	830
	Excursion	578
	GIT	442
New York–Kinshasa	First class	$1486
	Economy	960
	Excursion	688
	GIT	558
New York–Nairobi	First class	$1660
	Economy	1100
	Excursion	784
	GIT	600

A few sample itineraries utilizing allowable stopovers: Take a regular first class or a regular economy class New York–Nairobi ticket and you can plan a really elaborate itinerary, embracing stopovers in Europe as well as Africa. The following itinerary embraces more cities than you might want to visit, but, give or take a few dollars' possible extra fare for excess mileage, could be scheduled on a New York–Nairobi round-trip first class or economy class ticket, New York–Paris–Rome–Athens–Cairo–Khartoum–Addis Ababa–Nairobi–Dar es Salaam–Lusaka–Kinshasa–Douala–Accra–Abidjan–Bamako–Dakar–Las Palmas–Casablanca–Lisbon–New York. Note that North, East, and West Africa are all well represented and that even southern Africa is touched upon with a stop in the Zambian capital of Lusaka, from which an inexpensive excursion could be made to Victoria Falls.

But even with bargain-rate group-inclusive tour fare, the seven maximum allowable stopovers can be spaced out so as to permit tremendous geographical diversity, as with this itinerary on a New York–Nairobi GIT ticket: New York–Athens–Entebbe–Nairobi–Abidjan–Bamako–Casablanca–New York—a routing embracing Europe as well as North, West, East, and southern African points.

Ways to go: Where one goes—and how one goes—are matters of personal taste and preference in Africa as everywhere. One can travel *independently*, "free-lancing" arrangements, transportation, accommodations, and sightseeing as one goes along—a method recommended only for the vagabond-type traveler with unlimited time and flexibility as to routing and destinations. For it must be borne in mind that despite the density of air networks to and within Africa, there is nothing like the frequency of flights that one finds in Europe, the United States, the Caribbean, and parts of Asia and the Pacific. Away from the really beaten path, flights can be few and far between—one, two, or three a week are not uncommon. Additionally, first-class and de luxe hotel accommodation is limited in most cities, while accommodation in the lodges of the national parks and game reserves is nothing like what it should be, in high season. Therefore, these other methods of travel in Africa are more to be recommended: One can travel *with a group on a package tour*—this is probably as popular in Black Africa as in Eastern Europe and the Soviet Union; and one can travel *with a prearranged individual itinerary* (known in the travel industry as an "F.I.T."), including advance hotel and sightseeing bookings en route, if desired.

Package tours of Africa: Tour packagers are at their most imaginative on this of all the continents, with visits to new destinations and new combinations of destinations appearing each travel season. There are many advantages to the package. All of the details are taken care of—transportation, accommodations, meals, basic sightseeing. Frequently, by the use of excursion or GIT fares plus mass-purchasing of rooms, meals, and sightseeing, costs are lower than they might be if one travels independently. There are a good many tour packagers. They wholesale their tours to retail travel agents from whom individuals may book. It is always wise to select both an agent and a packager who are not only members of the American Society of Travel Agents (ASTA), but to whom Africa is a specialty. Here is a selection—by no means a comprehensive list—of packagers who specialize in Africa to an appreciable extent: Adventures Unlimited at Abercrombie & Fitch, New York; American Express, New York; Thomas Cook & Son, New York; Donald L. Ferguson Travel, Coral Gables, Florida; Hemphill Travel, Los Angeles; Henderson Tours, Atlanta; Natural History Tours/Executive Travel, Inc., Chicago; Percival Tours, Los Angeles; Raymond & Whitcomb, New York; Travcoa, Chicago; Vision Travel, New York.

Driving in and through Africa: Certain areas of North, East, and southern Africa are equipped with modern highways, as, indeed, are virtually all the urban areas of substance on the continent. Still, a motor tour of Africa or even of any major portions thereof remains something of an adventure, and by no means for everyone. One needs a variety of documents, a serviceable car, and a strong constitution. It is possible to go by car from the Mediterranean to the Cape of Good Hope. One route is from Tangier, in Morocco, to Cape Town, via West Africa and Central Africa; it should be undertaken during the tropical dry season—between November and April. Another route is from Cairo to Cape Town via East Africa. Either can be accomplished in about a month, but friends of mine who are veterans of the Tangier–Cape Town trek recommend ten to twelve weeks—enough time for frequent stopovers at points of interest along the way. Road conditions vary from excellent to unbelievable. Further information: International Division, American Automobile Association, 750 Third Avenue, New York.

Hotel rates, like all costs, vary from season to season. By and large, though, the price of accommodation in first-class hotels in Africa remains lower than in Western Europe and the United States. Of the more popular tourist countries, Kenya is probably the most expensive in this regard—although one gets value for the money. Singles in the better Nairobi hotels average eighteen or nineteen dollars, doubles about thirty dollars. Safari lodges in the

Kenya national parks are somewhat less, as are rates in neighboring East African countries. West African hotels might average about sixteen dollars single, twenty dollars double, with tabs running a bit higher in Abidjan than elsewhere in this region. Rates in southern Africa are similar to those of East Africa, wth the odd exception of those in Mozambique, which are the cheapest by far of the entire continent. Moderate best describes the North African situation, too, with top-class singles going for twelve to fourteen dollars in Morocco, doubles for only slightly more; and not dissimilar tabs—a bit higher, perhaps—in Egypt.

ALGERIA

République Populaire et Démocratique d'Algérie

Entry requirements: *A visa; no health certificate is required, but the usual inoculations are recommended.* **Best times for a visit:** *November to May are the ideal months—mild and much like the climate of Mediterranean France. Summer in the north is hot but not excessively so, but the south should be reserved for the non-summer months.* **Currency:** *The dinar: 4.9 dinars=$1.* **Principal European language:** *French, with Arabic and Berber dialects the languages of the Algerians. English is spoken in leading hotels, transport terminals, and resorts.* **Domestic transport:** *Good roads above the Sahara region, a fairly extensive rail network in the north, and a well-organized air service connecting major centers.* **Further information:** *Office Algérien d'Action Économique et Touristique, Algiers, Algeria. Trans-Sahara motor trips (for government rules, special permits, etc.)—Compagnie Générale Transsaharienne, 15 Rue Michelot, Algiers, Algeria, and Société Africaine de Transport Trolicoup, 26 Bis Rue Sadi Carnot, Algiers, Algeria. Embassy of Algeria (Algerian Interest Section) 2811 Kalorama Road, Washington, D.C.*

INTRODUCING ALGERIA

One of Africa's biggest countries—it is three times the size of Texas—Algeria is home to some fourteen million people. Algeria used to have the highest proportion of Europeans of any of the North African countries, but since independence most of the European settlers have left, leaving the Algerians to develop the economy and manage the commerce that used to be in the hands of the Europeans. Algeria has known foreign occupiers from the earliest days of its long history; the Carthaginians; the Romans; the Vandals; the Arabs—who came in the sixth century, bringing Islam and the Islamic culture with them; the Turks, who arrived in the fifteenth century; the Barbary pirates, who actually pulled the strings during the reigns of the Deys of Algiers; and finally the French, who entered Algiers in 1830 and had conquered the entire country—including the Sahara regions of the south—by 1909.

France brought many *colons* to Algeria, and mainly for their benefit, and for the benefit of the French economy, built modern cities, railroads, piers, and factories. She did not begin to concentrate heavily on improved health, sanitation, and education facilities for the heavy Moslem majority until after World War II—during which time Algeria served as headquarters for the De Gaulle Free French government. (Neighboring Morocco and Tunisia had French administrators who were pro-Vichy.) But the postwar concern for the Algerian populace was a case of too little, too late. The war inspired the establishment of a nationalist movement, as it did in so much of Africa and Asia. And the French were not about to go along. Guerrilla warfare reared its ugly head, beginning in 1954. Thousands of lives—Algerian and French—were lost before the war was ended and independence achieved in 1962. The Algerian conflict, one of the saddest of the postwar period, became a model of guerrilla warfare, with the expert Algerian National Liberation Front pitted against De Gaulle's forces and the all-too-powerful near-fascist ultras of Algeria's colonial community. Today Algeria is governed by a National Revolutionary Council headed by President Houari Boumédienne, who gained power after a military coup in 1965. His aim appears to be to develop a socialist state while retaining the country's religious traditions and maintaining good relations with foreign powers. Algeria depends heavily on the Soviet Union for weapons, on China for on-loan physicans (more than 160 Chinese doctors were working in rural Algeria in 1972), on France for technical assistance, and on the United States for economic development—often though the

United States severed diplomatic relations with Algeria, for a period, as a result of Algeria's part in the Arab-Israeli war.

In 1972, the Standard Oil Company (New Jersey) signed a four-hundred-million-dollar agreement with Algeria for crude oil deliveries, and another U.S. firm, Commonwealth Oil Refining Company, made an eight-hundred-million-dollar deal with the Algerians, at about the same time. The hope was that these major business transactions would pave the way for others, bringing the two countries closer together.

YOUR VISIT TO ALGERIA

Algiers: The Arabs called it Al-Djezair, a description of the tiny islets which cluster in its harbor, and which the Turks linked to the mainland by means of a long dyke, which they later fortified. The French, not finding Al-Djezair easy to pronounce, or spell, corrupted it to Alger, and later named the entire country after the city, calling it Algérie. And the English, naturally enough, Anglicized the French-created names. Call it what one will, Algiers is at once Arab, Turkish, and French. Best approached by sea, it rises in tiers from the low harbor—now mostly modern and bustling. The new city is quite as Gallic in many ways as Paris, both as regards architecture and *joie de vivre*—long-windowed buildings with tiny balconies, delightful open-air cafés, *luxe* boutiques and department stores, superb restaurants, *boîtes de nuit, dancings, bistros,* and prosperous garden-bordered residential sections. There are two excellent museums, the Maréchal Franchet d'Esperey, and the Bardo, with exhibits telling the drama-packed story of Algeria's past, from Carthaginian times onward; there are the great mosques and churches (some of which are ex-mosques, to the justifiable chagrin of the Moslems, who contrast Algeria with neighboring Morocco, where Marshal Lyautey forbade Frenchmen to even enter mosques, let alone convert them to Christian churches); the magnificent summer and winter palaces of the governor-general, imbedded in jewel-like gardens; the Medersa—a Moslem theological university; and—for splendid views of the tiered city, the harbor and the islets at its base, and the waters of the Mediterranean —the Saint-Raphael Park and the terrace of Nôtre-Dame d'Afrique Church. There remains the most famous attraction of them all, the Kasbah, with its steep narrow streets, its dimly lighted cafés, its many houses of prostitution, its rather pathetic flea market, the difficult-to-see tiled patios and interiors of wealthy residents' homes, the hand-crafted merchandise of the *souks*, and, most memorable, the people of the Kasbah—silent, veiled ladies; long-robed men, and pert youngsters with enormous brown eyes, sometimes in miniature versions of their elders' costumes, sometimes in European shorts, too often in nondescript tatters. Other attractions? Well, there is the Admiralty in the Old Harbor, dating back to Turkish days, the lush Jardin d'Essai du Hamma (botanical gardens, to you), the race tracks, yacht basins, tennis courts, golf courses, and excellent bathing beaches. Stay for as long as you like, but reserve time for visits to other parts of Algeria, all accessible from the capital.

Zeralda and Moretti: These seaside towns, both short drives from the capital, are two of a number of small resort areas being designed by the Algerian government's chief architect, Fernand Pouillon. Zeralda, thirteen miles west of Algiers, has shining white villas and winding streets that open up to beautiful views of the sea. Moretti has Romanesque arches, Moorish motifs, and a new hotel overlooking the sea.

Kabylia: Lying between Algiers and Constantine is Kabylia, a rugged mountainous region whose Berber peoples have resisted—with amazing success—the inroads of invaders from the time of the Romans. In certain regions, descendants of the Arabs have intermingled with the indigenous residents, but in many, there has been no intermixture, and the Berbers remain fair and blue-eyed, and their women unveiled, just as they were before the arrival of Islam. Mostly farmers—of olives, figs, barley and chick-peas—the Kabylia people are superb craftsmen as well, with their specialties silver jewelry inlaid with enamel, carved furniture, and traditionally decorated pottery. This is as good a place as any to become convinced that not all North Africa is parched desert. The Djurdjura peaks are snow-covered from December until May, and skiers have seen to it that slopes are available for the practice of their avocation. Down at sea level, the beaches are quiet and inviting to swimmers. And all about are neat farms and pleasant villages. The best hotels are at *Michelet*, in the interior, and *Djidjelli*, on the coast.

Constantine: At the eastern fringe of Kabylia is Constantine, one of the most unbelievable towns in the world. Originally Phoenician and formerly called Cirta, Constantine received its present appellation from the Turkish emperor of that name (the very same who unmodestly gave Constantinople *its* name). It is ingeniously constructed atop a fantastically steep rock, accessible—in the old days—only by means of a single, easily defended slope, but otherwise surrounded by deep, moatlike canyons in the manner of a medieval castle. Invaders of old had a tough time taking Constantine. But the French changed all that. When they finally occupied it themselves after a bloody battle in 1837, they built a series of bridges over the moat which are masterpieces of the engineer's art. The city now includes nonrocky suburbs, as a result. But it is the heart of Constantine—the pinnacle, one might say—that never fails to awe visitors, who circle its boulevards, traverse its bridges for downward views into the canyon depths, and occupy themselves otherwise with more conventional sightseeing: the cathedral (once again, a former mosque), the Place de la Breche—in the center of town, the Gustav Mercier Museum, the ornate Ahmed Bey Palace, and of course, the Medina—or Moslem quarter—and the *souks*. Nearby are the ancient Roman towns—now restored ruins—of *Timgad*, *Djemila*, and *Tebessa*, the traditional Berber villages of the *Aurès Mountains*, and the busy little city of *Philippeville*, which serves as Constantine's port.

Oran: Algeria's second city—exceeding 300,000 in population—is Oran, blessed with an unusually mild winter climate and an unusually cool summer one, fine Mediterranean beaches, a thriving harbor, and an unexpected surfeit of Spanish monuments—fortresses, churches, houses—which are souvenirs of an Iberian invasion followed by a good bit of immigration a few centuries ago.

This is not to say the Arabic influence is missing; on the contrary, Islamic culture and architecture reaches a peak here, with the Mosque of the Pasha, the Old Kasbah neighborhood, and the *souks*. Aïn-el-Turck and Bouisseville are the leading beaches.

Bône: Easternmost of the major ports, Bône was known as *Hippo Regius* in Roman days, and was the home of St. Augustine, who wrote and preached there, and in whose honor a modern basilica has been erected, which interests visitors. Otherwise, there is little in the town, aside from animated sidewalk cafés (especially at night) on the Cours Bertagne, the coastal *corniche* and Promenade des Caroubiers, and bits of ruins from the old Roman town. The countryside is lovely, however, and excursions can be made into the hills and mountains, and to smaller coastal resorts.

Tlemcen: Drop the "t" when you attempt to pronounce this. Not far from the Moroccan frontier city of Oujda, Tlemcen is blessed with a 2500-foot altitude and is one of the few Algerian cities with a comfortable year-round climate. It is visitable in any season, and it has more than good weather to recommend it. Known as *Pomaria* (the Orchards) in Roman times, it is still the center of a region of green, blossoming countryside, with a Moslem population more conservative and tradition-bound than that of any other major town of the country. There are any number of splendid mosques which date back to the twelfth and thirteenth centuries (including Mansourah, of which little more than the tall, square minaret remains, and El-Eubbab, still opulent with lavishly embellished walls of tile mosaic). There is an important archaeological museum, the venerated Tomb of Rabb, to which the local faithful make May pilgrimages, the strange Grotto of d'Aïn Fezza, and outlying woods that are considered holy by the Moslems. The Medersa—or college—keeps alive handicrafts traditions (carpets, curtains, embroidered leatherware) by teaching their techniques, as well as religious subjects. There is a daily produce market teeming with activity and a blaze of color, frequent Moslem festivals, and of course the *souks*, well stocked with Tlemcen's handiwork.

Sahara oases: A trip to Algeria without a visit to oases in the desert would be like a holiday in France which omitted Paris. There are a number of easily accessible oasis towns in the northern regions of the Sahara, and the chief town of the southern Sahara is now accessible by air. Closest to Algiers is *Bou-Saâda,* just 150 miles south of the capital, in a lush valley surrounded by the arid, rugged desert hills, with small, neat, cubicle-shaped houses, white and glistening in the sun; *souks* selling hand-woven *djellaba* robes and other wares; delightful hotels and swimming pools; splendid dances, performed frequently, by women of the Ouled-Nails tribe, clad in flaring silk robes; and a border of palm groves leading into the desert, which is accessible either by foot or camel. Farther distant is *El Hodna,* a vast salt lake absolutely guaranteed to create an effect of mirages. *Biskra* captivated tourists long before André Gide's glowing commentaries made it famous. Even the Romans—who called it *Vescera*—found it a little paradise. It was later an archbishopric during the early Christian era, and a Turkish stronghold in later centuries. The weather is perfect from November through April, and besides fine hotels, swimming pools, cafés, and even a casino, there are Moslem *fantasias* (festivals), a palm grove of some two hundred thousand date-bearing trees, a ruined Turkish fort, nearby villages, and a number of swirling desert dunes accessible via camel. Permeating the dry climate: a quiet charm which not even foreign tourists have dissipated.

Laghouat: Gardens, gardens, gardens—*laghouat* is Arabic for "gardens," and this charming town is full of them, as well as groves of date palms, figs, oranges, and pomegranates. It is an ancient Moslem settlement, with a white-walled Medina, a number of important mosques and tombs, and Ouled-Nails, headquarters of the town's dancers, who perform every evening. Nearby are the *Mountains of Moloh* and *Aïn Mahdi,* seat of the Tidjania Moslem sect and a center for pilgrimages. Craft specialties are striped *jerbis* tapestries and rugs, sold in the *souks* and at the White Sisters' crafts school.

The Mzab region: This is a complex of seven northern Sahara towns, with *Ghardaïa* the biggest and most easily reached. It is built on a semicircle of rocks at the foot of a mountain with snow-white, tightly clustered houses on steep terraces, and a mosque whose design is reminiscent of those in Mali, to the south. The people—rigidly orthodox Moslems of the Ibadite group—crowd the frenetic market place and *souks*. Beyond are the other lovely towns of the region, established in the barren desert eight centuries ago by Berbers driven from Kabylia in the north.

Tamanrasset: This isolated town—now closer than ever before to the north, thanks to air service—is the center for tours through the vast stretches of the southern Sahara—endless dunes of sand which appear to be mountains more often than not; the Hoggar peaks—which *are* mountains; breathtaking fortresses guarding little oasis settlements in the Colomb-Béchar area; long, silent camel caravans, inviting pools shaded by swaying palms, and the handsome, hospitable desert people, whose way of life remains much as it has been for many centuries—invaders, conquerors, and nationalist movements notwithstanding.

SHOPPING

Though each region of Algeria has its own specialties, samplings of almost all are available in the *souks* of Algiers, Oran, and Constantine. Tlemcen features its own distinctive wares, and the oasis towns, theirs. Look for rugs, hand-woven cloth, *djellaba* cloaks, babouches (slippers), beautifully worked leather, copperware, jewelry in gold and silver, a great variety of pottery, small pieces of furniture, some with fine inlay work. Bargaining is the rule.

CREATURE COMFORTS

Good hotels, restaurants, bars, night spots, casinos, cafés are found in the large cities and resorts. Smaller places, with less choice, are nonetheless generally well equipped, if not luxuriously so.

HOTELS—**Algiers:** The Aletti and St. George are both de luxe;

other leaders are the Angleterre, Albert I, Oasis, Suisse Central Touring, Nice, and Regina. **Constantine:** The Transatlantique is excellent, and the Cirta comes close; others—de Paris Grand, d'Orient et Saint George, Panoramique. **Bône:** Grand Hôtel d'Orient, Grand Hôtel de Nice, Grillon, and Touring. **Oran:** Grand, Martinez, Windsor. **Tlemcen:** Transatlantique, Villa Rivaud, Villa Marguerite. **Kabylia** (Djidjelli)—du Casino, de France, du Littoral (Michelet)—Transatlantique. **Bou-Saâde:** Transatlantique. **Biskra:** Transatlantique, Oasis, du Chef, Sahara. **Laghouat:** Saharien, Transatlantique. **Ghardaia** (Mzab): Transatlantique, Atlantide. **Tamanrasset:** Transatlantique.

ANGOLA

Entry requirements: *A visa, obtainable from Portuguese consulates, plus a health certificate (smallpox, yellow fever) and an onward ticket.* ***Best times for a visit:*** *Temperatures vary in so big a land, but, generally, the most desirable months are those of the dry season—May through September.* ***Currency:*** *The Angola escudo, on a par with the Portuguese escudo—about 29 to $1.* ***Principal European language:*** *Portuguese, with French and English secondary.* ***Domestic transport:*** *Air service to leading towns, as well as an extensive rail network, and some mediocre roads.* ***Further information:*** *Casa de Portugal, 570 Fifth Avenue, New York; Associacão Comercial e Industrial de Angola, Luanda, Angola.*

INTRODUCING ANGOLA

Angola is immense. Its area is equal to a sixth of that of the United States, and it is fifteen times as big as its mother country, Portugal, with an Atlantic Ocean coastline of 1000 miles. Still, its population is little more than five million. It was decimated by the slave trade; many Brazilians are descendants of Angolans, for when the Guinea Coast of Africa began to decline as a source of slaves, Angola filled the breach.

Slavery did, of course, do more than depopulate the country. It enervated its inhabitants, left them without initiative, encouraged some of their leaders to collaborate with foreign slavers, ripped apart much of the social fabric, and many facets of traditional culture, so much so that little is now known of the pre-European period. The slave trade was, after all, not a short-lived tragedy; it lasted for several hundred years, and it robbed many Africans as well as many Europeans of any respect for human life, semblance of human dignity, or any regard for the worth of the individual. The numbers of people involved were not hundreds, but thousands, many thousands each year over a long period. Angola has never quite recovered, and it is only in recent years that Portugal has made any attempt to develop it. For a long time it was a prison colony, which helped lessen its prestige in the motherland, in contrast to Mozambique. Still, it is known that the Portuguese, when they first came in the fifteenth century, discovered substantial Iron Age civilizations. But the archaeologists have a great deal of work to do before more details of these cultures are known.

Like Mozambique, from which it is separated by Zambia and Rhodesia, Angola is officially designated an "autonomous region" of Portugal, but the terminology is largely academic. Though closer geographically to the mother country, it is the less developed for tourism; its capital is—some believe with government intent—off the beaten path of most international airways traversing Africa. Still, its port cities are visited by ships of many countries, and tourists are welcome. Those who have gone have been delighted to find excellent accommodation and, again as in Mozambique, a continental European façade intertwined with the atmosphere of sub-Sahara Africa.

For many years Portugal maintained a harsh and repressive rule over Angola, a situation that in 1961 led to a revolt in the north. This revolt, which quickly spread to other parts of the country and engaged nationalist sympathizers from Black African nations, persists to this day. Portuguese troops continue to combat guerrillas, although the fighting is now limited to certain areas and there is little open combat. One result of the continuing fight for liberation is that Portugal, although unwilling to grant independence to her African territory, has promoted a degree of economic and social reform. Forced labor, long a tradition in Angola, is at long last being discontinued, and the Angolans have been granted some local autonomy. One of the reasons for Portugal's reluctance to give up her African colonies is Angola's recently developed mineral wealth. Although most of the people are still engaged in subsistence agriculture, deposits of offshore oil, iron ore, diamonds, copper, and manganese are beginning to produce profits.

YOUR VISIT TO ANGOLA

Luanda: A great deal of the Angolan interior—it rises from the seacoast in successive steps to high plateaus—is as yet undeveloped, from the parched desert of the south to the dense forests of the north. But one would never know it upon arrival at Luanda, the capital and chief city. This is the oldest town on the coast of West Africa; to many, the most attractive; and not without its share of modernity. Proud of its reputation as the City of Bougainvillaeas, it was originally a fort and has gradually been built up, in tiers, not unlike Tangier. The lower, or Old Town, is an area of cobbled streets, miniature squares and open-air cafés, and old houses roofed with gay, round tiles. The newer quarters are slick and streamlined, with vivid, Portuguese-designed skyscrapers along the broad boulevards and generously proportioned squares. Luanda is pleasant for strolls, which should be leisurely enough for stopovers en route. Worth seeing are the charming Chapel of Nazareth, dating back to 1644; the venerable São Miguel Fort, which guards the harbor, and three important museums: the Angola Museum (by far the most important and most interesting), the Zoological Museum, and the Bunda Museum. The waters off the city's coast are an angler's paradise, and tourists may rent boats and hire guides at the Fishing Club, not far from the principal bathing beaches. Still other fishing grounds—for real *aficionados*—are along the south coast—rich with fish but less accessible.

Excursions from Luanda: Luanda is organized enough for tourism to offer some fascinating excursions, which can be made either by car or tour bus. One would be along the coast to *Belas,* and then by boat for a look at its inner bay. Or one can travel to *Caxito,* through the fishing village of *Cacuaco* to the modern

Mabubas Dam, one of the relatively few manifestations of rural development in the colony. In two days an excursion can be made to the *Quicama Game Reserve*—animal-filled and one of the least visited in all Africa—and in three days one can go by rail and bus to the town of Malange and the nearby *Duque de Bragança Falls,* on the Lucala River, among the most beautiful and impressive on the continent. They are not as wide or as high as the Victoria Falls; they are even more remote, and in a considerably less developed area, which is richer in tropical foliage than that near the Victoria Falls. The name is a pleasant change too. So many of Africa's natural wonders are named for British monarchs that it is a pleasure for a change to come upon one which honors, if not an African, at least somebody other than an Anglo-Saxon. Besides the game reserves like Quicama, where no animals can be killed, there are others, specifically earmarked for hunters, and a number of Luanda agencies make specialties of conventional safaris—averaging more than $100 a day in cost—to the tropical forest regions of *Cabinda* in the north, and the semi-arid regions of the south, near *Moçamedes.* Special equipment is of course necessary, as are licenses for shooting. Most agencies offer all-inclusive rates and provide the services of a professional hunter, servants, and de luxe camping facilities which may not include the kitchen sink but *do* include electric refrigerators and portable canvas bathtubs.

Other cities: Angola's principal towns, besides Luanda, include 6000-foot-high *Nova Lisboa,* a mountain resort with a pleasant, dry climate; modern *Lobito,* the busiest of the ports; and neighboring *Benguela,* a delightful old city which has aged gracefully in the three centuries since it was founded and abounds in mellowed monuments of earlier centuries.

SHOPPING

Open-air markets in the major cities, and smaller towns as well, are good sources for leopard- and zebra-skins, carved heads and other figures, mostly of wood, and hand-worked ivory items. Bargaining is the rule. Bazar Angola and Lojinha dos Presentes are among Luanda's better souvenir shops.

CREATURE COMFORTS

Count on gracious service, cleanliness, and, at times, even modernity. The Portuguese, while hardly progressive as a colonial power, are good innkeepers and hospitable hosts in Africa as at home. **Luanda:** The Continental leads; Globo and Turismo follow. **Lobito:** Terminus, Belo Horizonte. **Benguela:** The Mombaka, modern, attractive, and de luxe; **Nova Lisboa:** Ruacana. **Cabinda:** Grand Hotel Cabinda.

BOTSWANA

Republic of Botswana

Entry requirements: *No visa is required for visits up to two months.* **Best times for a visit:** *May to September, the dry months, are best.* **Currency:** *South African rand: 0.714 rands=$1.* **Principal European language:** *English, which is the official language.* **Domestic transport:** *There are good paved roads; there is internal railroad service and air service.* **Further information:** *Embassy of Botswana, Washington, D.C.*

INTRODUCING BOTSWANA

About the size of Texas, and bordering Rhodesia and Namibia as well as South Africa, Botswana is largely desert—the Kalahari—and for this reason has a population of less than 700,000, the great majority being African. It was in Botswana (then called Bechuanaland) that Dr. Livingstone—who worked there as a missionary for several years—married a missionary's daughter. And it was through here that the British marched on their way north to occupy Rhodesia. They annexed the area in 1895, and they held onto it until 1966. South Africa would have liked to incorporate it, and Rhodesia, its northern neighbor, had designs on it too. But its people preferred protectorate status, rather than domination by the white minorities of either of their big neighbors. In 1966 the country became an independent member of the British Commonwealth and changed its name from Bechuanaland to Botswana. Botswana depends mainly on dairy farming and stock raising, which account for most of her exports, but production has recently been started on a huge diamond site in the north, and copper and nickel depositions are being developed in the east. It is hoped that with improved stock-breeding methods and education of farmers in modern techniques Botswana will become self-sufficient in food production. Although Botswana, of necessity, maintains close ties with neighboring South Africa, her president, Sir Seretse Khama, is committed to policies of nonracialism and is himself married to a white Englishwoman.

YOUR VISIT TO BOTSWANA

Botswana is safari country—both photographic and hunting, particularly in the north. Botswana has been described as having the "largest herds of plains game in Africa today." There are more than twenty operators running safaris in the country, and various tours—from half-day to two weeks or more—can be arranged. In the center of the northern area, not far from *Maun*, a sunny town of some six thousand people, is the *Okavango Swamp*, famed for wildlife, with lagoons filled with flamingoes and pelicans and a great variety of animals, including impala, warthogs, and wildebeest. *Lake Ngami*, two hours from Maun, is also worth a visit. The 4,500-square-mile *Chobe National Park*, one of Africa's least-crowded game parks, has a comfortable lodge in Kasane on the banks of the Chobe River. The Game Reserve offers fine fishing, bird watching, and animal hunting—with a camera. It is the home of waterbuck, the rare Puku antelope, and hundreds of zebra, buffalo, and elephant. Occasionally one may see a Bushman, about thirty thousand of whom survive in the desert, living a spare existence and usually avoiding strangers.

Other areas: Also of interest to the tourist is the capital of Botswana, *Gaberone*, a new city of about fourteen thousand carved out of the bush with British aid. The capital, which eventually will house twenty thousand people, has modern shops, office buildings, a hospital, government offices, and comfortable hotels. *Francistown*, the country's commercial center, is a good starting point for trips to the Okavango Swamp.

SHOPPING

Skins, reed, and gameskin mats, Bushmen's beaded "Majumboro" shirts, curios, and carved objects can be found in public markets and in shops in Gaberone. Prices are usually reasonable, and bargaining is the rule.

CREATURE COMFORTS

HOTELS—**Gaberone:** President, Gaberone. **Francistown:** Grand, Tati. **Maun:** Riley's. **Kasane:** Chobe Safari Lodge, modern, attractive accommodations in main lodge or cottages.

BURUNDI

République du Burundi

Entry requirements: *A visa, obtainable from Belgian consulates where Burundi has no diplomatic representation, plus a health certificate (smallpox and yellow fever) and a police certificate.* **Best times for a visit:** *The dry seasons—June through August, November through March—are best, but the rain in the other months is only intermittent. There is little humidity because of the high altitude.* **Currency:** *Burundi franc: 87.5=$1.* **Principal European language:** *French, with Flemish second, and some English. Swahili is much spoken.* **Further information:** *Burundi Embassy, Washington, D.C.*

INTRODUCING BURUNDI

Like its neighbor to the north, Rwanda (see page 279), the Republic of Burundi is noted for its dramatic terrain and for a history of tribal discord between the two major ethnic groups: the tall, aristocratic Watusi and the more numerous Bahutu. However, whereas in Rwanda the Bahutu slaughtered or forced most of the Watusi to leave the country, in Burundi they remain the ruling class. And despite a few abortive coups and flareups of violent conflict, the two groups manage to coexist. Until 1966, when the independent monarchy of Burundi became the Republic of Burundi, the country was run along feudalistic lines, in which Bahutu mortgaged their services to the all-powerful Watusi, in exchange for cattle. The monarch, or *mwami,* ruled over the land, quite literally the lord and master of the normal-sized Bahutu. The Watusi did little menial work; the Bahutu farmed the land

and even constituted the ensembles of the famed Watusi dance companies. This caste system existed in both Rwanda and Burundi but was far more rigid in Rwanda. Burundi is primarily an agricultural country—coffee is the major crop—and only 2 percent of the population lives in anything resembling an urban center. Like Rwanda, it has few villages; family groups live on the steep hillsides in thatched mud huts surrounded by banana trees.

Burundi, like Rwanda, was originally part of German East Africa. It was ceded to Belgium in 1916, and in 1946, as the southern sector of Ruanda-Urundi, it became a UN trusteeship under Belgian administration. Independence came in 1962, and with it a series of assassinations, a succession of governments, and general tribal unrest. In 1966 Watusi Premier Michel Micombero overthrew the monarchy and declared Burundi a republic, with himself as President. He is on record as being opposed to feudalism and tribal conflict, but there still is a good deal of unresolved animosity between the two ethnic groups. It manifested itself in 1972 when deposed twenty-five-year-old King Ntare V was killed after returning from exile in West Germany, in connection with an attempt by monarchists to restore the throne.

YOUR VISIT TO BURUNDI

Bujumbura: On the northern shore of Lake Tanganyika, the capital, Bujumbura (formerly Usumbura), is a modern town of some 100,000 inhabitants and the center for excursions to other parts of the country. The Belgian administrators were justifiably proud of the façade of the capital. In less than half a decade it has been turned into a functional administrative center with an immense new airport and terminal, an ingeniously designed college—Holy Spirit—on a mountain overlooking the town and the lake, a little yacht basin at the water's edge, and residential quarters and business sections while, if not strikingly handsome, are at least functional and solid. Aside from these attractions, and the public market—bustling, vibrant, peopled by Watusi, Bahutu, and pygmoid—there is little to hold the visitor for more than a day or two.

Other attractions: As in Rwanda, the visitor can enjoy the spectacle of the Watusi dancing (see page 280), or the pleasures of simply observing these handsome people and their elaborate and refined culture. Their crafts—the most delicately woven baskets in Africa, intricate beadwork, subtle wood carving, sturdy iron spears—are of great beauty. Their dress—dramatic headbands, sweeping cloaks, elongated hairdos—is striking. And they are very often extremely handsome, with imposing physiques and fine facial features. *Kitega,* at an altitude of almost six thousand feet, is worth a visit. It houses a museum of Burundi lore and a restored fort dating back to German days.

SHOPPING

Hotel lobbies and terraces in towns throughout the country usually offer curios for sale—most of them authentic—and the open-air markets are always a good shopping source. Bargaining is the rule.

CREATURE COMFORTS

HOTELS—**Bujumbura:** The Paguidas—long the leader, has been modernized, and some rooms have air conditioning; there are bungalows, too; dining room, bar. The Burundi Palace is a very good No. 2. Chez Charles is the best restaurant, with excellent Belgian-French fare—and with plans for the construction of an adjoining motel.

CAMEROON

République Fédérale du Cameroun

Entry requirements: *A visa, obtainable from French consulates where Cameroon has no diplomatic missions, plus a health certificate (yellow fever and smallpox) and an onward ticket.* **Best times for a visit:** *The dry season extends from November through April. But a visit need not be avoided even during the rainy months, for the rain is not incessant, and the countryside is then at its greenest and freshest—though some roads are impassable.* **Currency:** *The CFA franc: CFA 280=$1.* **Principal European language:** *French in the east, English in the west.* **Domestic transport:** *Roads connect principal towns, some of them dirt-paved, and there are a few hundred miles of railways, the best connecting the two major cities. Generally, travel by Cameroon Airlines is recommended.* **Further information:** *Chambre de Commerce et d'Industrie du Cameroun, Douala, Cameroon; Service de l'Information de la République Fédérale du Cameroun, Yaoundé, Cameroon.*

INTRODUCING CAMEROON

The only country in the world named for a shellfish, Cameroon, which became a republic in 1960, is about the size of California. The traveler who misses it—and it is still considered a little off the beaten tourist path—is foregoing the experience of finding in one relatively small land a microcosm of all tropical Africa. He must content himself, though, with luxury facilities only in the two major towns.

Until January 1, 1960, the Republic of Cameroon was the

French Cameroons. The reader might well wonder what happened to that final "s" in the transformation. It has simply been removed arbitrarily. I doubt whether anyone knows how it ever got there to begin with. The word is, after all, an anglicization of the Portuguese for "shrimp." The waters surrounding the country's metropolis, Douala, abound in these creatures, and it was after them that Fernando Po—a Portuguese who was the first European to visit the Cameroons, back in 1472—gave the country its name. In Latin, the shellfish is *callinausa turnerano*; in Portuguese, it is *camarão*; after the Germans colonized the country in 1885, they changed the spelling to Kamerun.

Came World War I, and German possessions in Africa became League of Nations mandates. Part of Kamerun—the eastern sector—passed into French hands and became Cameroun. It remained that way, becoming a United Nations Trust Territory, still administered by France, after World War II.

The French always kept their sector an entity in itself. They never attempted to make it a part of what was French Equatorial Africa, with which it shared several frontiers. They began, after World War II, to prepare it for independence. In 1956 they conducted a country-wide election for the legislative assembly, which was the first in Black Africa to be chosen by voters, regardless of race or religion. There was completely universal suffrage—all men and women over twenty-one were eligible to vote, and a huge proportion took advantage of their franchise. The following year the country became self-governing, with its own administration largely in control, but under the jurisdiction of a French High Commissioner. Eventually the French agreed to ask the UN Trusteeship Council to grant the country complete sovereignty, which came as New Year's gift to the Cameroonian people in 1960.

In 1961, in a UN-supervised plebiscite, the southern part of the British Cameroons voted to join the Republic to form the Federal Republic of Cameroon, comprised of two states: East and West Cameroon. The northern section elected to join Nigeria. Independence has seen considerable progress under a series of five-year development plans; the most recent, of President Ahmadou Ahidjo, has included tourist development through—among other things—the creation of Cameroon Airlines and arrival on the scene of Sheraton hotels.

YOUR VISIT TO CAMEROON

Lush forests in the south . . . an elevated plain in the center . . . rocky crags in the mountainous north—this is the diversity of the Cameroonian countryside. There is variety, too, in its peoples—aristocratic Moslem Foulbés contrasted with animist Kirdis in the north . . . Pygmies in the depths of the equatorial forests . . . the Bamilekes of the west, whose collective organization has produced great skills in agriculture, the dance, and highly organized religions . . . the Doualas, for whom the great port city is named, who are largely traders and sailors, with a rich song-dance tradition, and many other groups, sub-groups, and sub-sub-groups, speaking a variety of languages and dialects.

Douala: In the shadow of volcanic, 13,000-foot Mount Cameroon, West Africa's highest peak, Douala is the republic's economic capital, chief port, and commercial center. It straddles the Atlantic, and the estuary of the Wouri River, flowing down from the interior. It is not without charm, nor on the other hand, is it a city where one need linger very long. Besides the public buildings and squares, the African sectors and markets, the open-air cafés and restaurants, the frenetic loading operations at the piers—heavy beams of mahogany, barrels of palm oil, bails of cacao, and the lovely view of the immense bridge over the Wouri—there is little of sustaining interest. One can, though, be comfortable, and relaxed. Just watching the world parade by from the sidewalk terrace of the Akwa Palace Hotel is time well spent.

Yaoundé: Rising in tiers over a series of hills in the southern interior is Yaoundé, the capital. It is considerably smaller and quieter than commercial Douala, and it is also a good bit cooler, with an average year-round temperature of 71 degrees—not easily come by in tropical Africa. The visitor without government business may see the city in a day, spend a comfortable night in the town, and be off without delay, either for the north, or on one of a number of excursions in the area. One might go to *Ebolowa,* to see cocoa plantations in the middle of an interminably immense forest. Another could be a trip to the small but pretty bathing resort of *Kribi.* Or the destination might be *Dschang,* a health center at a 4000-foot altitude on the Bamileke Plateau, not far from the gigantic *Ekom waterfalls* and a fascinating village with a fascinating name: *N'Kongsamba.*

The North: If I had time for but one destination in Cameroon it would be *Maroua,* capital of Diamare country in the north. There are few luxury-hotel facilities, but there is a great deal else. This is a city of more than 20,000 in the heart of the country's Moslem-dominated area. The Lamíbe is the ruler of a hereditary aristocracy, with as rigid a caste system as one could find anywhere in the world. The ruling group—the Foulbés—live in a complex in the center of town; the less exalted Boúrnouans have a quarter of their own on the outskirts, beyond which are the more modest neighborhoods of the animist peoples. A tour of each sector is a field day for the amateur sociologist or art buff. Maroua's widely celebrated artisans include coopers, jewelers, embroiderers, shoemakers, blacksmiths, leatherworkers, potters, tanners, dyers, and weavers. They work in family units, and their products can be purchased—ideally, *after* one has seen them being made—at the Artisan Center of the Diamare Museum, with its exhibits of Hamitic Moslem and animist Sudanese cultures, including a garden display of the six major types of regional dwellings.

From Maroua, the excursion possibilities are fraught with interest. There is the village of *Mokolo,* built among rocky crags, with a market featuring shields of skin, musical instruments, and—on Wednesdays only—touching ceremonies at which the young men of the area select their fiancées. There is the *Centre Massif* region, with terraced farms on the mountain slopes not unlike those of the pre-Columbian Incas. There is the *Waza Forest Animal Reserve*—420,000 acres of forest and savanna teeming with easy-to-view animals ranging from warthogs to panthers. And there is the *Logone Valley*, with brilliantly costumed Foulbés in its villages, and *Pouss*, with its huts virtually hidden in palm groves and the impressive palace of the area's sultan. Nearby is *Yagoua*, whose residents include women with enormous saucer-plate lips—a fashion now almost extinct among Africa's peoples. Weather conditions must be considered before planning trips in the north, and market days in the villages—always a riot of color and excitement—are invariably worth a detour.

SHOPPING

What *not* to buy can be a problem in this country. Crafts include those described in the section on *Maroua* (above), obtainable at the Artisan Center there, plus masks, ceramics, canoe prows, sculptured dance scepters, bronze statuettes, carved wooden panels, and ivory sculpture. The public markets are always browseworthy, and upon occasion, itinerant vendors on hotel terraces have something purchasable. Bargaining, outside of established shops, is the rule.

CREATURE COMFORTS

HOTELS—**Douala:** Hotel des Cocotiers, with a view of Mount Cameroon; Akwa Palace, not opulent but central, with a busy sidewalk café; Relais Aériens; Residence de Joss. **Yaoundé:** Hotel du Mont Fébé, luxurious, set on a hilltop three miles outside of town, and under Sheraton management; Independence Hotel. **Kribi:** Du Commerce, Beach. **Dschang:** Pavillons. **Ebob1wa:** Du Ntem. **Maroua:** Relais de Kuliao, Camp Hotel, Salak Airport Hotel, rooms in private homes. **Mokolo:** Rest Camp.

INDEPENDENT RESTAURANTS—**Douala:** Le Paris, Les Relais Aériens à l'Aéroport, Al Vesuvio, Le Lido, Lotus. **Yaoundé:** Safari Club.

CENTRAL AFRICAN REPUBLIC

République Centrafricaine

Entry requirements: *A visa, obtainable from French consulates where the republic has no representation, a health certificate (smallpox and yellow fever), a letter from your bank to indicate that you're solvent, and an onward ticket.* **Best times for a visit:** *November through May, the dry season, is best.* **Currency:** *The CFA franc: CFA 280=$1.* **Principal European language:** *French, with some English spoken in leading hotels and transport terminals.* **Domestic transport:** *There are no railroads, some poor roads, and an air network, and the Ubangi River is navigable at certain times of the year.* **Further information:** *Office National Centrafricain du Tourisme, B. P. 655, Bangui, Central African Republic.*

INTRODUCING THE CENTRAL AFRICAN REPUBLIC

A middle zone between the humid forests and the semidesert the Central African Republic is for the most part a gently rolling plateau with a wide variety of landscape. Many different kinds of wildlife can be found in the heavy forests and rolling grasslands of this little-known country deep in the heart of Africa. Unfortunately no longer called Ubangi-Shari, after its two major rivers, the Central African Republic was one of the four territories of French Equatorial Africa until 1958, when it became an autonomous member of the French community. Two years later, on August 13, 1960, it became an independent republic. Inhabited largely by subsistence farmers—with some primitive pygmy tribes—and largely undeveloped during seventy years of colonial rule, the Central

African Republic is arbitrarily ruled by Africa's most eccentric and unpredictable dictator—General Jean-Bedel Bokassa, who in 1966 seized power in a bloodless coup. Although his long-impoverished country is beginning to show signs of economic progress, the Bokassa regime is hardly one to be applauded. Cabinets are shuffled constantly—one year saw four foreign ministers. A recent Mother's Day saw the execution of all prisoners convicted of murdering women. The general keeps a pair of thirty-five-thousand-dollar limousines, as well as a pair of mistresses, and wears as many as twenty-five full-size medals on his chest. Security is tight, with citizens fearful of contacts with foreigners.

Agriculture—predominantly coffee and cotton—is still the main enterprise, but there is a growing diamond-mining industry and a number of small-scale manufacturing concerns. Progress is also being made in education and health care. Limited transportation and the country's landlocked position have somewhat hampered foreign investment and trade, but the Central African Republic does receive aid from France.

The Central African Republic's future economic success seems to lie in the exploitation of her natural resources. Diamonds bring in some twelve million dollars each year. Uranium deposits found in the eastern part of the country are expected to yield profits, and the rich forestland represents a great potential for the development of a timber industry.

YOUR VISIT TO THE CENTRAL AFRICAN REPUBLIC

The capital, Bangui—now a town of about two hundred thousand—is perfectly located for excursions to the most interesting parts of the republic. A low, broad city straddling the banks of the Ubangi River, with the green forest serving as a backdrop, Bangui deserves at least two or three days of a thoughtful traveler's itinerary. Walking its flamboyant-lined avenues is the best way for looks at the central market (particularly just after sunrise, when it is at its busiest), the river port, where porters load cotton, coffee, sisal, and palm onto steamers, the Chamber of Commerce building, with its immense modern frescoes of African life, the quiet and tropical municipal park, the Boganda Museum, and the Corniche Promenade, along the river's edge. See, too, the various African sections of the town and its environs—the Moslem sector, Mamadou M'Baïki, with its unusual market; Kina, with its Catholic Mission; the villages of n'Dres and Boy-Rabé, and—most important—the African Arts and Crafts Center.

Excursions from Bangui: The possibilities for trips from the capital are virtually limitless, but here are a few suggestions: a boat trip down the Ubangi River to the rapids of *Zinga,* from which there is a road through the forest to *M'Baïki,* with coffee plantations and sawmills, and, farther on, forest pygmy camps, made of light wood covered with leaves; a motor journey some sixty miles to the north, to the village of *Bouali* and its famous waterfalls on the M'Bali River. Higher than Niagara, the falls are floodlit, in the best French tradition, from December to June. All about are the people of the new republic, most of them in neat thatched villages—hospitable, and delighted to welcome visitors who, if they would learn of African forest life, will cruise leisurely on the highways, always on the lookout for feasts and fetes that are inevitably celebrated with dancing and music. There are two national parks—*Bamingui* and *Bangoran,* covering two and a half million acres, and with good roads and resthouses, and, smaller but equally well populated with game, *St. Floris.*

SHOPPING

Carved wood—much of it very good—in a variety of shapes. Try Perroni in Bangui for a good selection of ebony and ivory works of art.

CREATURE COMFORTS

HOTELS—**Bangui:** Rock, handsome, luxury class; Minerva; Safari. **Bambari:** Hôtel des Chasses.

CHAD

République du Tchad

Entry Requirements: *A visa obtainable from French consulates, where Chad has no diplomatic mission, plus a health certificate (yellow fever and smallpox), and an onward ticket.* **Best times for a visit:** *The dry season—November through April in the center, mid-November through mid-March in the south—is ideal for a visit. In the north, toward Lake Chad, there is some rain every month, but considerably less humidity than in the south.* **Currency:** *The CFA franc: CFA 280=$1.* **Principal European language:** *French, with English spoken in leading hotels and transport terminals.* **Domestic transport:** *There is good internal air service; few paved roads; no railroad.* **Further information:** *Service d'Information, Fort-Lamy, Republic of Chad.*

INTRODUCING CHAD

Three times the size of California, the Republic of Chad has a diverse population of races and cultures: North African, Black African, European. Its northern borders touch the southern frontiers of the Libyan desert, and its southern territory links it with the equatorial forests. Modern Chad is a twentieth-century phenomenon. Its major towns came into being only seven decades ago, and the rest of the world knew little of the territory until it figured so prominently as a Free French-Allied stronghold during World War II. In 1959 Chad, long a part of French Equatorial Africa, became an autonomous member of the French Community. In 1960 it was proclaimed a republic.

Chad is named for an immense lake—the eleventh largest in the world—with an average depth of but five feet. It was not, of course, always that shallow, but alluvial deposits from the rivers of the area, all of which converge upon it, continue each year to dry it up. The country's landlocked situation (it is a thousand miles from the nearest seaport) and its inadequate transportation facilities (there is no railroad, and highways tend to become flooded during the rainy season) make Chad one of the remotest of African nations. Although it is not lacking in natural beauty, it is an undeveloped country with few natural resources and an economy that still largely depends on the French, who own most of the businesses and shops. There are about ten thousand Frenchmen in Chad, and the country would be hard-pressed without French aid and subsidies. Most of the people are engaged in subsistence farming, stock raising, and fishing. Almost all other goods must be flown into the country, a situation that makes for extremely high prices.

Chad's problems are aggravated by continuous friction between the Moslems in the north and the Bantus of the south, who control the government. The continuing presence of more than two thousand French troops, who are helping the northern rebels, has led some observers to call Chad France's Vietnam. French President Georges Pompidou, on a state visit in 1972, pledged continuing support to the country.

Additionally, Chad has had difficulties with Libya, its neighbor to the north; it broke off relations in 1971, charging that the Libyans were behind an attempted coup to oust François Tombalbaye as President. Despite the country's internal difficulties, it holds great interest for the tourist in the form of abundant wildlife, the great variety of its people, a capital city with a chic Franco-African atmosphere, and Lake Chad itself, one of the strangest of Africa's natural attractions.

YOUR VISIT TO CHAD

Fort-Lamy: With about 100,000 residents, Fort-Lamy is the biggest city of the republic, its capital, and a major transport terminus for persons and cargo arriving via air, water, foot, and camel. Lying at the confluence of the Shari and Logone rivers, it is hot and dusty, with a façade of glistening white European-style buildings and mud-walled African sectors. The heat is dry, and there is little humidity, so that Fort-Lamy is anything but torpid. Its own inhabitants and the constant stream of visitors are gay, effervescent, busy buying and selling during the clear, bright daylight hours, and equally as occupied at amusing themselves after dark. There is nothing of architectural significance in Fort-Lamy, except for the separately enclosed quarters of the varied racial, religious, and tribal groups, and the public buildings and squares in the European-built sector. What makes the town so eminently worth visiting is its people—particularly on market days and holidays. One can simply sit over a cool drink and watch all manner of activity on the sandy streets: sultans from outlying regions on horseback, surrounded by sworded courtiers of their retinue; lovely women in flowing gowns perched atop camels, delicate-featured Bororo and Foulbé tribesmen, verbose Hausas in long *boubou* gowns and pantaloons, ascetic Moslem professors with their young pupils. And the animals: goats, horses, sheep, rams, oxen. And the bright-eyed children, laughing, cavorting, dressed in variations of their parents' traditional costume, intrigued with the presence of visitors, and with their cameras.

Trips from Fort-Lamy: Walk Fort-Lamy's streets, amble through its markets, relax in its cafés for a day or two, before moving onward. There are any number of excursions available, from a half day to a fortnight. *Lake Chad* itself—dotted with immense islands and tiny islets made of twigs and papyrus brought together by rapids and whirlpools—should be first among them. In a day or two one can visit fishing villages about its shores, and even see the cliffs and peaks of the Hadjer-el-Mamis region. Other trips can be made to villages along the banks of the major rivers, and if one has the time and the energy, one destination should be the *Tibesti Mountains* in the north. This range's peaks tower some 14,000 feet above sea level, amid a region of cliffs and gorges. The people of the Tibesti are the strange Tibus, wanderers who live in tent huts made of matting and built on the frameworks of bent branches.

Fort-Archambault: Named, rather romantically, for a young French army lieutenant who died of fever during a turn of century campaign, Fort-Archambault is smaller than Fort-Lamy, but of equal importance for the visitor. On the banks of the Ubangi-Shari, its location signals the end of the savanna-forest region of the south and the beginnings of the northern desert. Here too there is a mosaic of peoples—the Saras with raised tattoos on their bodies—each a work of art; more Hausa, Arabs, and other representatives of tribes to the south, each in quarters of their own, separated from those of their neighbors by walls of straw. Fort-Lamy is in the heart of some of the finest animal country in the Union. Among its residents are a number of professional hunters and safari outfitters, who can easily arrange for bush expeditions as short as a day, as long as a month. Nonhunters—visitors who like myself prefer photographing animals rather than shooting them—are accommodated quite as well as the gun toters. I would suggest at least a day in the bush, particularly for the visitor who will not have the opportunity to visit other game areas during his African journey.

Other Chad highlights include *Abéché,* an important commercial town with a distinctive Arab flavor; *Ouara,* with ruins of an ancient regional sultanate; *Ennedi,* with its centuries-old rock paintings; and *Mousgoum,* a village with unusual shell-shaped conical mud huts.

SHOPPING

Carpets, draperies, pottery, jewels, and leatherwork can be purchased in the public markets, where bargaining is the rule.

CREATURE COMFORTS

HOTELS—**Fort-Lamy:** La Tchadienne, on the outskirts, luxurious, air-conditioned; Chari, modern, very attractive; Grand. **Fort-Archambault:** Eascale, Massenya. *Note:* Although restaurants in Chad are excellent, be prepared for high prices.

CONGO

République Populaire du Congo

Entry requirements: *A visa, available from French consulates where the Congo has no diplomatic representation, health certificate (yellow fever and smallpox), police certificate, and financial guarantee.* **Best times for a visit:** *The dry season runs from mid-May to late September and mid-December through January.* **Currency:** *The CFA franc: CFA 280=$1.* **Principal European language:** *French, with English spoken in leading hotels and transport terminals.* **Domestic transport:** *There is internal air service between cities; railroad and road facilities are limited.* **Further information:** *Service d'Information, Brazzaville, Congo.*

INTRODUCING THE CONGO

Thick equatorial forest, the kind so dense that the sun rarely penetrates through to the ground, a capital city that has an unmistakably French air and is one of the most modern in tropical Africa—this is the Congo. It was named for the great river, and until recently was dependent on it and its tributaries as a link between its forests, plains, and mountains. Claimed for France in the eighteenth century by Savorgnan de Brazza, it was once a part of the immense French Union of Central African Republics, which included Chad, Gabon, and the Central African Republic. The Congo attained independence in 1960 and has had a turbulent political history since then. Each of the three governments that have been in power since independence have had to grapple with serious financial and political problems—tribal conflicts, unemployment, economic underdevelopment—and each has existed in an atmosphere of high intrigue, with coups, abortive and otherwise, coming from both the left and the right. The present government, headed by President Marien Ngouabi, who is also head of the nation's one political party, the Congolese Labor Party, is committed to a policy of "revolutionary socialism." However, although there are signs throughout the country of the alliance with the Communist nations—Russian and Chinese advisers, a large Russian-built hotel and maternity hospital, prominently displayed photographs of Mao—the Congo is still economically dependent on France, and French companies still own most of the country's industry. It is a largely urbanized country, with more than one-fifth of the population living in the two major cities, Pointe Noire and Brazzaville. The Congo has made progress in political and economic reform, but it remains to be seen whether Africa's first people's republic can solve its ethnic and social problems and develop into a prosperous, progressive nation.

YOUR VISIT TO THE CONGO

Brazzaville: Facing Kinshasa, capital of Zaïre just across the river, Brazzaville had a tremendous spurt of growth in the 1950s. It remains a country cousin to Kinshasa. There are nowhere near as many skyscrapers and not nearly so much bustle. The Belgians built Kinshasa with function more than amusement in mind. They crossed the river for relaxing evenings in Brazzaville, and were quite as ready as any visitor to admit that it is quite the more delightful of the sister towns. Brazzaville was, until late 1958, the capital of all French Equatorial Africa, and it can thank this circumstance for much of its modern façade. It is, as well, a river port—the Congo (now called the Zaïre by the Zaïreans in the neighboring republic across the water) winding through the dark forests of the Mayumbe region links it with the coastal Pointe Noire, second city of the republic and site of its biggest harbor. The churling waters of Stanley Pool lie at Brazzaville's feet. There are, as well, residential streets ablaze with the red shades of the mango trees, the gay hibiscus blooms, and trees whose names evoke the tropics: lemon, orange, avocado, papaya, guava. The former governor-general's headquarters, now in use by the new government, is a handsome French Colonial building. And there are other monuments: the cathedral, dating back to 1887; the turn-of-the-century town hall; and the zoo—quite as popular, even in Africa, as those in less animal-filled countries; the market, homes, and unusual art school in the Poto-Poto district, the Art and Handicrafts Instruction Center, and the views of Kinshasa across the river from the Brazzaville banks of the great river. A day or two can easily suffice for the casual visitor, but there are excursions for those with additional time. Short ones—of less than half a day—can be made to the *Congo Rapids,* to the great hydroelectric works at *Djoué,* and to the pyramid monument to de Brazza—France's answer to Henry M. Stanley. Day-long trips might be made to *Linzola,* the first mission in the interior of the country, dating back to 1883; to the tiny village at lovely *Lake N'Zamboula,* revered as a sacred place by many Africans; to the virgin forests which surround the *Bouenza Waterfalls;* and to *M'bé* and *N'Gabé,* residences of the chief of the Bateké tribe. And of course for the unfortunate traveler not able to make a proper visit to the neighboring Republic of Zaïre, a requisite would be a cross-river safari to Kinshasa; boats run regularly and take a half hour to reach the other side.

Other towns: Other Congo cities are the aforementioned *Pointe Noire,* with its chief attractions the busy Atlantic Ocean piers, from which gold, ivory, coffee, palm oil, and rare woods are exported, and two superb bathing beaches and excellent deep-sea fishing. *Loango,* once the main coastal town and the port of entry to the interior in the days of the explorers, is now a decadent, rarely visited place, not unlike Saint-Louis in Senegal, which lost out to Dakar as Loango did to Pointe Noire. There is one *national park—Odzala*—and there are throughout the country, and never far from the major towns, the great equatorial forests, deep gorges, waterfalls, cascades, and at intervals—along the river and its tributaries—tiny European-run trading posts, invariably with a solitary visitor's hut for itinerant travelers.

SHOPPING

Polychrome masks, carved wood figures, paintings, ceramics, and other crafts from Brazzaville's Poto-Poto Art Center and School of Art and Handicrafts.

CREATURE COMFORTS

HOTELS—**Brazzaville:** Rélais Aériens, motel-style and modern; the newer Soviet-built Cosmos; the central and attractive Olympic. All these hotels are air-conditioned and have swimming pools. The downtown Mistral, and Ma Campagne, on the outskirts, are top restaurants. **Pointe Noire:** Mayumbe—luxurious, excellent cuisine and wines.

DAHOMEY

République du Dahomey

Entry requirements: *A visa, obtainable from French consulates where Dahomey has no diplomatic representation, plus a health certificate (smallpox and yellow fever) and an onward ticket.* **Best times for a visit:** *The dry season—January to April—is the pleasantest time, but even during the remaining months of the year the rains are only intermittent, and need not deter visitors. The climate is hot and humid at all times.* **Currency:** *The CFA franc: CFA 280=$1.* **Principal European language:** *French, with English spoken in leading hotels and transport terminals.* **Domestic transport:** *Good roads connect major centers in this tiny country; there is a limited air service, a coastal steamer system, and a rail network.* **Further information:** *Service d'Information de la République du Dahomey, Cotonou, Dahomey.*

INTRODUCING DAHOMEY

Before it became a semi-autonomous republic in 1958—and a sovereign state in 1960—Dahomey had been the smallest of the eight provinces of French West Africa, and the most densely populated. It has an Atlantic coast line of but 70 miles and extends only 430 miles from north to south. But, as is often the case, big things come in small packages, and Dahomey makes up in interest what it lacks in size. It had cities, palaces, arts, and highly organized societies of its own, long before Europeans arrived on the scene.

It was not, from all reports, a peace-loving society; it even included among its fighting forces brigades of women—centuries before the WACs or WAVEs came into being. Still, its proclivity for warfare was no more deplorable than in, say, France, Britain, and other leading Western countries.

The early-bird Portuguese were the first white visitors to Dahomey in the sixteenth century. In search of slaves—which was so often their mission in Africa—they came upon a bustling coastal city and dubbed it Porto Novo (new port), although, of course, it was new only to them, not to the Africans who had lived in it for some centuries. Later they, and their successors, came upon Abomey, ancient capital in the interior. But it was not until the French took over the area, toward the end of the nineteenth century, that the African Kingdom of Dahomey came to an end.

The Republic of Dahomey is aligned with four other former French West African provinces. Though each is sovereign, they are banded together in a loose political federation, the Council of the Entente. The other members are the Ivory Coast, Niger, Upper Volta, and Togo.

YOUR VISIT TO DAHOMEY

Cotonou: Though not the capital, Cotonou is Dahomey's commercial center, major port, and air terminus. And it contains the best hotels in the country. Besides its interesting markets and European business sections, it boasts an unusual African fishing quarter, located on a beach fronting one of the lagoons which separate it from the sea. But there is no need to devote more than a day or two to sightseeing; one's time can better be spent on excursions to Abomey, the ancient capital to the north; Porto Novo, the current capital, also on the coast; Ouidah, an ancient city which contains a fort still held by the Portuguese; and the villages of the north.

Abomey: Abomey was the capital of the ancient kingdom. Its kings lived in a hundred-acre fortified palace compound, the remains of whose high, thick walls (thirty feet high and six feet deep) still stand. There is a fascinating museum of Abomeyiana within the walls of the palace. After looking at the exhibits, it is easy to believe that Abomey at the peak of its greatness exchanged ambassadors with the court of Louis XIV. It ranked with the Kingdom of Benin—now a part of Nigeria—as one of the greatest of the West African societies. And although its kings were to traffic in slaves and practice cruelties quite as savage as their European contemporaries, Abomey's past was not without distinction; its sculptors and artisans, working for the main on royal commissions, executed some of the continent's most superb art. Although it began to decline many decades earlier, it was not until French troops conquered it in 1892 that it finally fell. The people of Abomey still pay homage to their former kingdom at annual ceremonies before the crumbling walls of the palace. Within, are restored chambers—the throne room, the statuary hall, the jewelry hall among them. Each is rich with collections of traditional arts and crafts, ranging from furniture and textiles to arms and jewelry.

Ouidah: A few miles west of Cotonou lies Ouidah, the country's oldest port and one of its most history-filled cities. The Portuguese first visited it in 1580 and the fort which they built—*St.-Jean Baptiste de Adjuda*—to this day remains Portuguese territory. Ouidah thrived in succeeding centuries as a slave-trading center. Many of the Negroes of Cuba, Martinique, Guadeloupe, and Bahia, in Brazil, are descendants of Dahomey Africans. It is, today, a small and quiet town. Its streets are bordered with fruit trees and brilliant-hued blossoming plants. Each of its quarters has a character of its own—Tove, the oldest; Maro, mainly Moslem; Ahoundjigo, French—among them. Ouidah's greatness has passed; its chief attraction today is the great charm which comes to towns steeped in history.

The north: The peoples of upper Dahomey have not the same rich past as their southern compatriots, but they are, nonetheless, very worth getting to know. The most interesting among them, in many ways, are the Somba, whose men wear little more than a loincloth and a wrist bracelet. Their women cover themselves with skirts of leaves suspended from slender string belts. The Somba live in patriarchal family groups in two-story castle-like compounds called *tatas,* the walls of which are embellished with circular turrets. Animals and equipment occupy the ground floor, while the family members live above. The principal activity of each unit is centered about the enclosed courtyard. Somba villages are in the neighborhood of *Natitingou,* accessible by plane from Cotonou—and by fairly good roads, as well. And elsewhere in this region are waterfalls, game reserves, and villages of other northern peoples including Berba, Nyende, and Youbou.

SHOPPING

Iron figures, woodcarvings, masks, jewelry, leatherwork, handwoven textiles, and other *objets d'art* can be purchased at the Artisan Center in Abomey, and at markets in Cotonou, Porto Novo, and Ouidah, as well as at the markets in the smaller towns and villages, including those of the north. Bargaining is the general rule.

CREATURE COMFORTS

Hotels and Restaurants—First-class hotels are the renovated Hotel de la Plage and the modern Hotel Croix du Sud, both in **Cotonou.** Other hotels in that city are the Hotel du Port, with swimming pool, and the Provence, conveniently located in the center of town. In addition to the hotel restaurants, good choices for eating are the Pam-Pam, Le Capri, and Les Trois Paillotes, on the road to Porto Novo. There are smaller inns and rest camps in the other principal towns; accommodation for them should be booked in advance from Cotonou.

EGYPT

Entry requirements: *Visa, obtainable from Egyptian consulates, plus health certificate for smallpox, and—if coming from yellow-fever and cholera areas—proof of inoculations against those diseases.* **Best times for a visit:** *Cairo and the north pleasantest from October through April; the south (Luxor, etc.) is ideal from December through March. However, Americans used to the heat of United States summers will find summer days in Cairo about like those at home, and can even bear the south during that period. The heat, away from the coast, is dry and not humid, and I personally would not let the climate prevent me from visiting Egypt at any time of year.* **Currency:** *The Egyptian pound: 0.348 pounds=$1.* **Principal European languages:** *English and French; a good deal of both are spoken. Arabic is the official language. Count on little communication difficulty.* **Domestic transport:** *Fair to good trains (including sleepers), only some of which are air-conditioned; a safe and modern domestic airline, with sometimes inefficient ground personnel (double-check departure times, etc.); an extensive road network; and Nile River steamer service.* **Further information:** *Egyptian Government Tourist Office, 630 Fifth Ave., New York; Egyptian State Tourist Administration, 5 Adly St., Cairo, Egypt.*

INTRODUCING EGYPT

Egypt is the one African country whose glorious past has been fully—and justifiably—appreciated by the rest of the world for many years. There is no other science like Egyptology, which is devoted to the study of but one country's ancient civilization—and named for it. Volumes have, of course, been written about ancient Egypt—and more can be counted upon to appear, for the archaeologists never stop digging, and continue to pop up with exciting new discoveries. (The University of Chicago, for example, has a permanent building of its own, for the use of university-sponsored expeditions, on Luxor's main street. Guides driving by with American clients point it out matter-of-factly, announcing, "To the right, The University of Chicago.")

With the exception of Mesopotamia—about which much less is known—Egypt's is the oldest of the world's civilizations, and without doubt one of the greatest. The exciting part about a visit to the country today is that so many remnants of Pharaonic dynasties still remain; the dry climate of the Nile Valley has been a remarkable preservative. One of the earliest known dates in the history of the universe is that of the adoption of the ancient Egyptian calendar: 4241 B.C. There were thirty ancient Egyptian dynasties. During those millennia—for Egypt's history is best described in terms of thousands of years, not centuries—nomadic peoples clustered about the banks of the Nile, settled down, devised a sedentary agriculture that included the use of domesticated animals, united their tribal structures into national organizations, the better to defend themselves, and began the creation of a culture in which they not only developed a highly complex (albeit ruthlessly authoritarian) system of government but, as well, a written language, and skills in the fields of architecture, engineering, agriculture, painting, sculpture, furniture construction, clothing design, metalwork (including jewelry), town planning, and—well, you name it, and the likelihood is that the Egyptians knew it. A guide of mine, during a visit to Luxor, repeated at five-minute intervals, as one marvel after another was approached, "Nothing new under the sun. . . . Nothing new under the sun." He was irritatingly repetitive—as guides can be—but there was a great deal of truth in what he said.

Egypt's thirty dynasties were preceded by a long period of separate kingdoms, intricately organized, and located in both northern and southern Egypt, along the Nile. This prehistoric period ended about 3100 B.C., with the founding of the First and Second dynasties (3100–2700 B.C.). Relatively little remains of that early period, other than scattered desert tombs and small flint and bone pieces. With the first two dynasties came a period of consolidation. A ruling family of Upper Egypt united the kingdoms of the north and south, established a capital at Memphis, and began the long series of Egyptian dynasties which lasted some three thousand years. Menes is traditionally known as the first Pharaoh. The long succeeding period of dynasties are broken up into periods.

During the Old Kingdom (2700–2200 B.C.) lived Zoser, builder of the first pyramid at Sakkara, and Cheops, builder of the Great Pyramid at Giza. The First Intermediate Period (2200–2050 B.C.), followed by the Middle Kingdom (2050–1800 B.C.), led to the Second Intermediate Period (1800–1550 B.C.) when the Hyksos invaded Egypt and ruled about a hundred and sixty years. The Eighteenth Dynasty (1570–1305 B.C.), which followed the expulsion of the Hyksos, is famous for its Queen-Pharaoh, Hatshepsut, who built many beautiful monuments such as Deir el-Bahri in Luxor, and numerous temples and obelisks, and for the conqueror, Thutmose III, who expanded the borders of Egypt into Asia. During the Empire (1465–1165 B.C.) lived Akhenaton, who established the worship of one god, and Tutenkhamon, whose magnificent gold tomb furniture is one of the marvels of the Egyptian Museum in Cairo. The famous Ramses II, builder of the Rameseum of Abu Simbel, and of numerous temples and monuments, lived during the Nineteenth Dynasty (1305–1200 B.C.). The Twentieth Dynasty (1200–1090 B.C.) and the Post-Empire Period (1150–663 B.C.) preceded the Persian Conquest in 525 B.C. At this point, the young warrior-genius, Alexander the Great, arrived on the scene and conquered a greatly weakened Egypt in 332 B.C. His successors, the Ptolemies, made Alexandria the fountainhead of the Hellenic world, and reigned for two centuries, when the Romans took over, despite the rather well-chronicled intrigues of Cleopatra with Caesar and Mark Antony, designed to regain Egyptian power. When Ptolemy XIV, the child of Caesar and Cleopatra, was killed by Octavian, the Ptolemy dynasty ended. Roman decline ensued a few centuries later and, under Byzantine rule, Christianity flourished, with Alexandria vying with Rome and Constantinople as one of the three chief Christian towns of the world. The Coptic Church—still an important minority religious group—developed during this period; many of its great old monasteries still dot the land.

But Christianity was not destined to remain dominant. Just two decades after the emergence of Islam in the Middle East, Arabs—militant and strongly religious Moslems—swept into an again weak Egypt and almost literally absorbed it. They founded Cairo, made it their capital, and ruled—one dynasty after another—from A.D. 639 until 1250, when their former Turkish slaves—the Mamelukes—usurped power, and in the two and a half succeeding centuries managed to run Egypt, despite court intrigues and murders, which resulted in the throne's being occupied by no less than forty-seven princes! Still they, like the Arabs before them, were great builders, and by the time the Ottoman Turks took over in 1517 the Islamic *ambiance* of Egypt had already been substantially established. Napoleon invaded Egypt in 1798. The British joined the Turks and got him out shortly thereafter, but in 1875—after the construction of the second Suez Canal (the first was constructed two thousand years earlier—"nothing new under the sun")—the British again became interested in Egypt, and in 1882 found an excuse to land in Alexandria. They consolidated control in the early years of this century, and declared Egypt a "protectorate" during the First World War, but postwar nationalists were successful in getting Britain to agree to independence, which came in 1923, along with the establishment of a monarchy whose last king—the dissipated playboy, Farouk—was unceremoniously thrown out in 1953, and succeeded by the revolutionary government of General Naguib, who in turn was replaced by a co-conspirator, one Colonel Gamal Abdul Nasser, in 1954. Egypt's more recent history is all too well known—its domination of the Arab League, its compulsive hatred of Israel and something it terms "the world Zionist conspiracy," the abortive French-British-Israeli invasion, abrogation of the Suez Canal treaty and nationalization of the canal by Egypt, humiliating defeat at the hands of the Israelis. In 1958 Egypt and Syria formed a "federation," establishing the United Arab Republic, with General Nasser at its head. However, in 1961 Syria withdrew from the U.A.R. but Egypt retained the official name. A decade later, in 1971, Egypt, Libya, and Syria formed the Federation of Arab Republics, with Cairo designated as the capital. The country's role in the 1967 Six-Day War cost her the Sinai Peninsula and the Gaza Strip, as well as a substantial part of her fighting forces and military equipment. More and more in the past decade, Nasser turned to the Soviet Union for economic, technical, and military assistance. It was that nation rather than the United States, as originally planned, that enabled Egypt to complete the billion-dollar Aswan High Dam, officially opened in 1971. This relationship with Russia has continued after Nasser died in 1970, under his successor, President Anwar el-Sadat, whose plans for Egypt revolve around an ambitious ten-year development program aimed at doubling national income and industrial production by the end of the seventies, coupled with a reorganization of domestic affairs to allow for "total confrontation" with Israel. (This included an austerity program, begun in 1972, whereby shops selling luxury imports were closed, TV channels were cut from three to one, late-performance movies were stopped, and late-hour public transport was curtailed.) The Aswan High Dam project promises a vast amount of electrical power for the development of industry as well as helping to stabilize the Nile waters and thus allow for improved agriculture, and, hopefully, a better life for the mass of impoverished Egyptians who suffer from years of broken promises and unfulfilled expectations.

For the tourist, Egypt remains fascinating to visit, despite its contemporary foibles, because of its great past (a past which had a great effect on ancient empires to the south such as Cush and Meroë, and, indirectly, on other more distant African cultures), a fascination which is all-encompassing, extending even to the

Egyptians themselves: pesty kids on the streets of Cairo, *fellahin* in the fascinating but appallingly poor villages of the Delta and the South, coffee-drinking intellectuals in the cafés and on the campuses.

YOUR VISIT TO EGYPT

Where to begin in Egypt? Here's how to size up what lies before you: the country itself is almost one great mass of desert. Its lifeblood is, of course, the Nile—the longest river in the world, traveling more than 3400 miles from its source in Uganda to its mouth at the Mediterranean. The great majority of the thirty-four million Egyptians live on a narrow strip of land bordering the Nile and rarely more than 15 miles wide, except in the triangular region of the Delta, in the north. In other words, less than 15,000 square miles out of a total of 400,000 is inhabited. The rest is the Libyan Desert, west of the river, the Arabian Desert, to the east, and the mountains of the lonely, arid Sinai Peninsula, to the northeast. The Aswan Dam has already harnessed some of the Nile waters and helped Egypt's economy. So have land-reform measures of the post-Farouk period, and beginnings at industrialization. But poverty is no more shocking anywhere in all of Africa. Nor are the riches—in the great cities and rural estates of gentlemen farmers—anywhere else more striking. How so? You'll see, when you start out—as most visitors do—in the capital, whose population of almost three million makes it the biggest city in Africa, the intellectual, cultural, and political center of the Arab world, and, for the curious traveler, one of the most important cities on the globe. Just one explanatory word on terminology which is often confusing: *Upper* Egypt is *southern* Egypt. *Lower* Egypt is *northern* Egypt. The flow of the Nile—from south to north—is responsible for these designations, one of but many indications of the eternal truth in the maxim, "Egypt is the Nile, the Nile is Egypt."

Cairo: There is no other city in Africa as sophisticated about visitors as Cairo. They have been coming, for one reason or another, for many centuries. And they play an important role in the economic life of the community. In no other tourist center—not even Paris—are they as easily discernible to the locals. Wherever one goes, there is someone trailing a few feet behind—either a dragoman (guide) who wants a few hours' (or days') work, or a vendor of postcards, or a small boy wanting to shine your shoes, or an itinerant peddler with cheap bracelets and little miniature pyramids, or—and don't laugh, it can happen to you—a simultaneous combination of all of these. They must be dealt with firmly—assuming you don't want their products or services, and usually you don't, for you have just had your shoes shined, seen those same postcards three summers ago in Paris, already bought more trinkets for the home crowd than you know what to do with, or just escaped from the chaperonage of a dragoman and want to be alone. At any rate, my own tested procedure for getting rid of Cairo street pests is very simple: simply *shriek*, "No!" A polite "No, thank you," an attempt to ignore the fact that you're being followed, or even a rather firm "*no*"—none of these is adequate, as they would be in any other city of the world. These Cairo characters assume—until told otherwise explicitly—that the only conceivable reason you are spurning them is that of cost. And cost is something that they believe must be discussed; a convenient price can easily be arranged, if only you will have the goodness to stop for a moment and listen. The fact that cost is not the only reason in the world for not wanting a shoeshine or a bronze sphinx does not enter the mind of your pursuer. You *must explain* in no uncertain terms, or he will not give up. My shrieking technique is guaranteed to do the trick. Small boys will giggle but depart, and their elders—possibly after soothing you by saying, "Ah, sir, you are *naar-voos* . . ." —will get the point too. I go into this much detail on this matter only because it is one which can easily spoil one's stay in Cairo.

At any rate, there is considerably more to Cairo than its ambulatory salesmen. Even for the most adamant of museum boycotters, the Egyptian Museum is a requisite—ideally, the first destination of a newcomer. Truly one of the great museums of the world, it often induces revisits; many of its fans never quite satiate themselves with its fantastic treasures. For the visitor without much time—say, only a morning—it would be wise to concentrate on those sections which display the magnificent contents of the tomb of King Tutenkhamon, discovered in Luxor in 1922, and surely the archaeological coup of this century. King Tut, it is important to remember, died in his twenties and was, therefore, one of the poorer Pharaohs, having had relatively little time to acquire as many riches for his after-death than other monarchs. Still, an entire room is devoted to his glittering jewelry. And there is the splendid gold mask of his head, his chair—as subtly designed as chairs made millennia later—the gilded shrine containing his entrails, statues of him in black and gold leaf, his mummy and that of his lovely young queen in ornate coffins, and much else. Other galleries of the museum—and this is too rich a collection to take in on a single trip—contain relics of other dynasties, from papyrus scrolls to solar boats to immense statuary. Egyptian collections in all other museums—including the Metropolitan in New York and the British Museum in London—pale in contrast. The Cairo institution brings ancient Egypt to life as no other does, and is the perfect introduction for visits to other monuments of the country's past.

These would include, of course, the trio of pyramids at Giza—most important of the eighty such structures in Egypt, and the Sphinx which sits majestically beside them.

The pyramids are, of course, royal tombs. The first and oldest was built by Cheops (Khufu) about 2600 B.C. It is 450 feet high, a stony mass of two million, three hundred thousand separate blocks covering 13 acres. Its smaller companions, probably built in the same century, belong to the Pharaoh Chephren (Khafre) and Mycerinus (Menkure). It is said that a hundred thousand people—gigantic teams of forced labor—worked together to build these pyramids. The Sphinx, built during the reign of Chephren and perhaps a likeness of this Pharaoh, was carved from a jut of rock left by builders quarrying for stone. It has the head of a human being and the body of a recumbent lion. It measures 240 feet long and 66 feet high. The Sphinx has withstood the wear of centuries amazingly well, though the face has been badly mutilated—some say, by the invading Arabs who were simply taking literally the Koranic edict against the reproduction of human faces.

All that remains of Memphis, the first capital of united Egypt, are the pyramids and tombs of *Sakkara*, its necropolis, or burial place. Here the highlights are the step pyramids of Pharaoh Zoser, those of the Pharaoh Unas and Meren-Ra, a recently discovered forty-seven-hundred-year-old funeral chamber, perfectly preserved, tentatively attributed to Pharaoh Sanakht and the tombs of Ti, Ptahhotep, and the Serapeum—where sacred bulls were buried.

Moslem Cairo is of great interest, even to the visitor who knows other North African and Middle Eastern cities. Its mosques are among the most elaborate in the world. They include El Azhar, dating back to A.D. 971, with a huge Koranic university of twenty thousand students, which makes it the intellectual center of the Arab world; Ibn Tulun, even older than El Azhar, and from whose minaret tower one has a fine view of Old Cairo; Sultan Hasan, a fourteenth-century masterpiece; El Muayyed, with its graceful twin minarets; and the nineteenth-century Mohammed Ali—with its immense courtyard, and the adjoining El Gawhara Palace, with its frescoed walls, and sumptuous alabaster bathroom. The Citadel, on which the Mohammed Ali Mosque stands—high on the slopes of a steep hill, commands a superb view of much of Cairo and the Nile, and has a drama-filled history of battles and intrigues covering eight centuries.

Still more to see in Cairo? By all means: four important museums, besides the Egyptian Museum: Islamic Art (gallery after gallery of exquisite Islamic treasures from all over the Arab world); Coptic (the only museum devoted solely to the rich early Christian culture of Egypt and its neighbors to the south, including Ethiopia, where half the population is Coptic Christian); Modern Art (interesting principally because of the building itself, a lovely old mansion); and the unintentionally amusing displays of the Wax Museum, particularly that of Cleopatra, as she might have been portrayed by Theda Bara. There are also several venerable city gates, or Babs, including thousand-year-old Bab Zweila, plus Bab El Futuh and Bab El Nasr; many old houses, now open as museums, including El Kritliyya, Ibrahim es-Sehnary, and Gamaled Dine; the Tombs of the Caliphs, with miniature mosques and mausoleums; the ruins of the Babylon Fort—only remnants of the Roman period—and the seven, little-visited ancient Christian churches that surround it, including El Mouallaka, Abou Sarga and Sitt Barbara, plus a Jewish synagogue that was originally a Coptic church; the palaces recently vacated by King Farouk and now either museums or government offices, including overornate and at times vulgarly garish Abdin; the resthouse near the pyramids, in ancient Egyptian style; and the interesting Persian-Ottoman-Moorish-Egyptian-Islamic Manial Palace, on Roda Island; and the most overrated bazaars in North Africa—the Musky, anticlimactic for any visitor who has experienced the *souks* of Tunis, Marrakesh, Algiers, or Tripoli, and with merchants whose arms are all too often employed to pull in pedestrians. The small shops clustered about the big hotels along the Nile have the same merchandise, and, while hardly as genteel as Madison Avenue boutiques, are at least operated without the crude "every tourist is a sucker" attitude of those in the Musky.

Luxor: Having seen the Egyptian Museum, the Pyramids, and the Sphinx in Cairo, the visitor is partially prepared for the splendors of Luxor—but only partially. This glittering forty-century-old treasure trove must be seen to be believed. Luxor is the site of ancient Thebes, where kings outdazzled each other in the course of a six-century period of one-up-manship never quite equaled in subsequent eras of history. Even allowing for the erosion of a great deal of the glitter, enough remains to put the visitor in a state of semishock, so awesome and magnificent are these relics of a great civilization.

"Only the grains of sand," wrote Homer, "outnumbered the wealth enclosed within Thebes." He did not exaggerate, and although much is now missing—stone roofs on the temples, *décor* of gold and silver on the walls, gold plate on the gates—there is still a great deal to see.

Within the pleasant town of Luxor, on the right bank of the Nile, are the Temple of Luxor, the complex of buildings which constitute the Temple of Karnak, and the remains of a royal road linking the two. Built by Amenhotep III and Ramses II, Luxor Temple now sits quietly, just opposite one of the town's big hotels, amidst a park where veiled Egyptian ladies bring their youngsters to play. Its columns and statuary are outranked by those of the much larger Karnak group, which is approached by an avenue lined by a series of small sphinxes, many of which still stand.

Across the river—in winter, tourists are transported in a modern steamer, but off-season they make the journey in ancient-design boats with both sails and a pair of oarsmen—are the funeral temples of Rameseum, Deir el-Bahri, Medinet Habu and Seti; the underground royal tombs in the Valley of the Kings and the Valley of the Queens, the Tombs of the Nobles, and the Colossi of Memnon.

Most important of the funeral temples is Deir el-Bahri, built by Queen Hatshepsut—enormous, sweeping, many-columned, and dramatically set beneath the crags of a towering rock cliff. The four most important of the kings' tombs are those of Seti I, with its fabulously ornamented corridor walls, Ramses VI, Amenophis II, and of course, Tutenkhamon—the most perfectly preserved, and containing those relics not now on display in the Cairo Museum. In the nearby Valley of the Queens, requisites should be the tomb of Prince Amenherkhopsef, son of Ramses III, and that of Queen Nefertari, wife of Ramses II—most astonishingly beautiful of the lot. In the Tombs of the Nobles, four Theban court officials' burial places are outstanding: those of Ramose, Amenophis IV's governor; Khaemhet, a keeper of the granaries; Menena, a scribe of Tutnmosis IV, and Rekhmara, a Theban governor, whose tomb is the most complete of the group. The famed Memnon Colossi are quite as imposing as photographs make them out to be, set as they are on the open desert, with the outline of a village some distance beyond. They are likenesses of

King Amenophis II, wearing the classical headgear—called *nemes* —of the period, and each is 60 feet high.

Other attractions along the Upper Nile: Denderla Temple, on the site of a provincial capital of Pharaonic days; Edfu Temple, one of the best preserved of the Ptolemaic period; Kom Ombu; Abydos, where excavations are still being made of tombs of the first Pharaonic dynasty.

Aswan: Aswan, site of the new Aswan Dam as well as the smaller dam, is also a winter resort, frequently the goal of travelers anxious for a rest after the rigors of Cairo and Luxor. Worth seeing here, besides the dam, are the sites of ancient quarries, Elephantine Island, across the Nile from the city; and Saint Simeon Monastery, which doubled as a fortress in the old days, and where the stone-floored monks' cells remain well preserved. The temples of Philae Island—most important of Aswan's relics—are submerged much of the time by the waters of the Nile, but plans have been made to dismantle them stone by stone and rebuild them on the nearby island of Ajlika.

Abu Simbel: About 166 miles south of Aswan, Abu Simbel is the site of the famed Great Temples of Ramses II, one dedicated to him and the other to his wife, Nefertari. When the Aswan Dam was built these two magnificent temples were rescued from the rising waters of Lake Nasser forming behind the dam. In a project financed by over fifty countries and taking six years, the temples were moved stone by stone and reconstructed two hundred feet above Lake Nasser. There is a new hotel in Abu Simbel, and hydrofoils travel to the town from Aswan.

Alexandria: Now a relaxed, attractive modern city of more than a million inhabitants, and the chief port of Egypt, Alexandria is bypassed by most American tourists, particularly those who enter the country by plane at Cairo. Still, a train ride north from the capital to the second city is time well spent. Much less frenetic than Cairo, and with a cooler climate, Alexandria is home to a substantial European community—British, Greek, French, Italian. It is also a resort mecca for Egyptians, who flock to its myriad of beaches—mile after mile of them, fronting the Mediterranean, with the finest that of Montazah, near the former palace of King Farouk, now open to visitors as a museum. The second royal residence, Ras-el-Tin, is also a museum today. Other attractions are Pompey's Pillar (which is believed to have been erected by Emperor Diocletian), the ancient Egyptian Catacombs, dating back to the second century A.D., and last, but hardly least, the excellent Greco-Roman Museum, which is as important to an understanding of those periods in Egypt's history as the Egyptian Museum in Cairo is in regard to the Pharaonic era.

Port Said and *Suez*, at opposite sides of the Suez Canal, are of interest mainly for their commercial prominence as ports, and because of the canal which they border; otherwise, the quicker the exit from them, the better. Other major cities—little known but each exceeding 75,000 in population—include *Faiyum, Tanta, Zagazig, Asyut*, and *Mansura*. None is of unusual interest to the casual visitor.

SHOPPING

Virtually every Musky Bazaar shop and every shop in downtown Cairo and in that city's Nile River hotel area carry the same merchandise. At all, rigid bargaining is essential. The Musky Bazaar merchants are the most difficult and are best avoided; with some others, doing business can be a pleasure, often taking on social aspects, when small boys appear with frosty bottles of Coca-Cola, or little cups of the delicious sweet, black Egyptian coffee. Interesting buys are camel saddles, copper and brass trays of varying sizes, alabaster carvings including tiny replicas of the pyramids which are simple and attractive, reproductions of scarabs which make good paperweights, great varieties of jewelry (necklaces, bracelets, rings, cuff links), luggage of varying sizes in soft camel leather, cigarette boxes and chests with mother-of-pearl inlay work, heads of Nefertiti and many other items—interspersed with quantities of junk. Much of this merchandise is machine-made, and things often *look* better than they are. Examine construction and workmanship before making purchases. Check zippers on luggage, findings on jewelry, stitching on leatherwork. And don't hesitate about going from shop to shop before making a decision. Those within the hotels have ridiculously high prices, as would be expected, but they're excellent for introductory browsing. Alexandria merchants are often more relaxed than Cairo's, and the same is true of those in the tiny shops along Luxor's main streets. Outside of Luxor, in the Valley of the Kings, men and boys from the villages often approach tourists with locally made reproductions of ancient relics, which—even if new —are often attractive, and worth bargaining over.

CREATURE COMFORTS

HOTELS—**Cairo:** Hotels in the capital run the gamut in price and degree of luxury, and many are excellent, with European cuisine, excellent service, and fine appointments. The Nile Hilton combines both Pharaonic and Islamic *décor* with American plumbing, complete air conditioning, houses a rooftop nightclub, and several bars and restaurants, including a good coffee shop. All rooms are with balcony and sumptuous bathrooms. The even newer Sheraton is handsome and luxurious, with all facilities. The sleek modern Shepheard's—nothing like its much-lamented, old-fashioned predecessor—adjoins the older, still excellent Semiramis. Others: Ambassador, Nile, Scheherazade, El Borg, Cleopatra Palace, Kasrel Harem, Mena House—the last two on the road to the Giza pyramids. **Luxor:** The Winter Palace, on the Nile, is the traditional favorite—elderly, spacious, comfortable, and with excellent meals. Second is the Luxor—first-class but unexciting; the Savoy is smaller and simple. **Aswan:** The Cataract and the Grand are the top two. Others: Kalabasha, Amun. **Alexandria:** The Palestine leads in the luxury class. Other good choices are the Cecil, Windsor Palace, Beau Rivage, San Stefano. **Port Said:** Casino Palace. **Suez:** Bel-Air-Misr. **Abu Simbel:** Nefertiti.

RESTAURANTS—Both Cairo and Alexandria are dotted with pleasant cafés for coffee and *apéritifs,* both sidewalk, indoor, and a combination of both. Cairo also has excellent restaurants, in addition to those of the Nile Hilton, the Sheraton, Semiramis, Shepheard's, and other hotels. They include the Kursaal, Groppi's, Le Grillon, Omar Khayyam (on a houseboat), Estoril, A l'Americaine —all with mainly European menus—and the Khumais, with delicious Egyptian specialties—breads, rice dishes, broiled pigeons, etc.—served from large brass trays to diners seated on expansive hassocks.

Nightclubs—Cairo nightlife—for the visitor with an adequate bankroll—passes the time pleasantly. Leading cabarets—often featuring Oriental belly dancers—are the Mokkattam Casino, Sahara City, Fontana, Abdine Palace, and Auberge des Pyramides. Those with dance floors include the handsome Belvedere Room atop the Nile Hilton, the cabaret of the Sheraton, the lovely alfresco rooftop dining room of the Semiramis, and the Mena House near the Pyramids. Watch the papers for events at the Opera House during the winter season.

ETHIOPIA

Empire of Ethiopia

Entry requirements: *A visa, obtainable either in advance from Ethiopian embassies or consulates, or—happy and inspired idea—upon arrival at Addis Ababa or Asmara International Airports; plus a health certificate (smallpox and yellow fever) and an onward transportation ticket.* **Best times for a visit:** *There are two rainy seasons. The "Big Rains" extend from mid-June through September, while the "Little Rains" fall in February and March. Neither is so intense that visitors need stay away. And bear in mind that most of Ethiopia is so highly elevated that it is cool and comfortable the year round. Temperatures have an average range of between 60° and 80° F., but I would say that the latter figure is a high one, except on the sultry Red Sea coast—where it could be considered low.* **Currency:** *The Ethiopian dollar is one of the most stable on the planet. It has long equaled approximately 40 U.S. cents; Eth $2.50 equaling about one American dollar.* **European languages:** *English—a good deal of it—and Italian, with Amharic—a Semitic language with its own alphabet—the official language.* **Domestic transport:** *Ethiopian Airlines, operated with management assistance from TWA, maintains one of the most extensive domestic routes of any African carrier, flying to some thirty points within the empire. Roads in this mountainous country are relatively few, and the principal railroad is that linking Addis Ababa with the important port of Djibouti, capital of the Territory of Afars and Issas, on the Red Sea coast.* **Further information:** *Ethiopian Airlines, 200 East 42nd Street, New York; Ethiopian Tourist Organi-*

zation, P. O. Box 2183, Addis Ababa, Ethiopia; National Tourist & Travel Agency, P. O. Box 1944, Addis Ababa, Ethiopia; Imperial Ethiopian Embassy, Washington, D.C.

INTRODUCING ETHIOPIA

Ethiopia is surpassingly beautiful, enchanting to visit, and unlike any other land in Africa—or elsewhere, for that matter. Geography has had a great deal to do with its distinctiveness; high mountain barriers have, until recent years, helped it remain loftily isolated from the rest of the world. But it was not always so. Ancient Ethiopia was a great power, and from it emanated a highly developed culture that is now believed to have influenced civilizations in great areas of sub-Sahara Africa.

Parts of modern Ethiopia were incorporated in the ancient kingdom of Cush, much of which embraced what is now the Republic of the Sudan. Some seven centuries before Christ, King Piankhi of Cush—which then included Egypt in its realm—incorporated the lands to the south, going as far, it is conjectured, as today's Uganda. Cush became a world power, if only briefly, but it was not vanquished until the third century A.D.

Helping to cause Cush's downfall was the city-state of Axum, whose remains are among the greatest of Ethiopia's antiquities, and whose forces also crushed the great city-state of Meroë, in the fourth century A.D. Axum remained a power, it is now believed, until the rise of Islam in the sixth century. From that period on, until the fourteenth century, Ethiopia's recorded history is largely a blank, and archaeologists are only beginning to fill in the gaps. At any rate, there is now a body of scientific opinion that believes that Axum's civilization may have had far-reaching effects in Africa.

Possibly of Axumian derivation are hillside terracing of farms, dry-stone building, the construction of elliptically shaped temples, and the practice of carving phallic ornaments on the foreheads of men's funerary statues. All these facets of southern—and even western—African cultures may have had their beginnings in ancient Axum.

At any rate, venerable Ethiopia—which was populated by Semitic peoples from southern Arabia centuries before Christ—is about as rich in history as it is poor today in per capita income (which is under sixty dollars per year). It is, as well, one of the oldest Christian countries in the world. King Aizanas of Axum minted coins with the Christian cross in the fourth century, and it was probably during his reign that the first Christian church was built at Axum in A.D. 340. It was in the fourth century that the Ethiopian Orthodox Church had its beginnings, tracing its origins to a pair of Syrian clerics who were shipwrecked in the Red Sea, found their way into the interior, and converted the royal family.

The church is one of five Oriental Orthodox bodies that split with their fellow Christians at the Council of Chalcedon in 451. Called Monophysite churches (and including the Indian Orthodox, Armenian, Coptic, and Syrian churches), they refused to go along with the council's theory that Jesus was both human and divine, and characterized his nature instead as "one incarnate nature of God, the Word." Close to half of Ethiopia's people are today Christians (about a third are Moslem, the remainder animists), and the Christian clergy—much of it part-time and only semiliterate—numbers 170,000. Though still rich, a major landholder, a national unifier of diverse tribal and linguistic groups, and a major link between the institute of the monarchy and the masses, the church is today losing ground with an increasingly sophisticated educated class, impatient—particularly its youthful segment—for economic betterment and a quicker leap into the late twentieth century.

Though on the defensive contemporarily, the Ethiopian Church —and the country's Christians—have long been the powerful national majority. (Interestingly enough, Ethiopia is home to a little-known and tiny but nonetheless fascinating minority, the so-called Black, or Falasha Jews, some twenty-five thousand strong. They live in and about Amober, in the interior, north of ancient

Gondar, consider themselves quite as Ethiopian as their non-Jewish compatriots [they are dark-skinned and speak Amharic], believe that their ancestors found their way to Ethiopia at the time of the Exodus, base their theology virtually entirely on the Old Testament, were not known to the outer world until the late nineteenth century, when they were surprised to learn there were other Jews besides themselves, and only at that time gave up their ancient practice of animal sacrifice.)

It was a Christian emperor of the Amharas—the majority group —who received the first European visitors, a Portuguese delegation determined to find the legendary Christian monarch whom they called Prester John. Emperor Menelik II finally welded together the Ethiopian Empire, but not until 1889. Ethiopia became a member of the League of Nations in 1923, and was invaded by the Italians, while a shocked world looked on, in 1935. Emperor Haile Selassie, exiled to England, returned in 1941.

Haile Selassie is one of the most remarkable of personalities, even to his detractors. He was born in 1891, the 225th in a consecutive line of Solomonic rulers. And if you think that "Solomonic" has to do with the King Solomon of the Bible, you are right. The Ethiopians consider their monarch descended from Solomon and the Queen of Sheba, who was believed to be the Ethiopian Queen Makeda of Axum. From the time he ascended the throne in 1930, Haile Selassie has been not only the ruler of Ethiopia, he has typified Ethiopia in the eyes of the entire world. No other monarch of the modern era, save possibly Queen Victoria—and she in a very different manner—has had such impact. Haile Selassie set out to modernize his ancient land, and his program has been a strange meld of the conservative and the progressive.

Throughout the long decades of his reign he has been criticized by progressives both within and without his realm as a reactionary, and by the reactionaries—particularly the rich, powerful landowners of his own class, as too liberal. He gave his people their first written constitution; set up a Parliament, which he addresses annually in a Westminster-like Speech from the Throne; and has attempted to modernize agriculture, introduce land reform, make starts at industry, and educate on a mass basis. Ethiopian Airlines, which he started after World War II, has united his almost roadless country as no other single enterprise could. The university bearing his name in his capital—the first university in the country—has not only created a class of young intellectuals, but has brought about an articulate, organized opposition to his policies, to the point where he has had, at times, to close the doors of the institution he himself founded and housed in one of his own palaces. As his country entered the decade of the seventies, it remained a land of staggering problems. A third of the agricultural area was still owned by the imperial family and the government, another third by the still-backward Ethiopian Church, elements of which continue to oppose Haile Selassie's land reform programs. Diseases like leprosy remain prevalant in remoter provinces. The heavily Moslem province of Eritrea continues, through a well-organized secessionist movement, to embarrass the government with its militancy, even though the government claims the secessionists do not represent the Eritrean masses. There have been border disputes with neighboring Somalia and Sudan.

Still, there has been progress. Since army elements loyal to the emperor crushed an attempted 1960 coup led by a disloyal army element under the nominal leadership of the Emperor's plump, ineffectual son, Crown Prince Asfa Wosen, there has been no difficulty in this respect. (Indeed, the crown prince and the crown princess are reconciled with the Emperor. When I was received by His Imperial Majesty, along with other press guests invited to the official opening of the Addis Ababa Hilton in 1969, the crown prince and crown princess were with the Emperor in the receiving line, and at other events of the opening, which coincided with the thirty-ninth anniversary of Haile Selassie's reign.) Though of another era and political stripe, the Emperor continues to merit the respect of fellow African leaders. Stanch Africanist though he is politically, and in many respects culturally, he has presided over an imperial court that could not be more European. On the day each November that he opens Parliament, the entire diplomatic corps is in the gallery in full formal regalia, despite the morning hour. At the reception I attended in one of his two Addis Ababa palaces, for the diplomatic corps, he stood alongside his throne to personally receive each one of several hundred guests (introductions were made by an equerry), then accepted a gift from the dean of the diplomatic corps, immediately after which—poof!—scores of footmen in eighteenth-century-style livery appeared as if out of nowhere with great platters of canapes and immense trays filled with goblets of champagne.

Withal, Addis Ababa is the site of the headquarters both of the United Nations Economic Commission for Africa, and of the politically progressive Organization of African Unity. This capital-of-Africa cachet is a tribute to the Emperor's popularity on the continent, as have been frequent requests by co-African leaders to him to act as conciliator in disputes on the continent. Short, slim, bearded, sober-visaged, he is fluent in a number of languages, including English, and has been an intrepid traveler. At the 1971 party in Persepolis given by the Shah of Iran, the star of the show—and there were scores of rulers and heads of state present—was none other than Haile Selassie. He had just come from Peking, and was able to personally quash then prevalent rumors to the effect that Mao Tse-tung was dead. The big question: Who will lead Ethiopia after Haile Selassie's death? And how?

YOUR VISIT TO ETHIOPIA

Addis Ababa: Known locally as "Addis," Addis Ababa (Amharic for "New Flower") extends over a range of sweet-smelling eucalyptus-covered hills at a level of 8200 feet, in the center of the country. Indeed, its setting is almost ethereal. Although the overwhelming majority of its inhabitants still live in mud-walled huts, the façade of the core of the city has become remarkably modern in recent years, and the visitor will be eminently comfortable.

No city has been less planned. The villa of a well-to-do family might be in the middle of a block of simple thatch-roofed huts, with cookstoves on the front doorstep. The high-powered motor-car may be right alongside a herd of goats being led in from the country. The airport bus might share the road with basket-laden donkeys, the principal beasts of burden. The Ethiopians, inordinately polite, greet each other with a blend of the low Japanese bow and a kiss on both cheeks in the manner of the French awarding the Croix de Guerre. Everywhere are attractive, gracious people—lovely, golden-skinned women dressed in the *shama,* a gauzy, white wraparound with colorfully embroidered borders; rugged-faced men, their *shamas* draped over white breeches; curious, good-natured children anxious to greet strangers to their town with wide, infectious grins.

To watch these people as they wend their way down the steep, verdant hills—often carrying enormous piles of eucalyptus branches to be used for fuel—is, to many visitors, one of the chief attractions of the city. But there are others. Its modern aspects cannot be overlooked. Africa Hall is the handsome art-filled structure housing both the Organization of African Unity (virtually all independent African states are members, save the racist ones like South Africa and Rhodesia) and the United Nations Economic Commission for Africa, and is open to the public. There is a strikingly modern City Hall, the auditorium of which the locals are understandably proud. There are two smallish but first-rate museums. One is the Archaeological, or National Museum, and the other is the Institute of Ethiopian Studies, quartered at Haile Selassie I University; traditional Ethiopian painting, strangely similar to that of Byzantine Europe, is a highlight at both museums. Special permission, not difficult to obtain, is needed to visit the gardens of the Jubilee Palace, about which roam the imperial lions. Parliament is open to visitors. So is the handsome, capacious Opera House (best visited, of course, when there's a performance). Elaborate St. George's Cathedral, principal place of worship for the Ethiopian Church, is set in a quiet park of its own; other Coptic churches like Trinity and St. Stefanos are also inspectable. The so-called New Market is the country brought to the city—and not to be missed, particularly on Wednesday and Saturday, the biggest days. Nor is the view of the city to be gained from the summit of Mount Entoto, with its own church.

Environs of Addis Ababa: The Ethiopian countryside is spectacularly beautiful. A popular by-car itinerary takes one through the mountains to *Debre Zeit,* a tiny town perched atop the crater of a volcanic lake, with drinks or lunch available at the Grand Hotel. En route one passes traditional farmhouses where one can stop for chats with, and photos of, their inhabitants. *Addis Alem* is west of the capital, and was where Emperor Menelik II lived; to be seen are both an imperial residence and church, the former exhibiting religious treasures of the period. Farther along is *Managesha National Park,* a drive-through game sanctuary where the lures include monkeys, leopards, and a variety of antelopes. At *Koka Dam* and the lake it has created in the Rift Valley one can see both the new and the old, including Gelila Palace, an ex-imperial palace turned hotel.

Awash National Park: Though Ethiopia is way behind East African neighbors like Kenya, Tanzania, and Uganda when it comes to game parks, it has developed a comfortable tented camp, with full dining facilities, in Awash National Park, about 150 miles east of Addis Ababa, and accessible by road or charter plane. To be observed are crocodiles and hippos in the Awash River, monkeys, warthogs, oryx, greater kudus, gazelles, zebras, hyenas, leopards, cheetahs, and that rarely seen crossword-puzzle favorite, the aardvark.

Asmara is the chief city of Eritrea, the former Italian territory that has been incorporated into Ethiopia as a province of the Empire. Second only to Addis Ababa in size, Asmara has a delightful European overlay, the Italian influence from earlier days having been surprisingly persuasive. Highly elevated like the capital—Asmara is at 7500 feet—it is proud of its comfortable climate. Palm-fringed Haile Selassie I Avenue is the attractive, *al fresco*-café-dotted central thoroughfare. There are good restaurants, comfortable accommodations, a bit of night life, a smiling *am-*

biance. And fifty miles downward—really downward—from the rarefied Asmara eminence lies the Red Sea port-resort of *Massawa*. One can go by car (the ride is memorable) or fly in twenty minutes. Massawa occupies a pair of islands and peninsulas, is the site of imperial Navy Headquarters, of good beaches just outside of town, of facilities for deep-sea fishing and for yachting, and of hot-as-hell weather, 100° F. is all too typical, and it can get ten or even fifteen degrees hotter. Happily, air conditioning is prevalent.

The Historic Route Quartet has become the standard Ethiopian itinerary—and with good reason. It's by air, utilizing scheduled Ethiopian Airlines flights. Start in Addis Ababa and work your way north to Asmara or start in Asmara and work your way south to Addis Ababa. Start any day. And make overnight layovers at each of the four links in the Historic Route chain. Going north from the capital, the first stop (unless you wanted to pick and choose, going to only one or two or three of the four) would be *Bahar Dar*. The attraction here is the relatively little-known phenomenon of nature known as the Blue Nile Falls, or as they are called by the Ethiopians, Tissisat. They are some two hundred feet high, emit a spray that extends ninety feet heavenward, and are located at Lake Tana, the source of the historic Blue Nile. But there's more: a network of islands on which are perched ancient monasteries, some filled with lovely icons and the kind of hand-written and illuminated Bibles and prayer books that are so distinctively Ethiopian. *Lalibela* would be the next stop. It's a remote mountain town named some eight centuries back for a man who was such a gifted builder-king that he became a saint of the Ethiopian Church. His handiwork is mind-boggling: eleven churches hewn from solid rock. Small today, Lalibela is inhabited almost entirely by Coptic priests—several hundred of them, to be sure, and their families. They live in *tukuls* (circular two-story houses built of stone and roofed in thatch). The priests themselves are splendid to behold, garbed in brilliant hues, with much gilded embellishment, and in the case of the top-ring high priests, rarely seen without elaborate umbrellas held over their heads, as signs of respect. The priests double as guides. Generally they'll spend half a day at the lower-down group of churches—Biet Medane Alem (Our Savior) with its twenty-eight carved columns and high altar with arks for Jesus, Abraham, and Isaac; Biet Marian (Virgin Mary), with its elegant paintings; and such others as Biet Giorgis (St. George's), in the shape of a great Greek cross. Later, one sees the upper-group churches, the most memorable of which is Biet Gabriel—thanks to a precarious approach, a log bridge over a fifty-foot drop. Everywhere one turns, youngsters offer minor treasures—hand-lettered and illuminated prayer books and long scrolls, and handsomely worked silver crosses. The terrain makes for rough, bumpy, and dusty going. But no matter. *Gondar:* Thanks to the difficulty of access during the not inconsiderable pre-Ethiopian Airlines period of some five centuries, Gondar remains an intact medieval town of remarkable splendor, with European-Moorish influences easily discernible. No one is quite sure how the kings of Gondar ever got to inaccessible Gondar in the first place, let alone how they built as they did. Still, there it is: palaces and churches and turrets and tombs and battlements, even a royal bath. And not far away live the Black Felasha Jews; their communities may be visited on excursions. An Ethiopian phenomenon, they thought they were the only Jews extant until the outside world discovered them in the late nineteenth century; their way of life and their biblical theology is very briefly described on page 120. *Axum,* whose early glories are described on pages 119–20, remains a monument of Ethiopia's early greatness. To be marveled at are the unique *steles,* considered to be stairways for the souls of the dead; obelisks—the highest is sixty-seven feet sculpted from solid granite, and a maze of additional slim vertical structures of one shape or other. The inner walls of St. Mary of Zion Cathedral are lined with splendid murals, and on display are ancient artifacts of jewel-studded gold. There is a water tank two millennia old, and a ruined palace, as well.

Dire Dawa and Harrar are a pair of towns east of Addis Ababa that typify Moslem Ethiopia. Invariably, Dire Dawa, with its airport, is the first gained. It is the commercial center of Hararge

Province, hot and tropical, and still with the shade trees and high-ceilinged, veranda-fronted houses of its original French designers. Dire Dawa dates from the time when the French set up headquarters there, while building the railroad linking Addis Ababa with Djibouti. To be seen are the palace of the Duke of Harrar, used by the Emperor on official visits; a shop-packed old town that serves as trading center for the area; and a considerable modern façade. Harrar is vastly more exotic and Old World, with a zingo market—handicrafts and bolts of cloth and produce and ceramics and the famed local baskets and silverware, and with baggy-trousered ladies all about and men in sarong-like skirts. There are a pair of palaces—Menelik's and Ras Makonnen's—both nineteenth century; a cathedral and twin-tower mosque, the modern imperial military academy, and—I kid you not—a community of itinerant hyenas that wander about the streets at night, fed regularly—before an audience of wide-eyed tourists—at the Old City Wall by a nameless if hardly uncelebrated character known simply as the Hyena Man.

SHOPPING

The arts and crafts of Ethiopia reflect the county's rich and distinctive culture. There is nothing else quite like them anywhere in Africa. Perhaps the most typical and the most popular of purchases are pictorial histories depicting the story of King Solomon and his wife, the Queen of Sheba, from whom the country's emperors consider themselves descended. These are done in sequence panels in traditional style on canvases of various sizes, and with varying degrees of proficiency in workmanship. Well painted, they look splendid framed and hung. Metal crosses in the elaborate style of the Ethiopian Church, and in many sizes, are also attractive. So are tiny tryptichs, wooded and delightfully painted, hand-forged hunting knives, in finely tooled red leather sheaths and handles of ivory and ebony. The basketry of Ethiopia is among the very finest in Africa. Paintings of religious scenes—St. George (the Ethiopian patron saint) and the Dragon are very popular—and of village life, done on thick, rough, hand-fashioned parchment are handsome. They come in various sizes, none of them large. Prayer books and Bibles, hand-illuminated in Amharic, illustrated with gaily colored paintings and bound by hand in wooden covers, are unusual and beautiful. So are religious scrolls on parchment, similarly lettered and illustrated. The gossamer-like *shama* costumes, and the brightly embroidered tapes with which they are embellished, may be of interest. Sources in Addis Ababa: Foremost is the riotous, colorful New Market, at which you bargain, bargain, bargain, allowing yourself plenty of time for browsing. Second is the price-fixed Empress Menon Handicrafts School, under imperial sponsorship, and where you may watch artisans at work in their shops and studios adjoining the retail salesrooms. Others are the retail shop off the lobby of Africa Hall (which also sells crafts from other African countries) and the shop called Belvedere. Perfectly beautiful reproductions on post cards of Ethiopian paintings are on sale inexpensively in the Archaeological Museum and the Institute of Ethiopian Studies Museum. There are, as well, shops in the hotels, frequently with interesting wares. And everywhere beyond, in the streets of both cities and remote towns and villages, one finds itinerant vendors, both youthful and adult. Frequently, they're selling minor treasures; never shoo them away until you inspect the merchandise!

CREATURE COMFORTS

First, bless the Italians. Uninvited occupiers they most certainly were. But they stayed on, some of them, or else returned, as hoteliers and restaurateurs, and the visitor must be grateful to them for bringing their genial brand of innkeeping and their great cuisine into this African land, not only to the major cities, but to remote locales, as well. Second, bless Hilton International. The Addis Ababa Hilton is one of the most beautiful Hiltons in the world. And I speak as one who has lived in, eaten in, drank in, or at least inspected virtually every one of them. A loan to the Ethiopian government, owners of the hotel, facilitated by the United States government, made the Addis Ababa Hilton possible. It is located diagonally across the street from the Jubilee Palace, whose occupant, Emperor Haile Selassie I followed every phase of construction avidly, and personally declared the hotel open at inaugural ceremonies. The hotel has style and taste and substance, from its interestingly patterned façade to the guest rooms, each up-to-the-minute but with Ethiopian *décor* prominent in the design motifs. The same goes for public rooms—local marble and locally woven rugs and paintings and sculpture and folk art in the lobby, Harrar Grill (surely the most elegant restaurant in East Africa), not-too-informal coffee shop, and charming cocktail lounge. Even the swimming pool is out of the ordinary, being in the same thick-cross shape of St. George's Church in Lalibela. It should go without saying that this is *the* place to stay in the Ethiopian capital. The Ghion, which had been the leader in pre-Hilton days, appears to have let itself slide, losing out to the newer Wabe Shabelle and the also-modern Ethiopia, with the elderly, Italian-managed Ras still comfortable. Restaurants? The Hilton's Harrar Grill is No. 1, hands down. Its continental European dishes are delicious and beautifully served, and if you order a day or so in advance (or, say, at breakfasttime for dinner that evening), they will prepare Ethiopian specialties for a party of at least two or three persons. The Ethiopia Hotel dining room is good, and that of the Ghion, like that of the Hilton, serves both Ethiopian and European food, doing quite a good job with both, particularly the former. The Ghion also has a coffee shop. The coffee (which, incidentally, takes its name from an Ethiopian town of Kaffa, and is believed to have originated in Ethiopia) is brewed over charcoal and served in tiny cups, seasoned with a cinnamon-like local herb. There is good Italian food at the Pizzeria Napolitana, Castelli's, and Villa Verdi; French cuisine at Maxim and Le Vieux Logis; Omar Khayyam, for Middle Eastern dishes; China Bar for Chinese food; and the Addis Ababa Restaurant, modest but clean, and decorated with Ethiopian artifacts, for national dishes. (Aside from coffee, the national dishes include *tej*, a sweet/sour meadlike beer derived from fermented honey, and *wat*, the national stew of the empire, with varying meat and poultry bases, accompanied by the spongy bread called *injera*. *Wat* is always served on a smartly designed, distinctively shaped basket-like stand, and you eat it with your fingers, piled on a piece of *injera*. Hostesses sometimes do the honors—popping a sample of this combination—into favored guests' mouths. For coffee or tea breaks: Enrico's, justifiably noted for its own-baked pastries. There is dancing at the Hilton, the Wabe Shabelle, and the Ras hotels and at such *boîtes* as the Mascotte and the Domino Club. **Asmara:** There are a pair of hotel leaders, both modern: the Nyala, with a roof garden, and the Imperial; both have comfortable rooms with bath, good restaurants—Italian-accented, in this Italian-accented town, and congenial bars. Lesser hotels are the C.I.A.A.O. and the Albergo Italia. Outside of the hotel dining rooms, good restaurants include the San Giorgio and the Capri, both Italian; the Mosobe Work, for Ethiopian dishes, and the inexpensive but good Caravel, with an international menu. **Massawa:** The undisputed leader here is the handsome, air-conditioned, beachfront Red Sea Hotel, with a swimming pool, and an exceptional Italian restaurant—in a country full of good Italian restaurants; specialties include the elaborate antipasto, homemade pasta served with excellent sauces, and fresh-caught seafood dishes. **Bahar Dar:** The Ras Hotel is it—bungalow style, no-nonsense Italian-style meals. **Lalibela:** The Seven Olives Hotel is simple and unpretentious but nonetheless inviting enough, and clean; lights out when the power supply is cut off—at 10 P.M. nightly. **Gondar:** The Itechic Menen Hotel is hardly chic, not one of its rooms having a bath of its own; okay for overnight, though. **Axum:** The Touring Hotel is modest but clean; still, if you time things right, arriving in Axum early enough, you may be able to push on after sightseeing Axum, to Asmara—and solid comfort—for the night. **Dire Dawa** and **Harrar** both have links in the Ras Hotel chain, with the Dire Dawa one the pleasanter of the pair.

GABON

République Gabonaise

Entry requirements: *A visa, obtainable from French consulates, where Gabon has no diplomatic missions, a health certificate (yellow fever and smallpox), and an onward ticket.* **Best times for a visit:** *The dry seasons—mid-May through September, and mid-December through January—are preferred periods. During other months there is rain, but it is seldom constant, so that one planning a visit then need not be deterred.* **Currency:** *The CFA franc: CFA 280=$1.* **Principal European language:** *French, with some English spoken in hotels and transport terminals.* **Domestic transport:** *Good air service connects major centers; there is steamer service on the rivers, and a fair road network.* **Further information:** *Office National Gabonais du Tourisme, Boîte Postale 403, Libreville, Gabon; Syndicat d'Initiative, Libreville, Gabon.*

INTRODUCING GABON

What the Nile is to Egypt, the forest is to Gabon. It is one immense mass of verdant equatorial forest, with thousands of species of plant life vying for growing space and forming a green ceiling which keeps the brilliant sun from penetrating to the ground—at least in many areas. Gabon's forest is overpowering, with a strength and beauty and timelessness which make a visit to it unique, even in a continent where great forests are hardly a novelty.

Withal, this little country—it is home to just about half a million people—is one of the richest in Africa. It decided, after becoming a semi-independent state of the French Community in 1958, to go it alone as a completely sovereign republic, in 1960.

Whereas its former fellow territories—Chad, Congo, Central African Republic—are poor and in need of continuing outside economic aid, Gabon may well be able to take care of its own small population, and thrive. It is rich in timber, oil palms, petroleum, and some of the biggest deposits of manganese and high-grade ore in the world. The iron ore is still unexploited, but all the other natural resources are being tapped frequently in collaboration with France, or resident Frenchmen, who remain an important part of contemporary Gabon, under the administration of President Albert Bongo, who despite his Francophile sentiments also seeks both American and other European investment in his little country.

YOUR VISIT TO GABON

Libreville: Libreville—or, if you want to translate—Freetown, in English—remains proud of its beginnings. It was established in 1849, more out of necessity than by prior plan, by a French naval officer whose government had sent him to the area in search of slave ships. The officer—Lieutenant Bouet-Willaumez—needed a headquarters for his operations, and negotiated with coastal chiefs, who gave him the land on which Libreville now stands. It received its name a decade later when the lieutenant brought ashore a shipful of slaves which his men captured—and liberated. He set them up in his little naval station. His successors penetrated the interior, soon had all of the territory, and eventually all of French Equatorial Africa. It is all back in African hands again, of course, but for France, this still small but now fast-growing city has a special significance. The old white buildings which were built as barracks for the naval personnel a century ago still stand, and the harbor, despite its modern facilities, is still dominated by rows of waving coconut palms. The town straddles the estuary of the Gabon River, and where it is not bordered by water, it is flanked by the luxuriant, fast-growing forest, which, if unchecked, would be at the water's edge in no time, just as it was before the town was founded. The beaches make for fine bathing and sunning, and just a few miles away—via a road hacked out of coastal forest—is *Cape Esterias,* with its rocks sheltering sea urchins, oysters, and lobsters. Aside from these natural attractions, the town is one of pleasant government buildings, the pretty squares which are a feature of any French-designed city, and comfortable accommodations. Short-time visitors to Gabon with no time for a visit to its other major centers would do well to drive into the interior to the little town of *Kango,* on a road leading through the forest, past tiny Gabonese villages.

Port-Gentil: The second city of the republic, Port-Gentil is dramatically perched on a finger-like peninsula, overlooking a magnificent bay on the one hand and the mouth of the Ogooué River on the other. It is a long, narrow town, with the Boulevard Maritime its main thoroughfare, and the traditional public buildings—Town Hall, Chamber of Commerce—on center squares, with bright bungalows and the attractive Church of Saint-Louis not far away. Nearby is a recreation area for swimmers, yachtsmen, and underwater fishermen in quest of tarpon, barracuda, shark, and merou. And here too is one of the largest plywood factories in the world.

Lambaréné: Still small, but about the most important town of the interior, is Lambaréné. It can be reached rapidly on daily flights from Libreville or Port-Gentil, but the traveler with a little time might like to approach it by steamer, proceeding along the Ogooué River from Port-Gentil. Besides being the site of the ramshackle, old-fashioned hospital founded by the late Dr. Albert Schweitzer—"the last of the great white fathers"—(Africa is full of many more modern and hygienic hospitals operated by Europeans whose policy toward Africans is not paternalistic and patronizing, as is the case at Lambaréné), Lambaréné has other monuments: Protestant and Catholic mission stations, a modern, twentieth-century hospital, and a tiny European community—all surrounded, of course, by the heavy green forest, among whose inhabitants are elephants and gorillas.

Setté-Cama: The least well known of the coastal towns is Setté-Cama, reached by air from both Libreville and Port-Gentil and of interest to the visitor because it is both a deep-sea fishing center *and* but a stone's throw from game reserves teeming with gorilla, elephant, buffalo, and other animals—all accessible from one's car, and easily photographed. For the visitor who will not have the opportunity to go farther into the interior, or to visit animal parks elsewhere in Africa, a quick flight to Setté-Cama for a day or two's drive into the savanna is recommended.

Okanda National Park, deep in the center of the country is still another excellent game reserve; it can be reached by plane, but not, of course, as easily as coastal Setté-Cama.

SHOPPING

Stone sculpture (from M'Bigou), carved wood and ivory, leatherware, vases, masks, musical instruments, and hunting knives are the outstanding craft products, and are obtainable in the public markets in the towns and villages, from itinerant salesmen in front of the hotels, and from the Maison Luxe curio shops in Libreville and Port-Gentil.

CREATURE COMFORTS

Hotels—**Libreville:** The modern, completely air-conditioned, 154-room seafront Inter•Continental has all facilities—pool, casino, *boîte,* Rotisserie restaurant, coffee shop; Du Roi Dénis—modern, luxurious, fully air-conditioned, fine food, and pleasant bar. Le Gamba, Central, and Hotel Louis are other choices in the capital. Noteworthy: La Pailotte Restaurant-*boîte;* Le Kinquelle—for Gabonese specialties; Le Komo—snacks and a cinema. **Port-Gentil:** Grand Tarpon—de luxe, with excellent restaurant and bar; Auberge de Phare; Dahu Restaurant, on beach in outskirts. **Lambaréné:** l'Ogooue—modern, good restaurant and bar; **Setté-Cama:** Camp Hotel—clean and simple.

THE GAMBIA

Republic of The Gambia

Entry requirements: *A visa obtainable from British consulates where Gambia has no diplomatic representation plus a health certificate (smallpox and yellow fever) and an onward ticket.* **Best times for a visit:** *November to June, the dry season, is best. July to October tend to be uncomfortably sticky.* **Currency:** *The pound: 0.417=$1.* **Principal European language:** *English, the official language, is widely spoken.* **Domestic transport:** *The principal means of transportation are steamboats that go up and down the Gambia River, which is also navigable by ocean vessels part of the way. There is some regional air transportation, and roads are being improved to accommodate the growing tourist industry.* **Further information:** *Government Tourism and Information Bureau, Bathurst, The Gambia.*

INTRODUCING THE GAMBIA

The Gambia (the "the" is there because the country takes its name from the Gambia River and is really a river valley) is a tiny country that, except for a short coastline, is entirely surrounded by Senegal. Finger-shaped, it ranges from five to twenty-five miles in width and is less than 250 miles long. The Gambia River, navigable from one end of the country to the other, bisects the country vertically and is the chief artery of transportation into the interior. But despite its size—it is Africa's smallest country—The Gambia has managed to survive economically, even balancing its budget, since becoming independent in 1965. Aside from a highly profitable smuggling trade in textiles, transistor radios, whiskey, and cigarettes, The Gambia's only industry is the growing of peanuts, which accounts for 95 percent of exports. However, in recent years, a brisk tourist business has been developing, mainly with the Swedes, almost three thousand of whom arrive by the chartered planeload each year. They are drawn here by the country's low living costs—a two-week, all-inclusive vacation can be had for a few hundred dollars—and the attractions of the beautiful beaches, not the least of which is the nude sunbathing allowed all along them.

The Gambians are noted for their courtesy, their realistic attitude about themselves and their minuscule country has helped lead to a stable political situation. The Gambia, which became a republic in 1970, is one of the few African nations to enjoy a multiparty system and free elections. Its economic condition, though fragile, is improving steadily. An official summed up in this way: "The average Gambian's common sense about the limits of this country, about austerity and his role in it, helps us keep in good financial health."

YOUR VISIT TO THE GAMBIA

Bathurst: This sleepy Victorian capital of close to forty thousand residents is on an island at the mouth of the Gambia River. Its vast natural harbor, which is being developed with the help of foreign loans, attracts cruise ships in increasing numbers. The city itself has a distinct British air, and visitors can enjoy watching such picturesque sights as changing of red-coated guards outside the palace of the governor-general and international soccer and cricket matches—the Gambians are great cricket enthusiasts, and have even defeated the national team of Nigeria, whose population is 150 times that of The Gambia. The streets of Bathurst, named for Wellington's generals, are laid out in neat rows, although one is more apt to see tin huts lining them rather than modern buildings. There are a few good hotels, and with the burgeoning tourist trade, plans for more facilities are in the works.

Outside of the capital are miles of relatively empty white-sanded beaches, with dense rain forest that comes within a hundred feet of the water's edge. There is good cast fishing at many of these beaches; Mile Three Beach is one of the most popular. A three-hour launch trip upriver takes the visitor to historic St. James Island, where he can see the old British slaving fortress and perhaps enjoy a cookout among the ruins. The entire country can be visited by steamboat that goes up and down the river in five days.

WHAT TO BUY

Japanese and Hong Kong goods can be bought in Bathurst at close to Hong Kong prices. The new Craftsmen's Village offers local wares—carvings, jewelry, tie-dye cloth—at reasonable cost.

CREATURE COMFORTS

HOTELS—**Bathurst:** The Palm Grove, small and friendly, has a beachside location; the Atlantic, opened in the 1950s, is The Gambia's oldest.

GHANA

Republic of Ghana

Entry requirements: *A visa, obtainable from Ghana consulates, or British consulates where Ghana is not represented, plus a health certificate (smallpox and yellow fever) and an onward ticket.* **Best times for a visit:** *The south is generally without rain, except in May, June, and October; and even at these times, the rain is not incessant, and need not deter visitors. The north—always drier than the humid coastal areas—has rain in August and September.* **Currency:** *The cedi, fluctuating in value, and equaling about seventy-eight U.S. cents.* **Principal European language:** *English, which is also the official language, and is widely spoken.* **Domestic transport:** *Daily flights connect the major cities; there are good all-weather roads throughout the country, a fairly extensive rail network, and steamer service along the coast.* **Further information:** *Ghana Information Office, 565 Fifth Ave., New York; Ghana Information Services, Accra, Ghana; Ghana Tourist Bureau, Accra, Ghana.*

INTRODUCING GHANA

Nigeria is infinitely larger, Sierra Leone is much newer as a sovereign state, the French Community republics have the appeal which comes from their being so relatively unknown, and Liberia has a unique American ancestry. But Ghana still stands alone in West Africa. It was, after all, the first European colony below the Sahara to achieve independence. It is the country which gave impetus to the nationalist movement that swept Africa. It chose as its name that of an ancient African empire which achieved greatness more than a thousand years ago, and it possesses today a rich indigenous culture. It has—despite vicissitudes—made fantastic progress in its brief history.

Roughly the size of Minnesota, which is not large by African standards, Ghana (known as Gold Coast Colony before independence) is home to over nine million persons, the great majority of them Black African. Although there are doubts still expressed as to whether ancient Ghana incorporated the territory of modern Ghana, there seems little disagreement that today's Ghanaians are linked by direct descent with the people of the old empire which flourished in the western Sudan regions of Africa until it was overthrown by Moslem conquerors from the north in 1076. And many of its people are believed to have migrated southward to what is now central and coastal Ghana.

The first Europeans to visit the country were a shipload of Portuguese traders in 1471. They stumbled onto a profitable trade in gold and their followers built Elmina Castle in 1482—the first of a chain of fortresses which still stand, imparting an incongruously old-European façade to the country's coast. The discovery of gold, even in those days, remained no more a secret than it did in later centuries elsewhere in the world, and before long all the major European powers got into the act—Dutch, Danes, Swedes, Prussians—and finally the British, by which time slaving had become quite as profitable as gold to traders. More than a million Africans had been tossed like cargo into the holds of ships bound for distant ports before the Danes and British declared slave trading illegal. All the Europeans left the scene, the ubiquitous British excepted. They established themselves along the coast, and in 1901 very gradually subdued the powerful Ashanti people of the interior. Just a few years earlier, in 1886, the non-Ashanti tribes of the Northern Territories had become British-"protected."

The independence movement was a post-World War II development. In 1949 an all-African committee was appointed by the British to explore constitutional reforms which would lead to self-government and, as a result, elections were held in 1951 with an African majority gaining for the first time a considerable measure of responsibility. Three years later a new constitution made the Gold Coast virtually self-governing, and in 1956 a new legislature voted for independence, and the British acquiesced—as they had indicated they would. Ghana came into being on March 6, 1957, as a full-fledged dominion of the British Commonwealth. Dr. Kwame Nkrumah—African-born, American- and British-educated, and the product, like Nehru, of a jail sentence for his political activities—became the first prime minister; he had already held that position during the preceding years, while the last of the British governors, Sir Charles Arden Clarke, was still the ultimate authority. Later, in 1960, Dr. Nkrumah, as the candidate of his Convention People's Party, won election as the country's first President under a new constitution. Though now a republic, Ghana, like India and Pakistan, remains a member of the Commonwealth, but, unlike dominions such as Australia and Canada, its citizens are no longer subjects of the queen.

In the first few years of its sovereignty Ghana made tremendous strides. Crash education programs, designed to wipe out adult illiteracy as well as to educate the young, were undertaken with great success and set a model for other undeveloped states to follow. Similar improvements were made in roads, hospitals, social services, housing, and town development. But it soon became apparent that a terrible price was being paid for these improvements. Less than two years after taking office Nkrumah, who considered himself Ghana's *Osagyefo*, its Redeemer, had taken on the role of dictator, with authority to rule for life. He began building up huge foreign debts in an effort to accelerate industrial and agricultural progress. Increasingly his government was characterized by extravagance, corruption, and suppression of freedom, including the jailing of political opponents.

By 1965 Ghana was fast approaching economic ruin, and the following year Nkrumah was deposed by a military coup. (He took up exile in Guinea, where President Sékou Touré made him honorary "co-president," and where he lived quietly until he died of cancer in April 1972 at the age of sixty-two.) A National Liberation Council, made up of army and political officers, took over the country and the task of shoring up Ghana's failing economy. In 1969, fulfilling an earlier pledge by the National Liberation Council, a civilian government was elected, headed by Prime Minister Kofi Busia. Thus, the first of Britain's African colonies to gain freedom became the first African country to shift peacefully from military rule to civilian constitutional government.

Since the unseating of Nkrumah, there had been a slow but steady economic recovery, with improvements in balance of trade, increased productivity throughout the country, and a government-spurred tourist promotion program, built around the modern facilities of the State Hotels Corporation properties.

Still, though, there was discontent with the progress being made by the Busia government. In early 1972—just after Mrs. Richard Nixon had paid a visit to Prime Minister and Mrs. Busia, after attending the inauguration of Liberian President William R. Tolbert, Jr.—a group of army officers staged a *coup d'état* against the democratically elected Busia administration. Colonel Ignatius K. Acheampong, leader of the revolutionary group, gave "general mismanagement" as the chief reason for the action. An earlier 44 percent devaluation of the currency and a rigid austerity program were believed to have been the principal factors leading to the coup. Ruling as part of a nine-man, mostly military National Redemption Council, Colonel Acheampong promised a return to democratic government "as soon as circumstances permit."

YOUR VISIT TO GHANA

Accra: The capital and chief city of the country, Accra is the natural starting point for a Ghana visit. It had just begun to take on the appearance of a modern town in the years immediately preceding independence, and it has continued to make strides since then. The contrasts—from the not-so-old days when it was a languid colonial capital, to its newer importance—are striking, and from them one can see how, with intelligent planning, a new modern city can replace a ramshackle one. Accra is blessed with a coastal location; and the sea front of Ghana is one of the most idyllically beautiful of any African state. Shopping areas are graced by sleek-lined department stores, smart boutiques, and wide, well-illuminated streets. The administrative area, with the headquarters of government institutions, is handsomely foliaged and dotted with well-kept buildings: Parliament House, the Supreme Courts Building, a well-preserved remnant of colonial days, the fine Central Library, and the ultra-functional ministries. Elsewhere one finds other evidences of growth—new banks, office buildings, government-sponsored housing developments both within the town and in the suburbs.

The Arch of Independence, built along the lines of the Arc de Triomphe in Paris and the Washington Square Arch in New York, is in the newest section of the town. The president makes his home and headquarters in a gleaming white, thick-walled castle built by the Danes in the seventeenth century, and still called Christiansborg, as is the Parliamentary Palace in Copenhagen. Worth inspecting too: the Ghana Museum, a circular building operated by the government and offering the visitor a capsulized picture of Ghana's history and culture; the superb white beaches—Labadi being the most popular with visitors—which, it must be stated, can be dangerous for bathing because of the undertow; the Accra Community Centre, often the scene of concerts and recitals, and with a public snack bar; two additional ancient forts—James (1673) and Usher (about as old)—both now prisons; the modern sports stadium, and, on the outskirts of the city at Legon, the beautiful University of Ghana. Its Terminal Gardens are the loveliest in the area, and its dining halls, dormitories, and lecture buildings are all open to visitors, with academic-gowned students usually the guides.

Accra's *nightlife* is about the liveliest in West Africa. There are only a few legitimate theaters, but there are a number of pleasant open-air cinemas, sophisticated restaurants and nightclubs, and even more delightful, innumerable dance halls, where the easy-to-learn Ghana "Highlife" is danced through the wee hours. Saturday night is the biggest of the week, and the visitor who does not stop in and participate in the merriment is missing a sampling of the robust, hearty flavor of urban Ghana. It is important to remember that strangers dance with strangers at these balls; it is not considered at all untoward for a gentleman to approach a lady who is with another party. The dance halls are usually open-air, or partially so, and the chief refreshments are beer and soft drinks.

There is, of course, an Old Accra—best typified by the harbor where ships, unable, because of currents, to berth at dockside piers, still unload cargos into small boats whose crews row up to the beachline and alight with immense boxes and crates toted on their heads. The system has not changed for centuries and is as different as night from day, when compared with the spanking new harbor operations at the modern ports of *Tema* and *Takoradi*. Near the harbor are Accra's poorer neighborhoods—streets where fishermen spread their immense nets to dry, and where merchants drive a hard bargain from their stalls and shops. The latter are—in this instance, and a most unqiue one in contrast to Moslem Africa—women. The men, while hardly slouches, have still not been able to take over as small-business owners, although, it may be noted, many of them probably have no desire to do so. Having a wife as the family breadwinner is not without advantages.

Along the Ghana coast: Good highways link the coastal communities on either side of Accra, and make day-long—or even half-day—excursions possible for visitors. *To the west* of the capital is the port of *Takoradi*, some 142 miles distant. It is just a few miles from *Sekondi*, where most Takoradi workers live and where the country's oldest schools are located. As one drives along, the route is dotted with tiny fishing villages—friendly, ramshackle, and with the attractiveness of a coastal setting made vivid by line-ups of marvelously decorated fishing craft which double as play areas for the scantily clad youngsters who welcome visitors with wide smiles, sparkling eyes, and delightful senses of humor. This is castle country too. Fort San Sebastian in *Shama*, dates from 1660 and is of Portuguese origin. Fort William at *Anamabu*, with its beautifully proportioned interior court, has been cleverly put to use as a children's vacation center, open to visitors. Other ancient monuments on the route are the castles and forts at *Axim*, *Dixcove*, *El-*

mina, Cape Coast, and *Komenda.* Takoradi and Cape Coast are the chief towns, both with hotels.

East of Accra, the countryside is verdant, hilly, and a center of cocoa cultivation. The first cocoa tree was brought from the little island of Fernando Po in 1879. Cocoa is Ghana's chief crop, and the country is now the leading cocoa producer of the world. This is, besides a farming area, the neighborhood of some of the country's leading sculptors and artists. Here too is Akropong Training College, the first institution of higher education in the country. Also worth a glance is Tema, one of the most modern ports of West Africa. North of Tema, on the Volta River at Akosombo, are the famous Volta Dam, which produces hydroelectric power, and Lake Volta, the largest manmade lake in the world. The hydroelectric plant, with its related aluminum-smelting facilities, is well worth a visit. Way to the east is *Trans-Volta Togoland region,* which includes the former British-governed United Nations Trust Territory of Togoland (not to be confused with the independent Republic of Togo, formerly French-governed). British Togoland became incorporated with Ghana, as a result of a plebiscite, in 1956. It is ideal for a brief excursion from Accra, with the destination its capital—*Ho* (not to be confused with Bo, in Sierra Leone) and the nearby mountain town of *Amedzofe,* from which there is a superb view of the Togoland Mountains, best viewed from the Government Rest House. This pleasant shelter looks over the valleys, plains, and farms of the area, as well as the distant Volta River.

Ashanti: Ghana's central province, midway between the coastal areas and the Northern Territories, is Ashanti, whose people are justifiably proud of their ancient culture and history, and the traditions which they still observe. The Asantehene and his predecessors have for long been the nominal rulers, with their symbol of sovereignty the Golden Stool, believed to have come down from heaven in answer to the prayers of the priests. More than half of Ghana's cocoa is grown in Ashanti and a large portion of its timber comes from its thick forests. Craftwork—gold, pottery, basketry, ivory, and wood carving—is among the most brilliant in Africa.

Headquarters for a visit is *Kumasi,* the regional capital, a pleasant day's drive over good roads from Accra. Highlights: the modern Central Hospital and the College of Technology, of which Ghanaians are understandably proud; Kumasi Fort, built by an Ashanti king in 1820, and the scene of battle after battle with the British; The Ashanti Cultural Center, a museum-type institution of Ashanti culture; and *Bonwire,* a nearby town which is the center of the *kente*-weaving industry. *Kentes* are the brilliant toga-like cloaks still frequently worn by Ghana men. Each is a composite of a myriad of small, hand-woven squares of heavy silk. Not to be missed in Ashanti are any ceremonials which might be in progress, and, if possible, a visit with the current Asantehene at his palace.

The Northern Territories: This is the least-visited and the most insular of Ghana's regions. *Tamale,* the regional capital, has grown considerably, but is nothing like Accra or Kumasi, despite its Teachers' College and modern airport. It is adequate for short stays during which excursions can be made to villages like *Savelugu* (13 miles) and *Tolon* (18 miles)—preferably on a market day. This is a part of Africa which has had little more than a half century's contact with the outside world; it is hardly for the luxury-living visitor, but for the less demanding a tour of it can be unusually rewarding.

SHOPPING

Ghana's arts and crafts are outstanding, and include *kente* cloths ($200 minimum!), superb tiny figures in iron and gold at one time used as gold-weight measures and made for centuries by means of the ancient "lost wax" process; hide-covered drums, carved heads and other woodenware, including attractive serving platters; basketry, ivoryware, silver filigree jewelry, leatherwork, ceramics—much of it still made without benefit of potter's wheel. Best Accra source: the government-operated Industrial Development Corporation (I.D.C.) shop. In Kumasi, Tamale, Cape Coast and other major towns, local offices of the Ghana Information

Services are glad to direct visitors to good shops and artisans' workshops.

CREATURE COMFORTS

HOTELS—**Accra's** best hotels are the modern, refurbished Ambassador; the Continental, near the airport; and the Meridian—twenty miles out. **Kumasi's** best hotel is the Kingsway; there is also the government-run Chalet Resthouse, similar to those in **Tamale** and **Ho. Takoradi:** Atlantic, Travellers Hotel, Busuah Beach Hotel. **Cape Coast:** Catering Rest House, Travellers Inn, Elmina Motel, Owusua Hotel. The State Hotels Corporation operates a chain of motels upcountry.

NIGHTLIFE—**Accra:** open-air nightclub and casino at the Ambassador; Bokom Club, in the Continental Hotel, the Lido, Weekend, Paradise, Tiptoe Gardens, and Weekend dance halls, and—definitely recommended—the Sea View Hotel, for its Saturday-night dances. **Kumasi:** the Casino, the Sentimental Saloon, the As Usual, the Way Fairies Inn, and the Decency Bar are just a few of the nightclubs. And if you find *their* names delightful, watch for those on the public buses—or "mammy wagons" all over the country!

GUINEA

République de Guinée

Entry requirements: *A visa, obtainable from Guinean consulates, plus a health certificate (yellow fever, smallpox) and an onward ticket.* **Best times for a visit:** *January to April—the dry season—is ideal.* **Currency:** *The Guinean franc: 280=$1.* **Principal European language:** *French, with English spoken at air terminals and bigger hotels.* **Domestic transport:** *Flights to major centers, trains, extensive road network.* **Further information:** *Ministry of Information, Conakry, Guinea; Embassy of Guinea, Washington, D.C.*

INTRODUCING GUINEA

Not big by African standards—it is about the size of Oregon—Guinea is West Africa in miniature: palm-fringed coastal areas, magnificent equatorial forests, formidable mountains, elevated plateaus, arid savanna; the religions of the animist, Moslem, and Christian; the cultures of a great many tribal peoples as well as the European and the Middle-Easterner; wild animals and turbulent waterfalls, modern hotels and tiny *campements,* mines and harbors, tiny farms and fishing villages.

Prehistoric Guinea knew civilizations ranging from Neolithic to "Pebble." And centuries later parts of its territory were included within the Ghana Empire while it was at its peak a millennium ago—when gold from the Siguiri region of Guinea helped make it rich. Mali, Ghana's successor in the twelfth century, also included parts of Guinea within its realm, and its last capital, Inani, was within Guinea; it was during this period that Islam came to the country's towns—where it has remained a powerful force. Later, in the fifteenth and sixteenth centuries, the first of the Europeans—the Portuguese—arrived on the coast, which they named *Rivières du Sud* (Rivers of the South), and about the same time, the pastoral Peul people conquered parts of the region, where they still remain. Mali, under attack from Europeans, Peuls, and later Moroccans, disintegrated, and in the seventeenth century the Peuls—gradually gaining strength—set up a feudal empire, Moslem-oriented and intricately organized into nine provinces. Later, in the mid-nineteenth century, the Europeans—French, Portuguese, Germans, British—fought over the Guinea coastal area; the French won out, only to face bitter resistance in the interior from the forces of the Guinean soldier-leader Alamy Samory Touré and his successors. The Colony of French Guinea was created in 1891, but fighting in certain areas continued until the start of the First World War. Development followed the European colonial pattern—roads, railways, and buildings were constructed by forced African labor, and an enlightened type of rule was to emerge only gradually, reaching its peak after World War II, when political parties were allowed to organize, and Guineans began to elect deputies for the Paris parliament, and for their colony's own legislature as well.

When General De Gaulle gave the provinces of French West Africa and Equatorial Africa a choice in 1958—join the French Community or become independent without continuing to receive French aid—Guinea's leader, Sékou Touré, rallied his people to vote for a complete schism with the mother country. De Gaulle, petulant and infuriated at this defection—the only one in the French African Empire—cut off funds at once and withdrew French administrators and technicians as soon as they could pack their bags. Guinea, with Touré as its first President, became the third independent country in West Africa.

France pulled out; England and the United States, while recognizing Guinea's sovereignty, hesitated about offering aid and sending technical missions. The Touré government, hardly Rightist in its point of view, had no compunctions in calling upon the Soviet bloc for help, and while the Western powers were still worried about offending France, the Soviets, the Chinese, the East Germans, the Czechs moved in with trade delegations, technical help, arms. The Westerners finally came through themselves—but a little late. Since 1958, Guinea, potentially rich in minerals and water power, has attracted Western investment, which has helped make the country one of the world's leading producers of bauxite.

Sékou Touré, along with Ghana's Nkrumah, was an early exponent of the African Unity movement. He promoted a short-lived alliance with Ghana and Mali, and in 1966 granted asylum to the deposed Nkrumah, giving him the honorary title of "co-president" which he retained until his death in 1972. Touré, handsome, forceful, one of the first African heads of state to visit the United States officially (he insisted that the State Department include the South in his itinerary, and it did), is a fervent nationalist, rules Guinea with a strong hand—his political party is the only one—and his country has had a turbulent political history since gaining independence. Late in 1970 Touré accused Portugal—probably with good reason—of backing an invasion into his country, an affair that aroused sympathy around the world. A UN investigating team concluded that the invasion was indeed led by white Portuguese from next-door Guinea-Bissau. In January 1971 Touré sentenced nearly one hundred Portuguese and Guineans to death for their alleged roles in the attempted invasion, and this action was but one of a number of purges of Guineans, with estimates of the executed and jailed running as high as 6000. Guinea, contemporarily, remains anxious—security is tight, tourism nil (the small resident foreign community includes the black American civil-rights militant, Stokely Carmichael, and his wife, South African-born singer Miriam Makeba), politics zealous, consumer goods scarce.

YOUR VISIT TO GUINEA

Guinea is a land of four distinct regions, each of which deserves a sampling from the visitor. There is the *Fouta Djallon* (Middle

Guinea), with its high plateaus, mountains, waterfalls, and rapids. There is the *Sudan Region* (Upper Guinea) with its great arid plains and savannas. There is the *Forest Region,* dense and animal-filled. And there is the *Coast* (Lower Guinea), which contains the capital, as well as myriad rivers and swampy archipelagoes which drain into the sea, and inspired the Portuguese to dub the region "Rivers of the South." Transport within Guinea is a peg above many ex-French areas; Europeans hied to its hills on holidays, and even outside the capital, there are several centers with good hotels.

Conakry and the coast: Guinea's capital became an international beehive soon after independence. Diplomats, technicians, businessmen, private visitors from all over the world—America, Western Europe, the Soviet bloc, Africa, China—made their way through its once quieter thoroughfares, gathered for drinks in its bars, conferences in its modern office buildings, functional ministries, and the still charming, French-built Présidence—for long the home of colonial governors, and now the presidential palace. Today Conakry shows the strain of over a decade of economic and political struggle. Black-market prices and extensive rationing have led to widespread discontent and many Guineans have fled their country for more prosperous areas. Some of the sections of the capital are now decaying and deserted.

Conakry is built along the sea. Its most delightful sector is along the parklike Corniche, an artery which follows the water line from one end of town to the other. Coconut palms sway in the breeze, towering above benches scattered on strips of lawn. And in the distance, just visible, are the *Iles de Loos,* now the site of extensive bauxite-mining operations but, in earlier centuries, a European headquarters for slavers and raiders of the mainland. Excursions to Loos, which take a full day, can be made by small steamers. The city itself is small enough to traverse by foot. Its main areas include the European-style shopping areas which border the central squares, the truly African residential neighborhoods, where families cook, launder, and chat on the small, neat front lawns, respond genially to visitors' greetings of "*Bon jour, ça-va?*" and react to the "invasion" of their recently obscure town with equanimity and poise. The market, *en plein aire*, has the robustness and strength of all-African markets. The IFAN museum's exhibits of Africana should be a requisite. And the beaches—some within the town, with cafés bordering them—and some without (like *Camayenne*) are perfect for half a day's relaxation. There is, as well, the coastal countryside, easily accessible by car, along good roads. This is a domain of a thousand streams—some almost dry, some more marsh than waterway—which rise in the hills and come down to empty into the sea. Resident here are the Soussou, known for their prowess as traders; the finely attired Baga, who are fisherfolk; the agricultural Landomouman. Each of these peoples has its own way of life, its own mode of dress (copper rings in the noses of some, plaited straw belts on the women of others), and its own villages, most of which are groups of houses elevated on skyscraping piles. In some—*Forécariah*, for example, whose buildings are of long-lasting dried mud—metal rings, used by slave traders to chain their captives, remain.

Away from the coast, but not too far into the interior, are a number of interesting destinations. One is the *Fria* bauxite mines and the new city alongside them near *Kimbo*. A trip to Fria can be made in a day's excursion from Conakry, but *Kindia* requires a minimum of two days. Its Pasteur Institute—the scientific pride of the republic—is interesting, and its environs consist, it would seem, of an endless series of waterfalls, one lovelier than the next.

Fouta Djallon (Middle Guinea): The great mountain range which gives this region its name is one of the most imposing in Africa. It is here that the thousand rivers of the coast originate as silvery brooks, gaining in width and strength as they hurtle over rocks in their path and jump over—as waterfalls—great precipices. Here, one's headquarters might well be *Dalaba*, developed as a health resort by the French, always cool, thanks to its 4000-foot elevation; attractive too, with villas reminiscent of the Côte d'Azur, and a beautifully situated hotel which is one of the pleasantest in Guinea. The surrounding countryside is dotted with cascades, gorges, waterfalls—and the villages of the hospitable Fulah (or

Peul) people, with their elegantly coiffed women and handsome men. Mostly shepherds and farmers who thrive on a diet of semolina, milk, and honey, they are the descendants of conquerors of the indigenous residents of the area—craftsmen, potters, blacksmiths, wood sculptors, weavers, and jewelers. They are another example (others abound in East Africa) of the subjugation of a highly developed people by warlike invaders. For the Fulah came long ago from the East. Today, though, they live in harmony with their more talented ex-subjects. And their neat towns and villages welcome visitors; these include *Timbo* (once their capital) and *Mali*, bearer of the name of that once great empire. *Mamou*, itself a rather pedestrian administrative center, is interesting mainly because of the villages and natural wonders which border it. And *Dabola* (not to be confused with the abovementioned Dalaba) makes a comfortable headquarters too.

Sudan Region (Upper Guinea): The emerald-hued mountains of the Fouta Djallon are a far cry from the arid plains of this region, where vegetation is sparse, animal life profuse, and the waters of the Niger and its tributaries the lifeblood of the agricultural economy. Here, one's headquarters might well be a town whose name is African, although it may not at first seem so: *Kankan*—overwhelmingly Moslem in façade, with a skyline of mosques, a populace not without its share of Islamic theologians and scholars, and the bustling Milo River harbor. Kankan's animist inhabitants are great dancers, and include in their repertoire the famous fire dance, in which participants immolate themselves—after an hour or two of highly athletic action—in a flaming fire, emerging, strangely enough, without burns. Other centers in this area are *Siguiri*, in the midst of a well-to-do region of both farms and gold mines; *Faranah*, with its hippo pools, and *Dinguiraye*, alive not only with hippo but with elephant, antelope, and even leopard. All about are little villages and farms whose owners live in circular bamboo-shoot huts, wearing abbreviated but functionally sensible clothing.

Forest Region: Dominated by great trees which blot out the sun and often exceed 200 feet in height, and by the *Nimba*

Mountains soaring almost 6000 feet into the air, the Forest Region is a land of tiny villages whose peoples have had considerably less contact with the outer world than those of other areas of the republic. Many forest people still live almost exclusively by hunting and fishing, but in other areas lands have been cleared and farming has become the chief means of livelihood. Clothing is, as one would expect, minimal, at least in the unfarmed areas, where diet is sparse and life is an unending struggle. But in the agricultural sectors, culture is more highly developed, songs and dances richer, village life worth exploring, crafts—particularly dance masks—outstanding. *Kissidougou* is a good center for excursions, and so is *N'zérékoré,* where the dominant ethnic group is the Guerze, animists with elaborate and fascinating rituals, the best known of which are the not infrequent initiation ceremonies, at which young people become full-fledged members of the community.

SHOPPING

Carved ivory, wood sculpture, leatherwork, ceremonial masks, iron figurines—at sidewalk stalls in downtown Conakry, at the public market in that city, and at similar locations in towns and villages throughout the country. Bargaining is the rule. Actual stores are virtually all state-owned. An interesting exception worth knowing about is Socomer (Société Mixte Guinéo-Yugoslave)—a PX-kind of paradise for everyone in Conakry with hard foreign currencies to spend.

CREATURE COMFORTS

HOTELS—**Conakry** has a trio of good hotels. The G'Bessia, not far from the airport, with a restaurant-*boîte,* bar, and air-conditioned rooms, is considered No. 1. The pre-independence Hôtel de France, central and seafront, was one of the best examples of French Tropical Architecture in Africa when it went up, and remains a leader, with air-conditioned rooms, restaurant, and bar.

The Camayenne, featuring terraces with its air-conditioned rooms, as well as a restaurant and bar, is No. 3. Le Provençal Restaurant serves French food, with seafood specialties. **Camayenne Beach** (near Conakry): Camavenne. **Dalaba:** Fouta Djallon. **Mamou:** Buffet. **Kindia:** Buffet. **Dabola:** Campement-hôtel. **Kankan:** Conakry-Niger. **N'zérékoré:** Campement-hôtel. **Kissidougou:** Campement-hôtel. Small, simple rest camps at smaller centers throughout the country.

IVORY COAST

République de Côte d'Ivoire

Entry requirements: *A visa, obtainable from Ivory Coast embassies, consulates, or the Ivory Coast Visa Office, 521 Fifth Avenue, New York, plus a health certificate (yellow fever and smallpox).* **Best times for a visit:** *December through April are the dry-season months; it is rainy May through July; quite dry in August and September, and showery in October and November.* **Currency:** *The franc (CFA): $1=280 CFA.* **Principal European language:** *French, with English spoken in the major hotels and transport terminals.* **Domestic transport:** *Air Ivoire connects the principal towns. Roads are generally good, but some in the interior are impassable during parts of the rainy season.* **Further information:** *Office National du Tourisme, Boîte Postale 1173, Abidjan, Côte d'Ivoire; Embassy of the Ivory Coast, 2424 Massachusetts Avenue, N.W., Washington, D.C.; Air Afrique, 683 Fifth Avenue, New York, and Abidjan, Côte d'Ivoire.*

INTRODUCING THE IVORY COAST

Don't look for great stacks of elephant tusks at Ivory Coast ports. There are still elephants to be seen in this republic's rain forests, but the trade in ivory—from which the country's name is derived—is past history. The modern Ivory Coast is one of West Africa's richest countries, thanks to its exports of rare woods, diamonds, manganese, and palm products. How rich? A visit to the capital city and chief port will tell. But besides the bounce and vitality of skyscraper-filled Abidjan, the Ivory Coast has other tourist attractions. Few visitors to this part of the continent leave without making its acquaintance—and rightly so.

The peoples of the country had evolved an elaborate Iron Age culture long before the first Europeans dropped anchor along the coast four and five centuries ago. They worked gold in the remarkable "lost wax" casting process, with results quite as superb as those of better-known Benin in neighboring Nigeria, and they were no slouches, either, in brass and iron, as well as in the decorative arts—masks, carved wood, and weaving.

Interested only in what they could make a profit on—that is, ivory and slaves—European traders never bothered to venture much beyond the coastal settlements until the mid-nineteenth century. It was not until 1893 that the French were able to declare the area a colony, and only within the past few decades has it made substantial contact with the technology of the West.

Until 1958 the Ivory Coast was the most pro-French of the provinces of French West Africa. Largely because of the influence of its leader—Félix Houphouët-Boigny—all of the provinces except Guinea voted to remain semi-autonomous members of the French Community, upon its creation. Houphouët-Boigny had been the most pro-French of the African legislators to hold posts in Paris cabinets.

Quiet-appearing, trained as a physician, the son of a chief, and a wealthy plantation owner, Houphouët-Boigny had served in half a dozen French cabinets before becoming the only African with cabinet rank in De Gaulle's Fifth Republic. He was strongly against full independence for the Community members, with a point of view exactly opposite that of Guinea's Sékou Touré and Ghana's Kwame Nkrumah. He argued—and at first with success—that Community states should be independent with regard to running their domestic affairs, but that the other appurtenances of sovereignty—a foreign service, armies and navies, postage and currency, etc.—were fields in which the French were better equipped to deal. Africans, he said, should concentrate on internal development. There were too few of them trained to staff elaborate diplomatic corps whose members would serve abroad as ambassadors and deprive their country of their services at home.

There was some logic in the Houphouët arguments, and most of the other Community members listened for a while. But they—and their leader—soon changed their tune. Senegal and Sudan (now called Mali) announced in early 1960 that they were opting for complete sovereignty. Houphouët himself came to America on an official visit just after Guinea's Touré, and no doubt perceived how modest was his reception—as a relatively unknown leader of a non-autonomous state—in contrast to that of the President of a sovereign republic like Touré. The American trip may not have been decisive in his change of mind, but at any rate, it was not too many months later that *all* the autonomous Community republics followed Guinea, Senegal, and Mali to complete independence. Houphouët's Ivory Coast joined with Niger, Upper Volta, and Dahomey in banding together as the Council of the Entente, through which they negotiated with France on the details of their changed status. France's most loyal African leader had about-faced and allowed the winds of change to blow his country, and its followers, to independence.

But Houphouët was too clever a leader to allow independence to work against his country's economy. On the contrary. Although the life of the villager upcountry has been little changed as yet (indeed, the indigenous cultures of the Ivory Coast are among the most undiluted in Africa), the Ivory Coast has shown economic gains virtually unparalleled in Black Africa. Houphouët's plan has been relatively simple. He has encouraged—and keenly promoted—foreign private enterprise and technical expertise. He has continued to emphasize coffee production (his country is No. 3 in the world, with its species of bean luckily ideal for instant coffee), the while diversifying with other tropical crops. And, with help from European friends, he has boldly set his country—it is still 80 percent illiterate—on the path of industrialization, building modern harbors along the coast and power stations in the interior, the better to make possible factories turning out a wide range of products, from processed foods to assembled automobiles.

With the profits, Houphouët quite obviously believes in spending in ways that are visibly discernible. His capital city has become one of the most skyscraping and swinging in Black Africa. He is building dams and housing projects and new schools and cloverleaf highways. Something like 25 percent of the budget is going into education, with a television-teaching system—patterned after that pioneered by the United States in American Samoa during the sixties—earmarked for use in elementary schools throughout the country.

The Ivory Coast is a one-party republic; all eighty-five members of its unicameral parliament are members of the Democratic Party. Unhappiness with this lack of a legal opposition manifested itself in 1963 when a revolt against the government was quashed. But there have not been any similar events of consequence since that time. (Although there were not a few Ivorians and foreigners who winced in 1971 when Houphouët, who has become the most conservative of the major French-speaking African leaders, urged his fellow Black African neighbors to consider trade and other relations with white-ruled, apartheid-policy South Africa). In 1967, the Ivory Coast became the first Black African country to float a loan—and a ten-million-dollar one at that—on the Eurodollar market. In 1969, work began on the one-hundred-million-dollar Bandama River power project, the aim of which is to open up development of the central portion of the interior. And plans are under way, too, for the construction of an absolutely massive riviera along the coast, outside of Abidjan, which would be unequaled not only in Africa but on any of the continents.

Even now, though, this West African state—humidity and all—has become a magnet for visitors, both pleasure and business. The President himself is a booster of an expanded tourist plant and industry. Accommodations are modern not only in the capital (which is the case in many lands) but at points throughout the interior, as well. Ivorians, quick to welcome their guests, are outgoing, loquacious, hospitable, and confident of their country's future.

YOUR VISIT TO THE IVORY COAST

Abidjan: Within a few short decades this one-time fishing settlement has become one of Africa's handsomest and most effervescent cities. With a population hovering about the half-million mark, it is also one of the largest in the western part of the continent. Abidjan is a green-and-white town: pristine skyscrapers towering under the brilliant sun; streets—when not obscured by the scaffolding of new buildings being constructed—bordered by parks and gardens, and surrounding pleasant, bench-filled squares; a waterfront incongruously nonurban in certain areas, with coconut palms blowing gently over an intricate network of blue-green lagoons, and boisterously modern in others—with an ingeniously designed harbor. Abidjan has the vitality of Lagos, but it is a French-inspired city without the squalor which the British did little to mitigate in the capital of Nigeria.

It is easiest to take Abidjan sector by sector, for the divisions are explicit ones. The area best described as downtown is known also as the Plateau. Here one finds a humming shopping area. The principal public buildings, and the immense Square Bressoles, with its Plateau Market, at which Ivorian handicrafts and other commodities are on sale; the Hotel du Parc is right across the way. Abijan's markets are among the most fascinating of any urban area in Africa. Besides the Plateau Market, there are those at Adame, and the teeming, two-story maze of bazaars in the Treichville suburb. See them all; they constitute a whopping slice of Ivorian life not otherwise easily come by.

Grander aspects of Abidjan are to be seen, as well. The President's Palace is one of the most opulent on the continent. Because, before independence, Abidjan was simply a provincial city in the vast territory known as French West Africa (of which Dakar was the capital) it had no governor's residence for the President to move into. One had to be constructed. Though not ordinarily open to the public, tours may be arranged on weekdays; the key telephone number is 286-93. Equally impressive is the elaborate and costly National Assembly. A look at the interior is possible at certain hours on weekdays when the Assembly is not in session; telephone 221-57.

Abidjan's National Museum contains one of the finest collections of traditional art in Africa. It is a descendant of the old museum of the Institut Français d'Afrique Noir which the French—who greatly appreciated the richness of African art—wisely established in key centers of French West and French Equatorial Africa. The Ivorian government took it over after independence, and if it has plans to build any more fancy public buildings in Abidjan ere long, I wish it would give top priority to a new home for the museum. The exhibits—there are a total of twenty thousand objects—are so jammed into the available space that it is difficult to appreciate them as one should. And the budget for the museum is apparently so tight that there appear to be no qualified persons on hand to offer guidance or help on the collections, in either French or English. One of the leading museums of African art in Africa deserves better.

Out in the residential section of town called Cocody, one finds the beautiful campus of the University of Abidjan (it has half a dozen faculties, including medicine and engineering), and the campus—indeed, that it may be called—of the remarkable Hotel Ivoire complex, which deserves a visit even from those who are not registered as guests, so extensive are its facilities. These include a superduper supermarket and what must surely be the only ice-skating rink in tropical Africa. I have never gotten the message of the Parc National du Banco, north of Abidjan, although you may, to be sure. But there are any number of excursions destinations on the lagoons outside of town that are agreeable. *Boulay Island* is a popular spot, and with good reason. You can take picnics or lunch at the simple restaurant-bar on the beach; the swimming is first-rate. *Grand-Bassam* is mobbed with Abidjanians on Sundays, so go during the week if you can; it was an administrative center during colonial times. Nearby is a lovely fishing village called *Azuretti*. The beaches are lovely (although the water is rough and can be dangerous) and there is a good restaurant, La Taverne Bassamois, where one may lunch.

Man: The name of a town set amidst the thickly forested mountains in the west of the country, not far from the Guinea border, Man knew no Europeans until as recently as 1897. The great forest served as protection for its peoples, and even though the town itself has grown considerably since the French "penetration," the region remains quite as it was—indescribably beautiful patches of forest alternating with more open savannas dotted with the unique Elephant Plant—so named because of its giant size—in the rolling mountains. The principal natural curiosity is a big tooth-shaped rock named by a pioneering punster, *Dent de Man.* This is panorama country (the view of Man and Mounts Dan and Touras from the peak of Mount Ton Koui: *c'est magnifique!*). This is excursion country for drives through the forest, the savanna, and the villages. And this is dance country—or ballet country, if you will. For ballet *is* the term for the subtly choreographed dances of the young girls in the villages, and those of their masked elders as well. The Dans are the principal ethnic group of the area, and the visitor is advised not to leave until he has come upon a village fête where dancing is part of the program. Not far north is *Touba,* where giant dancers on stilts perform behind the most splendid masks of the Ivory Coast, obtainable in the great market, along with gold and silver work.

Bouaké: The second city of the republic, Bouaké is smack in the center of the country, amid the forests of the interior. It is distinguished chiefly by a cotton mill which is the pride and joy of the community, and which most visitors are shown through regardless of their interest in cotton mills; an agricultural experimental laboratory; a tall TV tower that has become a landmark; and one of the noisiest open-air markets in Africa, ablaze with brilliantly clad people and merchandise running the gamut from bicycles to monkey meat. Outside of town—and this is the region of the Baoulé people, animists who believe in a Supreme Being and whose religion is one of the most interesting in West Africa—one will find, besides their villages and farms, a solitary mosque strangely decorated in shades of black, white, and yellow, and some terribly scientific experimental farms which, while hardly exotic, indicate the extent of this remote region's development.

Other destinations with modern hotels that are easy of access and from which excursions can be made to culturally rich areas include *Daloa,* chief town of the northwest; *Korhogo,* the unofficial capital of the far north, in the heart of hunting territory (warthogs, antelopes, wild ducks); and *Abengourou,* the little metropolis of the east. Travel agencies in Abidjan sell interestingly planned *package tours,* all-inclusive and a good way to have a look at the little-traversed interior; inquiries may be made on the scene in Abidjan, or through one's own travel agent at home. One of the best of these trips is to the game reserve at *Bouna,* some four hundred miles to the north of the capital.

SHOPPING

In a word: excellent. Abidjan has two things going for it in this respect. The first is that the Ivory Coast, as well as neighboring countries like Mali and Upper Volta, are among the best in all Black Africa for traditional handicrafts and folk art. The second is that Abidjan has become the richest city in West Africa, attracting more monied people than any other. That money is responsible for bringing exceptionally good merchandise to town, both Ivorian and from elsewhere in West Africa, particularly the relatively little-traveled interior. Look for wood carving—masks, headpieces, stools, and the like. Additionally, there are little iron figurines, made by means of the ancient "lost wax" process that has been known in West Africa for centuries; gold and silverwork; articles in leather—including good-looking men's and women's sandals; and basketry. The hands-down best source of *quality* masks and woodcarvings—some of it of museum caliber—is La Rose d'Ivoire. The principal shop is in the lobby and basement of the Hôtel Ivoire (the best things are in the basement) and there is a small branch with a choice selection of the better pieces, downtown on Rue Nour Al Hayat, near the Hôtel du Parc.

Monsieur Christian Debeneste, the owner, imports masks from the interior of the Ivory Coast, and neighboring countries like Mali and Upper Volta, as well. Of course, he also stocks cheap tourist trivia. But his expensive things are the real item. His is one of the few retail commercial outlets in Black Africa where you will find the kind of art that museum curators and art-gallery dealers must usually go into the bush to obtain. And he is expert at packing and shipping. Highly recommended. Then there are the markets. They are all fun to explore, bargain in, even make purchases at. And they are an adventure—hot, sweaty, smelly, Abidjan at its most authentic. The most tame is that of the Square Bressoles, facing the Hôtel du Parc, in the Plateau. Tame, that is, in that it is open-air, and uncrowded. The merchants are the most aggressive in the republic. You must be firm with them to the point of rudeness, and bargain furiously for anything you see that you like. On sale are masses of souvenirs, from sandals (these are among the best bets) to corny carvings. The larger Plateau markets, along the Boulevard de la République, facing the modern Town Hall, are more typically local—lots of textiles, and other requisites for the Abidjanians, some of which you might find most interesting. In Treichville, at the immense, two-story market building, you'll find ceramics and food on the ground floor; upstairs there are textiles, coins (many of them old ones—collectors go wild when they see them), and clothing, including caftans and bubus (long gowns), for both men and women. Additional bubus are to be found nearby in the bazaars of the Moslem community; bargaining is the rule. In Adjamé there are still more markets. The largest building is quite similar to that at Treichville, but the Market Bromakote specializes in woodwork and is unusual. Remember that Adjamé and Treichville close at 2:00 P.M., having opened at 6:30 A.M. The Plateau market opposite Town Hall shuts down, except for foodstuffs, at about noon, but the souvenir stalls opposite the Hôtel du Parc stay open all day. Conventional shops are open from 8:00 A.M. to noon, 3:00 P.M. to 7:00 P.M. Outside of Abidjan, there are large public markets in the towns (that at Bouaké is an all-Africa standout), and one frequently encounters itinerant vendors of handicrafts—masks and the like—outside hotels or in the shopping areas of smaller communities. It is from such sources that one can often make excellent and authentic buys. Always have a look—and with a smile.

CREATURE COMFORTS

In a country that has amassed so much wealth, and that attracts so much wealth, it should come as no surprise to find first-rate accommodations. And in a country where the colonial occupiers had been French, and where many Frenchmen still are resident, it should come equally as no surprise to find good food and wine. Here are the highlights. **Abidjan:** The Hôtel Ivoire is owned by the Ivorian government and operated by Inter•Continental Hotels, the Pan Am subsidiary that is exceptionally strong in Africa. It is, as I have mentioned earlier in this chapter, a unique establishment, occupying what might well be termed a campus of its own. There are two principal buildings, the original (twelve stories) and a newer thirty-floor tower; between them they contain five hundred superspiffy air-conditioned rooms with bath, many with absolutely superb views of downtown Abidjan, the lagoons, and the Atlantic beyond. There is a big swimming pool, surrounded by a café on its own level, with another café one flight above. The fanciest restaurant in the complex is the Toit d'Abidjan, not quite on the roof, but on the twenty-third floor of the tower, with French food in a super setting. Aux Quatre Coins du Monde is another restaurant, this adjoining the hotel's casino. And on you go—Le Pili Pili, an informal eatery with African and international dishes, le Rendezvous cocktail lounge, le Petit Boulevard for coffee or tea and pastries in the shopping arcade. And there are a six-hundred-seat movie theater, a two-thousand-seat convention hall, a ten-lane bowling alley, Black Africa's first and only ice-skating rink, gym, sauna, heliport, marina, and—coming up—an eighteen-hole golf course. Inter•Continental staffs and operates the whole shootin' match beautifully. Following would be the Hôtel du Parc. For long the leader before the advent of the Ivoire, this centrally located hostelry has spruced up its public rooms and its eighty guest rooms. Virtually all have private bath or shower. There are two handsomely decorated French restaurants, and a canopy-covered café overlooking the Square Bressoles that is a major congregating place. Also very pleasant is the eighty-room Relais de Cocody, a link in the African chain operated by Air France. It has a pool, exceptional restaurant, bar-café, and lovely lagoonside location. Following, in my ranking, is the Grand Hôtel, on the lagoon but more central than the Relais, and with a pair of good restaurants. Club Mediteranée members will be attracted to their organization's six-hundred-room Ivorian outpost sixty miles from the capital, on the Assinie Lagoon. *Restaurants* in Abidjan? Those in the leading hotels—Ivoire, du Parc, Relais, Grand—are all very recommendable. Additionally, for French food, consider Le Petit Auberge and Le Vieux Strasbourg (with Alsatian specialties). Mekong is popular for its Vietnamese dishes. Pizza is, of course, Italian, but serves a lot more than pizza. The Palm Beach Hotel, near the airport, is very big on seafood. Middle Eastern dishes, mainly Lebanese, are to be had at Walbeck. Tante Sally, in Treichville, is very good for Ivorian specialties, like chicken with peanut sauce or lamb in palm kernel sauce, served with *foutou*, a plantain or banana paste, that is the national staple. There is no shortage of nightspots. Smartest is Au Quatre Coins du Monde in the Ivoire. But the discothèque called Submarine—and when you see it you'll know why—is very popular. And so is the Boule Noire, with Ivorian entertainment and a heavily local clientele, in Treichville. More? Well, there are the Scotch Club and the In Club. The thoroughfare popularly known as the Rue Douze, or Twelfth Street (no longer its official name, but no matter) is full of bars of every description, some run by Guineans, Ghanaians, or Nigerians, and one, Chez Françoise, is headquarters for the Eurafricans of Abidjan, and a diverting stop-off spot. Upcountry hotels are an Ivorian surprise package. They've gone up in recent years as part of the government's tourism development program. **Bouaké's** is the Bouaké. **Korhogo's** is the motel-like Mont Korhogo. **Man's** is the most attractive Cascades, with a swimming pool. At **Daloa,** it's Les Ambassadeurs. **Gagnoa** offers Le Fromager, and **Abengourou's** is the Indénié, with pool. **The Assouinde Beach** Hotel, fifty miles east of Abidian, is a 300-room, full-facility resort complex—among the first (late 1972) of those to be developed by the government's Seitho tourism-promotion agency.

KENYA

Republic of Kenya

Entry requirements: *A visa obtainable from the Kenya Government Tourist Office, 15 East 51st Street, New York; the Kenya Embassy, Washington, or other Kenya diplomatic or consular missions; plus a health certificate (smallpox, yellow fever) and proof of onward transportation.* **Best times for a visit:** *There are rainy seasons between March and May, and November and mid-December, although I wouldn't let them deter me from a Kenya visit if I were in the neighborhood. The Indian Ocean coast is generally hot and humid, but the elevated portions of the interior (including the region around Nairobi) is considerably cooler and more temperate. Nairobi temperatures run from the low eighties in February to the mid-fifties in June and July. Mombasa, on the shore, hovers around ninety in February and March, the hottest months, but can go just below seventy in July and August, the coolest time, and the most popular vacation period at coastal resorts.* **Currency:** *The Kenya shilling, worth about fourteen U.S. cents, with about seven shillings to the American dollar. The shilling is at par with the Uganda and Tanzania shillings, and although the* coins *of these three countries are interchangeable—usable in each of the countries—the* notes—*or bills—of each are legal tender only in the country of issue.* **Principal European language:** *English, widely spoken, and a co-official language along with Swahili, which is considerably more widely spoken and the* lingua franca *of the area embracing Kenya, Uganda, Tanzania, and Zaïre.* **Domestic transport:** *Kenya has what is probably the most extensive network of paved roads of any East African country, with Nairobi the* *focal point. One can motor from the capital to any number of important destinations, including Mombasa, on the coast. There is the historic railroad leading from Mombasa to Uganda, in the interior. Worth knowing about is the unorganized, unscheduled, but extremely popular and convenient system of "Peugeot taxis"—privately operated cars whose owner-chauffeurs drive them through the most heavily traveled areas of the country, picking up and discharging passengers along the way. Hotels, lodges, and travel agency people are generally* au courant. *Far more comfortable, of course, are the scheduled flights of East African Airways to major areas not only of Kenya but of neighboring countries, as well; EAA is jointly owned by the governments of Kenya, Tanzania, and Uganda. Nairobi has an extensive taxi fleet; if one's destination is at all out of the ordinary, or away from the city center, it is well to have it written clearly on a slip of paper, and to have been briefed in advance on routing, for some drivers are newcomers to town, and know neither it nor the English language well.* **Further information:** *Kenya Government Tourist Office, 15 East 51st Street, New York; Permanent Secretary, Ministry of Tourism and Wildlife, P. O. Box 30027, Nairobi, Kenya; East African Airways, 576 Fifth Avenue, New York, and P. O. Box 41010, Nairobi, Kenya; Embassy of Kenya, Washington, D.C.*

INTRODUCING KENYA

Kenya is the most developed, the most visited, and the most publicized country in East Africa. Indeed, it leads all of tropical Africa in the touristic sweepstakes. But until just a few years before the turn of the century, it was *terra incognita*—at least beyond the settlements of its Indian Ocean coast, where the Arabs and the Portuguese had been trading, pillaging, and slaving for centuries, in cities that they are reputed to have established but that archaeologists now conclude—with strong evidence—were African in origin.

Even in the interior, largely ignored before the British entered the scene, there is evidence of developed African cultures, communities, and settlements. One, for example, was Engaruka, on the Kenya-Tanzania frontier, now believed to have been a city of more than six thousand stone houses, with a population of more than thirty thousand, and a thriving, terrace-type agriculture, whose inhabitants were ancestors of the Mbulu people, still living in the neighborhood. Engaruka was probably built about three centuries ago and fell when marauded by Masai warriors from the north. It is now considered typical of East African Iron Age civilizations, and it is believed that civilizations like that of Engaruka were linked to those of the Indian Ocean coast. There is little doubt, among the experts, that the East African interior had been settled for centuries by urban peoples working with stone and iron for their own use as well as for export, growing grain and raising cattle.

But all this research is so relatively new that most Europeans living in Africa are still not familiar with it—and many would disbelieve it if they heard it. Europeans did not penetrate beyond the coast until Queen Victoria was nearing the end of her reign, although the Portuguese had built the great stone Fort Jesus in Mobasa in 1592, only to lose it to the sultans of Muscat and Oman, and of Zanzibar, who controlled the area until the arrival of the British in 1877. It was not until 1883 that a European visited the Kenya highlands; shortly thereafter British and German traders followed. But it was the British East Africa Company that was mainly responsible for the development of modern Kenya. In 1895, the London government took over responsibility for the company's territory, and built the railroad from Mombasa, on the coast, to the then protectorate of Uganda, in the interior.

The principal stopping-off point en route was a tiny settlement of shacks and tents named Nairobi ("land of the cold waters" in the Masai language), whose European inhabitants were mainly camp followers, construction workers, and assorted hangers-on.

As Nairobi grew—and it is now the largest city in East Africa between Cairo and Johannesburg—so grew Kenya. There is no doubt but that the British are responsible for the development of modern Kenya. They brought to it Western concepts of commerce, architecture, education, hygiene, industry, and religion. But it could not have been done by the small minority of Britons without the collaboration of the great mass of Africans and another imported minority, the Asians—mostly descendants of East Indians who were brought in mostly to serve as laborers on the railway.

Still, the settlers kept the cream for themselves. Only their group was allowed to farm the fertile "White Highlands." They controlled the Legislative Council. They reserved the amenities of their cities—hotels, restaurants, other public places—for themselves. They set up a rigid color bar and a dual wage scale. Still, they educated a small African élite, which became articulate enough to convince other Africans that they were being exploited in many ways. Dissatisfaction spread faster than concessions to Africans from the colonists.

The situation erupted in 1952 with the Mau Mau terrors. Members of a secret African society murdered on a mass scale—mainly Africans, but whites as well, of course—and engaged in other acts of plunder. Retaliation by the settlers was as terrifying as the acts of the Mau Mau, and the colony was under a state of emergency until July 1958. As horrible as it was—more for the great mass of law-abiding Africans than for the Europeans—the Mau Mau uprising led to reforms. Africans were allowed to participate more in government. The color bar began to be lifted, even though it was still enforced—albeit illegally—in some public places almost until the eve of independence, there having been no area in the bulge of tropical Africa with a more powerful, loquacious concentration of white racists. African leaders—most notably the late Tom Mboya, then president of the Kenya Federation of Labor—began to emerge and attract wide followings. Political parties—African, Asian, European, and multiracial—developed, and African representation on the Legislative Council increased. In early 1960, a

Kenya Constitutional Conference took place in London, paving the way for a sovereign Kenya. The following year, Africans gained a Legislative Council majority. Jomo Kenyatta—a British-educated member of the dominant Kikuyu tribe that was reputed to have formed the basis of the Mau Mau strength, and long imprisoned as an alleged Mau Mau leader—was released, only to enter the Legislative Council as head of the political party known as the Kenya African National Union (KANU).

Early in 1963, the popular white-bearded Kenyatta and his KANU followers won out in national elections over the opposition, Kenya African Democratic Union (KADU), and at year's end, Kenya became a sovereign state within the British Commonwealth. Its first Prime Minister was Jomo Kenyatta. Only a year later, that Prime Minister Kenyatta became President Kenyatta. The country gave up the monarchial status it had chosen at independence to become a republic, still affiliated with the Commonwealth. The opposition KADU party voluntarily disbanded, and the infant republic became a one-party country. The single-party situation was not entirely felicitous, and an unhappy political situation evolved. The alliteratively named Vice President, Oginga Odinga, long an associate and supporter of the President, but a member of the Luo tribe, which was beginning to resent the political dominance of the strong Kikuyu tribe, resigned his position, charged KANU with being overly Western-capitalist-oriented (even though it had espoused what it terms a policy of "African Socialism"), and emerged as leader of the new Kenya People's Union. The year was 1966 and the country was not without the problems any new, developing nation faces as it attempts to mature.

Kenya had a lot going for it, to be sure. The British had developed it to the point where it was by far the most advanced, economically and otherwise, of the East African states. The climate of the elevated central plateau, on which Nairobi is situated, is bracing, healthful, and conducive to enterprise. Transportation and communications were good. Perhaps most important, the rich white farmers agreed to sell their land to the government, so that it could be resettled by blacks, who lost no time in making a go of their new farms, concentrating on revenue-producing export crops like coffee, tea, cotton, and sisal. The situation of the Asian minority proved more difficult. The descendants, by several generations, of East Indians brought over to build the railroad, the Kenyan Asians had become prosperous businessmen, some modest, some anything but. Their success, in a land where the majority—the Africans—remained impoverished and almost completely without any kind of foothold in the business community, led to the government policy of Africanization being carried over from the civil service (where it worked well) to the private business sector. Asians, even many who had taken out Kenyan citizenship, found pressure put upon them to leave the country. And although they were nominally British subjects, the United Kingdom, bowing to the pressure of reactionary MPs with bigoted working-class constituencies, put limits on entry, with the result that Kenya Asians found themselves, increasingly, in a pillar-to-post world that they did not make.

Meanwhile, President Kenyatta faced political problems, despite his tremendous personal popularity, the wide base of his support, and his enlightened policy of "Harambee" (Swahili for "Let us pull together"). He was to find that old prejudices were not far from the surface. In 1969, Tom Mboya, born a member of the Luo tribe, and by then Minister of Economic Planning, was shot in the chest as he emerged from a Nairobi drugstore and died en route to a hospital. His assassin, it developed, was a member of the dominant Kikuyu tribe. The loss of Mboya was tragedy in itself. I first met him when he visited the United States on a lecture tour in 1959, and later, in the course of researching the first edition of this book, I interviewed him on home base in Nairobi. He was bright, forceful, logical, one of the most prescient of the pioneer group of young African nationalists. He knew independence was going to come to Black Africa. And he knew that the new nations would blunder as they progressed to maturity. To the anti-independence forces—and Mboya was from a land filled with white settlers who did not relish giving up comfortable situations—Tom

Mboya repeated over and over again with considerable patience: Every people deserves to be free in order to make its own mistakes. His philosophy seems hardly profound or even original today. But as recently as the late fifties and early sixties, when even educated Africans were regarded as savages who, upon achieving control, would bring their nations to immediate destruction, the Mboya doctrine was heady stuff. Given a different set of political circumstances, Tom Mboya might well have been the first President of Kenya. As it was, it was not at all unlikely that he would follow Jomo Kenyatta, as the second.

Mboya's death had wide repercussions. It was the impetus for a renewal of the divisiveness of tribalism. Former Vice President Odinga, himself a Luo like Mboya, so muddied what had been reasonably clear political waters—by pandering to tribal prejudices—that his former friend of so many years' standing, President Kenyatta, arrested him, keeping him prisoner for eighteen months. In so doing, he severely impaired Kenya's image as the most stable, progressive, and democratic of the new East African states, anxious to attract foreign industrial investment as well as to continue expansion of an already impressive tourist plant.

But Kenya has incredible staying power. Despite its somewhat blurred image as a democratic state, despite the confused, the complex, and the unhappy situation of its Asian merchant class, and despite a birth rate that is one of the highest in Africa and that makes for a population expansion so rapid that considerable accomplishments in such areas as education, social welfare, and health are mitigated, Kenya continues to go forward.

Its eminence in the field of tourism is an African phenomenon. More than a score of international airlines serves busy Nairobi Airport, with routes directly linking the country with Asia, Europe, America, and the northern, western, and southern regions of the enormous African continent (the list includes both major American international carriers, Pan Am and TWA). International hotel firms are on the scene, including both Inter•Continental and Hilton from the United States. The national parks in the interior expand, and so, concurrently, do facilities on the lovely beaches of the tropical Indian Ocean coast.

Kenya has always attracted strangers—from the early Phoenicians, and the later Portuguese down through the centuries to the colonizing Britons, and more recently, the romantics as exemplified by Hemingway and the insensitive bigots of the Robert Ruark School. Europeans resident today must either have taken out Kenyan citizenship (and quite a few have indeed done so) or hold specialized-type jobs with explicit government permission to be in the country only so long as no Kenyan is available to perform the same task—which must be one that the government considers essential. Even so, whites remain resident who, when asked the population of the capital, will reply with a partial figure, that of the *white* population, and an explanation that it is difficult to count the blacks, what with their being so transient. No, the wonder is that the Kenya government is as patient and well-mannered and moderate as it is, given the nature and the background of the country's involvement right up to this morning's paper, with the European. And I speak as one who will always be appreciative of the Europeans' contributions to Kenya. (No other country of Black Africa north of Zambia has had such a populous white-settler class; in most, whites constituted only a tiny administrator group.)

The short-time visitor finds the Kenya scene stuff of which movie scenarios used to be written—exotic and colorful and bizarre, and rarely, if ever, these days, uncomfortable. The people alone are a special treat: well over half a hundred diverse tribes of the interior plateau; the farming and fishing Nilotic peoples, like the Luo of the west, the splendid-looking, fine-featured Nilo-Hamitics like the legendary Masai on the frontier with Tanzania; the nomadic Somalis of the far north, the India-descended Asians of the cities and towns—Hindus and Moslems and turbaned Sikhs; the robed Arabs of the venerable coastal communities. But there are the animals as well, photographed today, happily, far more than they are hunted, and protected by one of the most forward-looking of conservationist governments. Indeed, what other republic is officially protecting a beloved resident in its forests by means of a presidential proclamation. It seems that Ahmed, the continent's most famous elephant—and the star of a feature film—had been the subject of reports that he was being hunted for his great tusks. Letter-writers from throughout Kenya and abroad set to work, with the result that by decree of President Kenyatta, Ahmed "under no circumstances may be hunted or harassed by any person."

YOUR VISIT TO KENYA

Kenya has for so long had a reputation as the pre-eminent touristic destination of all Africa, that it has had a difficult time keeping abreast of the demand for its facilities. The government, through the Kenya Tourist Development Corporation, has wisely encouraged the construction of additional facilities, however, at the same time concerning itself with matters ecological, so that the country does not build and pollute itself out of business.

Time was when all East African itineraries began and ended in Nairobi, with destinations in neighboring Uganda and Tanzania touched upon only lightly, or very often, completely neglected. Recent years, though, have seen considerably more air traffic routed to the Ugandan and Tanzanian capitals, and the newer Kilimanjaro International Airport in northern Tanzania, near that republic's most noted national parks. Nairobi, though no longer the nucleus it once was, still remains in the center of things. It should, of course, be on every East African itinerary. And so should other Kenyan locales. I have a soft spot for Treetops; for me it will never have any serious competition. I shall always remain fond, also, of the Masai-Amboseli Game Reserve, for it was the first of the East African animal parks that I visited; it has a modern lodge now, but the earlier tented camp happily remains for those who would sample a more authentic species of safari. The Indian Ocean coast, with Mombasa its focal point, is a facet of Kenya most Americans have no idea exists, more's the pity. There are, as well, the immense, two-section Tsavo National Park, with its modern facilities; the more remote areas, typified for me by Lake Baringo; and a number of lesser destinations for the traveler with plenty of time and curiosity. Highlights follow.

Nairobi: Nairobi is, for better or for worse, the hopes and fears, the fun and folly of East Africa. It is all of the conflict and contradiction of an emerging continent rolled into a single good-looker of a town—elevated and green and cool and most assuredly contemporary. Britons in residence, I recall from my very first visit before independence, thought of Nairobi as *their* town, distinct numerical minority though they were. The initiative that made the town was, of course, theirs, as were the capital and the technology. But it was the Indians imported from the subcontinent across the sea, and the Africans of the vast majority whose country Kenya was to begin with—and still is—who built the city. Interplay between these groups was a feature of the lively life of pre-republic Kenya, and sovereignty has not changed the situation. Indeed, it has added the element of party-tribal politics to the scene, assuring continued effervescence.

Today's Nairobi intrigues one, first because of the interactions of its mixed-bag populace—African professors and students at the university, Asian merchants in the shops, clipped-accent British types in the travel agencies and the bars. A magnificent Masai—tall and handsome and splendidly coiffed and costumed—enters a curio shop to sell some of his family-made handiwork as you enter to buy. A turbaned Sikh—surely the authentic Punjabi article—was, you learn in conversation at his shop, Nairobi born and bred.

Nairobi is a substantial enough city to warrant the institution of the half-day sightseeing tour (United Tours runs these—and well). These are mostly undertaken, to be sure, in station wagons rather than buses. But they are scheduled every-morning activities, and as such are not easily come upon in urban Black Africa. You may, of course, proceed independently. The heart of town is an area of wide, boulevard-like thoroughfares lined with uncommonly attractive, clean-lined, contemporary structures. I doubt whether this capital of a sovereign republic any longer calls itself a "royal" city, even though it was awarded that honor by the Crown in

1950—the first to be granted a town in the then-colonial empire. Still, the British-inherited ritual and ceremony has not been discarded. The mayor (and, incidentally, this office's occupants have included Margaret Kenyatta, daughter of the President), on formal occasions, appears in robe and white ruff, with the seal of office on a neck chain. And the imposing City Hall is patterned on those of the former mother country, with chambers not only for mayor, city council, and administration, but with additional amenities that Americans—whose city halls are purely for city business—are surprised to see, such as auditoriums and halls for balls and receptions, as well as an open-to-the-public terrace restaurant-café. The Parliament Buildings went up in the early fifties to house the colonial Legislative Council, but were enlarged just after independence. Dominated by a twelve-story clock tower, their principal attractions are the handsome New Chamber, which is the seat of the unicameral legislature, and the Chamber of Meditation, decorated by a wall-size mural of the Kenyan landscape, and used as a prayer or meditation room by members of Parliament of all religions.

The City Market is a big, modern, two-story structure in the heart of town which, serious shopper or not, one wants to inspect. The main hall on the ground level is mostly for produce—vegetables and fruit as well as other foodstuffs, and flowers, as well. Of even more interest are the balcony stalls, most of which specialize in handicrafts. The market's customers are of quite as much interest as its wares.

The former Coryndon Memorial Museum, dating back to 1910, in a substantial two-story stone building, is now the Kenya National Museum, and one of the most important in tropical Africa. Exhibits tell the East African story, as regards flora and fauna, and perhaps even more interesting, handicrafts and folklore. A snake park, perhaps of less universal appeal, but with a rather terrifyingly comprehensive representation of the species, is across the street.

Though without the tradition of the older and more globally noted Makerere University in Kampala, the University of Nairobi occupies a lovely campus with faculties of arts, science, architecture, medicine, veterinary medicine, and commerce. Plays and concerts open to the public are presented in its Taifa Hall, and there are attractive, sculpture-dotted gardens. The well-equipped National Theatre—itself the locale of the city's most important dramatic and musical attractions—is adjacent to the university, as are the headquarters of Kenya Radio and Television. State House Road cuts through that quarter of the city that is the poshest. It is named for the residence of the President, which, during colonial days, had been Government House, and home to the Crown-appointed governors. There is a lovely arboretum in the area, and just near it, the studio of the Kenya Arts Society, where you might like to look in on classes, take in the current exhibition, or buy crafts at the retail shop. There are houses of worship for virtually every major faith (possibly excepting the Buddhists), with immense All Saints (Anglican), and Holy Family (Roman Catholic) Cathedrals, traditional-design mosques like the Jamaii and Ismailia, the Cutchi Gujarati Hindu Union, Jewish Synagogue, First Church of Christ (Christian Scientist), and additional places of worship for a number of Protestant denominations. Shopping is centered downtown in and about Kenyatta Avenue, an area that appears as full of safari and tour operators and travel agencies (well over eighty!) as of shops and stores. Accommodation, not unsurprisingly, is the best in East Africa; the restaurant and nightlife scene is likewise; these matters, too, are elaborated upon later on in this chapter. But what is perhaps Nairobi's biggest treat is:

Nairobi National Park: Like the city itself, Nairobi National Park had been honored with a "royal" designation before independence. And deservedly so. No other city in Africa, or anywhere, for that matter, has an honest-to-goodness wild-animal refuge ten minutes from its downtown area. There they are, within the shadow of a city of more than a third of a million people: pride after pride after pride of lion—gloriously maned papa, plain-Jane mama, deceptively playful-looking cubs. If it is afternoon, they have had a lunch of one sort or other (zebra and antelope are favored entrées) and are simply resting in the sun, either asleep or staring right back at you as you snap them from within the Land-Rover that is your transport. (The park's only rule of consequence: Stay in the car.) But the lions are only the stars. In supporting roles are great herds of zebra, hardly beauteous baboons that will climb right on your roof, lovely gazelle, meandering giraffes, ugly, spotted hyenas that eat what the lions leave of their prey—and are followed in turn by the always hovering vultures. If you are lucky—very lucky—there may be leopard or the even swifter cheetah. You may alight from your vehicle near the river pools where rangers guide you, on most days at least, to see resident hippo and crocodiles. Operated in conjunction with the park is a unique Animal Orphanage; it is precisely what its title implies: a haven for deserted, injured, or abandoned wildlife. Kenya kids love the place, but no more than their parents or, for that matter, foreign visitors.

Treetops has been a Kenya classic for a long enough period to have lured a lady we all know of, back in 1952, and circumstances would have it that during her overnight stay, her father died. She arrived at Treetops as Princess Elizabeth, she departed as Queen Elizabeth II, and there's a plaque there, on the tea terrace, that tells the story. Treetops, over the years, has remained absolutely first-rate: without gimmickry, excellently staffed, good value, African tourism at its most memorable. The Treetops tour is a two-parter of necessity. Because it is a hotel tucked into the branches of an immense Cape chestnut tree overlooking a tiny lake and saltlick in the midst of a wilderness region of Aberdare National Park, one simply cannot drive up to it, as though to an ordinary country inn. What happens is this: Check-in is at an affiliated hostelry, the beautifully operated Outspan Hotel, near the town of Nyeri, north of Nairobi. Arrival should be in advance of lunch in the high-ceilinged dining room which, with its sumptuous buffet, has become an East African culinary institution. Heavy bags are checked at the Outspan (neither space nor need for them at Treetops), and that day's Treetops group assembles to meet the senior hunter or one of his associates, under whose supervision guests are put aboard Land-Rovers, escorted by one of the hunters, loaded rifle on shoulder just in case. Minutes later, the vehicle pulls up within view of Treetops. So as not to disturb whatever game may be in the immediate vicinity, the final approach to the hotel is by foot, silently and over a narrow path. The ascent then, to the several elevated decks. Bedrooms are tiny but snug cubicles, mostly without private facilities, which are hardly necessary for the maximum stay of but one night. They all have potentially exciting views, though. The hunter and his hostess-assistant urge that the windows of rooms remain locked until after dark, the reason being baboons—a dozen plus of a garrulous clan that retires to its woodland home only after dark, appearing on the alfresco tea deck during the time tea and homemade scones are served to guests. Viewing then—from the outer decks or the picture-window lounge over drinks. Yes, you *are* indeed given a score card, and I kept the one from my last visit: one elephant, two rhinoceros, ninety-five buffalo, seventeen warthogs, four hyenas, thirty-five waterbucks, fourteen bushbucks. In between, one enjoys a six-course dinner with wine in the compact, ingeniously designed dining room; and in the wee hours, most visitors force themselves to get a few hours of sleep, although some stay up the night long, for the area is flood-lighted. Breakfast is early and simple: biscuits and coffee, and precedes the drive back to the Outspan, for a more substantial meal, and baggage is unchecked.

Lake Baringo is a two-hundred-mile-square body of water smack in the arid, sparsely inhabited Rift Valley, some 120 miles due northwest of Nairobi. Until an enterprising British couple relatively recently took it upon themselves to build a lodge, the lake and the surrounding countryside had been virtually *terra incognita* to most Kenyans, much less to visitors from abroad. But the lodge has added a destination of considerable significance to the Kenya scene. There is no regularly scheduled transport to either lake or lodge; one must make arrangements for a visit in advance through the lodge's Nairobi representative, Safari Air Services, Wilson Airport, Nairobi (P. O. Box 1951, if you are writing). At first glance, the lakeside landscape appears almost lunar. It is craggy and rough and anything but lush. But it is hardly without interest. Three little-known tribal groups make their home in the area. The onetime-warrior Pokot people live to the north; the Njemp—relatives of the Masai—to the southeast; and the Tugen, to the west. Excursions to their villages are a requisite, and—if enough advance notice is given—their dancers will perform for lodge guests. Near-neighbor to the lodge is Jonathan Leakey, son of the noted archaeologist (see p. 333) and operator of an unusual snake farm, whose star tenants are cobras, adders, and mambas, all of which can be seen being milked. The lake itself is home to crocodiles, hippo, and quantities of fish, not to mention an unusual variety of birdlife, including the nesting grounds of the immense Goliath herons. The lake's islands—all visitable—include one long inhabited by bats, another by a solitary old man and his fourteen wives, and others filled with hot springs and abnormally tall desert roses. There is, despite the croc/hippo populace of the lake, waterskiing on its surface, and swimming—yes, swimming—from the lodge's beach is a popular pastime, the theory being that people are much less attractive to the crocs and hippo than the abundant fish. And there is still another attraction: It is Lake Hannington, forty miles south. The lures are incredible masses—countless thousands—of pink flamingos resident in a lake whose shores seethe with boiling sulphur springs, one of which is a veritable geyser.

National parks beyond Nairobi: *Masai-Amboseli Game Reserve,* on the Tanzanian border in the shadow of the eternally snow-capped wedding cake that is Mount Kilimanjaro (Africa's highest: 19,340 feet) is the granddaddy of the Kenya game parks, and because of its magnificent situation and its still-operative, traditional-luxury-style tented camp, my favorite of the lot. There is no better Kenya locale for black rhino, but there are, in addition, great quantities of elephant, giraffe, and zebra; such species of antelope as the little Thomson's gazelle ("Tommies"), Grant's gazelle, lesser kudu, eland, and bushbuck; and warthogs—the comedians of the plains—scurrying rapidly, their ropelike tails rising vertically into the air. And lion, cheetah, and leopard, as well. The photographer is in paradise, not only because of the animals that can be snapped with Kilimanjaro backdrop, but because of the Masai who live in the area—fine-featured, tall and slim with elaborate hairdos kept in place by ocher-dyed mud and grease; enormous earrings and ankle bracelets, with cattle the mainstay of their economy, and indeed of their diet. The Masai nutritional mainstay is blood and milk, both obtained from the livestock. There are Masai villages—some of tiny, baked-mud huts—throughout the reserve. *Masai Mara Game Reserve* is in the southwestern part of the country, adjacent to Tanzania's Serengeti National Park. It is best known for its immense herds of buffalo, zebra and antelope—thousands upon thousands of them, as well as considerable quantities of lion in abnormally large prides, numbering as many as twenty or thirty. Elephant, rhino, leopards, cheetah, and giraffe are also on the scene, and the accommodation is in a modern lodge. *Tsavo National Park* is so enormous—embracing more than eight thousand square miles in southeast Kenya (it is by far the largest in the country and one of the largest extant)—that it is divided into two parts. The principal lures are astonishing quantities of elephant—estimates go as high as twenty thousand—and the bulk of the country's black rhinos. But there are, additionally, herds of buffalo, zebra, and antelope of various species, lion, leopard, cheetah, crocodile, and giraffe. Both sectors of the park offer accommodation in several modern, well-equipped lodges. *Samburu Game Reserve:* This is a relatively little-visited reserve—small (forty square miles) but choice, in that it is home to animals rarely seen elsewhere, such as Grevy's zebra, oryx, gerenuk, and the reticulated giraffe, in addition to great herds of elephant, lion, leopard, and cheetah. The near-desert park flanks the Uaso Nyiro River, and the area is home to the Samburu people, who wear distinctive red cotton sarong-like garments, paint their necks and shoulders in a matching hue, and parts of their faces in contrasting white, with their hair elaborately coiffed, their ears ringed, and a spear inevitably in their right hands. Accommodation is in an imaginatively designed riverbank lodge, with a swimming pool built of local materials. *Lake Nakaru National Park* is the site of what is considered by ornithologists to be the finest bird spectacle on the planet. Located just a few minutes' drive from the town of Nakuru, one hundred miles northwest of Nairobi, the eighteen-square-mile so-called "soda lake" attracts to its murky, plankton-filled waters more flamingos, both the greater and lesser varieties, than any other body of water, anywhere. The plankton, which they eat, is what draws them, and at peak times, when the SRO sign is really out, there have been as many as an estimated two million in residence. That, to even the most amateur bird-watcher, is a lot of hot-pink. But the flamingos are not all. Some three hundred species of bird live in the neighborhood. Accommodation is not in the park proper, but in *Nakruru town*, seat of government of Rift Valley Province, No. 4 in size in Kenya, and in the choice Highland farming country that had been white-settler territory before independence.

Mombasa and the Indian Ocean coast: Mombasa was a thriving city long before the British arrived in Kenya, and still bears the marks of its varied occupiers, and the charm that only age can bring. Dominating the town is the high-walled Fort Jesus, Portuguese-built four centuries ago and a prison until, shortly before independence, it was wisely converted into a regional historical museum. But Mombasa is not without other attractions: its Old Harbor, still reserved for the dhows that sail each winter from Persian Gulf ports with cargoes of rugs and spices and with crews in costumes right out of the *Arabian Nights*; the New Harbor, with berths for modern sailing ships; Kilindini Road, whose landmark is a double arch of giant, pseudo-elephant tusks and in and around which is a commercial district and the atmospheric Old Town quarter. Mombasa is actually an island city, connected to the mainland by causeways and bridges. With its tropical climate, its coastal location, its great age, and its heavy Arab overlay, it is as unlike Nairobi as is, say, Los Angeles from San Francisco. The pace is slower and the attractions fewer: cathedrals, both Catholic and Anglican; mosques and Hindu and Jain temples; an agreeable after-dark café and coffee-house life, and what must surely be a higher proportion of streets named for African leaders than any other city on the continent. Like Nairobi, which renamed one of its streets for Tom Mboya after he was assassinated, Mombasa has done likewise. And again, like the capital, there is a street named for President Kenyatta. But there are, as well, thoroughfares named after Nasser, Haile Selassie, Patrice Lumumba, Kwame Nkrumah, Julius Nyerere, Kenneth Kaunda, with more to come, I am sure. Flanking the town, alongside its lovely white-sand beaches, are first-class resort hotels, and catering both to local and continental European clienteles. Some seventy miles to the north is *Malindi,* a port since the fifteenth century, when Chinese ships anchored in its harbor, and for some years now a popular beach resort, again, as with Mombasa, attracting Kenyans, others resident in East Africa, and sun-starved visitors from Europe. There are direct Nairobi–Malindi flights. The route from Mombasa —there is bus and tourist-taxi service daily—takes one through verdantly foliaged coastal villages of bare-bosomed women and friendly children, small, congenial, and informal. Malindi itself hugs the cliffs that overlook the Indian Ocean; most of its hotels have pools as well as their own beaches on the sea. In late 1971, Malindi made news around the world when a team of Italian and American scientists launched a 114-pound satellite to probe the earth's magnetosphere from the Italian government's launching platform in Malindi's Formosa Bay. Ten miles south of Malindi is *Gedi,* or at least the remains of Gedi; it was an ancient Afro-Arab city that is now preserved as a national park. The Great Mosque, part of the palace, and other dwellings have been reconstructed, and there is a small museum of some of the finds from the excavations, including some interesting household utensils, with the remainder in the Fort Jesus Museum in Mombasa. Gedi is believed to have been founded in the late thirteenth or early fourteenth century, to have reached its peak period in the fifteenth century, and to have been abandoned—possibly as a result of invasion by the Galla people of Somalia—in the early seventeenth century.

Other destinations: Mount Kenya—at 17,058 feet, the second highest in Africa—and the region around is the setting for two national parks. *Mount Kenya National Park* comprises the land on the mountain above the eleven-thousand-foot level. Safaris are made to the snowline, by horseback and, on occasion, by a mutual animal called a zebroid—a blend of horse or donkey and zebra, used as a pack animal. From Secret Valley Game Lodge, on the mountain, one can observe leopards who make nightly visits for a meal of meat put out on the trees directly in front of the lodge. Another lodge in the area is the Mount Kenya Safari Club, near Nanyuki. Despite its fine situation, in the shadow of the always snowy (and invariably fogbound) peak for which the republic is named, and a substantial physical plant, the club, at least when I stayed there, had an unwelcome *ambiance*, with an air about it of the *pukka-sahib* white man's sanctuary of the old Empire, even though, of course, it may no longer, by law, practice racial discrimination. *Aberdare National Park* is the other park of the region. It is the site of the earlier-described Treetops, and also of a game-viewing hotel known as The Ark, newer to be sure, but without the Treetops' charm. Takeoff point for this game-viewing spot is a onetime private home known as the Aberdare Country Club, and with nothing like the facilities—or, indeed, the superlative kitchen—of the prelude to Treetops that is the Outspan Hotel. Of possible interest to dedicated anglers—for Nile Perch and tigerfish—would be *Lake Rudolf*, in the extreme north bordering the Sudan and Ethiopia, accessible by air, and with lodge facilities.

BIG-GAME HUNTING

The shooting safari remains both a Kenya specialty and a rich man's diversion. A month's safari can cost between four thousand and five thousand dollars, although it can be cheaper if one opts for simple camping rather than the luxury of such amenities as hot water, electricity, and refrigeration, and elaborate meals with wine, served by uniformed waiters. Planning a safari is at least as complicated as arranging for a trip around the world, and you need a good six months' time. Because of the admirable conservation policies of the Kenya government, licensing regulations are complex; animals are officially classified either "dangerous" (these include the so-called Big Five—buffalo, elephant, leopard, lion, and rhinoceros) and non-dangerous. (May I at this time point out, apropos of nothing, that the buffalo one sees in Africa are not—as so often commonly assumed—*water* buffalo. They are a peculiarly African species, neither the "water" variety of Southeast Asia nor, of course, the bison of North America.) The government has licensed more than eighty professional hunters (no hunting safari is allowed without one as an escort), and I suggest that if you are interested you write for a list to the Kenya Government Tourist Office (address at the beginning of this chapter) or the Licensing Officer, Kenya Government Game Department, P. O. Box 241, Nairobi, Kenya.

SHOPPING

Kenya falls down here, at least as regards African handicrafts. There is quantity, to be sure. But far less quality than in neighboring Tanzania, Uganda, and Ethiopia. There is, to be blunt, an excess of tourist junk that is appalling, and somehow or other, the government, to better the image of the cultural talents of its people, should do something about it. One has the feeling that there are enormous factories in the bush where countless carvers are turning out limitless woodcarvings of distinctively African things like letter openers, bookends, cocktail toothpicks, and the like, not to mention commercially over-polished, standard-design heads, figures (Masai are Very Big), and animals. It does, to be sure, take two to tango, by which I mean that the entrepreneurs would not contract to have the stuff made and market it if there were no takers. Still, one has only to look at the caliber of the output encouraged by the Uganda Government in its handicraft shops. And if the Kenyans wanted to go farther afield, they might take a look at the Permanent Exhibition of Arts and Crafts in Copenhagen to learn how the Danes turned a tawdry souvenir industry into a showcase for their people's talents. I must add that not all of the carved wood is junk, and that there are some of the fine carvings of the Makonde people—Tanzania's wizards—imported, and more costly, of course, than in Tanzania. The Masai and the Kikuyu, whose ancestors have worked with imported beads for generations, are highly skilled at making necklaces and collars, bracelets, earrings, and other jewelry. The Kikuyu are, as well, makers of extraordinarily good-looking baskets. Bracelets of elephant hair, the traditional good-luck charm of professional, amateur and would-be hunters in East Africa, are inexpensive, authentic, virtually weightless for air travelers, and make excellent gifts. (They are, more's the pity, being prettied up by jewelers with gold and other metallic fittings.) Animal-skin products remain popular, but happily many people are no longer buying products made from skins of such endangered species as leopard. Zebra-skin rugs are everywhere to be seen, and so are an increasingly varied production of articles made from parts of the elephant, quite as ugly as the elephant itself is magnificent. Additionally, there are European-made souvenirs—glassware, bowls, ashtrays, and the like, engraved or painted with animals, for which there is an apparently enormous market. One sees contemporary paintings of varying quality in the art galleries. There are other objects—gourds and tie-dye and *batik* textiles, trinkets and household implements encountered in shops, markets, and from itinerant vendors. Lastly, there are the safari outfitters—shop after shop selling safari jackets, with or without matching skirts and trousers; wide-brimmed safari hats, suede, rubber-soled shoes, and—for hunters—guns and ammunition. The Nairobi shop with perhaps the most imaginative selection of handicrafts is Studio Arts, on Standard Street. There is a tendency toward the precious and the cutesy-pie, perhaps, but the quality is good, and the stuff is handmade and never vulgar. The City Market is a requisite, even for the most avid nonpurchaser. The main floor is mostly foodstuffs and produce, but the upstairs balcony contains stall after stall of handicrafts—good, bad, and indifferent. This is the principal Nairobi source for the earlier-mentioned Kikuyu baskets. The craft shop of Maendeleo Ya Wanawake—a national women's group—on Muindi Mbingu Street is interesting. Rowland Ward is more African-motif than African—to say the least. The specialty is glassware with engravings of animals; silk scarves, ties, and cuff links with similar motifs, and—these last-mentioned really are attractive—simple white demitasse cups and saucers with various species of African birds as their decoration. Good old Bata is on the scene with Kenya-made suede, rubber-soled shoes—ideal for trips into the bush, and inexpensive. Safari-outfitters include Alibhai, on Kimathi Street and in the Inter•Continental Hotel; and Bentley's, across from the Hilton; but there are many, many others. Jax of Kenya, in the Hilton, specializes in hand-blocked cottons with African themes, tie-dye fabrics, *kangas*—those muslin rectangles worn, both as dresses and as headgear, by coastal women, with gay print designs, and *vitenge*, the Indonesian-style *batiks* that are a mainstay of the female wardrobe in this part of the world. The East African Wildlife Society, with its headquarters up one flight in the shopping arcade of the Hilton, is an estimable nonprofit, nongovernment conservation group. It sells a variety of articles—jewelry for both men and women, silk scarves, blazer badges, shoulder patches, lapel pins with the society's insignia (national parks buffs wear these on their safari jackets, along with similar pins with the insignia of the various parks—bought at their shops), Christmas cards, maps and literature on birds and animals. Proceeds from all sales benefit the society's program. Additionally, the society's magazine, *East African Wildlife Journal*—individual copies and subscription—is on sale, and society memberships are solicited. There are retail shops in both the National Museum and the Kenya Arts Society's studio on Arboretum Road; the former sells traditional crafts, the latter contemporary prints, wood-blocks, and hand-worked articles—aprons and the like. In *Mombasa*, what you want to do is make the rounds of the myriad of shops in and about Kilindini Road, bargaining strenuously. The stocks are heavy on animal skins, and imports from India, as well as the usual things seen in Nairobi. Good-looking, cheap, and attractive as women's gifts are hand-embroidered skullcaps from Zanzibar. A source of handicrafts is the Home Industries Center of the Batuibak Christian Council, on Sir Ali Street, opposite the Castle Hotel. Elsewhere, there are curio gift shops in the larger hotels and the lodges of the national parks and game reserves. (One of the very best in Kenya is the shop of the Outspan Hotel, Nyeri; if you can, get the charming proprietress to tell you of the events that transpired in the area when the word came from London that King George VI had died, while his daughter, now Queen Elizabeth II, was a guest in nearby Treetops.) Remember, too, that there are duty-free (and other) shops—for liquor, particularly—at Nairobi Airport.

CREATURE COMFORTS

In a word: super. Kenya leads East Africa when it comes to sheltering and feeding its visitors. And the accommodations scene is an ever-expanding one.

HOTELS—**Nairobi** has a number of first-rate hotels. The Nairobi Hilton, a striking, circular-design building with an enviably convenient location in the heart of downtown, is surely one of the very top urban hostelries in all Africa. There is something about it that makes everyone—Kenyans and visitors alike—take to it. The big lobby is animated and inviting. The coffee shop is one of the town's principal congregating places; the mezzanine bar-lounge likewise. And there are a pair of additional, more formal restaurants. Guest rooms are Hilton-handsome, at once modern and functional, but with African twists to the *décor*. Service is smiling and alert; highly recommended. The Inter•Continental Nairobi has many fans, too, both local and visiting. Less than a ten-minute walk from the core of downtown, it features terraces with all of its rooms, restaurant and coffee shop, skilled management, and a pair of bars that are the handsomest in town. One, the Big Five Cocktail Lounge—named for the Big Five group of animals—has a smart safari motif, while the other is a pub right out of London. The Inter•Continental is home-base for the Headquarters Safari tours operated by Jane and Buz Chapin's Adventures Unlimited at Abercrombie & Fitch in New York, on which you headquarter at the hotel, making flying excursions each day to different game parks and other East African destinations. The New Stanley Hotel, quite as centrally located as the Nairobi Hilton, was, before the newer hotels went up, for long the town's top hostelry. And it remains good—with what is perhaps the most lively sidewalk café in East Africa, its noted Grill, and a spirited *ambiance*. The Norfolk is an atmospheric mock-Tudor structure hard by the university campus and National Theatre, not far from downtown. It has a pool, comfortable rooms as well as detached cottages on the pretty grounds, a popular restaurant and café, and was for long the Nairobi home away from home for the white Highland farmers of pre-independence days. The futuristic-design Panafric is a part of the BOAC-affiliated global chain. It is not central, but has such facilities as a swimming pool, restaurant and snack bar, and cocktail lounge. Also modern, and central as well, is the Ambassadeur, hardly French despite the name, but with full facilities. Dining in Nairobi can be very pleasant. All of the leading hotels are reliable, and with coffee shops as well as more elaborate eateries. Of the lot, the Hilton stands out, with its big, lively coffee shop that caters day and evening to a marvelous cross section of Nairobi; its delightful, moderate-price Tsavo Restaurant, and its posh and handsome Amboseli Grill. The sprawling mezzanine cocktail lounge is nice, too. Noteworthy, also, is the Grill of the New Stanley (Friday lunch features smorgasbord) and its alfresco Thorn Tree café, where you are just as likely to meet someone from home as you are at the Café de la Paix in Paris. The Norfolk's Lord Delamere terrace snack bar is congenial and ever-busy, as are the earlier-recommended bars of the Inter•Continental. At the Panafric, the menu is at once French-accented and Kenyan, with the local specialties including the ground-beef dish called *sukuma wiki*, served with saffron rice and *irio*—a corn and peas mélange. My favorite in-town restaurant is Alan Bobbe's Bistro, a smallish place where one must book in advance, and then only if one is a French-food buff. Mr. Bobbe is an Englishman who knows his *cuisine classique*, utilizing good Kenyan ingredients—oysters, beef, pork, vegetables—to turn out splendid meals; highly recommended. Very good indeed for

Italian-style dishes is the Swiss-Italian-owned Lavarini's; specialties include dishes of the various pasta expertly sauced, of veal, and of well-prepared vegetables; prices are moderate. Country excursion for a meal? Yes, if the destination is to Limuru and the Kentmere Club, a onetime private home, with its garden still lovely, and truly exceptional kitchen. After dark, Nairobi offers dinner and dancing at the leading hotels, repertory theater at the Donovan Maule Theatre, (with its own café), a variety of programs at the National Theatre, the movies, of course, and semi-seedy spots like the Sombrero Club with striptease and a nicely mixed clientele; the Starlight—a heady mix of indoor dancing and garden drinking and largely African-populated, and the dominantly Asian Bonanza Club, with first-rate rock. Watch the daily papers—the *East African Standard* and *The Nation*—for current activities. **Treetops** is described at length earlier on in this chapter; to reach it one must first go to the Outspan Hotel at *Nyeri*; this is a first-rate country hotel-*cum*-swimming pool in its own right, with comfortable rooms with bath, and one of the best restaurants in Kenya; highly recommended. **Lake Baringo's** Lake Baringo Lodge is one of the most unusual hostelries in East Africa; I detailed its attractions earlier in this chapter. Suffice it to say here that its limited number of rooms all have private bath, it operates a good eat-when-you-like restaurant featuring such local delicacies as hippo steak (it's good!) and more conventional viands, as well. Dress is as casual as can be, *ambiance* quiet and restful. Book through Safari Air Services, Nairobi, whose guiding light, Judy Houri, is one of East Africa's most knowledgeable—and attractive—experts on all matters touristic. **Masai-Amboseli Game Reserve** offers a choice. My favorite is the traditional-style Safari Camp—surprisingly luxurious, and great fun. But there is, as well, the modern and comfortable Amboseli Lodge. **Masai Mara Game Reserve's** visitor headquarters is at the handsome Keekorok Lodge—all rooms have bath and terrace; swimming pool, fine dine-wine-lounge facilities. **Tsavo National Park:** At Tsavo East is Voi Safari Lodge, BOAC-affiliated and one of the most luxurious such facilities in East Africa, with a handsome restaurant, kicky bar-lounge, lovely bedrooms all with bath, and swimming pool, the whole set on an eminence overlooking a water hole at which game can be seen drinking both during the day and—under floodlights—at night. At Tsavo West's entrance is the smart-looking Tsavo Inn; all rooms have bath, and there's a pool. Within Tsavo West is Ngulia Safari Lodge, a part of the BOAC hotels group, beautifully situated at a near-three-thousand-feet altitude on the edge of the Ndawe Escarpment with super views and beautiful interiors—the bedrooms all with baths and balconies, high-ceilinged bar-lounge and restaurant, and a swimming pool, as well. The Taita Hills Game Lodges are a handsome pair of ultra-modern Hilton International hostelries in the Taita Hills area, about a three-and-a-half-hour drive from Nairobi, and just two hours from Mombasa. They lie between Tsavo and Amboseli national parks. One of the pair, Salt Lick Lodge, is built over a two-hundred-foot-wide salt lick in four separate, interconnected, stilt-heightened tower blocks, from which guests may watch the wildlife from lounges as well as from the restaurant and bar. Nine miles away, with a fine view of Mt. Kilimanjaro, is Taita Hills Lodge, built around a courtyard and swimming pool, with a pool nearby—formed by damming a river—for the neighborhood hippo, crocodiles, and exotic fish. **Samburu National Park:** The charming Samburu Game Lodge is on the banks of the Uaso Nyiro River, at an altitude of three thousand feet; comfortable rooms in cottages, each with private bath, riverside public rooms, swimming pool. **Nakuru:** Stag's Head Hotel, comfortable, with all facilities, and convenient to nearby Lake Nakuru National Park. **Mombasa:** The close-to-town Oceanic, once the loveliest hotel on the coast, is not what it used to be—although it is relatively modern, with pool, restaurants, bar, and elevated setting. The heart-of-town Castle Hotel on Kilindini Road is a nice old-fashioned place, agreeable for a snack or cool drink. Outside of town, on its own wide, white-sand beach is the modern Mombasa Beach Hotel, a Caribbean-style luxury establishment—long and low-slung, with attractive rooms, pool overlooking the beach and Indian Ocean, restaurant, nightly entertainment. It has a number of competitors including the also-attractive Nyali Beach Hotel, with similarly luxurious and extensive facilities. **Malindi,** to the north, offers several casual hotels, all seaside, and including Lawford's, all of whose units—in African-style *bandas*—have baths and whose pool is in the shape of the continent of Africa; and the Eden Roc, also with baths attached to all rooms, and a fine garden setting overlooking Malindi Bay. At **Lamu,** an Arab-*ambiance* island out at sea that may be reached by charter flight from Malindi, one finds the intimate and informal Hotel Peponi, Danish-operated, on the beach, and with a good restaurant featuring lobster and other local treats. **Mount Kenya National Park:** Secret Valley Game Lodge, for unusual game-viewing way up on the mountain; the Mount Kenya Safari Club, luxurious to be sure, but with service so wanting that during my last visit, rooms had notices advising guests to contact the assistant manager when requests went unfulfilled. **Aberdare National Park:** Earlier-described—and recommended—Treetops is the lure here; The Ark is a newer competitor, gained by means of a preliminary check-in/lunch at the Aberdare Country Club. **Lake Rudolf:** Angling Club, a lakeside lodge catering to fishermen.

LESOTHO

Kingdom of Lesotho

Entry requirements: *No visa is required for a visit of less than three months.* **Best times for a visit:** *The dry season, from May to September, is best.* **Currency:** *South African rand: 0.714 rands=$1.* **Principal European language:** *English is the official language.* **Domestic transport:** *There are good roads, limited rail service, and a government-run internal air service (as well as small government-owned planes for charter).* **Further information:** *Embassy of the Kingdom of Lesotho, Washington, D.C.*

INTRODUCING LESOTHO

The former British protectorate of Basutoland, Lesotho is a landlocked country completely surrounded by South Africa—beautifully mountainous, except for a low-lying agricultural area in the west. The population of one million is made up mostly of Basutho, a Black people noted for their high literacy rate. The Basutho people are intensely nationalistic and have been ever since the reign of their greatest monarch, King Moshesh, who was responsible for welding together the nation in the early part of the past century. He ruled it autocratically from 1820 until he died in 1870. Not wanting his land to become gobbled up as a part of one of the white-dominated states of South Africa, he turned to the British for protection, and in 1884 they assumed formal control. The descendants of Moshesh remain the aristocracy of Lesotho, and the present head of state, young, bespectacled, Oxford-educated King Moshoeshoe II, and the Prime

Minister, Chief Leabua Jonathan, both claim to be direct descendants.

Basutoland became Lesotho in 1966, when it gained independence from Britain. In 1970, the Prime Minister, Chief Jonathan, seized power, after an apparent defeat in the country's first election. He jailed his opponent, suspended the constitution that had been in effect since 1965, and succeeded in forcing the King out of the country and into a temporary Dutch exile for a period. He has espoused firm friendship with racist South Africa, on which Lesotho is necessarily very dependent.

Lesotho's main economic activity is agriculture, although the country suffers increasingly from drought and soil erosion. Lesotho continues to seek foreign aid and investment to bolster the agriculture and to help expand mining and manufacturing industries. Tourism is in its infancy.

YOUR VISIT TO LESOTHO

Maseru: The capital is a small, pleasant town, but with few attractions. From it, however, car trips can be made to the foothills of the *Maluti Mountains*; ascent of the peaks is possible only by those hardy enough for horseback riding and open-air camping under canvas. The Malutis' highest peak—Machache—soars 11,000 feet into the air. Easier to visit is the mission station of *Thaba Bosiu,* historic battle site of the country, and burial place for the late, great Moshesh and many of his descendants.

Other highlights: Ancient Bushmen paintings at *Ficksburg* and excellent specimens of dinosaur tracks in *Leribe* and *Maletsunyane Falls,* 80 miles from Maseru, 630 feet high. *Most interesting:* The Basuto themselves—good-looking, blanket-covered, and, more often than not, riding along the steep mountain roads atop sleek ponies.

Good fishing is available throughout Lesotho. The *Orange* and *Caledon rivers* are well stocked with trout. The *Makhaleng stream,* less than forty miles from Maseru, is an excellent spot for rainbow trout.

SHOPPING

Beadwork, woodcarvings, colorful Basutho blankets, traditional, conical straw hats, and angora rugs are available at the Government Handicrafts Center in Maseru.

CREATURE COMFORTS

HOTELS—**Maseru:** The Holiday Inn—probably the first such to be the subject of a postage stamp—with air conditioning and swimming pool, is the best bet. Lancer's is comfortable. **Butha Buthe:** Crocodile. **Leribe:** Mountain View. **Oxbow:** Oxbow Ski Resort. **Teyateyaneng:** Blue Mountain.

LIBERIA

Republic of Liberia

Entry requirements: *A visa, obtainable from Liberian consulates, plus a health certificate (smallpox and yellow fever), and a police certificate.* **Best times for a visit:** *The pleasantest months are November to February; the rest of the year is intermittently rainy, but not so wet as to discourage a visit from the traveler in that region of Africa at the time.* **Currency:** *The dollar, at par with the U.S. dollar, and used interchangeably with it.* **Principal European language:** *English, which is also the official language of the country, although it is little spoken in the interior.* **Domestic transport:** *Domestic airlines serve some interior communities, and roads are being built to new industrial and mining installations, one of which is connected to the capital by the country's only railroad. There is a feeder air service connecting Roberts Field—the major airport—with Monrovia, some 50 miles distant, as well as a new highway. Passengers arriving at Roberts Field are advised to determine clearly the price of either the feeder plane or a taxi before embarking for Monrovia—with the assistance of airline personnel, if possible. Some planes now land at James Springs Payne Airfield, just three miles from Monrovia; from there, fares to the city are much cheaper.* **Further information:** *Consulate General of Liberia, 1120 Avenue of the Americas, New York; Liberian Government Information Bureau, Monrovia, Liberia.*

INTRODUCING LIBERIA

There is probably no country with a more unhappy past than the Republic of Liberia. It is only just now beginning to emerge as a modern state, after decades of neglect and ill-concealed ridicule from the rest of the world, coupled with a record of internal corruption and forced labor.

Tourist territory? Why not? Liberians are friendly and hospitable, and there is a luxury hotel in the capital, so that visitors can be eminently comfortable. But one does not go to Liberia to sightsee in the conventional sense. Here, after all, is the only country outside of the United States with its capital named after an American president, its form of government patterned after that of the United States, its official language English, its currency the equivalent of the U.S. dollar, and—most important of all—its founding fathers American.

Liberia came about as the result of an idea of a group of white Americans who thought they had found a solution for the disposition of slaves whose masters were voluntarily freeing them. They founded the American Colonization Society in 1822, when their agents negotiated treaties with African chiefs on what is now the Liberia coast, and between that year and 1860 some 11,000 freed slaves were sent to the new country. They were a minority: most American Negroes had no interest in settling on the African coast, and the Abolitionist movement understandably opposed the Liberia idea, claiming that in the south it strengthened slavery by removing the free Negroes. There was little colonization after 1860, but the society was a kind of trustee to Liberia until it was dissolved in 1912.

Neither it nor the American government went out of its way to do much for the country, though. The descendants of the American settlers, called Americo-Liberians, became the Liberian aristocracy and exploited the indigenous peoples of the interior, whom they still consider "uncivilized," with the same kind of patronizing attitudes of many European colonials in other parts of Africa. The country made virtually no progress until the start of World War II. The only time it was paid any attention, internationally, was in 1930, when a scandal erupted over the exportation of forced labor from the country. The League of Nations investigated, and in 1931 corroborated charges that the government had connived in a still thriving slave trade. The President and Vice President resigned as a result, but Liberia's efforts to clean house—and develop technologically—were minimal until World War II, when the United States modernized the chief harbor, built an air base, and sent a public-health mission.

Firestone, which had begun cultivating rubber plantations in the 1920s, set up a modern community for its own personnel but did little for the Liberians—except pay them low salaries—until recent years, when it agreed to increase its taxes to the Liberian government, set up schools, hospitals, and scholarship programs, and actually train Liberians for positions of some responsibility. With more American help, iron-ore deposits began to be exploited, and U. S. Point Four technicians appeared on the scene. The government sensibly encourages foreign investment, and the economy is at last beginning to develop.

But Liberia has a long way to go—in every direction. President William V. S. Tubman—in office since 1943—ran the country heavy-handedly and almost singlehandedly until he died in July 1971. Nine African heads of state attended his funeral, and there was a nine-man official U.S. delegation, including—appropriately enough—Firestone Rubber's Raymond Firestone, and a number of American black leaders, the NAACP's Roy Wilkins among them. Tubman was succeeded by his Vice President, younger and more progressive William R. Tolbert, Jr. (Mrs. Richard Nixon represented the United States at his inauguration in January 1972).

Much of what is known about the interior of Liberia has been learned by the foreign Christian missionaries, both Catholic and Protestant. President Tubman was the first President who ever ventured away from the coast into the provinces and the first to bring Afro-Liberians (as the people of the interior are known) into the government. Although the country, with a little over one million people, is still dominated by the approximately thirty-six thousand Americo-Liberians, strong efforts are being made to bring tribal people into positions of power.

YOUR VISIT TO LIBERIA

Monrovia: The capital, this city was named for U. S. President James Monroe (its original name was Cristopolis). Its older buildings are patterned after those of Louisiana, with local variations, including tin roofs and exterior colors of yellow, blue, and red. This is a town which did not know a hotel until World War II; where telephone service—even to the major airport—is a recently developed phenomenon; where bribery—minor and major—manifests itself in all manner of transactions; where there are probably more Christian churches per capita than in any other African capital, and where the police dress like New York City cops.

The most attractive part of the city is that which faces the sea, where most of the embassies are situated, and from where there is a fine view of the port and the ocean. Not far away are the bathing beaches, bordered by coconut palms; Sinkor is one of the best. Also worth seeing are the modern capitol, the city hall, and the National Museum. Of unusual interest are the African Performing Arts Center, whose director for some time was the American dancer, Pearl Primus, and the skyscraping, Tubman-built Executive Mansion, the annual upkeep of which is reported to be a quarter of a million dollars.

The interior: The visitor who would see the new Liberia might embark for the *Bomi Hills* iron mines, some 45 miles distant, and accessible by rail, and *Mount Nimba*, 4500 feet high and near the Guinea border, where digging is going on for what is reputed to be some of the richest iron-ore deposits in the world. Also worth a visit: the Firestone operations near Roberts Field, as modern and efficient as Monrovia is not; the smaller and newer Goodyear rubber plantations; and the cocoa and coffee plantations of the Liberia Company, 180 miles into the interior—the original inspiration of a firm founded by a former U. S. Secretary of State, the late Edward R. Stettinius. Other foreign-operated enterprises include banana and rubber plantations financed by German, Swiss, and Dutch firms. This is the new Liberia, a facet of the country's personality not evident in easygoing Monrovia. But that is not to say that the visitor cannot enjoy himself while in the capital; there are several dance palaces—informal but fun—for after-dark relaxation, in addition to the handsome beaches.

SHOPPING

Carved wood, ivory, leatherwork, iron figurines—at Lanahil Shop, Charlie No. 9, Tamoir Charlie's, and Robert Sulzer Memorial Art Center, near Payne Airfield. Bargaining is the rule, particularly with the "Charlies"—the Liberian term for traders.

CREATURE COMFORTS

HOTELS—**Monrovia:** The sumptuous 106-room Ducor Inter•Continental Hotel is the answer to a traveler's prayer—fully air-conditioned, with bars, nightclub, restaurant, and even a cinema of its own. Next best is the centrally located and air-conditioned Carlton. More modest hotels are the Traveller's Roost and the Hotel de France. Pan Am's Roberts Field Hotel, at the airport, has a bar, restaurant, and swimming pool. Restaurants in Monrovia: Atlantic, Incognito, and Salvatore's, a popular Italian eating place. Travelers going into the interior may make arrangements with heads of religious missions in Monrovia to stay with their up-country representatives; a small fee is usually charged for the support of the mission.

LIBYA

Libyan Arab Republic

Entry requirements: *A visa, obtainable from Libyan consulates; no health certificate is required, unless the visitor is coming from a country suffering from epidemics of "Internationally Notifiable Diseases" (whatever they may be). Play safe, though, and be protected by the usual inoculations.* **Best times for a visit:** *December through March is the coolest period; the principal summer months are hot but without rain; and the spring and autumn months are best avoided—winds (called* ghibli*) blow in from the desert at these times, bringing with them oppressive heat and fine particles of sand as well.* **Currency:** *The pound: 0.357 pounds=$1.* **Principal European languages:** *Italian and English, in that order; Arabic is the official language.* **Domestic transport:** *Planes connect the major cities. A road runs along the entire Mediterranean coast, there are a few stretches of railway, and desert tracks extend south to the Republic of Chad.* **Further information:** *Ministry of Information, Tripoli, Libya; Embassy of Libya, Washington, D.C.*

INTRODUCING LIBYA

Imagine a land, largely desert, one-quarter the size of the United States, with but fewer than two million inhabitants. This is the Republic of Libya, made up of three distinct provinces which were joined together under the auspices of the United Nations, in 1951, to become a sovereign state. Because so much of Libya's enormous territory is desert, its attractions—mostly near the coast—are limited and can be visited in a relatively short period. This is not to say, though, that they are not significant. A country that has known occupiers representing virtually every great world civilization—from the Phoenicians onward—is not to be dismissed lightly.

It is easy to realize how much is yet to be learned about the African past when one considers that it was only in mid-1960 that some University of Pennsylvania archaeologists discovered the ruins of an ancient Punic—or Phoenician—city directly beneath the remains of Leptis Magna, one of the great Roman settlements on the Libyan coast, and the site of scientific exploratory activity for many years—unlike vast regions of sub-Sahara Africa which have yet to be even faintly tapped.

If there is a country that has known more occupiers than Libya, Libyans would like to know about it. Name a great power, and Libyans—originally Berber peoples—have known its warriors, its colonizers, and its builders. Phoenicians, Romans, Greeks, and Vandals were its masters in ancient times; Islam—as represented by Egypt, Morocco, and Arabia—took over in the Middle Ages, followed by Spain and the crusading Knights of Malta in the sixteenth century, whose successor was the Ottoman Empire, which —though it let Libyan pashas retain a good deal of power—held on until 1912, when Italy took over, as a result of winning the Turko-Italian War.

The Italians did relatively little to help the Libyan economy develop, or even to employ Libyans. Their aim was to gain some breathing space in the homeland by shipping colonists to Libya and offering them the choicest jobs. They did build some roads, hospitals, public buildings, and schools in the 1930s, and would probably still be on the scene if it were not for World War II, when Libya became a battleground, and went to the Allies after the Axis defeat there in 1943. France was assigned its southern sectors, and Britain the coastal regions, with the Americans kicking in on aid programs and representing themselves through their presence at *Wheelus Field Air Force Base*, subsequently vacated. After the war Libyans began demanding independence, through the United Nations. The great powers debated the ifs, whys, hows, and wherefores for an inordinately long time, and finally agreed to a UN decision granting sovereignty to these Moslem people, rather paradoxically, on Christmas Eve, 1951. Prior to that time, the country's three provinces—Tripolitania, Barqa (formerly Cyrenaica), and Fezaan—had buried their age-old differences sufficiently to elect a Barqan, who was leader of the powerful Sanussi, an orthodox Moslem group, its first monarch. King Idris I, scholarly, elderly, little given to press-agentry, at the time the only Libyan with enough nationwide support to hold the country together, ruled until 1969, when he was overthrown by a military coup. The new military regime introduced strict social reforms: no alcoholic beverages, all street signs, restaurant menus, and the like printed only in Arabic, nationalization of banks. Thus American and British military bases were closed, and the Italian community of thousands—leftover from the colonial period—was ousted. Headed by Prime Minister Muammar el-Qaddafi, a good-looking colonel who was twenty-nine when he took over, and a zealous orthodox Moslem, Libya is aligned with the militant Arab nations in the conflict with Israel, and the revenue from some of the country's oil reserves is given to Egypt as a subsidy (with Egypt and Syria it makes up the 1971-founded Federation of Arab Republics). Although Libya is a nation of great wealth—it is the fourth largest oil producer in the world with an oil income of $2 billion a year—many of its people still live in the Middle Ages, and the majority are unaware of their country's riches. The government plans to change this with a dynamic program of economic and social reform and increased industrial and agricultural production. As one government member has said: "Our leaders are young. They have the possibility of leading our people straight from the age of the camel to that of automation without having taken off their *jelabbas.*"

YOUR VISIT TO LIBYA

Tripoli and Tripolitania: Known in Arabic as *Tarabulus el Gharb* (Tripoli of the West) to distinguish it from the Tripoli in Lebanon, Tripoli is the only modern survivor of the three ancient Roman towns (or Tripolis) of the Libyan coast, the others being

Leptis Magna and Sabratha, whose splendid ruins have been restored in recent years. In Libya the desert extends from the interior directly to the edge of the sea, and Tripoli is set amid one of its chief coastal oases: a forest of palm and olive trees, and great varieties of cactus. Its buildings—many painted immaculate white, others in soft pastels—gleam against a background of tan earth, green foliage, and the blue Mediterranean waters, all of which makes for one of North Africa's most attractive cities. Following the North African pattern, there is an Old (Medina el Kadima) Town and a New Town. The Medina, on a promontory that was the site of the Roman Tripoli, is dissected by narrow, winding arched alleyways, few of them wide enough for even a small car, and many so narrow that there is room for a pedestrian or a donkey—but not both. Most Libyans, as a walk through the Medina will tell, wear white, toga-like robes called barracans, the ends of which are thrown over the left shoulder, toga-style. Older men flap the ends over their heads, and women—still Old School Moslems—cover their faces as well, leaving only a tiny gap for one eye to peep through. There are, of course, some Western-dressed Libyans, mainly men, but even they wear a red fez—or *tarboosh,* as it is called in Libya. But the Medina of Tripoli offers more than glimpses of its inhabitants. Here are long gallerys of *souks,* or market stalls, some enclosed shops, some open booths—to which their owners beckon customers for glimpses of beautifully handwoven carpets, barracans, jewelry. Not to be missed by the visitor is the Suk as-Sayaga, where the goldsmiths and silversmiths hawk bracelets, earrings, and *kholkhols*—heavy ankle bracelets worn by Bedouin women. Away from the *souks* are the dwellings of the Medina—low, whitewashed, with latticed windows—many of them exquisite examples of Arab and Turkish design.

Other Tripoli highlights: the Bathhouse (Hammum) of Sidi Dargut, dating from 1605, the Mosque of Shaib-el-Ain (1699), and the two-storied house of Ali Pasha Karamanli, with its quiet courtyard and tile-decorated walls; the several *fonduks,* or inns—old galleried buildings which sheltered caravaneers from the desert. And, too, the Roman arch of Marcus Aurelius, at various times since its erection in A.D. 164, a general store, fish market, and movie theater—and now beautifully restored as the monument the Romans intended it to be. Away from the Medina, and a part of the New Town, with its lovely waterfront boulevard named for Adrian Pelt—the Dutchman who arranged the transfer of European-held Libya to sovereignty in 1950—is the Castle, Tripoli's citadel for more than a millennium, the site of countless battles for its possession, and now one of the most fascinating museums in Africa, room after room telling the story of the new kingdom, as well as the functions of the old building itself, which has been fortress, mosque, Roman Catholic church, residence of rulers, and office building. Of particular interest to Americans is the old Protestant cemetery with the graves of five Yankee sailors, members of the crew of the USS *Intrepid*, which was blown up during the Barbary wars—a reminder that even America invaded Libya—the first time in 1804, and not again until 1942. That first landing is the one celebrated in the line in the *Marines' Hymn*, "to the shores of Tripoli."

Excursions from Tripoli: Besides the Mediterranean beaches which flank the city (Lido, Piccola Capri, Beach Club), there are three excursions which only the visitor in a great hurry can afford not to undertake. The first is to *Sabratha*, 42 miles to the west, along a fine road running through a fertile, picturesque green belt —the ruins of the Roman city which was built in A.D. 180, and which includes a forum, temples, houses, shops, and a superb theater in which the back wall of the stage is composed of a three-storied colonnade of Corinthian columns of variously colored marbles, outlined against the blue sea and sky. There is a museum of mosaics and statues found among the ruins, and a pleasant restaurant affording a panoramic view as well as refreshment. A little more distant from Tripoli—76 miles to the east—is *Leptis Magna*, even bigger and more imposing than Sabratha, probably because it was developed by Emperor Septimius Severus, a part-Negro Roman, who was born there. Here to be marveled at are palatial public baths, a vast forum, giant fountains, temple after temple, miles of paved streets, and a harbor with extensive quays. The amphitheater, excellently preserved, has a stage backed by finely carved rows of marble columns. The third in the trio of important excursions would be to the *Gebel country*, a wonderfully mountainous region dividing the coastal province from Fezzan, in the far interior. Along the way, one sees Roman dams and fortified farms dotting a wild countryside with scattered villages, including Garian, whose troglodyte inhabitants live beneath the ground, either in caves or at the bottom of artificial wells. Grim though these may sound, they are considerably cooler in summer and warmer in winter than conventional surface houses, in a region without air conditioning or central heating. Other Gebel attractions: the oasis of Wadi Rumia; the typically Berber village of Jefren, its castle perched like an eagle's nest atop a rocky crag near Nalut, and the remains of an early Christian church near Mudiryat. There are several modern hotels in the Gebel, and the roads are good.

Benghazi and Barqa Province: Considerably smaller than Tripoli, and severely damaged by World War II bombs, Benghazi is in itself hardly a desirable tourist attraction today, despite the intensive efforts being made to rebuild and modernize it. The eastern co-capital of the republic, the chief city of Barqa Province, and the ex-residence of the king (his suburban palace was an ex-Italian villa), it is the ideal base for excursions through the Green Mountain region to the ruins of the ancient Greek cities of *Cyrene* and *Apollonia.* With those cities, and two others, it was one of the Greek "Five Towns" many centuries ago. The provincial Antiquities Department is still excavating at Cyrene, which is dramatically situated on the side of a hill overlooking miles of farmland and the sea, and near the modern village of Shahat. Its chief monument is a splendidly located amphitheater, and it is only a thirty-minute drive from Apollonia, which straddles the sea to such an extent that part of its ruins are submerged, and inhabited today by both skin-divers and exotic-looking fish. *Ghadames,* in the interior, is a densely populated oasis town, whose founding has been attributed to Alexander the Great. Its Berbers—among the strictest Moslems in North Africa—live in houses enclosed by mud walls, and its principal visitors are itinerant blue-veiled Toureg tribesmen—in from the desert—who camp at the gates and often amuse themselves at evening dances, with music provided on *tobols* by their unveiled women.

Fezzan Province: Libya's least-developed and least-visited province, Fezzan—which is more than three times as large as England—is hot, dusty, and as fascinating as any region of the world that has had little contact with outsiders for many centuries. Since World War II it has been largely under French guidance, and travelers may now fly to its capital, *Sebha* (also called Fort Leclerc), via Ghadames. Sebha is home to the Moutassaref ("Possessor"), and the chief dignitary of the province. The French have made some progress by digging wells, building roads, establishing schools and public-health services. They have also had some success in eradicating the ingrained, ancient system of hereditary slavery. But the façade of Sebha—and indeed of all Fezzan—is little changed, thus far, as a trip to *Murzuk* indicates. Seventy miles south of the capital, is the religious center of Fezzan, dominated by a venerable Turkish fort, and not far from the village of Traghen, from which long camel caravans depart for treks through the desert to the Tibesti Mountains and the Republic of Chad, way to the south.

SHOPPING

Leatherwork, jewelry in gold and silver, hand-woven textiles, barracans (cloak-like garments worn by both men and women), *kholkhols* (heavy ankle bracelets worn by Bedouin women), carpets, with the *souks* of Tripoli the best source, followed by those of the other towns. Bargaining is the rule.

CREATURE COMFORTS

HOTELS—**Tripoli:** The main hotels overlook the lovely, palm-lined harbor and the Mediterranean, and are elderly but clean and attractive. Leaders are the Libya Palace and the Uadden;

Mediterraneo, Grant, National, Rex. A new Hilton hotel is planned for Tripoli. **Garian:** Gebel. **Jefren:** Rumia. **Zliten:** Gazzalat. **Benghazi:** Palace, Bernice, Lux. **Cyrene:** Jebel el Akhdar. **Apollonia:** Cyrene. **Sebha:** Palazzo. **Ghadames:** Aïn el Fars.

MALAGASY REPUBLIC (MADAGASCAR) AND NEARBY INDIAN OCEAN ISLANDS

Comoros
Mauritius
Réunion
Seychelles

Purists may not agree, but the islands of the east coast of Africa are generally associated with the continent, and Africa-bound visitors might want to include them in itineraries. Although philatelists have long known about the islands—some of the most rare and interesting stamps have been issued here—there is no question that they are among the world's least-visited territories. Each in its own way is scenically handsome and culturally rich, blending the influences of the Orient, Europe, and, of course, continental Africa. Giant of them all—and indeed a Goliath among all the world's islands—is Madagascar, now known as the Malagasy Republic, independent. To the north are the French-administered Comoro Islands, and the British Seychelles. To the south are the Mascarene Islands: the Republic of Mauritius and French Réunion. All are accessible by air from abroad.

Malagasy Republic: If one counts Australia as a continent, Madagascar is the world's fourth largest island, exceeded in area only by Greenland, New Guinea, and Borneo. It is some 360 miles wide and almost a thousand miles in length. The 240-mile-wide Mozambique Channel separates it from the mainland of Africa. A number of satellite islands—Sainte-Marie and Nossi-Bé among them—ring Madagascar's coast. They, together with major towns of the main island, are connected by a surprisingly comprehensive air network—one of the most extensive of any country, and a boon to the traveler with a minimum of time. This is an island republic of almost seven million people, most of whom are Malagasy descendants of Malayans and Melanesians who settled there many centuries ago. Europeans—mostly French—are in a small minority, probably not exceeding 50,000. The French, in one way or another, have had connections on the island for several hundred years, but the islanders—particularly the dominant Hova tribe—played them against the English in a power struggle, and it was not until 1896 that the French won out, deposed the ruling Hova queen, and took over. The island eventually became an overseas department of France, with representation in the Paris Parliament. During World War II it sided with the Vichy regime, and was occupied by the British from 1942 until the war was over, presumably to keep it safe from Japanese invasion. With the establishment of the French Community in 1958, it became a semi-independent republic at first, and then requested—and received—from Paris complete sovereignty in 1960. The island was one of the best prepared of the French overseas territories for independence. Between 1946 and 1958, F.I.D.E.S. (French overseas-development program) invested 270 million dollars in Madagascar for public improvements ranging from harbors to schools. The only unhappy note of more recent times was a 1970 agreement signed with white-supermacist South Africa, from which will come 6.5 million dollars for tourist development—with the tourists to be largely South African whites—bringing not only their money but their racist attitudes to a nonwhite and a still naïve land. French is, of course, the principal European language, but there is more English spoken than one might imagine. The language of the people is their own: Malagasy. Except on the coast, the island is largely temperate. It is most ideal, however, during the dry months, from May to September; expect some rain the rest of the year.

Tananarive, the capital, is an exceptionally attractive, French-accented city with a population of about a quarter of a million, built on seven peaks, in the elevated hills of the interior. The French have seen to it—as indeed they have almost everywhere they have been in Africa—that this capital looks like a capital: substantial, well-planned, comfortable. Flowering jacarandas and poinsettias line the streets and bring color to the parks and public gardens. There are a number of good restaurants, hotels, and street cafés, in the best French tradition. Tananarive is famous for the Friday market, called the *Zoma,* which is vast, colorful, and distinctly untouristy. Besides the open-air market there is a good deal to be seen while ambling along the steep streets—the palace of the former queen on the highest peak, with the National Museum adjoining it; the profusion of Christian churches, with services given in Malagasy in most of them, and heavy emphasis on group singing; the fashionable race track; hanging gardens overlooking lovely lakes; balconied houses rising one above the other; bazaar-filled streets peopled by exotically costumed Malagasy, some in beautiful *lambas,* or shawls, of silk.

Outside Tananarive: Make your island swing circular, and by air. Try and include *Tamatave,* the main harbor city—a modern town with suburban villages of great charm and nearby crocodile-infested lakes; *Antsirabe,* a delightful resort with thermal springs which French residents have made into a local version of Vichy; *Fianarantsoa,* an ancient mountain town; the east-coast port of *Manakara,* in a region of verdant forests, high peaks, and waterfalls; and *Fort-Dauphin,* the center of what is locally known as the Madagascar Riviera, and a perfect spot to conclude a Malagasy holiday. Wherever you go, notice how different the flora and fauna are from those of mainland Africa; look for rare species of fern, orchids, and the rare traveler's tree, which yields a potable beverage. And keep an eye open for lemurs and the strange animals known as *aye-ayes!* Like Brazil, this country is a bargain headquarters for semiprecious gems: topaz, aquamarine, amethyst, all obtainable at not more than a couple of dollars a carat at stalls in the open-air market. Also interesting: paintings of landscapes and of people by local artists, unusually good woodcarvings, woven raffia mats and baskets. Bargaining is the rule. In *Tananarive* the best hotel is the modern and handsome Madagascar Hilton, the first de luxe hotel in the Indian Ocean islands with a pool and an

18-hole golf course next door. Others are the Relais Ambohibao, Motel Agip, and the Colbert; in *Tamatave,* the Chez Martinez, Plage; *Fort-Dauphin:* Bellevue, Felli; *Fianarantsoa:* Sud; *Manakara:* C.C.B. Hotel. *Further information:* Alliance Touristique de l'Océan Indien (ATOI), 19, Rue Amiral Pierre, Tananarive, Madagascar.

Comoro Islands: Rarely visited, but now developing tourism, the Comoros might well be the most unusual stopover of an African holiday. Part of an archipelago of volcanic islands, they can be reached by air from Tananarive. The group includes *Anjouan,* with its central mountains rising to five thousand feet; *Moheli,* with its center at *Fomboni; Great Comoro,* the biggest of the group, with Kartata, an eight-thousand-foot, active volcano that can be climbed on a two-day expedition, accompanied by guides; and *Mayotte,* closest to Madagascar, with its center at *Mamoutzou. Dzaoudzi,* the chief town, is a good starting point for an island tour; its chief hotel is the Marine. *Further information:* Alliance Touristique de l'Océan Indien (ATOI), 19, Rue Amiral Pierre, Tananarive, Madagascar; French Government Tourist Office, 610 Fifth Avenue, New York.

Mauritius: Volcanic Mauritius, completely surrounded by coral reefs, had the French as its first European settlers but was for long a British Crown Colony. It attained complete independence in 1968. Still, the lingua franca—and the *ambiance,* to a great extent, is French. It is one of the most densely populated areas of the world, with about eight hundred thousand people, most of them of East Indian origin, living within its 720-square-mile area; it became a sovereign republic in 1968. Although the government of Hindu Premier Sir Seewosagur Ramgoolam is nominally anti-apartheid, it is listening to South African aid overtures, and may well succumb, as has Madagascar. Except for occasional winter storms, which sometimes cause tremendous damage, the climate is generally pleasant and comfortable. *Port Louis,* the capital and chief port, boasts a lush setting and a number of imposing monuments, including two cathedrals, a citadel, a Chinese temple, and the unusual Jummah Mosque. Most Europeans live in *Curepipe,* in the high interior; this is a good setting for excursions to the Botanical Gardens, laid out in 1767 at *Pamplemousses,* and the extinct volcanic crater at *Trou aux Cerfs.* There are a number of beach resorts, an interesting historical museum in the old town of *Mahebourg,* and verdant forest reserves in the *Black River Gorges. Hotels:* Le Morne Brabant, in the southwest corner of the island, is set on a bay and offers all water sports. Le Chaland, in the southeast corner, is also recommended. Port Louis—Golden Tourist Hotel, National, Mauritius; Curepipe—Park, Vatel, Les Mascareignes. *Further information:* Mauritius Government Tourist Office, Port Louis, Mauritius.

Réunion: The French now call Réunion an overseas department of the republic; it has been in their hands since 1639. Mountainous and volcanic, it has a population of some four hundred thousand—mostly Africans and Asians, with a tiny European minority. Ships call regularly at *Pointe-des-Galets,* and planes fly to *Saint-Denis,* the capital, from Tananarive, Madagascar. Besides Saint-Denis—charming, small, Franco-African—there are a dozen or so tiny but interesting towns, each named for a Roman Catholic saint, ringing the coast. The active *Grand Brule* volcano can be climbed, and there are thermal springs (for a post-climb rest?) at *Cilaos* and *Hell-Bourg,* both in the mountains. The climate is temperate for the most part; the terrain is scenically magnificent; and there are good but small hotels *à la Française. Saint-Denis*—Europe and Bourbon; *Cilaos*—Touristique; *Hell-Bourg*—Salazes. *Further information:* Alliance Touristique de l'Océan Indien, 19, Rue Amiral Pierre, Tananarive, Madagascar; French Government Tourist Office, 610 Fifth Avenue, New York.

The Seychelles: These islands have a new airport on Mahe Island, and there are special cruises that include visits to them. Other ships call at the Seychelles only occasionally. There are ninety-two islands in the group, the most important of which is *Mahe,* but even its population of thirty-five thousand is small, and its area is only 150 square miles. The Seychelles were taken over by the British from the French in 1814, but, as in Mauritius, the prevailing language remains French. The rugged granite terrain adds a great deal to the beauty of the islands. *Victoria*, the pretty little capital, is on Mahe, from which trips by boat may be arranged to other islands in the group. The people are mainly African and Asian, with a sprinkling of old-time French settlers and British civil servants. They created history when, in 1971, James Mancham, their Chief Minister, told the United Nations General Assembly that they did *not* want independence, that it would not be practical, and that they had "learned to like and understand the British." This is a land of tropical lagoons, splendid scenery, giant turtles, a mild climate—except from December to May, during the monsoons—and the kind of hospitality that only an isolated island people can dispense. *Hotels:* Pirates Arms and Continental in Victoria. *Further information:* Seychelles Tourist Bureau, Victoria, Seychelles; British Information Services, 30 Rockefeller Plaza, New York.

MALAWI

Republic of Malawi

Entry requirements: *An entry visa, valid for one year, is required.* **Best times for a visit:** *The dry season, from May to October, is best. From mid-October through the end of December there are intermittent heavy rains, and from January until the end of March the weather is apt to be steadily rainy.* **Currency:** *The pound, equaling about $2.80.* **Principal European language:** *English is the official language.* **Domestic transport:** *Air Malawi operates domestic flights. There are some roads, and steamer service on Lake Malawi.* **Further information:** *Embassy of the Republic of Malawi, Washington, D.C.; Ministry of Trade and Industry, Zomba, Malawi.*

INTRODUCING MALAWI

Malawi is one of the most beautiful of African countries, with windswept plateaus, palm-fringed beaches, green mountains, and huge Lake Malawi, which occupies a full third of the country. Malawi (formerly Nyasaland) was a member of the three-territory Federation of Rhodesia and Nyasaland until 1963, when the federation was dissolved. In 1964 Malawi attained independence, and in 1966 it became a republic within the British Commonwealth.

With one of the densest populations in Africa—four million people crowded into 36,481 square miles—Malawi has serious economic problems. British aid and the recent development of lumber and mineral resources supplement the raising of tea, peanuts, and cotton, the country's main crops. Malawi maintains friendly relations with the racist, white-ruled countries of Rhodesia and South Africa, both of which have contributed investment income to their neighbor. This peculiar friendship—Malawi was the first African nation to establish trade and diplomatic relations with South Africa—has understandably aroused the ire—and, frequently, the disgust—of self-respecting countries throughout Africa.

Malawi's Uncle Tom President, Dr. Hastings Kamazu Banda, a United States-educated and intensely pragmatic man who has figured prominently in the country's political history since before independence, made some sort of history when he paid an official visit to South Africa in 1971, having earlier sent an ambassador to Pretoria—the first black in that capital's diplomatic corps. South African President J. J. Fouche followed up Banda's visit to South Africa with a trip to Malawi in 1972—the first by a South African head of state to a sovereign Black African country.

YOUR VISIT TO MALAWI

Lake Malawi: Lake Malawi, 365 miles long, fifty-two miles wide, and formerly Lake Nyasa, is Malawi's chief attraction. Small resorts dot the southern and western shores, and are concentrated in the neighborhoods of *Salima, Fort Johnston,* and the delightfully named *Monkey Bay.* For the visitor with enough time, a highlight of a Malawi holiday would be an eight-day cruise around the lake on a Malawi Railway cruise ship. The route covers close to eight hundred miles, and there are stops at twelve ports in Malawi and two in neighboring Tanzania. Ports include the town of *Kota Kota,* on the western shore, one of the largest Bantu settlements south of the Equator; *Nkata Bay,* with its rich rubber plantation and lovely white-sand beach; and *Monkey Bay,* a resort area with swimming, sailing, and water-skiing.

Other areas: The *Kasungu Game Reserve,* with an area of more than eight hundred square miles, and an airport of its own, can accommodate overnight visitors or those making day trips.

Here one may see a variety of game, including lion, leopard, elephant, buffalo, and zebra. The *Lengwe Game Reserve,* only fifty square miles, is easily reached from the city of Blantyre and affords excellent close-up views of impala, antelope, the rare Samango monkey, and a particularly good assortment of birds. *Malawi National Park,* open all year round, is at an altitude of seven thousand feet and has an invigorating climate with surprisingly cold nights. The park can accommodate both day and overnight visitors.

Malawi's two main towns, Zomba and Blantyre, are also worth a visit. South of Lake Malawi, in the green hills of the interior, is *Zomba,* one of the smallest, and perhaps prettiest, capitals of the world. (It is being replaced as the seat of government by the new capital, *Lilongwe,* with the help of South African loans, in excess of eleven million dollars. The idea is to build up the impoverished north, where Lilongwe is situated.) And even farther south is *Blantyre,* the chief commercial town, named for Livingstone's birthplace in Scotland. Outstanding here is the great Church of Scotland church; it was built at the turn of the century by African converts and missionaries.

SHOPPING

Ceremonial masks, wood and ivory carvings, raffia work, beadwork, and pottery can be purchased in the markets. Bargaining is the rule.

CREATURE COMFORTS

HOTELS—**Blantyre:** The Mount Shoche Hotel is the country's newest and largest and is fully air-conditioned. Others: Ryall's Hotel, Nash's Private Hotel. **Limbe:** Shire Highlands Hotel, International Hotel. **Zomba:** New Zomba Inn, Ku Chawe Inn. **Lilongwe:** Lilongwe Hotel. **Fort Johnston:** Palm Beach Inn, Marina Beach Hotel, Cape Maclear Hotel. **Salima:** Fish Eagle Inn, Grand Beach Hotel.

MALI

République du Mali

Entry requirements: *Visa, a health certificate (yellow fever, smallpox) and an onward ticket.* **Best times for a visit:** *January to April—the dry season—is ideal, but the rainy months are often dry enough for sightseeing in certain areas.* **Currency:** *The franc: 555.5=$1.* **Principal European language:** *French, with English spoken mainly in hotels and air terminals.* **Domestic transport:** *Air service and roads, a railroad to Dakar on the Senegalese coast.* **Further information:** *Service d'Information de la République du Mali, Bamako, Mali; Embassy of Mali, Washington, D.C.*

INTRODUCING MALI

The site of Timbuktu, of Gao, and of other centers of the once great African empires (see pages 37–39), the Republic of Mali—formerly the French Sudan—is immense, landlocked, and one of the least appreciated of the new West African republics. In large part because of its interior situation, it was not conquered by the French until the early part of this century. It first flew the tricolor, as a formally established French territory, in 1904. After World War II political consciousness developed, with French encouragement, and in 1947 it elected its first legislative council. In 1958 the territory became the Sudanese Republic, a semi-autonomous state of the French Community, along with every other French West and Equatorial African province, except Guinea, which voted to become completely independent. Shortly thereafter, the Sudanese Republic joined with Senegal to become the Federation of Mali, which gained complete sovereignty in mid-1960 for a very brief period. In August of that year, the two states parted company, and in September of that year, the Sudanese Republic changed its name to the Republic of Mali.

Modibo Keita, President of Mali, quickly established a socialist regime, complete with Chinese adviser-technicians, but in 1968 Keita was overthrown in a bloodless military coup. The new government of President Moussa Traore has actively sought economic aid from both East and West and is dedicated to developing Mali's agricultural and mineral resources, as well as encouraging—but very slowly and cautiously—the growth of tourism.

YOUR VISIT TO MALI

Bamako: A city of some two hundred thousand people, Bamako is the capital of a dominantly Moslem country of about five million inhabitants who live in an area three times the size of Germany—desert in the north (a frontier is shared with Algeria), savanna in the south. The capital is on the banks of the great Niger River, which flows through much of the country. (It is also the terminus of an 800-mile railroad line from Dakar, but most visitors prefer to arrive by air.) The European-built sections of Bamako are modern, charming, and comfortable. And there is a considerable amount to see before departing for other destinations within the republic. Besides the African market and African residential sections, requisites would include the National Museum, replete with exhibits of prehistoric as well as relatively recent history; the Maison des Artisans (Artisans' House), established by the French in 1932 to revive flagging arts-and-crafts traditions, and offering instruction in the traditional style to young people in jewelrywork, leatherwork, weaving, sculpture, ironwork, and other skills; the *souks,* or markets, of the professional artisans—excellent for shopping; the tailor shops, where costumes of varying designs and materials are cut and measured for men, women, and children by scores of tailors, each with sewing machines in their open stalls; the port, busy with river fishermen, whose sleek, hand-carved pirogues dot its shores; an immense, imaginatively designed zoo in a verdant park of its own, and—at least for visitors with socio-medical interests—the Ophthalmology Institute, for research and treatment of prevalent eye diseases such as trachoma, and the Leprosy Institute. Bamako, with verdant public gardens, tree-lined avenues, some substantial public buildings, and fine old houses can make for an agreeable visit. Its immediate environs are delightful for short excursions too—the Oyako Waterfalls, the Korounkorokalé Grottoes—with exhibits of neolithic-age objects discovered within them; Lake Ouégna, and the forests of Lake Mandingues region, and La Boule National Game Reserve.

Mopti: Center of an unbelievably extensive Niger River fishing industry, Mopti—particularly between February and October—is a city of brilliant color. To its market, fishermen bring bale upon bale of salted, dried whitefish, for transport to many parts of West Africa. Away from the water's edge, a brisk trade is carried on in vegetables, fruit, meat, and all manner of spices and condiments. The panorama is one of action, noise, and the bright hues—flaming red, lemon-yellow, deep purple, royal blue—of the shoppers' costumes. Elsewhere in the town, walks along its streets reveal the minarets of the Komoguel Mosque and the peculiar architecture of the terraced dried-mud houses in that quarter. All about are the people of the town—animists and Moslems, Negroes and Berbers, as well as the small European minority.

The Dogon country: Not far from Mopti are the villages of the Dogons, amid poor, rocky country, still farmed as it has been for centuries by these animist people, who live in small, square huts of mud topped with roofs of thatch, and whose age-old religion includes among its paraphernalia superb—and sometimes rather terrifying—ceremonial masks. The people themselves are friendly and hospitable.

Goundam: One of the great cities of the ancient Songhai Empire, Goundam was elderly as late as 1492, a year during which—among other activities elsewhere in the world—the emperor of Songhai undertook a rebuilding program there, to bring the place up to date. The Moroccans, when they destroyed Songhai, took over Goundam in 1691, and later it was occupied by the Tauregs. The French came in 1894, by which time the town had long lapsed into somnolence. It is worth a visit, however, for its fantastic houses of dried mud and plaster in the shape of beehives. And Timbuktu is just down the road a piece.

Timbuktu: The twentieth century is manifesting itself in the strangest places, Timbuktu among them. Long known as one of the most inaccessible of the world's fabled cities, Timbuktu now possesses an airstrip wide enough to land DC-6s, and for all we know a Hilton-type hotel-*cum*-swimming pool may someday spring up on one of its narrow, dusty streets. But although Timbuktu is no longer inaccessible—one can fly there easily from Mopti—it is still a gateway to an exotic past. It is exciting to walk the streets of this venerable place—now a town of 6000, but once reputed to have had a population many times that, at the height of prosperity, during the heyday of the old Mali Empire. Even now, though, there is considerable activity. The camel caravans from the north still converge upon the market place. The Medersa, an Arab boys' high school, still teaches Koranic scripture to some three hundred boys. The Kjinguer-ber Mosque still attracts devout pilgrims from distant regions. And the inlet of the Niger, on which the town is built, still attracts the traffic of pirogues, navigated at incredibly high speeds, by skilled boatmen, manipulating high poles. They come each morning to one of the town's two markets—this one on the water's edge—with fresh grass for the animals of the nomads who have come to trade hides and salt from mines 500 miles north. Walking the streets, one sees veiled Taureg men, Black Africans, small boys reciting the Koran on shaded corners. Accommodations are simple, and one must put up with the searing sun and the ever-present sand, which seems to coat and permeate everything, but the lure of Timbuktu is its mystery and romance, not its luxury.

Gao: You will have to forgive residents of Gao if they look upon other cities of the world as youngish upstarts. Their town was founded in A.D. 670 and became the capital of the Songhai Empire four hundred years later. Though it is now one of the country's largest towns, it is quiet and off the beaten path—at least if one contrasts it with its period of glory. Still, there is much to be seen—and pondered over—as one walks the now wide, tree-lined streets, whose buildings are of flat-roofed dried mud (is there a better building material in such a climate?). Here one finds descendants of the ancient Songhai people—a Negro group, Moors, Tauregs, Bambara, and still others, with distinctive customs, clothing, religions, ways of life.

The market, in the center of the newer part of the town, is sparkling and animated, and is distinguished by a large animal population—camels, donkeys, horses, and cows among them. The port teems with pirogues. The Tomb of the Askias is Gao's *pièce de résistance*—a monument and mosque honoring the memory of two of Songhai's emperors. It is immense, pyramidal-shaped, and dates back some 600 years. Outside the town, and easily visitable in half a day, are the Green Island (l'Ile Verte), reached by an interesting pirogue ride down the Niger, and the Pink Dune (la Dune Rose), an immense hill of sand so named because at certain times of day its color is pink, at others yellow-brown. From the dune, also reached by pirogue, there is a superb view of the entire region—Gao in the distance, the river, and nearby villages.

SHOPPING

Mali craftsmen are among the most skilled in Africa at mask-making and woodcarving, at fashioning figurines in iron, and all manner of objects in soft, tooled leather, hand-woven textiles—including blankets and rugs; spears and lances. In Bamako, the Artisans' Souk, near the Maison des Artisans, is the outstanding source. Carved wood ceremonial headpieces of the Bambara tribe are especially good. Away from the capital, try the markets, and watch for street stalls, sidewalk displays near hotel entrances, and airport shops. Bargaining is the rule.

CREATURE COMFORTS

HOTELS—**Bamako:** Hotel de l'Amite—new and comfortable; Grand—modern, air-conditioned, central location; Le Motel, Le Lido, on the outskirts, Majestic. **Gao:** Atlantide, Transsaharienne; elsewhere: small rest camps or *campements,* usually with restaurants; book in advance from Bamako. Restaurants in Bamako: Chez Fanny (open-air), Lido (outskirts). **Timbuktu:** Tombouctou Hotel.

MAURITANIA

République Islamique de Mauritanie

Entry requirements: *A visa, obtainable from French consulates where Mauritania has no diplomatic missions, plus a health certificate (yellow fever and smallpox) and an onward ticket or letter of financial responsibility.* **Best times for a visit:** *This is a hot, dry country, with little rainfall the year round. It can be visited at any time, but July and August are recommended because of the Moorish festivals which occur then.* **Currency:** *The CFA franc: CFA 280=$1.* **Principal European language:** *French, with some English in leading hotels and transport centers.* **Domestic transport:** *Flights to major towns the preferred means of getting about. There are few regular roads, and many desert trails recommended only to motorists especially equipped for this kind of travel.* **Further information:** *Service d'Information de la République Islamique de Mauritanie, Nouakchott, Mauritania; Embassy of the Islamic Republic of Mauritania, Washington, D.C.*

INTRODUCING MAURITANIA

There's room to roam in the Islamic Republic of Mauritania. Considerably bigger than Texas, this country has a population of just a little over one million, no large towns, and a seat of government built from scratch since 1958. The country is eager for tourists and is proud of its modern capital and its four hundred miles of unspoiled beaches, but there is not yet a single luxury-class hotel in the entire republic. The great majority of dwellings, as a matter of fact, are portable, for this is a land predominantly peopled by Caucasian Moorish nomads. And they are its principal attraction for the visitor.

Until 1958, Mauritania was simply one of eight provinces of French West Africa. It chose to become a semi-independent republic within the French Community in that year, and in 1960 its government advised the De Gaulle regime in Paris that it was opting for complete sovereignty, under the terms of the Community constitution. Independence came in November of that year.

Only the southern part of Mauritania is fertile and arable, but great wealth lies beneath the desert that makes up nearly three-quarters of the land. Iron ore is being mined by Miferma, an international syndicate, and the vast copper deposits are being developed with the help of foreign investment and aid. In 1969 a desalination plant, Africa's first, was opened in Nouakchott. In 1971, the President—in office since independence, after being re-elected in 1966—was elected President at the Organization of African Unity; one of his early acts was a White House conference with President Nixon. The Moors are mainly pastoral shepherds, and the Negro minority are small-scale farmers. There are vastly more animals—300,000 camels, 1,500,000 oxen, and 8,600,000 sheep and goats—than people. Until very recently, the French had done very little to bring Mauritania into the modern world. It was the most neglected of the French West African territories. But Mauritanians, though poor today, are inheritors of a rich past. Within their borders are vestiges of the once great Empire of Ghana.

Islam, imported from the relatively near North African states, has been a part of the Mauritanian culture for more than a millennium. (It is the state religion of the new republic, but freedom of worship is guaranteed.) The town of Chinguetti, though virtually unknown today, was, in the fifteenth century, one of the top half dozen cities of the Moslem world. Its skyline was one of a dozen mosques, visited by Africans passing through on pilgrimages to Mecca. And on the site of Chinguetti stood the even more ancient city of Aboer, dating back to the seventh century.

YOUR VISIT TO MAURITANIA

This is a land where sand, desert, and dunes overwhelm the visitor almost everywhere he travels. It is offset by an occasional forest and oasis. And it is accented by the silhouettes of silent camel caravans, great herds of goats and cattle, and the profiles of fine-featured men, long-haired and long-bearded, their women in billowy robes, their black-eyed children, their tent cities, and their beautifully wrought arts and crafts.

Nouakchott: This means "selling-place" in the Berber language. It is the new capital, and the logical starting place for a visit. It was, until 1958, nothing more than a collection of mud huts in the scrubby desert, a few miles inland from the Atlantic coast. Mauritania's capital had been Saint-Louis, in the former French West African province of Senegal, just over the border. Now, just about completed, Nouakchott is a modern city of about fifteen thousand people, with wide streets, new public buildings, and fairly substantial residential areas. The attraction here is the population—nomads in from the desert to trade at the market, fisherfolk from the nearby coastal villages selling their catches, artisans at work in their stalls, and clusters of nomad tents on the outskirts.

Atar: The largest of the Mauritanian towns before the construction of Nouakchott, Atar is at once a metropolis of brown stone houses, a shopping center for Mauritania's finest crafts, and the departure point for the most fascinating of the country's towns—Chinguetti.

Chinguetti: There is no hotel here—only a tiny rest camp. Unless the visitor wants to rough it, he must make his visit within a day from Atar. And he should attempt to time it to take place in either July or August, the months of the annual Feast of the Guetna. This is the time of year when the dates are ripe, and nomads from many miles around gather in the town to eat their fill, and to make merry. Fires are lighted all over the town, over which mint tea—a requisite at Mauritanian banquets—is brewed. Rifles are fired, and there is a sixty-day round of dancing, music, prayer, feasting, and elaborate weddings. At the end of August the nomads gather up their flocks and their camelskin tents, mount their camels, and resume their wandering for another ten months. Chinguetti empties out, but even then it is worth visiting. It is, of course, nothing like what it was in the fifteenth century, when it ranked as a leading city of Islam (see page 227). Only one of its many mosques remain, with a tall, delicate minaret hovering over an enclosure hallowed in Mauritanian history. The sandstone houses, cube-shaped and mellowed by centuries of sun, are, more often than one would imagine, schools as well as homes. Elders instruct small groups of boys in the Koran within their walls. They write texts from the sacred book on planes of wood, and then recite them aloud.

Nouadhibou (formerly Port Étienne): The major port of the republic, Nouadhibou boasts a small hotel, a teeming market, an important fishing industry, and environs not unlike those elsewhere in Mauritania.

SHOPPING

There are no gift shops to speak of; buy direct from the artisans in the open markets. Workmanship and design are often excellent. Watch for: ironware figurines, intricately carved woodenwork, filigree jewelry in gold and silver, leather handbags, cushion covers, and wallets, and camel-hair rugs. Bargaining is, of course, the rule.

CREATURE COMFORTS

HOTELS—**Nouakchott:** The Oasis, small but comfortable, with restaurant; Hotel Marahaba, with restaurant and air conditioning. **Nouadhibou:** Clupea.

MOROCCO

Royaume du Maroc

Entry requirements: *Only a valid passport, for United States citizens—no visa and no health certificate required, although inoculations for the usual diseases are recommended.* **Best times for a visit:** *The months of September through May are ideal for a country-wide visit. The summer months, however, are excessively hot only in the south (including Marrakesh). Winter is very cool in the north, but delightfully mild in the south.* **Currency:** *The dirham: 5.06 dirhams=$1.* **Principal European languages:** *French in the greater portion of the country which had been under French control; Spanish in the small ex-Spanish area and in the onetime International Zone of Tangier (where virtually every tongue is spoken); English in hotels, travel bureaus, transport terminals, leading restaurants and night spots. Arabic is the official language.* **Domestic transport:** *Royal Air Inter, domestic division of Royal Air Maroc connects the major centers, as do modern buses. There is also a fairly extensive rail network, (many trains are air-conditioned), and some five thousand miles of remarkably good roads, car ferries link Tangier with several Spanish ports, and Gibraltar; and Casablanca, with still other European cities.* **Further information:** *Moroccan National Tourist Office, 597 Fifth Avenue, New York 10017; Office National Marocain du Tourisme, 22 Avenue d'Alger, Rabat, Morocco.*

INTRODUCING MOROCCO

The number of Americans who visit southern Europe and bypass Morocco remains legion. Though it is the westernmost of the Moslem countries, quite the most accessible to Americans, superbly well equipped for tourism, and one of the most fascinating countries in the world, Americans more often than not overlook it, except for a few who consider themselves brave souls when they traverse the Strait of Gibraltar for a glance at Tangier and a quick return to Europe. There is, of course, nothing the matter with a visit to Tangier—long or short. But it offers little more than an introductory sampling of what lies in store to the south. Morocco is, after all, the home of the descendants of those Moors who changed the faces of Spain and Portugal. The Alhambra of Granada has antecedents in every city of Morocco. The wrought-iron grillwork of Andalusian balconies is Moroccan-inspired. The flat-roofed houses of southern Portugal are of Moorish design. The very word *morocco,* which has become a synonym for leather, takes its name from this country.

Morocco's architecture and craft genius alone are enough to make a visit worthwhile. But besides its talented builders and craftsmen, Morocco has known great philosophers, mathematicians, astronomers, teachers, clerics, merchants, and sailors for many, many centuries. It has known fanatics and plunderers as well, but they brought with them to Europe many facets of a culture which many Europeans now take for granted and mistakenly accept as European-inspired.

Before the Arabs swept over North Africa and into Morocco in the seventh century, Morocco had already had a long, eventful history. Its indigenous Berber peoples had been colonized by the Phoenicians of Carthage a century before the Christian era began, and were superseded as conquerors by the Romans who called the area Mauretania. They lost out after six centuries to the ubiquitous Vandals, who met *their* Waterloo with the arrival of the Arabs. Arab and Berber dynasties controlled Morocco from that time until the latter part of the nineteenth century, when the Europeans began to get into the act. The French, British, and Germans were all interested in extending their domains across the Mediterranean, and worked out a series of complex deals among themselves—after much bickering—which ultimately gave *carte blanche* to the French. Presumably to restore order, the French—not without an armory of weapons—signed an agreement with the Moroccan authorities under which Morocco became a French "protectorate." The sultan was allowed to stay on as religious leader of the overwhelmingly Moslem population, but was otherwise a figurehead. Later, similar arrangements were made with the Spanish for the much smaller area of the country which they annexed. Tangier was declared an international zone, and run by a committee of consuls representing not a few but *nine* nations—Belgium, France, United Kingdom, Italy, the Netherlands, Portugal, Spain, Sweden, and the United States. Somehow or other, this turned out *not* to be a case of too many cooks spoiling the broth, and Tangier thrived as a free port and free currency zone.

But after World War II the nationalist movement gained strength, and the French—not at all graciously—gave in, after bloody demonstrations, as did the Spanish and the nine occupiers of Tangier. Only the towns of Ceuta and Melilla remain foreign-controlled; they are still Spanish. The tiny desert enclave of Ifni (capital: Sidi Ifni) was surrendered to Morocco by Spain in 1969. The current King, Hassan II, succeeded his father, Mohammed V, upon the latter's death in 1961. Mohammed V had been a strong and popular leader who straddled the line between the conservative Moslem culture and that of the modern West. His son suspended Parliament in 1965 and declared a state of emergency. In 1969 Morocco was granted association with the European Common Market, an arrangement that is expected to bolster Morocco's economy. In 1970 the state of emergency ended and a new constitution was adopted. But the following year, in July, a bloody revolt in Rabat almost toppled the throne. Top army officers attempted to overthrow Hassan in a raid on his palace at Skirhat, in the midst of an elaborate party, with many diplomats among the guests. Months later, the King arrested six cabinet ministers and a number of lesser officials on corruption charges, at which time it became clear that the chief reason for the July revolt was discontent with extravagance and hanky-panky in high places. In 1972, the people voted decisively for still another constitution, which would change Morocco into a limited constitutional monarchy. The decade of the seventies did not commence happily for Morocco—with a distrusted bureaucracy, agitation for reform from left-wing and other groups, and the centuries-long poverty of a people whose rich culture is one of the most remarkable in Africa.

YOUR VISIT TO MOROCCO

The great majority of Moroccans live much as they have for centuries, but the visitor will find—and not at exorbitant cost—luxury hotels, fine restaurants, modern transportation, deft service in principal cities and resorts throughout the kingdom. To give credit where it is due, it is the French whom today's visitor must thank for these amenities. Under the direction of a perceptive administrator, Marshal Lyautey, the French undertook to modernize the country without disturbing the folkways of its peoples, their homes, towns, villages, and even places of business.

As a result, a European quarter was built alongside the Medina, or Old Town, in all the major cities; railroads were constructed, hotels went up, restaurants opened, and the French language and culture were transported by settlers from across the Mediterranean to supplement—but not to replace—the heritage of the Moroccans. All of this took place while the Arabs and Berbers went about business as usual—dressing, eating, working, traveling, and praying much as they always had. Lyautey forbade any European-style construction in the Medinas, and strictly forbade any non-Moslems to enter mosques. He was the first of the important colonial administrators to show any appreciable concern for, and appreciation of, the culture and way of life of an occupied people. And though his point of view is one which many people today would consider little more than a combination of courtesy and common sense, it was unusual in its time. There are still parts of the world where it has not yet been emulated.

Tangier: Located just across the Strait of Gibraltar from southern Spain and Britain's Gibraltar Colony, Tangier, not so long ago was governed by representatives of nine foreign powers. Now it is a Moroccan city, just like any other. Its appeal to those visitors who frequented it with get-rich-quick schemes, is now lessened. But the flavor of Tangier is still delicious. It is the most cosmopolitan of the Moroccan cities, even today. One hears virtually every European language in its streets and cafés and on its beaches, as well as the Arabic and Berber tongues of its Moroccan residents. Its beaches are among the loveliest on the Mediterranean, its night life is gay and bouncy, and it is probably safe to say that it has more good restaurants, hotels and night spots than any other town in the kingdom. The center of the Medina, or Old Town, is the Grand Socco—a vast, color-splashed square which somehow manages to combine all of the sights, sounds, and odors of the Afro-Arab world. At the other end of the Medina is the Petit Socco, reached by a maze of tiny, winding alleys, covered *souks*—market stalls—on either side of them. The walk is hot and somewhat tiring, but there are cafés at the termination point for relaxation and a view of Tangier's multilingual, diversely costumed inhabitants. Up on a summit, high above the city and the harbor, is the Kasbah, ancient palace-fortress of the sultans, and nearby is an old café, perfectly situated for strollers anxious to sip Moroccan mint tea as they take in the view. The European sectors of the town are modern but otherwise undistinguished. Tangier is exciting for those to whom it is the first North African port of call. But if there is enough time on the visitor's itinerary for other parts of Morocco, a few days there are quite sufficient—unless one's chief interests are bistros and beaches, in which case a longer, relaxing stay is ideal.

Tetuán: Formerly the capital of what was Spanish Morocco, Tetuán is worth the 38-mile drive from Tangier, if only to gain an idea of how much less the Spanish developed their territory than did the French and the International Committee of Tangier. This is not to say that the city is without appeal. It is built on Mount Dersa, encircled by thriving farms and verdant gardens, and is home to seventeen mosques (Sidi Saïdi is the handsomest), and a fine old synagogue erected by the Jews, who rebuilt the ancient town in 1492—yes, 1492—after their expulsion from Portugal. The Jewish quarter—the Mella—is interesting strolling territory, and offers, as it does in every Moroccan city, a great contrast with the Arab Medina, in Tetuán's case bordered by great old gates. Riffian people (named for the Rif Mountains of the region) live in and about Tetuán. Their costumes are found nowhere else in the country: red-and-white-striped shawls, embroidered leather gaiters, and enormous straw hats—not unlike those of Thai farmers—with blue pompons hanging from them. Nearby: the Roman ruins of *Tamuda* and *Río Martín Beach*—15 miles of snowy white sands.

Ketama: A small village at an elevation of 6000 feet, in the Rif Mountains, Ketama is being developed as an international ski resort by an Italian firm, Agip Mineraria. Less than 140 miles from Tangier, the village is encased by groves of cedar trees. Its slopes are wide but rarely oversteep, and mild winds blowing up from the Sahara keep the temperatures moderate, so that there is snow only from January through March. During the remaining months of the year, Ketama—with its modern accommodations (including a luxurious motel) and handsome setting—can serve as a pleasant rest haven in between bouts of more hectic Moroccan sightseeing; Mediterranean beaches are but 25 miles distant.

Casablanca: Wealthiest, largest (three-quarters of a million people), most Western (skyscrapers are towering), with the most industry and a showplace of a harbor, Casablanca owes its modern façade to the French, who built it up from a small town to a great metropolis within the first decades of this century. Its name (meaning "white house" in Spanish) still describes it aptly, except that today many of the houses are considerably taller than was the case when Europeans named the place, simply by translating the Arabic title, *Dar el Beida*. Even the Medina in

"Casa"—as it is called throughout Morocco—has a New Look, for it was here that the French experimented and built a modern Arab quarter to supplement the still extant old one. Though the architecture is traditional—square, white, cubicle-shaped houses with no outer windows and an inner patio—the new Medina is unique in Morocco; no other city has one. On the outskirts of town is the Anfa Hotel (named for an ancient settlement on the site), where Roosevelt and Churchill met during World War II. It overlooks a series of smart beach clubs, all open to the public, and with salt-water pools cleverly built into rocks near the ocean's edge. Besides smart boulevards, shops, and office buildings, the mainly European sector is graced by a contemporary-style Roman Catholic cathedral, built on modified Moorish lines, and with stained-glass windows that are superb gems of that art. It is from Casablanca that transportation connections are best for visits to the four Imperial Cities—Rabat, Fez, Meknès and Marrakesh—each history-filled, tradition-laden, and the site of a royal palace.

Rabat: Closest of the imperial cities to Casablanca—it is about an hour's bus, car, or train ride away—is Rabat, the capital. Smaller, quieter, less bustling than its big neighbor, it is another gleaming white city, though devoid of skyscrapers. Its European quarter has elegance and charm quite unlike any other North African town. The French administrators who built it took care to make themselves comfortable in the pleasantest of surroundings, including brilliant gardens surrounding the buildings which once housed the French Residency and are now headquarters of the Moroccan government. Here are to be visited—besides the Triangle de Vue, the Belvedere, Essai, and Udayia gardens, the last with a delightful Moroccan patisserie-café—the Museum of Moroccan Art, the Bab er Rouah and Oudaiya Kasbah gateways, which date back to the great Almohades dynasty, and the landmark of Rabat—its Eiffel Tower and Statue of Liberty—the Tour (Tower) Hassan, designed to have been the largest in Islam, in Romano-Byzantine style, and the site of the modern albeit traditional-design King Mohammed V memorial—a splendid repository of Moroccan art. Though now in ruins, it may still be climbed. From its roof, there is a superb view of all Rabat as well as its sister city, *Salé,* just across the Bou Regreg River, guarded by centuries-old ramparts, and jampacked with neat white houses, a fascinating medina, and a Medersa—or Moslem college—with a patio dating back to the thirteenth century. Here too is the tomb of Sidi Abdallah ben Hassoun—patron saint of Salé—and nearby is the coastal Sidi Moussa sanctuary, and the two-hundred-year-old G'Naoua Kasbah, a fort built by Sultan Moulay Ismail. *Chella,* known in Roman times as *Sala Colonia,* is just outside Rabat, and popular as a promenade site for Moroccans as well as a sightseeing destination for tourists who find it incongruous for veiled ladies and djellaba-clad men to be strolling past its triple-arched gate, through its forum, baths, and wide streets. It is, understandably, hard to believe that Morocco had been as integral a part of Rome as the Italian homeland. There is one other Rabat highlight, which can be experienced only if the visitor is in the city on a Friday. On that day, each week—the Moslem sabbath—the King leaves his palace on an opulently decorated horse, and rides, accompanied by a glittering mounted retinue of scarlet-clad foot troops, to the Djamaa Abel Fez Mosque, where he presides over prayers. The pageantry is equaled in Africa only by the durbars of northern Nigeria.

Meknès: Encircled by some 25 miles of ramparts and bastions, Meknès is largely the heritage of Sultan Moulay Ismail, and the site of his tomb. Dominated by the immense, intricately decorated Bab el Mansour—the principal gate—it is a city of bigness: the big gate, big artificial lakes, a big royal palace, and even big gardens, mostly hidden behind equally big walls. Meknès's *souks* are distinguished by their carpet-makers' stalls; the rugs of the region are now among the most popular of Moroccan floor coverings in Western homes. Here too are embroideries unlike any other in the kingdom; with other local crafts, they are displayed at the Dar Jamai art museum. But it is the great gate—the Bab Mansour, its walls covered with the gay skullcaps of the hat sellers—that one remembers most in Meknès, along with the awe-inspiring bronze doors of the Bou Inania Medersa.

Fez: This is not only the city which gave its name to the red tasseled cap of the Moslem world. It is also the oldest of the Moroccan Imperial Cities. Sultan Idris II founded it in 808 as a trading post, but for many centuries it has been renowned as a leading intellectual center of Islam. Most of its Medersas and other educational institutions—Karaouine University is the best known—are open to visitors. The *souks,* whose streets are protected from the sun by raffia and straw arcades, are the narrowest and most winding of any in the country. Other highlights are the Karaouine Mosque with nearly 300 columns and 16 naves, the elaborate gateway of the Andalusian Mosque, and the gardens of Bou Jelud overlooking the old town, and, near the Dar Batha museum, and Dar Beida palace. Fez should first be seen in toto from the elevated road which encircles it; sunset is the ideal time of day for such a drive; the view is one of the most memorable in Africa. Near the city—besides the old towns of *Ifrane, Azrou, Khénifra,* and *Kasba Tadla,* is a phase of the new Morocco—the Bin el Widane, one of the highest dams on the continent.

Marrakesh: The farthest south of the quartet of Imperial Cities and the chief town of southern Morocco is Marrakesh—from which came the name Morocco, a purely European appellation. Had I a choice of visiting but one city in this country it would be Marrakesh, the most magnificent of them all. (Sir Winston Churchill spent many winter holidays there.) Marrakesh lies below eternally snow-covered Atlas Mountain peaks. It is surrounded by a palm grove embracing thirty thousand acres, and made even greener by the olive orchards of the Agdal and Menara gardens. And just to the south is the Sahara itself. Within the town, the newcomer is transfixed as he goes from one great monument to another in this thousand-year-old city founded by the Almoravides dynasty and embellished by the Saadians: the ingeniously designed pale green minaret of the Koutoubia Mosque—the most famous in Africa; the Ben Yussef Medersa, with its mosaics, marbles, and wood carvings; the superb tombs of the Saadian sultans in a palace of their own; the Bahia Palace, with its Moorish gardens and a *décor* reminiscent of

Andalusia in Spain; the lovely gate, Bab Aguenau; the sparkling El Mouasine and Eshrob ou Shouf ("Drink and Admire") fountains, and the *souks*—alive not only with the djellaba-clad townsfolk but the strangely costumed tribesmen down from Atlas slopes and Sahara oases, with their wives, children, camels, and donkeys, browsing among the stalls of the leatherworkers, shoemakers, dyers (oh, the brilliance of dyed yarn drying in the sun!), brassworkers, spice merchants, weavers, and even antique dealers—who often tempt visitors from abroad. Toward the end of the day, as the sun drops behind the mountains, the *pièce de résistance* of Marrakesh comes alive: the Place Djemaa el-F'na, which can be more easily described than pronounced. It is an enormous market square, with elaborately costumed water boys, snake charmers, holy men, public correspondents, musicians, dancers—all plying their wares or offering their services, wherever there is space enough, amid the crowds of strollers. Not far from this spectacle—the most intricately staged Italian opera could not begin to duplicate it—is Marrakesh's sleek, chic casino, and a string of fine hotels, one of whose gardens—the Mamounia—deserve a sightseeing visit. Beyond the town are any number of excursion points in the mountains, not the least of which, at least for skiers, is *Oukaïmeden*, on the slopes of the Toubal range.

Goulimine and the Bani oases: South of Marrakesh—the gateway to the desert—is Goulimine, the chief community among a string of oases collectively known as the Bani. It is here that the so-called Blue People live, dressed always in robes of blue, and with blue-tinted skin as well—a centuries-old precaution against the rays of the sun which is long since regarded as ineffectual, but still practiced for tradition's sake. The Blue People—mostly nomadic wanderers—fill the *souks* of Goulimine, particularly its Sunday camel markets. This town—vivid with the color of its people set against the neutral setting of the sands—is a departure point for the great caravans which trek south across the Sahara, and serves the same purpose for the visitor who would have a look at the other oases of the Bani region, as well as the fertile, river-bordered villages of the *Dra Valley*, and its chief town, *Zagora*.

Coastal resorts: A number of fascinating old cities border the Atlantic coast and double as coastal resorts. *Agadir*, until the tragic 1960 earthquake, was queen of the coastal resorts and has made a remarkable recovery. It is once again Morocco's leading resort—with accommodations running a wide gamut, even including a Club Mediterranée. Other resorts include *Fédala* (only 15 miles from Casablanca), which has known Europeans since the fourteenth century; *Mazagan*, a Roman trading post, a sixteenth-century Portuguese stronghold (with churches and remarkable cisterns from that era still extant), and a splendid, hotel-lined beach; and *Safi*, still with a Portuguese fortress and seafront castle, from whose dungeon tower one gains a fine view of the coast; *Mogador*, handsomely designed by a French architect for Sultan Moulay Abdallah, with *souks* of craftsmen specializing in furniture and wood marquetry, and again, fine beaches and hotels.

Moulay Idris and Volubilis: These two great cities—one among the holiest cities of Islam, the other a shell of a great third-century Roman settlement—are within just a few miles of each other, and within excursion distance of both Meknès and Fez. Volubilis, though in a better state of preservation than Tunisia's Carthage, cannot come close to Libya's Leptis Magna. Still, the Triumphal Arch of Caracalla remains imposing, good portions of the city walls still stand, and one can see bits and pieces of the forum, the Gallien Baths, and the dwelling houses, as well as sculpture, mosaics and bronzes in a little museum on the site. Moulay Idris is something else again—a city so revered by the Moslems that only members of the faith may live there. Visitors are, however, welcome between sunrise and sunset. Founded in 788 by the great-grandson of the Prophet Mohammed's son-in-law, it straddles the slopes of two rocky pinnacles and extends all the way down to the flat plains of an intervening valley. Its fairground is the frequent sight of *fantasias*, or fairs, the climaxes of which are horse races at which opulently turbaned, heavily bearded chieftains charge down a wide track, riding horses saddled in red and green gold-tooled leather, and shooting rifles into the air as they approach the finish line. Should you be lucky enough to be in the audience, you'll probably be the only non-Moroccan. There are no bleachers and no refreshment stands or rest rooms. One stands, with families in from the countryside, accompanied by children, livestock, round loaves of bread, and earthenware jugs of water.

SHOPPING

Of the major cities, Marrakesh generally offers the lowest prices in its *souks,* although there is great variety in every important town, and bargaining is *always* the rule, even in the more elaborate shops; the first price quoted by a merchant can easily be three to five times what he expects to receive. Best buys are hand-woven woolen rugs. Designs and weaving techniques vary, but the best are considered those of the Moyen-Atlas (Middle Atlas) region, with the Haut-Atlas (High Atlas) following. Although Marrakesh is in the latter region, both types can be purchased there. The bigger rug *souks* are usually reliable and well equipped to ship to America. No rug should be bought unless there is affixed to it—by wire and a metal seal—a green and white card which certifies its region of origin and its quality. These certificates are issued by the government and are necessary for any rugs passing through Moroccan customs for export. Also worthwhile are copper and brass trays, wrought-iron lanterns and chandeliers, and leather, leather, leather—that magnificent Moroccan leather, soft and smooth, tooled by hand in gold and red and green, in designs both classically simple and intricately elaborate. Look for desk pads and folders, wallets, book covers, women's handbags, change purses, glove-soft slippers as well as babouches—heavy white or yellow footwear which Moroccans wear as shoes. Items actually stamped in gold bear the legend, "Or 20 carats." Don't be upset if the shopkeeper is asleep on a mat when you enter his *souk.* He is simply napping between customers. As soon as one approaches, he arises, slips into his babouches, and is *à votre service.* Which *souk* for which product? Most are not labeled with the names of owner-artisans. There are dozens in each category in every city;

shop around and make your own choice—or, if in a hurry, flip a coin and hope for the best.

CREATURE COMFORTS

I have never stayed at a bad Moroccan hotel. The French built well and the Moroccans are continuing in that tradition. Cuisine is either French (a synonym for delicious) or Moroccan. The latter's many excellent specialties include *couscous*—steamed chicken, lamb, and vegetables with semolina; *pastilla*—a kind of meat (usually pigeon) pie, with almonds; skewered and roast lamb; delicious grilled sausages known as *merguez; tajines*—a casserole dish with either a meat or a fish/seafood base; the flat, chewy bread called *ksra;* rich pastries; mint tea (the traditional beverage of hospitality); and good wines, both red and white. Service is frequently deft, surroundings attractive, and very often, luxurious. **Tangier:** There are a number of *luxe*-category hotels. El Minzah—Moroccan architecture, splendid gardens, bar, restaurants, central location—is exemplary. So are the Rif and Les Almohades. Only a mite less posh are the Velazquez and the Grand Hotel Villa de France, with the Rembrandt, and the Africa among those following. **Casablanca:** El Mansour, a French-style skyscraper with all facilities, is the longtime No. 1—and deservedly so. Its neighbor, the Marhaba, is also very good indeed, and so are the Anfa, Plaza, and Transatlantique, with the beachfront Anfa Plage worth noting, too. **Rabat:** The Rabat Hilton is one of the most inventively and beautifully designed of Hiltons around the world; all facilities, of course. The Tour Hassan is quiet, opulent, a replica of a Moroccan palace with style and charm. Other leaders include the Balmina, Rex, Grand, and Royal. **Fez:** Palais Jamai, not a replica of a palace, but *actually* a former palace—world-famed, justly so, and with a modern one-hundred-room addition, and swimming pool. The modern Merinides and Holiday Inn are also luxury-class, with the Ramada and Zalagh following. **Meknès:** The elderly Transatlantique remains the luxury leader, with the small but attractive Dar Essaada, the Palace, and the Nice following. **Marrakech:** The Mamounia is one of the great traditional hotels. Its gardens are splendid, and so are facilities within. Es Saadi is a major competitor—luxurious and elegant. The Menara, Marrakech, and Almoravides are all good, too. The Ramada Inn and the Holiday Inn are motel-style. **Agadir's** long-established Marhaba remains tops, with the modern Almohades in the same luxury category, and the smart Kasbah, the Atlas, El Oumnia, and Mabrouk following. **Tetuan:** The Dersa is No.1, with the National trailing. **Safi:** Mimosas. **Ketama:** Tidighine. **Sidi-Ifni:** Ait-Baamran. **Goulimine:** Salam. (Club Meditérranee members note: There are club outposts at Agadir, Al Hoceima, Marrakech, Ouarzazate, Smir-Restinga, and Tangier.)

MOZAMBIQUE

Entry requirements: *A visa, obtainable from Portuguese consulates, a health certificate (smallpox and yellow fever), and an onward ticket.* **Best time for a visit:** *The dry season—April to October—is the pleasantest; at other times there is some rain and more humidity.* **Currency:** *The Mozambique escudo, at par with the Portuguese escudo. About 29 escudos=$1.* **Principal European language:** *Portuguese, with English a surprisingly popular second, thanks to the influence of neighboring Rhodesia and South Africa.* **Domestic transport:** *Roads and railroads are poor, but air service is efficient, widespread, and recommended.* **Further information:** *Propaganda Department, Mozambique Harbours and Transport Administration, Lourenço Marques, Mozambique; Casa de Portugal, 570 Fifth Ave., New York.*

INTRODUCING MOZAMBIQUE

Mozambique has known visitors for many, many centuries. Today the callers are merchant mariners whose ships fly flags from nations on every continent, as well as large numbers of tourists and businessmen from the neighboring countries of Rhodesia and South Africa. This Portuguese colony, with its long Indian Ocean coast, has known many peoples and many cultures—including those of its own peoples.

There were the very ancient travelers, Greeks among them, and the later Arabs of the medieval centuries. The Portuguese were the first of the Europeans, but they did not come until 1498, by which time the coastal cities had developed into Afro-Arab communities, in many ways as rich and advanced as many towns of Europe, prospering on a trade of gold brought from the kingdoms of the interior (like that of Zimbabwe) which they sold to the Indians, the Chinese, and the Arabs, importing their products in exchange.

The language of that era—Swahili—manifested the culture which had evolved: a blend of the Arabic with the indigenous African, with the dominance, archaeologists now believe, heavily African, and not the reverse, as most colonials today like to think.

Even before the tenth century, Arabs were trading at the late, great city of Sofala (near contemporary Beira), and then a part of the African kingdom of Waqlimi. There was, too, the interior city of Sena, which the Portuguese were later to discover, and whose ruins can still be seen.

Da Gama and his Portuguese successors plundered, murdered, exploited, in the European fashion of the time. They hit upon ports dealing in metals—iron, copper, and gold; shells—ivory and tortoise; and probably the richest of the commodities—and the most tragic—slaves. They took over as quickly and as ruthlessly as possible, destroying much, but getting rich in the process, and as they did so, they rationalized their record by coming to believe that their mission was a "civilizing one," one bringing their "superiority" to the "savagery" of Africa. The fact that they came upon settled cities, with tall houses, walled forts, elaborate palaces which they all but destroyed, managed not to conflict with the legends they effectively disseminated. Now there are but fragmentary ruins of the African civilizations with which the Portuguese came in contact.

The Portuguese have never left Mozambique, but it is only in recent years that they have begun to develop it. Even now, only the major cities are modern; most of the population of eight million—predominantly African—remains poor, illiterate, and often exploited by the great white plantation owners who practice a form of forced labor, or semislavery, calling it "directed labor."

Authorities officially deplore "directed labor" but seem to do little to discourage it. Their point of view—the official one in Portugal and the colonies—is that every able-bodied person must work, that idle hands do not help Portuguese economy.

Archaic and cruel as Portuguese policy is in many ways, it is without the rigid color bars of South Africa and Rhodesia. A tiny percentage of Africans takes advantage of the *assimilado* scheme, under which an African who is well enough educated and Roman Catholic may apply for full-citizenship status and the privilege of working at white-collar occupations at the white-salary scale. The hitch is that not enough such jobs exist, and the *assimilado*, even if he cannot get a favored job, even if the only work he can get is menial and with a minimal salary, must pay taxes at the white man's level. As a result, the ranks of the *assimilados* remain a drop in the bucket, and the overwhelming majority of blacks are kept down, economically as well as politically—even though miscegenation is not illegal.

Most other European-dominated countries are more advanced in every other way, but the Portuguese (with the French) are unique in their lack of bigotry on the basis of race. They remain paternalistic, believing that the Africans are descendants of savages who, like children, need "guidance." But at least there is an appreciation of African art, and there is an atmosphere in Mozambique which is gay, relaxed, and—despite the poverty and the dictatorial government—amazingly relaxed. It is what draws holidaying South Africans from their apartheid atmosphere and Rhodesians from their "partnership policy" setting. It is a blend of Afro-Portuguese charm and hospitality.

Mozambique, and indeed all the Portuguese colonies, are now called "autonomous regions" by the Portuguese, who somehow or other believe this terminology will convince the world that they are quite as integral a part of the mother country as are its metropolitan provinces. They are not, of course. In my experience, even Portuguese officials occasionally make a slip and call Mozambique a "colony"—quickly correcting themselves. Even Portuguese residents resent the government's piddling development program. It takes out a great deal more than it puts in.

Until 1964 there was no significant underground nationalist

movement in Mozambique, but in that year guerrilla uprisings, aimed at gaining independence, began in the north. Dominated by the Mozambique Liberation Front, popularly known as Frelimo, the guerrilla war was headed by Dr. Eduardo C. Mondlane until 1969, when he was assassinated. Despite this setback, the insurrection has persisted for more than seven years and by 1972, more than a quarter of the area of the countryside was reported held by Liberation forces, whose leaders set up schools and health facilities in places that had never before known them.

While not quite as big as its sister colony, Angola, on the west coast, Mozambique is still substantial—ten times as large in area as Portugal, and with an Indian Ocean frontage of 1100 miles. Of the two territories, it is by far the more developed for tourism.

YOUR VISIT TO MOZAMBIQUE

Lourenço Marques: The Portuguese are a century behind the rest of Europe, their government is autocratic, their policy toward Africans paternalistic, their industrial development minimal, their literacy rate low. One can go on and on. But there is no denying that, despite inadequacies, they know how to live graciously. Nowhere is this more evident than in Lourenço Marques, the capital of Mozambique, and the major port, as well, for the gold-rich Transvaal province of South Africa. This is a city of informal sidewalk cafés, great *praças* or squares, inlaid with mosaic-tile sidewalks similar to those of Lisbon and Rio de Janeiro; good hotels, miles of bathing beaches, and swimming pools, as well; restaurants which specialize in African-style barbecued chicken and succulent jumbo shrimp; cafés for dancing and for listening to *fado* singers flown from Lisbon; bullfights with participants also imported from the motherland; gingerbread-decorated public buildings which somehow are perfectly appropriate in Portuguese Africa, and gracious, courteous people—both African and European. Lourenço Marques is named for a Portuguese explorer who first visited it in 1544. For centuries it was nothing more than a military garrison. One of its old forts still stands and is now a museum, full of mementos of Mozambique history. It was not until 1897 that the modern city began to develop, for in that year it became the capital of the colony; up until then, the *island* of Moçambique, in the north, had served as the seat of government. Besides the fort's museum, there is another—the Alvaro de Castro, in an elaborate Manueline-style building. It ranks among Africa's most interesting, particularly because of its mounted specimens of wildlife in the bush, and for the display—unique in the world—of the various stages of gestation of the elephant. A Lourenço Marques tour might also include a visit to the modern Roman Catholic Cathedral of Our Lady of the Conception, the elegantly appointed reception rooms of the immense Town Hall, the bustle of the harbor, where ships are berthed from all over the world, the African quarters of the city—neat but simple—and the newer and of course richer residential sections of the Europeans. There are a number of excursions that can be taken into the surrounding countryside, but the most interesting is a day's trip to *Vila Luisa,* a little town on the left bank of the Incomati River. After arrival, visitors board a boat for a journey upriver and views of the great numbers of hippopotamuses and crocodiles that line its banks. The hippos concentrate on areas of their own, and generally keep their young with them at all times; occasionally they go ashore and sun themselves, and at other times they argue with each other, and considerably intense altercations ensue. The crocodiles are deceptively shy, and take refuge on narrow islands in the river, or else lie in wait on its banks for victims.

Beira: A two-hour flight north of Lourenço Marques is Beira. It is to landlocked Rhodesia and Malawi what Lourenço Marques is to the Transvaal: the chief port. Development of Beira has been phenomenal in recent years, and it is a modern town with pleasant hotels, fine shops, and the gracious squares which the Portuguese consider an essential in a city of any size. Besides its beaches and swimming pools, and its harbor, it is of touristic interest as a departure point for safaris into the Gorongosa Game Reserve.

Gorongosa Game Reserve: One of the least toured of Africa's animal parks, and one of the least developed, Gorongosa abounds in wildlife—perhaps because it is relatively unlittered by the presence of too many visitors. It can be reached by car in about six hours from Beira. The roads are not always smooth, but the countryside is lush and lovely, and at one point motor vehicles must be transported across the rapids of a shallow river by means of simply constructed rafts. Not far from the distant bank is a modern rest camp with a fine dining room and comfortable cabins. By the time one has taken a few drives through the reserve, it is almost inevitable that a lion—or indeed a whole pride of lions—will have been spotted. And, in addition, the area is alive with towering giraffe, great herds of shy zebra, immense buffalo, and many varieties of antelope. Though relatively small in area, Gorongosa is one of the greenest and most beautiful of Africa's national parks. Besides game-viewing at Gorongosa, which is exciting enough to please the most adventurous of visitors, it is possible to organize old-style safaris, for both shooting and photography, into unprotected game reserves such as *Chemba*, north of Beira. The rates are hardly for the budget traveler: one hunter charges almost $1300 for a single "client" on a fifteen-day trip, and about $1800 for a pair of clients; this can easily be upped by more than $200 for "extras," such as licenses and ammunition.

Moçambique Island: Not far from the Tanzanian border, in the north, is the tiny town of *Lumbo*, just across the water from the Island of Moçambique. Least exploited of the colony's attractions is the little-known island for which the entire colony is named. (It is actually no longer an island, having recently been connected to the mainland by a causeway.) It was to Moçambique that the Portuguese came in the late fifteenth century, and just a few years later they erected there the greatest stone fortress in that region of Africa. It covers the southern tip of the island, protecting it by thick walls from the mainland. Ancient rooms beneath the walls—the waves of the sea beating outside the slit windows near the ceiling—house venerable cannonballs, yellowing documents, rusted armor, and other memorabilia of the fort's long history. Elsewhere on the oblong island are the still splendid Governor's Palace, lovely colonial houses, their stucco walls painted in varying pastel shades; and an African community distinguished by its women, who wear heavy white facial makeup during the day to protect their skin from the sun's rays. Visitors may stay on the island or in Lumbo; at all events, one is wise not to miss a walk around the fortress in the moonlight, as well as a daytime exploration of its ramparts.

Vilanculos, Inharosso, and the Paradise Islands: Two coastal resorts, on the mainland between Lourenço Marques and Beira, and a group of islands—technically known as the Bazarutos—have been developed in recent years as holiday spots, with Rhodesians the principal visitors. All are small, informal, relatively simple insofar as accommodation is concerned, and fantastically beautiful. Vilanculos is the transport terminus for the group. Planes reach its airport from Beira, and also from Salisbury and other cities in Rhodesia.

Besides Vilanculos and Inharosso on the mainland—both with modern hotels and bungalow colonies—there are these islands, all reached by launch from either of the mainland resorts: *Paradise* (or Santa Carolina) *Island:* coconut palms, tropical vegetation, less than two miles in length, restaurant, bar, dancing, bungalow-type accommodation—and superb beaches and fishing; *Bazaruto Island,* 30 miles long, 20 miles from the mainland, and fishing, fishing, fishing, with swimming as well, and bungalows but no dining room (visitors bring their food with them from the mainland); *Magaruque:* sister island to Bazaruto, with same type of accommodations, and a series of secluded bays, coral banks, and almost isolated beaches.

SHOPPING

Lourenço Marques is the best shopping center in the colony. Concentrate your purchases here in either the African or European markets; both are patronized by people of all races. At the European market, check the gift stalls for hand-carved African figures in soft wood. At the African market, look for all manner of

African *objets d'art*—ivory, woodcarving, assorted trinkets, and, most important of all, leopardskins. Similar markets in Beira and the smaller communities may also yield minor treasures. Bargaining is the rule.

CREATURE COMFORTS

HOTELS—**Lourenço Marques:** The Polana remains tops, on a cliff overlooking Delagoa Bay, with two swimming pools, tennis, golf, dancing, lovely gardens, agreeable bar and *boîte,* and food which might be tastier were it not for the demands of the largely English-speaking South African clientele; Girassol; Cardoso; Tivoli. **Beira:** Embaixador—handsome Afro-Portuguese *décor,* central location, modern, with dining rooms, *boîte,* bars; Residencia Hotel Beira. **Moçambique Island:** Pousada de Moçambique.

NIGER

République du Niger

Entry requirements: *A visa, obtainable from French consulates where Niger has no diplomatic representation, plus a health certificate (smallpox and yellow fever) and an onward ticket.* **Best times for a visit:** *The northern desert regions are hot, hot, hot the year round. But the southern areas offer a choice: rains from June through September (when most roads and trails are closed) and the dry months the rest of the year, except for a little rain in October and May. Coolest months: December and January.* **Currency:** *The CFA franc: CFA 280=$1.* **Principal European language:** *French, with English spoken in leading hotels and transport terminals.* **Domestic transport:** *Good domestic air services, a road network, passenger steamers on the Niger River, no railroads.* **Further information:** *Service d'Information de la République du Niger, Niamey, Niger.*

INTRODUCING NIGER

Not to be confused with its neighbor, the Federal Republic of Nigeria, the Republic of the Niger—a former province of French West Africa became semi-autonomous in 1958, along with its fellow territories, and with three others (Ivory Coast, Dahomey, and Upper Volta), it negotiated for complete freedom from the Paris government in August 1960. The former mother country, however, continues to provide some economic and technical aid to this landlocked and isolated nation that is also the recipient of U.S. largesse—in the form of a bridge across the Niger River in Niamey.

Tourism had never been discouraged during French days, but it had not, on the other hand, been fully exploited. The situation has changed since independence. And the traveler who would enjoy acquainting himself with a little-frequented land which blends the Moslem culture of the Sahara with the indigenous societies of Black Africa—and which is the chief gateway to one of the world's newest and biggest game reserves—will find comfortable accommodations.

Niger's first-known European visitor was the granddaddy of the explorers, the Scottish Mungo Park, who trekked through the area as long ago as 1805, shortly before his death in what is now Nigeria. But centuries earlier—between 1591 and 1595—Niger was the scene of fierce battles between victorious conquering Moroccans and the last rulers of the great Songhai Empire.

The Moslem influence of more than a millennium has long been strong, and in certain areas today the predominant religion combines both animist and Islamic elements—not unlike that in Haiti, where voodoo and Catholicism are often peculiarly mixed.

This is an immense country—almost half a million square miles in area, but with a population of less than four million. Its biggest town has less than 70,000 inhabitants. And it has no railroads.

But it does have a personality which is a mélange of Africa and France, even though the French did not invade the region until the latter years of the nineteenth century, establishing a military post in 1902 and formally setting up a territory in 1920—there being some stubborn sultans and chiefs to deal with in that interim.

YOUR VISIT TO NIGER

Niamey: On the banks of the Niger River, which flows through a surprisingly small portion of the country which bears its name, Niamey is remarkable for its magnificent sunrises and sunsets, which impart a wealth of brilliant colors over the river water and the buildings which hug its edge. The government ministries are astride a plateau overlooking the lower quarters, which contain the shops and offices and a great open market place. The Niamey National Museum displays the works of Niger's craftsmen—leatherwork, silver jewels, many-colored blankets, and other wares. A visit need not be longer than a day and a night—if within that time arrangements can be made for tours to the "W" National Park, Tahoua, Agadès, and Zinder.

"W" National Park: "W" is not an abbreviation for a many-syllabled African name, nor even for a French one. It is simply the shape of the route of the twisting Niger River within the region of this immense 4000-square-mile park. The first French designation for the area was adapted as the official title when the park was conceived in 1937, and formally opened in 1957. Remember, when speaking of it, that the French pronunciation of "W" is *double-vay.* This is the only game reserve in the world whose territory is in three countries. Besides Niger, the park is also a part of both Upper Volta and Dahomey. Niamey, in Niger, is the major city which is closest to it, however, and the most convenient departure point for visits to it. Reach it by either car or via the Niger River. A speedboat can make the 140 miles from Niamey to the Barou Falls in less than a day, and there is a fully equipped paddle steamer which follows the same course on an overnight journey. To be seen along the way are deceptively lazy crocodiles sleeping along the banks of the river, herds of immense hippos bathing, snorting, and showering streams of water into the air when they surface; great varieties of fish and aquatic birds; and, very often hollowed-out-log canoes—or pirogues—containing fishermen, some of whom have paddled hundreds of miles to catch a supply which will last them for many months, in dried form. The villages of the Zarema peoples are all about; these sturdy former warriors are experienced farmers and skilled craftsmen, working in pottery, metals, basketry, and textiles. The landlubber can reach the park from Niamey via the "tourist route"—by car through the eastern region of Upper Volta to *Diapaga,* a kind of county seat on whose outskirts is an official park rest camp, well equipped and with a restaurant. From there, trips can be made through the roads of the park for glimpses of what is considered the greatest collection of wildlife in West Africa—elephants, antelopes in great variety, cheetahs, lions, leopards, baboons, monkeys, in addition to the aforementioned hippopotamuses, crocodiles, and birds. There are special areas beyond the park where hunting is allowed, but this is primarily a photographer's paradise; take plenty of film, and count on more close-ups than you might think possible—even *without* a telescopic lens.

Tahoua: Tahoua's distinction lies with its people. It is on the dividing line of Niger's chief cultures: the sedentary blacks and the nomadic Tauregs, both of whom converge on its narrow streets and in its vast market place—at its most frenetic on Sundays. The black animists can often be seen at religious ceremonies, and on elaborate processional marches as well. And the Moslem Tauregs pray five times each day, either in their mosques or from reclining positions on improvised prayer rugs, wherever they may be.

Zinder: The ancient capital of Niger (Niamey has had that distinction only since 1927), Zinder is rich in the history and traditions of the Moslem sultans who were the last rulers before the French occupation. It is being modernized, slowly but surely, but its venerable façade still dominates. Originally a hunters' community, the town through the centuries became a headquarters for invaders from the north, and most of its monuments of today date back to the eighteenth century. There is an ancient fort with a superb tower, an execution block, remains of once strong fortifications and their gates, and the Sultan's Palace, whose interior chambers are open to visitors. The Zengou is the business quarter—particularly exciting on Fridays when Taureg nomads, itinerant Hausa traders and townspeople of various creeds and colors meet to trade, browse, and enjoy themselves, attired in costumes which run the gamut in style and hue and with all of the animation, gesticulation, and verve which make the market places of Africa the very essence of each community's society and culture.

Agadès: Not far from the Aïr Mountains, and just south of the

Sahara, Agadès wins, thumbs down, as the most fantastic of Niger's cities. Historians have long doted on it, regardless of the period of their specialty. It was, they have concluded, a region of hunters in prehistoric times. It was a center of Iron Age society in later centuries. It has been inhabited by Berbers since A.D. 700, and beginning in the fifteenth century the Tauregs have been among its residents. There have been feuds and rivalries and battles among its peoples for as long as the historians can dig deep in their researches. And among these would be the twentieth-century French. It was only in 1905 that they were able to erect a fort, and it was not until 1919 that they laid down their arms after subduing the Moslem forces. Agadès is justifiably proud of its past, and it has made little change in its façade since it was conquered by the Europeans, or once again liberated as a part of the sovereign Niger Republic. The immense market place dominates the center of the town, crowded with nomads in from the desert, artisans at work on their specialties, short-order cooks—if they may be called that—preparing their specialties in the open air. Houses with upstairs terraces surround the market, and a sixteenth-century mosque stands above the entire scene. Its high, delicate minaret may be climbed by even the non-Moslem, for a fine view of the town and the plain surrounding it. Nearby are the remains of the sixteenth-century Sultan's Palace and—in contrast—the early-twentieth-century *Poste Militaire*, a symbolic souvenir of the battle which brought the tricolor to this remote desert outpost.

SHOPPING

Niger's markets are packed with the splendid arts and crafts of its peoples: ironwork, including spears; gold and silver jewelry, hand-woven fabrics, leatherwork, basketry, carved figures and heads. Besides public markets, look for vendors in air terminals, hotel lobbies and the sidewalks surrounding them. Bargain everywhere.

CREATURE COMFORTS

HOTELS—In **Niamey,** the modern and comfortable Grand Hotel du Niger and Le Sahel are both air-conditioned and have swimming pools, as does the smaller, older Terminus. RESTAURANTS—Le Saigon serves Vietnamese specialties; La Flotille, Russian food. Other good restaurants—with French food—are La Pagode and Les Roniers. **Agadès:** Hotel de l'Aïr.

NIGERIA

Federal Republic of Nigeria

Entry requirements: *A visa, obtainable from the Nigerian consulates, or from British consulates where the Nigerians are not represented, plus a health certificate (smallpox and yellow fever) and an onward ticket.* **Best times for a visit:** *October to March—at least in the south. The rainy season—March to November in the south, April to September in the north—need not deter visitors, however. Rains are not constant, and the countryside during this period is fresh and green. Count on the kind of humidity familiar to New Yorkers, Philadelphians, St. Louisans, and Washingtonians, along the coast.* **Currency:** *The Nigerian pound, at par with the United Kingdom pound: 0.357=$1.* **Principal European language:** *English, which is also the official language, and widely spoken.* **Domestic transport:** *Air service to major towns, and abroad, as well, via Nigeria Airways—aided, as of 1972, with management assistance from TWA, following considerable public criticism of its operations; a railway system of some 2000 miles which is one of Africa's best, and a good network of all-weather highways linking all regions.* **Further information:** *Nigerian Consulate General, 575 Lexington Ave., New York; Embassy of Nigeria, Washington, D.C.; Federal Ministry of Information of Nigeria, Lagos, Nigeria.*

INTRODUCING NIGERIA

Nigeria is, in a word, fantastic. It is the most populous of all African countries—with some sixty-six million inhabitants who constitute one sixth of the population of Africa. It was, until it became independent on October 1, 1960, the largest non-self-governing territory of the British Commonwealth. It is the largest black country in the world, one of the most dynamic and exciting to visit, and with a potential which may someday make it the political leader of the African nations. It is, as well, the country from which great numbers of black Americans are descended. Slaves were being exported from Nigeria as late as the mid-nineteenth century. Area? Stretch it on a map of the United States and it would cover the eastern portion, extending as far west as Illinois, as far south as the Carolinas.

Nigeria has been inhabited for many thousands of years. Relics of the Stone Age have been discovered near Jos in the central part of the country. And in the early 1930s a discovery at the tiny village of Nok—near Jos—was one of the most revolutionary of modern archaeology. Investigators came upon heads sculpted in ceramic—naturalistic, representational, life-size or near life-size. And not long after, very similar pieces were discovered throughout the Jos region, making clear that from the year 2000 B.C. to the beginning of the Christian era a society inhabited this region which was the predecessor of many later developments in religion, art, and social patterns. Nok—as it is now known—was probably the earliest of the iron cultures in West Africa, and discovery of its relics made it necessary for Europeans to admit that Black Africans did produce a naturalistic as well as impressionistic art.

Vast Nigeria was included in the realms of a number of ancient empires. Songhai used Kano as its easternmost trading post—and it became rich from its dealings in the hand-dyed cloth and leather for which it is still noted. Its fine walls and superbly designed old buildings remain today as memorials of its past greatness. The Hausa—still a major Nigerian people—built up a series of small states which federated into the Kebbi Empire during medieval times. And perhaps the greatest of Nigerian artistic achievements were products of the Benin and Ife city-states. Not far from the Atlantic coast, Benin was discovered by the Portuguese in the fifteenth century. They settled there as traders, became palace guests of the King of Benin, who visited Portugal during his reign and began an exchange of ambassadors. Reports of the period indicate that Benin was not radically different, in many respects, from contemporary Portugal. Its art was discovered by the British only in 1897, and it was not until decades later that they—and other Europeans, forced to accept archaeologists' findings—had to admit that it was African-designed and African-made, even though it consisted largely of great wall plaques and busts superbly cast in bronze. Even more recently, in 1938, more bronzes were discovered in the palace of the Oba of Ife. These were even finer than the Benin masterpieces, and considerably more naturalistic and representational. Experts have concluded that they too were of African origin. The two groups—Benin and Ife—are Nigeria's greatest art treasures. Many of the former are in museums throughout the world—including several in the United States—but the Nigerians have succeeded in buying some back.

Although the British had been in Nigeria since 1553, it was not until 1861 that they took over the settlement at Lagos (named, incidentally, by the Portuguese for what is now a little backwater town on Portugal's south coast) and constituted it a colony. At the Berlin Conference in 1885, when the colonial powers carved up Africa among themselves, the British were given carte blanche to take over Nigeria. In 1914 the southern and northern regions were amalgamated into the Colony and Protectorate of Nigeria, and that same year Britain was given the west portion of the ex-German Kamerun, which it began to administer as a region of Nigeria. In 1951 a new constitution gave Nigerians a token measure of self-government—but not enough to satisfy them. They succeeded in getting the British to introduce still another constitution, in 1954, under which the Federation of Nigeria came into being.

In 1960 Nigeria became an independent federal state within the British Commonwealth, and in 1963 it became a Federal Republic divided into four regions: North, West, East, and Mid-west. Since independence Nigeria has been troubled by tribal conflicts among the country's three major peoples: the industrious and talented, largely Roman Catholic Ibo, who predominate in the East; the urbanized, sophisticated, Yoruba of the West, and the Moslem Hausa of the North. In 1966 a group of Eastern army officers overthrew the government and formed a new government under Major General Aguyi-Ironsi, an Ibo. Later in the year Ironsi was murdered as a result of another coup—this time by anti-Ibo forces—and a federal military government was set up. There followed a period of violence in which thousands of Ibos were murdered and more than one million were forced to flee from the North to the Eastern Region.

In 1967 the military government divided the country into twelve ethnically determined states to replace the former four regions. Shortly thereafter the former Eastern Region, long dominated by the Ibo, who were much resented by other residents of the area, seceded from the republic, proclaiming itself the Republic of Biafra. Fighting soon broke out between Biafran troops and federal troops, and the country was plunged into a bloody civil war. For the next thirty months the world watched in horror as nearly two million people—many of them children—starved to death in the blockaded region of Biafra, despite massive relief efforts. The Biafran conflict was a tragedy as well for the five million non-Ibos in the East who were trapped in a situation from which they could not escape.

Biafra capitulated in January 1970, and strong efforts are being made to reintegrate the Ibos, who now control only one state, the East Central, and to rebuild the wartorn cities of Biafra. Nigeria is a potentially great and powerful nation with rich industrial, agricultural, and oil resources, and her future lies in a strong policy of unification. The federal government's attitude has been one of remarkable goodwill and conciliation. As Major General Yakubu Gowon, the handsome, young, and popular head of state, has said: "Nothing will deter us from building a strong and united nation, which will be the pride of the black man wherever he may be." But despite his humanitarian reconciliation program, his intelligence, and his goodwill, General Gowan has not had an easy time. While he devoted considerable effort to making friends abroad for post-Biafra Nigeria—visiting more than a dozen African states as well as Israel (on a Middle East peace mission with three fellow African leaders)—problems at home remained pressing. Corruption, in and out of government, and a traditional bane of West African life, continued. So did high unemployment. And inflation. And excessive spending by an apparently uncurbed army. And restless politicians anxious for a return to the kind of civil, representative government with which Nigeria was founded. Problems notwithstanding, Nigeria's friends continue to believe in it, and to wish it well.

YOUR VISIT TO NIGERIA

Given two full weeks, the visitor can tour the most interesting areas of Nigeria, utilizing the air routes. Here are the highlights—only the highlights.

Lagos: Earliest of the regions to know the Europeans, Lagos is the capital of Nigeria and its commercial center. The city of Lagos was once one of the most squalid of British African cities. Never with a large European community, it grew haphazardly and without careful planning, as did many of the British-colonized towns of West Africa. There was none of the concern for attractiveness which the French, Belgians, and Portuguese brought with them to Africa. Built on an island in a large lagoon, Lagos is connected to still another island—Iddo—by a bridge; Iddo is joined to the mainland too. Until the British stopped the practice, Lagos was so important a slave-trading center that its coastal area was known as the Slave Coast. It is only in recent years that this collection of shanties—or 'dobe shacks—has begun to be transformed into a city. Nigerians, with independence in sight, wanted a capital they could be proud of, and new construction is about as prevalent as it is in midtown Manhattan. (The real estate prices are comparable too.) Although Lagos still has one of the worst slums in Africa and beggars can still be seen in the capital, low-cost housing developments are replacing tin shacks as rapidly as they can be built. And Lagos can be proud of its plush, modern office buildings, its new luxury hotels, and its stores filled with consumer goods made in Nigeria.

Old Lagos has not, however, disappeared. The palace of the Oba (or chief) is much the same as it was when the Portuguese built it two and a half centuries ago. The immense public market —one of the most fascinating in Africa—still thrives, with wares running the gamut from marmalade to magic accessories (known colloquially as *juju* and including dried rats and birds, human and animal skulls, and other not-so-charming little charms). Modern department stores vie with tiny shops on the teeming business thoroughfares. And the Nigerian regional costume—brilliant-hued, loose tunics over matching trousers for the men, and long wraparounds for the women—adds flash and fire to the crowded streets and bridges. Relaxation? The town's environs abound in white-sand beaches, and there are facilities for fishing, sailing, and the sports which the British brought with them: polo, tennis, squash racquets, golf, and even billiards. Not to be missed under any circumstances are the National Museum, the largest in the country, housed in a fine building, with examples of the great Nigerian cultures—incomparable Ife and Benin bronzes, brass, and ivories, as well as woodcarvings, masks, and crafts of other regions and other eras; the National Hall, with its elaborately decorated doors; Omogbua Gallery of Art—both modern and traditional; and the Independence Building—Nigeria's tallest, with its exhibit of "made in Nigeria" products. Lagos at night is gay and informal, at least outside of the more stolid private clubs and homes of the British residents. Bars, dance halls, cinemas, festivals of varying types—all welcome the visitor. Whoever believes that the humid tropics makes for an indolent people has not visited Lagos! And if he would leave its teeming streets and proceed along its ocean-front marina to the modern harbor or *Apapa* across the lagoon he can see how it is keeping pace with contemporary commerce.

Western and Midwestern States: The former Western Region, now divided into two states, contains Nigeria's tallest skyscraper and is as well the site of its greatest traditional arts. *Ibadan*, with a population of over a million, is the capital of the Western State and the largest black city in the world—bigger than Lagos, and indeed larger than any other city between Cairo and Johannesburg. Enclosed by great mud walls, it is a town of drab little tin-covered houses, in great contrast to the trim, new Parliament House and ministries, and two of Nigeria's greatest institutions—the ultramodern Teaching Hospital and the University of Ibadan, one of tropical Africa's most important universities. Worth visiting, besides the academic buildings, are the strikingly designed Protestant chapel with its statue of the risen Christ, and the altar murals of the Roman Catholic chapel, with the Madonna and Child beautifully portrayed as Blacks. Another highlight of the Western State—besides drives through the lush green countryside and its villages—is *Abeokuta*, an ancient city whose thick walls were built as a fortification against slave-raiders, and whose leading chieftain—the Alake—occasionally receives foreign visitors. The traditional cloth-dyeing pits are an attraction of this town. Ife, spiritual capital of the Yoruba tribe, is known for its art treasures and its new university. *Benin*, the capital of the Midwestern State, has a museum full of its great bronze heads and plaques. Predominant throughout the two states are the two main groups of people—the Yoruba and the Edo. The Yorubas are among the most advanced of the African peoples and were living in large, well-organized urban communities long before the arrival of the Europeans. They are generally distinguishable by their blue clothing.

East Central, Rivers, South Eastern States: This is the area that, as the "Republic of Biafra," seceded from the republic in 1967. Before the war almost all the area was controlled by the Ibos, but now that it is divided into three states only the East Central, the poorest of the three, actually has an Ibo majority. There is a residue of hostility against the Ibos in Port Harcourt, the capital of the Rivers State, and throughout the area the Ibo problem persists. However, although one can still see scars of the civil war, the Nigerians have made strong efforts to repair and rebuild here in the East. With rare exceptions, the East had no powerful feudal chiefs such as the northern emirs or the western obas. It typifies the highly democratic and individualist society of much of West Africa, where the social organization was one of people and their elders rather than people and their chiefs. There is still a stronger sense of kinship within eastern tribal groups than in other areas. The Ibos—with a reputation in Nigeria for thrift, industry, and business acumen not unlike that of the Scots in the United Kingdom—are the traders of Nigeria. Ibo women are probably the most advanced of any eastern tribe; you'll see them all about at stalls and shop counters. There are no big cities in the region. *Enugu,* the capital of the East Central State, and *Port Harcourt* are post-World War I towns. *Calabar,* capital of the South Eastern State, and *Onitsha* in the East Central are the only old cities. The latter is distinguished by the Lady chapel of its Anglican Cathedral, designed by a British architect named Richard Nixon expressly for the tropical climate and the African setting of the city—and unique for these reasons, the British having generally favored buildings more suitable for Manchester or Birmingham in their African territories. Its other highlight is its public market, with some three thousand stalls, completed in 1957 at a cost of one and a half million dollars, and opened by Britain's Princess Royal—a fact appreciated by the market's traders, most all of whom are women, known as the Merchant Princesses of Onitsha. *Enugu* is distinguished mainly for its modern Parliament, or House of Assembly, the government ministries and modern schools, hospitals, and housing developments, and the rich coal mines, an unexpected surprise in tropical Africa.

Kwara, North Western, North Central, North Eastern, Benue Plateau States: These five states, along with Kano, once comprised the Northern Region, the latest to be occupied by the British (1903), and the last to attain self-government—just a year and a half before federation independence. It has had less contact with Europeans than any other region, but it has traded with Africans of the ancient empires of the Sudan—and with the Arabs and Berbers from north of the Sahara—for many centuries.

Its traditions are rich and proud, its culture complex and opulent, its faith predominantly Moslem, and its attractions for the visitor among the most glittering in all Africa. Pomp and circumstance? The following paragraph is a brief description of the *durbar*—or ceremonial procession—which took place in *Kaduna,* now the capital of the North Central State, on the occasion of self-government for the Northern Region in 1959. This account is *only of one group of marchers*—those from the Kano Emirate: ". . . It is led by the *shantu,* trumpeters who spur the warriors into action . . . followed by the *kuge* hornblowers . . . the scarlet-robed *y an bindiga* swordsmen . . . the mounted horsemen in chain mail . . . more warriors . . . the horses with bells jingling at their necks to frighten the enemy . . . the *yan kagura,* who acknowledge greetings paid to the Emir . . . the twelve *yan zage,* who hold the Emir's horse and carry his bed and chair . . . the Emir's personal bodyguard in red and green . . . the drum bearers on horseback . . . the *zinginai,* who fan the Emir, steady his horse and remove dust that may fall on him, and in their midst the Emir himself, mounted and wearing ostrich-feather shoes . . . shaded by his umbrella . . . followed by war drums so heavy they must be carried on camels . . . spearmen and lancers, and finally the main body of councilors, district heads, and domestic office holders." *Durbars* such as the one described above are rare these days, and the visitor who comes across one is indeed lucky. But even without such formal pageantry, this area is unforgettable. Kaduna was built at the turn of the century by the most famous of the British governors, Lord Lugard, who had hoped to make it capital of the entire federation one day. Its people are a cross section of the entire region—Hausa and Fulani—the principal groups who form the Moslem majority, plus people of some thirty different animist tribes, many of whom are now Christian. Besides the regional parliament and ministries, Kaduna is of interest principally for visitors on government business—except on an occasion such as the aforementioned *durbar,* when *any* visitor would be wise to go out of his way to be present. *Jos,* the capital of the Benue Plateau State, is at once a tin-mining center, developed by Europeans but based on the traditional smelting furnaces successfully worked by guilds of Hausa smelters for many centuries, a mountain resort, and a cultural center. At an elevation of some 4000 feet, Jos and the plateau which surrounds it are areas of fertile grasslands, rolling hills and interesting peoples. The Jos Museum is the principal repository of the Nok-culture relics and remnants of a two-thousand-year-old culture (page 259). Twenty-two miles distant from the town is *Miango,* noted for its views and the animist tribes who inhabit it. To the south are two spectacular waterfalls—the *Kurra* and the *Assob.* And happily—at least for the British—there are specimens of every variety of English flower in the gardens of the town, as well as wood-burning fireplaces in houses and inns, actually used on cool evenings! Jos is an oasis of temperate climate in a largely tropical country, and it makes for a refreshing stopover on a Nigerian tour.

Sokoto, the capital of the North Western State, is the traditional home of the Sultan of Sokoto, leader of all Moslems in this region of Africa, and of the Sardauna of Sokoto. It is to Sokoto that pilgrimages of Moslems are made each year, with its shrines the destination. This is semidesert country—with the Sahara not far away, and the Niger River nearby. Not unusual are camel trains of traders winding their way into the town from distant areas.

Kano: The city of *Kano,* capital of Kano State, has been a haven for travelers for more centuries than the United States is old. Kano was ancient when the great kingdoms of the Sahara were young. At the end of the desert caravan routes, it is the chief city of northern Nigeria, and one of the great ancient cities of Africa. What is now the State of Kano first became a Hausa kingdom in A.D. 999, and during the ensuing eight centuries was subjected by the great Songhai Empire from the west, and the Bornu Kingdom from the east. Its most noted emir of the early centuries was Muhammadu Rumfu, who not only consolidated Islam in the region and built the still used

Emir's palace, but is reputed to have had as many wives as King Solomon himself. The Fulani people conquered the Hausas of Kano in 1804, and the politics of the area took various shapes and knew various rules until the coming of the British at the turn of this century. They went about building a new town surrounding ancient Kano, and their contributions have helped the city become a modern industrial trading and transport center. But its ancient façade has been untouched. Great mud walls still enclose the Old Town, and within them are street after street of domed red-pink houses, their dried mud walls accentuated by tiny, slitlike windows and exterior walls decorated in geometrical patterns. Donkey and camel trains from adjoining provinces and countries—and from across the wastes of the Sahara just to the north—wind their way through one of the thirteen cowhide gates of the forty-foot-thick, eleven-mile-long wall to the market, which on busy days has as many as 40,000 customers and browsers in its stalls. Wares for sale? The ancient crafts of Kano—soft leather tooled with great skill, hand-woven cloth colored with traditional indigo dyes, intricate silverwork—all are still on sale to the tourist as well as the trader on camel back. Even refreshment stalls are traditional—meat is roasted over a glowing fire which was a forerunner by centuries of today's barbecue. Craftsmen sit cross-legged in their tiny stalls, at work on their specialties. To walk the streets—be you shopper or not—is to partake of an experience obtainable nowhere else in the world. This, after all, is Black Africa—not the Middle East, and not North Africa. Its culture is a blend of the Africans long indigenous to the region and the Africanized Moslem, on the scene for many centuries. It is easy to spend an entire day walking the streets, peering in the stalls, bargaining with merchants and artisans, watching the camel trains and donkey processions. But there are other attractions: the twin minarets of the dazzling white mosque in whose great square many thousands gather on feast days, the emir on horseback towering over them. There is, too, the palace of the Emir, amid a compound of 33 acres—high-domed, twenty-arched, brilliantly decorated, and surrounded by a twenty-foot wall. The *Arabian Nights?* Kano is *African* Nights—and days—and it is, fortunately for today's traveler, an important air terminus and with fine hotel accommodations.

SHOPPING

Kano: Silver, leather, hand-woven and dyed cloth, carved ivory, at stalls in the market, where bargaining is the rule. **Lagos:** Kano crafts, as well as woodcarvings and iron figurines of the other Nigerian regions, again at the public market. Gallery Labac has a collection of contemporary African arts and crafts, including the silver bracelets—typically West African—that are worn by men as well as women, and are widely available.

CREATURE COMFORTS

HOTELS—**Lagos's** leader is the 165-room, air-conditioned Federal Palace Hotel on Victoria Island, overlooking Lagos Lagoon, with dining room, bar, reception room, shops, dancing. Others include the centrally located Bristol, the Ikayi, on residential Ikayi Island, and, near the airport, the Airport Hotel (formerly the Ikeja Arms), with a good restaurant. **Ibadan's** best is the Premier; the Lafia and the Green Springs have air conditioning and swimming pools. **Enugu** and **Port Harcourt** are known for the beautiful Presidential Hotels. In Enugu, the Progress Hotel and the Atlantic are air-conditioned. **Jos:** Hill Station—first-class, with dining room, bar, and a climate so cool that air-conditioning is not necessary. Others: Plateau Catering Resthouse, Government Catering Resthouse, at suburban Vom. **Kano:** Central Hotel, 144 air-conditioned rooms, restaurant, bar. Airport Hotel, smaller, used mainly by airline passengers in transit, with some air-conditioned rooms, bar, dining room. Good meals and drinks at the Flight Deck Restaurant, at the airport. **Kaduna:** Hamadala Hotel. Lagos's best restaurant is probably the nineteenth-floor Quo Vadis, with a beautiful view of the harbor.

RHODESIA (ZIMBABWE)

Entry requirements: *No visa is required of American tourists. An onward ticket and a health certificate (yellow fever and smallpox) are required.* **Best times for a visit:** *The seasons are, of course, reversed, and the climate in most areas is generally temperate or near temperate. The American summer months are the pleasantest; during that season—June through September—there is virtually no rainfall, and days are clear and cool.* **Currency:** *The Rhodesian dollar: 0.714=$1.* **Principal European language:** *English—which is widely spoken.* **Domestic transport:** *Good air service to major centers, extensive road system.* **Further information:** *Rhodesia National Tourist Board, Salisbury, Rhodesia, and 535 Fifth Avenue, New York.*

INTRODUCING RHODESIA

The Republic of Rhodesia is one of Africa's most firmly entrenched white-supremacist countries, a land of vexing problems for both its white and nonwhite populations (the latter of which make up a whopping 94 percent majority and to many of whom the country is referred to as Zimbabwe—the name of a highly-developed old African city-state, now in ruins). Rhodesia is one of the most British countries in flavor and façade, despite the brief span of British settlement. It is, of course, Cecil Rhodes country. Still regarded as "The Founder" by white Rhodesians, he moved his Pioneer Columns north from South Africa to occupy the territory before President Paul Kruger of the Transvaal Republic (now a province of South Africa) could do so. It might be added that the Rhodes forces were not invited to come north, and that they met with a great deal of resistance before the indigenous Africans submitted to them. An analogy might be made—and frequently is, by Rhodesians—to that of European-origin settlers pushing west in America and wiping out Indians whenever expedient. But this does not make the manner of Britain's entry into the Rhodesias any more palatable than the bare facts indicate.

At any rate, South Africa, ever since Rhodes's forces went north, had its eyes on the rich Rhodesias area, and South Africans continue to exert a great deal of influence there, as do their racial policies. But in 1953 Rhodesia (then called Southern Rhodesia) and her two neighboring territories of Northern Rhodesia and Nyasaland federated and became a member of the British Commonwealth, much to the disgust of their African populations, particularly those of Northern Rhodesia (now Zambia) and Nyasaland (now Malawi), which did not relish being ruled by a white-settler minority. The British government assured the African majorities of Nyasaland and Northern Rhodesia that its "protection" could be counted on for so long as needed.

In the years 1945–62 somewhat better racial attitudes prevailed —in certain respects—in Rhodesia, and there was a bit of desegregation and some opening of opportunities to black Rhodesians. In 1964 the Federation was dissolved; Southern Rhodesia became just plain Rhodesia, and Northern Rhodesia became Zambia. In 1965 the white-minority government of Prime Minister Ian D. Smith unilaterally declared the country independent—a move that angered most of the rest of the world, Portugal and South Africa being the chief exceptions. Britain refused to recognize Rhodesia as a state and instituted a trade blockade in an effort to persuade the government to change its mind. Unfortunately, Britain's sanctions and those of the UN did not serve their purpose, and Rhodesia continued to function economically, importing goods from Portuguese Mozambique and other sympathetic countries and finding other loopholes in the blockade. (A particularly sad violation of the UN blockade was the 1971 U.S. congressional vote to allow the importation of Rhodesian chrome; the vote was engineered by a powerful Rhodesian lobby, working cleverly with racially prejudiced southern congressmen and senators—with silence from the Nixon White House. A United Nations General Assembly vote—106 countries strong—cautioned Washington, following the congressional action, that importing the chrome would be a breach of America's international treaty obligations. Even so, President Nixon signed the bill; his only concession to the worldwide opposition to it was to delay its implementation, pending completion of the Britain-Rhodesia reconciliation talks.)

In 1969 the Rhodesian government took another step in the direction of political apartheid by proclaiming a new constitution and voting to separate completely from the mother country. In 1970 Rhodesia decreed itself a republic—a republic that remains unrecognized by most countries. During this time it also passed a series of laws severely restricting nonwhite land ownership and prohibiting or restricting interracial worship and education.

Although its economy seems to be thriving, it remains to be seen what will be the fate of the majority of Rhodesia's people, more than five million blacks and Asians. These peoples' rights were the subject of late 1971 conferences between the Smith regime and British Foreign Secretary Sir Alec Douglas-Home, who came up with a settlement of their differences that would make African majority rule a possibility in a future so distant as to be almost mythical. Rhodesian blacks—Zimbabweans, as many prefer to call themselves—protested at home, in London, and even in New York, along with black Americans. The British sent a commission to Salisbury, under Lord Pearce, to gauge local opinion, and while it was there, the white Rhodesian government imprisoned a white ex-premier and his daughter who publicly criticized the settlement. It later undertook attempts crude and arbitrary to curb the black-led African National Council, formed to oppose the settlement. There was no denying that American playwright Imamu Amiri Baraka (Le Roi Jones) summed up the situation accurately: "Britain's attempt to palm off an agreement between itself and the white settlers . . . as an attempt at speeding up African self-rule is bizarre and degenerate in the extreme."

One need only glimpse at the way white Rhodesians interpret their country's past to get an idea of their attitude toward Africans. No one, not even the most anti-African settler, denies that this part of the world has been inhabited from the very earliest times. Stone Age studies reveal that the history of the region began a good half million years ago, and relics of that area—particularly Bushman paintings on rock—survive. But later history is something else again. Rhodesia's most famous antiquities are the Zimbabwe Ruins (see page 276), a cluster of brilliantly designed stone buildings near the "Pioneer" settlement of Fort Victoria. Zimbabwe is now maintained by the government as a national park, and tourists are encouraged to visit it. But the ruins are billed in folders as a "mystery" and a "riddle." In fine-point type, one can read that there is no question about the ruins' origin in the minds of the most distinguished archaeologists who have researched them.

But most white Rhodesians continue to feel about Zimbabwe as did their grandfathers. It is inconceivable to them that the "primitive savages" whom they have attempted to "civilize" could have built such a city. And it follows that these ruins were the work of outsiders. Two schools of thought persist: that they were built by ancient Phoenicians; and, even more preposterous, that they were in some way or another the works of Solomon and Sheba.

Be that as it may, the two latest investigators—Professor David Randall-MacIver (1905) and Miss Gertrude Caton-Thompson (1929 and in subsequent years)—have concluded definitely that Zimbabwe was designed by Africans, built by Africans, and lived in by Africans native to the area, who had developed a trading culture, exporting gold and importing cloth, with the cities of the Indian Ocean coast and the Asian countries beyond. They are, moreover, not truly ancient monuments. Parts of them may have been built as late as the early eighteenth century, and it is believed that they represent a fairly continuous regional Iron

Age culture of well over a thousand years. Zimbabwe does not stand alone as a monument to this heritage: other ruins in western Rhodesia—Dhlo-dhlo, Hami, Nalatali—are of roughly the same era, and the same is true of sites in the eastern region: Van Niekerk, Inyanga, Penhalonga.

YOUR VISIT TO RHODESIA

Salisbury: Capital of Rhodesia and the major transport terminus of the country, Salisbury is invariably the starting point for a Rhodesian visit. It does its very best to pretend that it is not in Africa, that it is, perhaps, just an hour or so distant from the cathedral city in Wiltshire for which it is named. And there is no denying that it is as modern as the Nile is long: trim, clean, with neat gardens, fountain-filled parks, soaring skyscrapers, surprisingly good hotels, a sprinkling of continental European restaurants, handsome apartment houses with Anglo-Saxon names, spacious homes for whites, and African housing sufficiently away from the center of things so that it must be looked for if it is to be seen.

There is not a great deal in the way of rubberneck sightseeing. The park on a hill atop the city which affords a fine view of the town is the Pioneer Memorial, flanked by a dignified marker whose legend urges visitors to conduct themselves in a "seemly manner" while on such hallowed ground. The Rhodesian National Gallery has galleries of contemporary African and of European art. Paintings and sculpture may be purchased at the Gallery's Workshop School.

Bulawayo: From Salisbury, the rest of Rhodesia's highlights are easily reached. These would include Bulawayo, the bustling, commercial center of the country, not quite as skyscraper-filled as the capital, but making rapid progress. One would do well to have a look at the National Museum (much better known to residents than the one in Salisbury), with Rhodesiana as well as relics of antiquities, and the Rebellion Memorial, which commemorates the Matabele Rebellion of 1896—a siege which it took the whites months of fighting to control.

Matopos Hills: Cecil Rhodes is buried on a rocky crag in the Matopos Hills, not far from Bulawayo. Much of the Matopo region is now a national park, with a great variety of wildlife—a lot of it visible to motorists. The area is a treasurehouse of Bushman paintings, which are protected by the National Monuments Commission. And a number of dams have been developed as recreational areas, with boating and fishing facilities. Maleme Dam is the most attractive of these, and contains a rest camp but no restaurant facilities; visitors must bring their own food and cooking utensils.

Khami Ruins: Only 12 miles from Bulawayo are the Khami Ruins, former seat of the Barozi dynasty which dominated the country several centuries ago. The buildings consist of a series of terraces supported by massive granite walls, many of which have an interesting checkerboard pattern.

Cyrene Mission: Just 22 miles from Bulawayo, the Cyrene Mission is eminently worth a detour. It is one of the relatively few places in the country where the African is taken seriously—in this instance, as an artist. Since 1939 Africans have been studying art at the mission and, besides doing their own work, have decorated the walls of the Mission chapel—both exterior and interior—with scenes from the Bible, interpreted from an African point of view. The movement has attracted enough art-world attention for there to have emerged a Cyrene "school" of art.

Kariba Dam: Built for the Rhodesian government by an Italian construction firm, along with a staff of several thousand Africans, is the fantastic Kariba Dam, hacked out of a gorge in the Zambezi River wilderness and a short flight from Salisbury. The dam's construction created Lake Kariba, the largest man-made lake in the world, and Kariba Township, a new city adjacent to the dam and the lake. Hotels—most of their rooms overlooking the water—have gone up, and guided tours of the dam are available, as well as boat rides on the lake and trips into the surrounding region. Worth a visit is the Roman Catholic church of St. Barbara, built by the Italian contractors of the dam to commemorate those who lost their lives while the dam was being built. The whole Kariba project typifies the vitality of Africa, and the modern direction in which it can move when there is proper impetus. It indicates, too, how Africans—most of them just out of villages in the bush—can be trained almost overnight to perform skilled jobs efficiently; their trainers, in this instance, were Italians, who, without the prejudices often common to the British, were able not only to teach them but to work with them down below in the mud, as well as on the surface. Kariba—which I watched being constructed—is an exciting chapter in modern African history.

Wankie Game Reserve: More than 6000 square miles in area, Wankie is one of Africa's lesser-known game parks, but is, nonetheless, home to numerous species of wildlife—particularly elephants. Not far from Bulawayo, it can be reached in a few hours' drive.

Zimbabwe Ruins: Now a national park, the Zimbabwe Ruins (see page 273) are a 17-mile drive from *Fort Victoria*, a town rich in pioneer lore and proud of what might be called the Rhodesian equivalent of a Wild West past. "Zimbabwe" means "great house" or "houses of stone" and was a name generally applied by the early Portuguese writers to the principal headquarters of important chiefs. No Portuguese is known ever to have visited it, but tales of its existence had been spread to the coast for centuries before it was discovered by a European, Adam Renders, in 1868. Six years later, Carl Maurch, a German explorer, spread the word abroad after his visit, and it was not until the investigations of Randall-MacIver and Caton-Thompson, in this century, that the "Phoenician" and "Solomon and Sheba" origins of the ruins were disproved. Before the Rhodesian government—at Rhodes's instigation—could put the ruins off-limits to get-rich-quick European prospectors, Zimbabwe's cracks and crevices were ransacked of untold quantities of worked gold, soapstone carvings of birds, and other priceless relics of what is now known to have been a rich mining civilization linked by trade with the cultures of the Indian Ocean coast. The ruins' most striking monuments are the Temple, an irregular ellipse 350 feet across at its point of greatest width, with a wall as high as 32 feet, and as thick as 16 feet. Its conical tower is 34 feet high, with a base circumference of 58 feet. Nearby, towering above the Temple, is the Acropolis, obviously designed as a fortification, and overlooking what is now known as the Valley of Ruins—the main residential area.

Inyanga National Park: Southeast of Salisbury, hugging the Mozambique border, and with the town of Umtali as its southern base, is the Inyanga National Park, a vast area of craggy mountains as high as 7000 feet, rolling downs, cascading waterfalls, and to boot, 2000 square miles of ruins, the most important of which are in the vicinity of Inyanga village. There are stone forts, deep pits believed by some to have been slave repositories but claimed by the Africans to have been kraals for cattle, with huts for their owners on the platforms. The remains of a contained community —now called the Van Niekerk Ruins—are in some ways reminiscent of Zimbabwe, although with architectural variations. Within the park is a former country home of Cecil Rhodes, now a hotel.

SHOPPING

Rhodesia is not outstanding shopping territory—at least for African crafts. An exception is the Workshop School at the National Gallery. Available also from markets and sidewalk vendors are carved wooden vessels, chests, and sculpture, as well as other crafts.

CREATURE COMFORTS

Tourist traffic from South Africa is heavy, so that facilities in Rhodesia are, by and large, modern and comfortable. **Salisbury:** The centrally located Jameson, with a de luxe wing overlooking Cecil Square, good restaurants, bars; Meikle's; Ambassador; George. **Bulawayo:** Carlton, Grand, Southern Sun. **Fort Victoria:** Victoria, Chiredzi. **Inyanga National Park:** Inyanga Mountains,

Troutbeck Inn. **Kariba:** Bumi Hills. **Wankie National Park:** Sun Safari Lodge, a modern, one-hundred-room inn with swimming pool and special game-viewing facilities. **Victoria Falls:** Victoria Falls Hotel—the elderly albeit updated leader; Victoria Falls Casino Hotel, nearby and modern. But why not cross the Zambezi to the Zambian side and stay at the more relaxed, more informal, more amusing Musi-o-Tunya Inter•Continental, at the falls' edge? **Zimbabwe Ruins:** Zimbabwe Hotel.

RWANDA

République Rwandaise

Entry requirements: *A visa plus a health certificate (smallpox and yellow fever) and a letter of recommendation.* **Best times for a visit:** *The dry seasons—June through August, November through March—are preferred, but during the remaining months the rain is only intermittent and need not deter visitors; there is little humidity, thanks to the high elevation.* **Currency:** *The franc: 100 francs=$1.* **Principal European language:** *French, with Flemish second, and some English. Swahili is widely spoken.* **Domestic transport:** *Some all-weather roads; air service to major points.* **Further information:** *Rwanda Embassy, Washington, D.C.*

INTRODUCING RWANDA

Landlocked Rwanda is Black Africa's most densely populated nation. Along with its southern neighbor, Burundi (see page 80), it is the home of the world's tallest people, the seven-foot-tall Watusi (or Tutsi) and the tiny pygmies. It is also one of Central Africa's most beautiful countries, with magnificent mountains and villages perched on the sides of terraced hills. Until World War I, Rwanda and Burundi were part of German East Africa. After the war, the two countries were mandated to the Belgians. Following World War II, they were made a UN Trust Territory, under the name Ruanda-Urundi, with Belgium continuing to administer the territory.

The Watusi, although a minority in the country, had long dominated the more numerous average-sized Bahutu (Hutu), and in 1959 Bahutu resentment of this domination led to a bloody rebellion and the overthrow of the Watusi monarchy. Thousands of the tall people were killed or forced to flee to Burundi and other countries. In 1963 the Watusis from Burundi tried to stage an invasion, which failed and only resulted in further massacres of Watusi in Rwanda. Again, thousands fled the country. Today the Watusis constitute only 9 percent of the Rwanda population, which is 60 percent Roman Catholic—probably the highest such percentage in Africa. In 1961, in a UN-sponsored election, the Hutu emancipation movement (Parmehutu) gained victory. The following year the UN granted Rwanda full independence.

Since independence, impoverished, overpopulated Rwanda—still the recipient of seven million dollars of annual aid from Belgium—has been making strong efforts to control tribal difficulties and to solve economic problems. President Gregoire Kayibanda's government is seeking to establish and maintain good relations with other nations of Africa and to develop agriculture and tourism.

YOUR VISIT TO RWANDA

Rwanda has few villages. Most of the people are clustered in self-contained farming compounds set in the hillsides. Despite this, there are centers of interest for the visitor. The following are the highlights.

Kigali: This quiet town of fourteen thousand, fifteen hundred of whom are Europeans, is possibly the most low-key capital in all of Africa. Surrounded by ancient hills, its chief value is to serve as a center from which to make excursions into the countryside.

Kisenyi: Of much more interest to visitors is Kisenyi, a resort on the shores of blue Lake Kivu, and sister city to Goma, just across the frontier in Zaïre. More informal than its twin, and with the advantage of the lake's principal bathing beach fronting its main thoroughfare, Kisenyi is the kind of town where the tired traveler might well relax, breaking his boating and swimming sessions with excursions to *Karisimbi* and *Mikeno,* active 15,000-foot volcanoes; and, perhaps, to a tiny nearby Watusi village for a dance performance. Traditionally done, these embrace several changes of simply splendid costumes which are nothing short of magnificent: banana-fiber headdresses, beaded sashes and chest bands, skirts of leopardskin, tiny wooden shields, tall spears, jingle-bell bracelets on ankles. Steps are complex and subtle; facial movements intensely expressive; leaps into the air higher than those of the most skilled European *premier danseur;* the sense of drama well-defined; the movements of hands, torsos, shoulders, waists, legs all beautifully co-ordinated under the watchful eye of a director—or ballet master, if you will—who follows the dancers about every moment of the alfresco performance. If there are Watusi in the audience, ask before you snap; they are generally very sensitive about pictures and, more often than not, refuse requests of strangers.

Other excursions from Kisenyi-Goma: See page 393 in the Zaïre Republic section.

Other attractions: Aside from its great dancing, Rwanda's choicest attractions are the beauties of its mountainous countryside: tiny villages on the slopes of mountains; idyllic valleys viewed from the twisting highways; the ubiquitous long-horned cow—symbol of wealth for the Watusis and never killed—in great herds along the roads, tended by young boys, sometimes under their elders' direction; passing parades of people, women—tall, erect, with beaded bandeaux adorning their heads, more often than not topped by great calabashes filled with water, pale-colored cloaks draped over their graceful figures; and the men—inevitably with pipes in their mouth and splendid spears at their sides. *Nyanza,* at an altitude of 6000 feet, was the home of the *mwami,* or king, of Rwanda, with its chief attraction the performances of his own company of dancers. *Ruhengeri,* near the Virunga volcanic range, is ideal for excursions to *Lakes Bulera* and *Luhondo*—both little visited by foreigners and extremely beautiful, as are the *Rwaza* and *Rusumu Falls.*

SHOPPING

Hotel lobbies and terraces in towns throughout the territory offer curios for sale—most of them authentic—and the open-air markets are always a good shopping source. Look for Watusi conical-topped baskets, banana-fiber headdresses, spears, beadwork-decorated drums, zebra-skin covers, carved wooden stools, wood-carving, and elephant-hair bracelets.

CREATURE COMFORTS

HOTELS—**Kigali's** leader is the modern, well-equipped Hôtel des Diplomates. The Kiyovu follows as No. 2. **Kisenyi:** Palm Beach.

SENEGAL

République du Sénégal

Entry requirements: *A visa, obtainable from the Senegal Mission to the United Nations, 280 Madison Avenue, New York; the Embassy of Senegal in Washington, or other Senegalese diplomatic or consular missions; plus a health certificate (smallpox, of course, but yellow fever as well, and—recommended but not mandatory—cholera).* **Best times for a visit:** *January to April—the dry season—is ideal, but the rainy months are often dry enough—or at least with enough intermittent dry spells—for sightseeing.* **Currency:** *The African franc (AFR); AFR 271=$1, subject to fluctuation, of course.* **Principal European language:** *French, with English spoken a good deal in Dakar, elsewhere mainly in hotels and air terminals.* **Domestic transport:** *Air Sénégal flights to major centers, some quite comfortable trains, a fairly extensive road system.* **Further information:** *Direction du Tourisme du Sénégal, Avenue Roume, Dakar, Sénégal; Sénégal Tours, Place de l'Indépendance (or Post Office Box 3126), Dakar, Sénégal; Air Afrique, Dakar, Sénégal; Embassy of Senegal, Washington, D.C.*

INTRODUCING SENEGAL

Senegal is very special. It is, to begin with, a part of the ancient Mali Empire (see page 37). It is Africa's westernmost country, geographically. It was the part of Africa to first know the Frenchman, whose culture, over four centuries, has blended into the indigenous ones with refreshing felicity. And although it has kept in reasonable touch with the times—as much as any of its neighbors, save possibly the go-getting Ivory Coast—it retains the kind of *ambiance* and pace with which it is comfortable, which becomes it, and which makes it, at least to one visitor, one of the most immediately likable and charming of African destinations.

Senegal is as contrasty as they come: Dakar, handsome and white-skyscrapered; venerable Saint-Louis, the languid island-city on the Atlantic that was for long the center of things; mosques of the moslems and cathedrals of the Roman Catholics; sleek European-style shops and vivid open-air markets in the traditional style; smart hotels and restaurants (nowhere in Africa have I had better French food) on the one hand, tiny *campements* in the bush, on the other; a populace embracing Sorbonne-educated intellectuals (the country's first President, Leopold Senghor, is a distinguished French-language poet), Koran-schooled Moslems, and still illiterate villagers.

For many visitors, Senegal—through its capital—serves as the gateway to tropical Africa; for others, it is the departure point for home. It is a remarkable land, making contributions uniquely its own to those who would know and enjoy West Africa.

European penetration into Senegal began in 1444, when the Portuguese navigator Denis Dias sighted Cape Verde. But it was not until 1617 that the Dutch settled on the Isle de Gorée, just opposite the mainland of Dakar. The French took the tiny island in 1677 and it remained in their hands—for the most part—until 1960. Mainland Senegal knew the French almost as early as did Gorée. Saint-Louis was settled in 1658—the oldest French Community on the continent of Africa. Dakar was still a fishing village until the mid-nineteenth century and did not begin to really sprout until the 1880s.

Senegal was formally declared a French territory in 1840. In 1947 its people elected their first legislative council, and in 1958 it became a semi-autonomous republic of the French Community, along with every other French West and French Equatorial African province except Guinea, which struck out on its own as a completely sovereign state. Shortly after the Community was formed, Senegal united with what is now the Republic of Mali (formerly

French Sudan) to become the Federation of Mali. Granted complete sovereignty in mid-1960 (along with the other Community members), the federation was short-lived; in August of that year its two member states parted company. The Senegalese feared that more heavily populated Sudan would overdominate the federal government; Sudanese leaders—far less European-oriented than those of Senegal—resented what they believed was the latter's overattachment to the French.

And so, after its brief honeymoon with Mali, Senegal started off on its own as a sovereign state. It had a new kind of smallness to reckon with, for it had long been the seat of government for the vast territory stretching from the Atlantic to the Congo that was French West Africa. Suddenly, with sovereignty, its borders were, in effect, shrunk; and its domestic market reduced from one serving some twenty million to that of its own population of some four million. Additionally, it had to face the prospects of every new state as regards political development and maturity.

It was extremely fortunate in this regard with its first President, the poet-politician Leopold Senghor, among the handful of African leaders who remained in office from the start of the eventful decade of the sixties straight into the seventies. Senghor's original Premier, Mamadou Dia, was not so lucky; by 1963 he had been ousted and his boss re-elected to a second term, with opposition parties shortly thereafter banned. In 1968, President Senghor was elected to a third term, along with an unopposed eighty-member Parliamentary slate for the one-chamber legislature.

By that time, however, the fledgling University of Dakar—the only institution of higher learning the French founded in Africa—had become substantial enough to have developed a questioning student body, one that was so unhappy with arbitrary one-party government that demonstrations forced it to be closed on two occasions, with a 1969 state of emergency a consequence. In 1970, the President wisely formed a new government, younger and from diverse sectors of the population. The Senghor-appointed Prime Minister, tall, slim Abdou Diouf—thirty-four when he took office—is a Dakar University law alumnus who studied also at the Sorbonne, as did the President and so many of Senegal's intellectuals. Premier Diouf talked to the African American Chamber of Commerce in New York in the course of a 1970 visit, appealing for the kind of investment from abroad, most particularly the United States, that would help diversify Senegal's long-time dependence on export income from its peanut crops. (You would not guess it from the high cost of a can of peanuts at the supermarket, but prices have declined for Senegalese growers.) The Premier urged more cooperation with Franco-American oil exploration projects, and asked potential investors to consider the country's potential in livestock, fishing, and—hardly to be overlooked—tourism.

The republic had its first big taste of tourism half a decade earlier when its capital was selected as the site of the first—and to date only—World Festival of the Negro Arts. Spring of 1965 saw Dakar alive with black artists, singers, musicians, dance troupes, and priceless displays of paintings, sculpture, and folklore from every corner of the globe with Africa-origin populations. The American representatives included the great Duke Ellington, who was the hit of the twenty-six-day festival, the late, sorely missed poet Langston Hughes, and ageless, American-born Josephine Baker, with additional excitement coming from the Russian contribution—a cruise ship tied up in the harbor that served as a floating hotel. It may be some time before Senegal will see the festival's likes again.

But it may well bring in the crowds as part of an ordered tourist development program. It has a lot going for it: the most convenient location of any country in Black Africa (Dakar's Yoff Airport is the major touchdown point for planes on United States/South America–Africa routes, and also for the carriers that fly between Europe and the Americas); a diversity of attractions, from its urbane capital to game-viewing reserves in the interior; a culturally rich populace, and an atmosphere at once largely stable and serene. Senegal's only international difficulties have been the result of geography. A next-door neighbor is the colony of Guinea-Bissau, where for a decade guerrillas have been rebelling against the Portuguese government, at a reported cost to Lisbon of some forty million dollars a year. Senegal has, of course, been sympathetic to the rebels, and has allowed some sixty thousand refugees to live on its side of the frontier. But in order to keep itself free of involvement in its neighbor's war, it had to send over a thousand soldiers to the border to make sure that Senegalese territory was not used as a part of a supply route from the Republic of Guinea to the Portuguese colony.

YOUR VISIT TO SENEGAL

Dakar: This gleaming white city jutting out into the Atlantic from its position on Cape Verde—the westernmost point of Africa—is considerably more than a great air transport terminus and harbor. It is one of the most fascinating cities in Africa, a fact sometimes overlooked by visitors who refuse to believe that what is often the first stop on their African itineraries can be worth close inspection. Today's Dakar is the result of hard work. The French labored for decades to make it the showcase of West Africa, and the Senegalese saw to it that it did not lose its African flavor.

The blend is quite delightful: appropriately designed skyscrapers constructed with the tropical African setting in mind; broad squares and seafront drives, lovely beaches, relaxing sidewalk cafés, and splendid French restaurants; a market that is outshone by none in Africa for brilliant color and frenetic activity; women's costumes (rakish, turban-like *moussoires*, flowing *bou-bous*) that are by far the most striking and stylish of any on the continent, with the men's garb (the male variation of the *bou-bou*, Moslem-derived from the *caftan* of Morocco, is typical) not far behind.

Dakar's landmark is the modern, rectangular Building Administratif, which the French built as their secretariat for the administration of all of French West Africa, not long before they realized that their African colonies were so close to freedom. Overlooking the sea, and fronted by a war-memorial statue depicting both African and French troops, it is one of the handsomest buildings in tropical Africa. Worth glimpsing, too, are the former palace of the governor-general of French West Africa (now the President's Palace, and guarded by sentries in magnificent uniforms—high hats, capes, and cloaks of scarlet, over baggy blue pantaloons), the clean-lined Palais de Justice, or law courts, the University of Dakar, schools that have been multiracial since considerably before independence, and—so that one will not have a lopsided picture—appalling slums in which many *Dakaroise* still must live.

There are beaches in town (Le Lagon is smack in the center, even if it doesn't seem so, *after* you've reached it), and out of town, N'Gor—alongside the hotel by that name—is outstanding. And there are, as well, mosques (the Great Mosque is the finest, and can be entered by non-Moslems even during services on Friday), and churches, including the Cathedrale du Souvenir Africain, with its lovely Chapel of Our Lady of Fatima. The National Museum ranks, among those in French-speaking Africa, with that in Abidjan, for the quality of its collection of African art. (And like that in Abidjan, it was founded back in colonial days by the Institut Français d'Afrique Noir, or IFAN, an admirable organization that typified the estimable French interest, both official and otherwise, in African cultures.)

Dakar is a very walkable city, particularly in the late afternoon or early evening. The streets bustle with *Dakaroise*, both African and European. And along some thoroughfares, *commercants*—aggressive and relentless but invariably good-natured and rarely without a sense of humor—hawk wares of ivory, wood, and leather. They delight in a good bargaining session, sale or no sale.

Beyond are any number of coastal fishing villages. The one to head for—there are afternoon tours—is *Cayar*, where the lure is a view of the vividly decorated, beautifully sculpted *pirogues* coming ashore over frothy high surf at day's end, their craft filled to the gunnels with the day's catch, their families waiting on the beach to greet them, clustering in and about the vast racks on which they will place much of the fish to dry. (Deep-sea fishing is not only for the Senegalese making a living from it. Sport fishing, to translate from the term the French use, is well-developed, and the government's Direction du Tourisme can provide the details to anglers.) Riding, sailing, golf, tennis, and yachting are also available within and without the city.

Île de Gorée: The traveler with a day to spare would do well to leave Dakar in the morning, equipped with swimsuit, towel, camera, and comfortable shoes. For one does not—indeed, cannot—ride about this lovely little island. Its narrow lanes and winding roads were built long before there were motor vehicles. And they have known the footsteps of countless thousands of slaves, as well as European slavers of many nationalities. Gorée today is little more than what Staten Island is to New York City—a residential suburb, mostly inhabited by commuters who enjoy its tranquillity and beauty after a day in the city. A circular fortress still guards the tiny channel to the landing pier. The handsome Greek Revival church has seen few repairs since it was constructed a century and a half ago, and one does well to pop inside for a look at the sanctuary. The houses, painted in pastel pinks and oranges and lemon-yellows and sea-greens, are still substantial, despite their great age. The museum tells the drama-filled history of the island. And in the Slave House (Maison des Esclaves) one can still see where Africans in chains were dropped through a hole into boats below for transport to ships lying out in deeper water, thence to be transported to the Americas and the West Indies. Gorée is tranquil today. Children scamper in the public gardens. Islanders and visitors relax at the small but pleasant beach near the wharf. Life is as easy now, as it was brutal in earlier days. This is a truly mellow place, with a beauty that only age can bring, untarnished even by the immoral occupation of its founders.

Saint-Louis: Representatives of the Compagnie des Marchands de Rouen et de Dieppe set up a trading post on an oblong island in the Atlantic just opposite the mouth of the Senegal River in 1659, and named it for their monarch, Louis XIII. Saint-Louis was the chief city of Senegal—and the capital of French West Africa—until the honors were transferred to Dakar in 1902. Gradually Dakar took over commercially as well, with its big harbor and the railroad which connected it with the interior. Saint-Louis's only claim to fame was as capital of the province of Senegal, and later as capital of neighboring Mauritania as well, for that largely desert territory was too poor to afford a seat of government within its own frontiers. Now, though, Saint-Louis is capital of absolutely nothing. Little but charm remains. The two-story stucco houses on the dusty streets, built by settlers in the style of the French provinces, are a little reminiscent of New Orleans, with grillwork balconies on the second floor, where the settler families lived, over the business quarters and servants' rooms on the ground floor. Bridges connect this quarter—on the rectangular island—with the mainland and with a lagoon fronting the ocean, which is largely populated by Moslem Africans who live by the sea. Each grave of their sandy cemetery is protected by a wall of fishnet. Saint-Louis can serve as excursion headquarters for trips into bordering Mauritania (page 228) or for shorter drives into the dry, desert-like countryside, dotted with the tent encampments of nomadic Moors and the thatched villages of Black Africans.

Casamance, the region tucked between Gambia and Portuguese Guinea, is perhaps the most favored area of Senegal for the observation of traditional village life. One may fly to the town of *Ziguinchor* or gain the area by means of weekly cruises on comfortable, yachtlike cruise ships out of Dakar. The area is one of thick forests and the villages of such groups as the Floups, Mandingos, Balantes, and Diolas. Their folk art, their dances, their architecture, their whole pattern of life has changed relatively little over the centuries. Casamance is visitable only during the dry season.

Niokola-Koba National Park: More than a thousand square miles of the Upper Gambian Basin have been set aside by the government as a game reserve. It is, as well, the region of the unusual Bassari people. The park, through which flow the Gambia and Niokola-Koba rivers, is less than four hundred miles from Dakar. One can go by overnight train, on certain days of the week, from which the route continues via car to the modern, air-conditioned little hotel at *Simenti* and tours of the park, with a small lodge within the park an alternate headquarters. Or one can, with less time, fly round-trip from Dakar–Simenti.

The Bisente are encountered in their villages and farms. They have remained extraordinarily faithful to old traditions. The men wear sheaths of braided palm leaves and a triangle of antelope hide around their loins; during feast periods, they add goatskin leggings, magnificent leather headdresses, and belts and bracelets of aluminum. The women wear small slips of woven material around their waists, belts of heavy bronze rings, numerous circles of aluminum wire (a relatively modern touch) about their arms and legs, and beautifully beaded headpieces and necklaces. Animists by religion, they maintain initiation rites that include elaborate preparation periods—particularly for the young men hunters—intricate ceremonies of a religious nature, and when it is all over, festive celebrations at which quantities of food and drink—millet beer—are consumed, with dances extending over a three-day period. Animal buffs will find the park filled with wildlife. The Buffon cob (a type of antelope) is the commonest species, but there are, as well, hippo, giraffe, buffalo, warthog, hyena, monkey, leopard, and lion.

SHOPPING

Because Dakar in recent years has not attracted the considerable wealth that is a feature of contemporary Abidjan, one does not come across anything like the quantity of good-quality African wood sculpture that is the case in the Ivorian capital. Still, there are to be found carved ivory, ebony statues (many of them mass-produced to standard models, as is the case in Kenya), jewelry of gold and silver (the very simple-in-design hand-fashioned identification bracelets in silver are very handsome), leatherwork (Senegalese sandals are super) and, for at-home or resort-wear back home, made-to-order *bou-bous,* or *caftans*—if you prefer to call them that—for both men and women. Find a good tailor and you can have yours in a day, but forty-eight hours is a more comfortable margin. There are several steps involved. You shop for the material you would like in the textile section of the public market, bargaining, of course, for your purchases. There are solid color cottons that make up well, and there are, as well, locally hand-printed (sometimes tie-dyed) fabrics that can be extraordinarily good-looking. You then take your material to a tailor. (I have used, with utmost satisfaction, Madame Ami Collet Guèye, who lives in the apartment house at 8, Rue l'Aperine. However, you must either speak French to make known your wishes, or have someone with you who does. Air Afrique and Sénégal Tours, on the Place de l'Indépendance, will gladly suggest other tailors.) After the garments are made by the tailors, they are sent to embroiderers, invariably men in Senegal, who work their magic around the collars and cuffs, using thread of a matching or contrasting hue of the color of the garment—or a shade you designate. Costs are a fraction of what you would pay for similar garments exported from countries like Morocco and Tunisia to Europe and the United States. The best-known source of what the French call *artisanat*, or folk art, or—to get right down to brass tacks—souvenirs—is the government-sponsored Village Artisanal de Soumbedioune, a collection of authentic-design thatched huts in which the various artisans make their wares and sell them. The concept of this village is indeed admirable. But there is a considerable letdown in the execution of the wares for sale. The merchandise is, by and large, tacky. Some of the textiles in production are commendable. So are the earlier-mentioned sandals, and the leather bracelets called gri-gris, and perhaps, certain of the ceramics and baskets. But the rest is not worthy of the great craft traditions of Senegal. High-caliber things are to be found in the shop operated by M. Claude Lamarsande in the mezzanine of the Meridien-Dakar Hotel; his sterling silver identification bracelets are particularly noteworthy. La Boutique on the Île de Gorée also has some interesting wares. There is a souvenir stall at Yoff Airport, where quality varies, but with the well-done odd item. And in downtown Dakar, there is the earlier-mentioned Public Market, and—more for manufactured than for hand-fashioned merchandise—the modern Printania department store. Beyond the capital, investigate the wares of itinerant vendors who set up shop outside of hotels, and, of course, the public markets; often, it's the provinces that have the most authentic stuff. Outside of the established shops and stores, bargaining is the rule, including, most definitely, Soumbedioune craft village.

CREATURE COMFORTS

Hotels and Restaurants—Senegal had for long emphasized quality as regards both hotels and restaurants. What it has needed is quantity, particularly in the case of hotels. This now seems assured, with the Hotel Teranga, an eleven-story, 268-room, fully air-conditioned hotel in the center of town, looking out to the Île de Gorée, and with facilities ranging from *boîte* to beauty salon; 1973 completion; and a Dakar Hilton is going up. The leader, pre-Terenga, for well over a decade has been the striking Meridien-Dakar (formerly the N'Gor), on a lovely beach of its own at N'Gor, up the Cape Verde peninusla from the city center. The main building is quite possibly one of the best examples of French Tropical architecture of the late fifties to be found in Africa. It was built to wow visitors to the then capital of French West Africa, with no stinting in its public areas—high-ceilinged and imposing. There is a very grand ocean-view dining room separated from the beach by lawns the length of a football field, which slope gently to the sea. An informal café is at water's edge. There are a private beach, miniature golf, tennis, a bar, beauty and barber shops, and a kicky disco known as the Salinas Club. Highly recommended. Almost adjacent—a brief walk away—is a newer, low-slung addition. And nearby is N'Gor Village; the key word here is village. This cluster of thatched African-style huts—unattractive, dank, and depressing within, difficult as hell to find one's way to, and with breakfast and bar service only, is adequate in a pinch—but no more. The long-established in-town favorite is the Croix du Sud, first-class rather than de luxe, but with comfortable rooms, all with bath, bar-lounge, and an excellent restaurant. Which leads one to restaurants. Dakar's, to my mind, are unsurpassed in French-speaking Africa. Particularly good for lunch is Le Lagon, where one is seated on a covered seaside terrace. Specialties are lobster and bouillabaise, but everything—beef dishes, salads, cheeses, wines, desserts, coffee—is absolutely first-rate, if hardly inexpensive. After lunching, you may change into your swimsuit, sun yourself on an open pier jutting into the Atlantic, and pop right into the water below for a swim, water-skiing or even skin-diving. Other good restaurants include the Baobob, in downtown Dakar; the Ramatou, outside of town en route to N'Gor; the venerable Hostellerie du Chevalier de Boufflers and the Relais d'Espadon—with its big seaside dining terrace—both on Gorée; and, for Senegalese specialties, with music and air conditioning to boot, Tam-Tam, downtown. The Senegalese are superb dancers. The National Dance Company of Senegal made a highly successful American debut in New York in 1971. And you do well to see the company, should it be performing on home base when you are in Dakar. But there are other dance troupes, as well, invariably worth seeing. **Île de Gorée:** Relais de l'Espadon—elderly, colonial-style, with a fine seaside location. There is a good restaurant and bar, and Senegal's deep-sea fishing club operates out of this location. Hostellerie du Chevalier de Boufflers is the ancient restaurant-café fronting Gorée's little harbor beach. There is a neat little bar where you may stop for a drink while making your sightseeing rounds. And the menu, not unsurprisingly, features seafood. **Saint-Louis:** Résidence, small but charming, and with a first-rate restaurant-café. **Ziguinchor:** Aubert, comfortable, with air-conditioned rooms with bath. **Simenti:** Hotel Simenti, modern and with a good restaurant and bar. **Niokola-Koba National Park:** Niokola Game Lodge—simple, to be sure, but quite literally, where the action is.

SIERRA LEONE

Republic of Sierra Leone

Entry requirements: *A visa, obtainable from British consulates where Sierra Leone has none of its own, plus a health certificate (smallpox and yellow fever).* **Best times for a visit:** *The dry-season months—November through May—are the best, but rain during the rest of the year is not incessant and need not preclude a visit.* **Currency:** *The leone: 0.83 leones= $1.* **Principal European language:** *English, which is also the official language, although many Sierra Leonis speak dialects based upon it, or African languages.* **Domestic transport:** *A small rail network, and an extensive, but hardly superior, road system lead into the interior; frequent internal air service.* **Further information:** *Government Information Service, Freetown, Sierra Leone; Sierra Leone Embassy, Washington, D.C.*

INTRODUCING SIERRA LEONE

Sierra Leone—Lion Mountain, if you'd like a translation—is the baby of the British Commonwealth. It received independence in April 1961, just a decade after its own people were allowed a majority in the colonial legislative council. The name it was given in 1462 by its first tourist, Pedro de Cintra, a Portuguese adventurer, has stuck, but there is little else to remind one that the first Europeans known to visit the country were of that nationality. The non-African tones are as British as overboiled cabbage and, in many respects, quite as unattractive.

Sir John Hawkins followed Senhor de Cintra by less than a century; his mission: slaving. He was followed by other slavers, but in 1787 the Society for the Abolition of Slavery stepped into the scene, determined to establish the colony as a haven for freed slaves. The first settlers were a group of four hundred freed men who had sought refuge in England—some of them were from the American colonies and Jamaica—accompanied by a squadron of English prostitutes, sent along to keep them company. Their descendants—called Creoles today—are the aristocrats of the country, and live principally along the coast. In sharp contrast are the indigenous Sierra Leonis of the little-developed interior, most of them members of the Mende and Temne tribes. The situation is not unlike that of Liberia in many respects, except that in that country the settlers and sponsors were American.

There had never been a large British community in the country, largely because of the hot, humid climate. But the British encouraged education and participation in government, and although it does not *look* it, Sierra Leone's background for sovereignty is one of stability which came about as a result of slow but substantial political development among an elite which is one of the best educated in Africa. As early as 1827 Fourah Bay College was training clergymen; it is one of the oldest colleges below the Sahara.

Sir Milton Margai—who had been Prime Minister under the British colonial governor, and leader of the Sierra Leone People's Party—continued to rule after Sierra Leone gained independence in 1961. His country's politics were quiet and temperate. Sir Milton died in 1964 and was succeeded by his brother, Sir Albert Margai. Unfortunately, Sir Albert reversed many of the gains made by his brother; his government was characterized by corruption and extravagance. In 1967 Siaka Stevens, the opposition leader, was elected Prime Minister, but he was soon removed by a military junta. Restored to leadership in 1968, Mr. Stevens has led the country into a period of prosperity and economic growth. In 1971 he declared Sierra Leone a republic, and that same year, the country made its first cultural stir in the United States, with the first American performances of the Sierra Leone National Dance Company.

The country's economy is largely agricultural, if one forgets the diamonds. Ah, the diamonds! Industrial ones, they are—not as glamorous as those used in jewelry, but not without value, either. The big difficulty is that they are generally just beneath the ground, so easy to mine—and to smuggle illicitly out of the country. Progress is being made, and *legal* sales are finally beginning to increase.

When not picking diamonds out of the soil, most Sierra Leonis cultivate it, as farmers. The great majority of the 2,600,000 inhabitants of the country are busy growing palm kernels, coffee, cocoa, and kola nuts. They are not distracted by tourists, and as yet not many have been lured to jobs catering to tourists.

YOUR VISIT TO SIERRA LEONE

Freetown is not likely to win a beauty contest. The small British administrative community holed itself up in the surrounding high Hill Station in pre-independence years, kept away from the town itself except when absolutely necessary, and did nothing to make the place at all attractive. What one sees is nothing more than a rather tawdry collection of buildings many of which are no more than glorified shacks. Close inspection will reveal a few edifices of some permanence—a gray, somber, graceless secretariat for the government; a rather absurd product of the 1930s—built to look like a ship at sea but actually State House—and a modern school, with clean lines and good proportions which would not be given a second glance in most towns but which sticks out like a sore thumb in Freetown. Shops are nondescript and with little of excitement to offer. What saves Freetown is its setting, something like that of Port-au-Prince in Haiti. It hugs the harbor (one of the biggest and best in Africa, holding 250 ships) but ascends rapidly into green, verdant hills, from which one has a fine view of the port in one direction, and the interior in the other. Only the well-to-do—diplomats and high-ranking Sierra Leonis—live in this lovely neighborhood, although the long-established and excellently regarded Fourah Bay University is not far below. Aside from a look at the town itself, the campus and principal buildings of the university, and the residential section on the hills, there is little else for the visitor, except the beaches on a quiet side of the bay. And they are, to be sure, most attractive. The country's beauty lies in the interior, whose mountains rise to a level of 6000 feet. You might want to visit the second city of the country, with a name which is probably among the shortest in the world: *Bo.* That is, unless you prefer *Ho,* in Ghana.

SHOPPING

Woodcarving (heads and figures), leatherwork, and other craft items at the market in Freetown, and occasionally from itinerant merchants with portable displays near the hotels. Bargaining is the rule.

CREATURE COMFORTS

Freetown: The Paramount Hotel—air-conditioned, clean, modern, and high on a hill overlooking the harbor—is the place to stay.

REPUBLIC OF SOMALIA AND TERRITORY OF AFARS AND ISSAS

Entry requirements: *A visa—for the republic, obtainable from Italian consulates where Somalia has no diplomatic missions; for the territory, from French consulates—plus a health certificate (yellow fever and smallpox).* **Best times for a visit:** *The coolest months are between November and March, with the interior highlands usually more comfortable at all times than the coastal areas.* **Currency:** *In the republic, the shilling: 7.14=$1. In the territory, the currency is the Djibouti franc (215 DF=$1).* **Principal European languages:** *Italian, in the former Italian territory, English in the former British protectorate, and French in the territory.* **Domestic transport:** *The republic has good roads and internal air service but no railroad. The territory has limited good roads; internal air service; and the Djibouti–Addis Ababa railroad, which includes on its route some points within the territory.* **Further information:** *Republic of Somalia Information Agency, Mogadiscio, Somalia; French Government Tourist Office, 610 Fifth Avenue, New York; Ambassade de France, Service de Presse et d'Information, 972 Fifth Avenue, New York—for the territory of Afars and Issas.*

INTRODUCING SOMALIA AND THE TERRITORY OF AFARS AND ISSAS

Somali Republic: This area—known as the Horn of Africa—constitutes the easternmost projection of the African continent. In ancient times, this was known as the Regio Aromatico, because of its fame as a source of spices such as frankincense and myrrh.

It forms a perfect "7" along the coast, which comes to an end just below the Equator, and until British and Italian Somaliland were united as the Somali Republic in 1960, it had been one of the least-visited parts of Africa.

This is the land of the Somali—tall, handsome, Hamitic-origin people, most of whom are nomadic shepherds. Before Europeans arrived on the scene, the coastal areas had been considered the property of the sultans of Zanzibar for several centuries. From the beginning of the European penetration, the history of the region was one of frequent unrest.

The British took over their region of Somalia—called until independence Somaliland Protectorate—in 1884, and they knew little but trouble from the Somalis until as recently as 1920, when things calmed down. For two entire decades their chief enemy was a fanatic Somali mullah whose cause was one of "holy war" against the European occupiers. By the time his forces were subdued, intertribal fighting had reduced the male population of the interior by one third.

By far the greater area of Somalia had been in Italian hands prior to independence. The sultan of Zanzibar sold his ports to the Italians in 1905, and they acquired other areas from the British in later years, only to have the Allies occupy their territory in 1941. After World War II Somalia went back to Italy as a United Nations Trust Territory, with 1960 set as the independence date. The Italians did a creditable job of fostering self-government among the Somalis themselves, and of developing the economy and standard of living. Some months before the independence date, British officials conferred with Somali leaders from their territory, in London. The result of the talks was a grant of independence to the Somaliland Protectorate, also for July 1, 1960, so that the two territories could unite and start off together on the independence road.

After independence the republic was troubled by border conflicts with Kenya and Ethiopia. This costly affair was settled in 1967 and the Somali Republic seemed well on its way to economic development. However, in 1969, the army gained political power in a takeover after the assassination of the country's President. The new government has taken strict anticorruption measures, and in 1970 it nationalized all foreign banks and oil companies.

French Territory of Afars and Issas: Though much smaller in area than the Somali Republic—only nine thousand square miles—the territory (formerly French Somaliland) is important. Its port of Djibouti is connected with Addis Ababa, Ethiopia, by a French-operated railroad, and is one of Ethiopia's chief links with the sea. Djibouti is, as well, the only French port on the route of the Suez Canal, and France may not yield it as readily as she did her other sub-Sahara African territories. About sixty-two thousand people, roughly half the population, live in Djibouti; the rest are mostly nomadic herdsmen.

YOUR VISIT TO SOMALIA

The Republic: Twice as large as Italy and by far the biggest of the three areas is the former Italian Trust Territory. Its best-known landmark is the dramatically high *Cape Guardafui*, Africa's most easterly point, and the northern extremity of the territory's 1200-mile Indian Ocean coastline. A considerable way to the south is the capital and chief port, *Mogadiscio*. Not without a pleasant Italian flavor, with a domestic airline and two new hotels, this is the most substantial of Somalia's cities. Flights are made to the principal smaller towns, which include *Hafun* and *Alula*, in the north; *Merca* in the Genale farming area; *Kismayu*, a port in the Juba region; and *Brava*, a town whose harbor caters to dhow traffic (these ancient-design sailboats are sailed by Arabs from Persian Gulf ports during the winter monsoons). This is the only area of Somalia where big-game hunting has been organized.

Hargeisa, the ex-capital of British Somaliland, is a tiny, unexciting town in the relatively cool interior, with not so much as a proper hotel to recommend it. It has probably received fewer visitors than any capital or ex-capital in all of Africa, and with good reason. There are government resthouses in the smaller towns, where officials have priority. The only true attraction of this region is its population—the customs and culture of the pastoral Somalis who constitute the great majority of the population. Its exotic exports are frankincense and myrrh.

Territory of Afars and Issas: One may be uncomfortably warm in *Djibouti*, the capital, but thanks to *la présence française*, one will at least eat well. Despite its heat, Djibouti is a pleasant city of gleaming white houses and mosques, set off by brilliant-hued plants and flowers. The French can be relied upon to bring a degree of charm to any area in which they settle, even one with a climate as oppressive as this. Outside of the capital, the major point of interest is *Lake Assal* which, after the Dead Sea, is the lowest spot on earth—if low spots interest you. A number of settlements are stopping-off points on the railroad to Addis Ababa, but they need not be requisites on even the most detailed of African itineraries.

SHOPPING

Hand-woven, specially dyed Benadir cloth, in two-meter lengths; woodcarvings, many of them inferior and produced for tourists, but some—including the type known as Asmedu—outstanding. The leading curio shop is Ricci's, in Mogadiscio, itinerant merchants are found near hotels, and Alitalia Airlines—good people to contact in this country—may have suggestions.

CREATURE COMFORTS

HOTELS—**Mogadiscio:** The Guiba and the Scebeli—completed in time for independence in mid-1960—remain the leaders. Both are fully air-conditioned, all rooms have baths, and there are good restaurants and bars in both; Italian management. **Djibouti:** Thanks to its French parentage, it is well equipped, with the Grand, the France, and the Djibouti Palace the leaders. **Hargeisa:** The elderly Oriental remains the leader.

SOUTH AFRICA AND NAMIBIA

Entry requirements: *The government is sticky about visas for anyone not white, or not on a purely touristic mission. Non-whites, journalists, and others on business are carefully investigated, and often visas for them must be approved by the government in Pretoria, which can take a month or more; the occasional token black gets in, when it suits the propaganda purposes of the government. White tourists, however, are welcome; tourism as an industry is expensively promoted. Apply for visas at South African consulates. Health certificates (smallpox and yellow fever) also required.* **Best times for a visit:** *The climate is mainly temperate, with hot summers, much like those in the United States, and mild winters, considerably less extreme than those in the northern United States. Seasons are, of course, reversed. The only drawback to the South African winter (United States summer) is the possibility of some rain in the Cape Town region.* **Currency:** *The South African rand: 0.714 rands=$1.* **Principal European languages:** *English—which is widely spoken—and Afrikaans, a Dutch dialect, are the official languages.* **Domestic transport:** *Air service to major centers, good roads, a rail network at its best with the Blue Train (Johannesburg–Cape Town). Bus tours to major points of interest.* **Further information:** *South African Tourist Corporation, 610 Fifth Ave., New York; 9465 Wilshire Boulevard, Beverly Hills, California, and Pretoria, South Africa.*

INTRODUCING SOUTH AFRICA

Southern Africa, we now know, was not a region of primitive savagery. The greatness of Zimbabwe, a part of present-day Rhodesia, is briefly described in another section of this book. But early African civilization extended south into what is now South Africa. Most white South Africans prefer not to trouble their consciences with the evidence. But there can be no denying that the ruins of Mapungubwe—discovered in the early 1930s by white South African farmers and later studied dispassionately by archaeologists—indicate that the present-day Transvaal was the site of an advanced Iron Age civilization which was developed during the first thousand years of the Christian era, by the ancestors of the Negro peoples still resident in this region.

The Mapungubwe discoveries, found atop a mountain just below the Limpopo River, were treasures in the literal sense—fragments not only of copper and iron and ceramics, but also of superbly wrought goldwork—thin plated pieces, beads, elaborate ornaments—and later a cemetery with remains of nearly two dozen skeletons, some of which were encased in skillfully wrought metal coverings.

Much remains to be done in the archaeological field; the present South African government would not, of course, be served by additional evidences of the richness of pre-European African cultures.

Europeans have been in South Africa ever since Portuguese Bartholomeu Dias first rounded the Cape of Good Hope in 1488. Successive ship captains appreciated its convenience as a midway point on the route to India, and in 1652 the Dutch East India Company founded the first permanent white settlement in the country at Cape Town, expelling the indigenous Bushman and Hottentot inhabitants and establishing a pattern of racial exploitation and discrimination that exists to this day. The British later entered the scene and, after several invasions, took over the Cape colony from the Dutch settlers—by then called Boers—in 1841.

But before then, many Boers migrated north to escape British domination. In the manner of the American pioneers, they traveled through uncharted territory in covered wagons and set up three republics of their own: the Transvaal and the Orange Free State in the interior, and Natal, fronting the Indian Ocean. To do so, of course, they either wiped out great numbers of Africans—including many brave Zulu—or forced others into relatively small reserves.

Natal was taken over by the British in 1843, but the other two Boer republics were left alone, and might have stayed sovereign had not diamonds and gold been discovered within their borders in the 1880s. British prospectors came in droves—infuriating the Boers, of course—and the situation exploded in 1899 into the Boer War. As a result of what turned out to be a rather hollow British victory, the Union of South Africa came into being in 1910. The two British territories (Cape and Natal) joined with the two Boer republics (Orange Free State and Transvaal) to become a federation of four provinces of the British Commonwealth; in 1926 the country was accorded complete sovereignty along the lines of Commonwealth dominions such as Australia and New Zealand. In 1961 South Africa withdrew from the British Commonwealth and became an independent republic.

But the Boers who came to call themselves Afrikaners, and who speak Afrikaans, a Dutch dialect, have never forgiven the British for winning the war, and as they gained numerical superiority over South Africans of British descent, so they came gradually to control the government. There are now more than twenty million people in South Africa: 19 percent white, 10 percent "coloreds," or people of mixed blood, 3 percent Asian, and the great remainder, 68 percent, pure-blood Africans, patronizingly referred to as "natives," or "Bantu."

Prior to—and after—World War II the opposition United Party, led by Jan Smuts was in power, and advocated close ties to Britain and support of the Allies in the war—not an easy task, as many Afrikaners in the Nationalist Party were ardently pro-Nazi. The United Party lost out in the 1948 elections, and since then the party of the Afrikaners—the Nationalists—has been in power, under a succession of progressively fanatic prime ministers—Daniel Malan, J. G. Strijdom, Henrik Verwoerd, and currently Prime Minister Balthazar J. Vorster, who has governed since 1966, when Verwoerd was assassinated by one of his white constituents—all of whom base their program on the policy of apartheid, an Afrikaans word for separateness. The races, never integrated to begin with, have been pushed farther and farther apart, and the non-white majority more and more repressed, exploited, and terrorized.

One act after another has been legislated, by means of Constitutional violations, including Supreme Court packing and the enlargement of the Senate to give it a preponderantly Nationalist majority. Legislation includes the Morality Amendment Act, the Prohibition of Mixed Marriages Act, the Population Registration Act—all to maintain "racial purity." There is also the Group Areas Act, which sets aside specific areas for the exclusive occupancy of each racial group. This is the act under which *Bantustans*—separate "countries" or "homelands"—would be established for Africans. Since these areas are mostly undeveloped, the government is trying to provide factories and industry on the borders, to which black workers can commute. Still, non-whites are being removed from residential areas within cities and must now travel several hours each day from their suburban "location" homes to jobs in the cities. In 1970 the Bantu Laws Amendment Act was passed, which prohibits whites from hiring blacks for certain positions, except in black areas or with special government exemption. Proscribed jobs include phone operators, cashiers and typists in shops, offices, factories, and hotels. All Africans must carry "reference"—or pass—books, which they are asked to produce incessantly. Imprisonment is the punishment for the slightest irregularity. The hated passbooks were the *raison d'être* for the Sharpeville riots—and others which followed—early in 1960.

These were staged by the Pan-Africanist Congress, an offshoot of the long-established and more moderate African National Congress. Leaders of both groups were imprisoned, along with hundreds of sympathetic whites, as a result of these riots, in which the police brutally opened fire on crowds of unarmed Africans, killing scores of people.

Opposing the government is not easy. The English-language press—in contrast to the pro-government Afrikaans-language press—is critical, but it suggests few alternatives to apartheid. Anyone considered a "troublemaker" or "agitator" can be automatically arrested under the Suppression of Communism Act, under which no charges need be proved. The Dutch Reformed Church of South Africa, to a large extent, supports the government, and condones its policies, as un-Christian as they appear to others. Most Afrikaners are communicants of this strong church. Only minority churches such as the Anglican and Roman Catholic have opposed the government, but so far, to little avail. (An Anglican Bishop of Johannesburg was deported from the country because of his anti-apartheid point of view in 1960, and history repeated itself in 1971, when the Anglican Dean of Johannesburg, Very Rev. Gonville ffrench-Beytagh, was charged with plotting to violently overthrow the government; he was acquitted, but left immediately for his native Britain.)

Despite the official and unofficial condemnation of apartheid by the UN and by individual nations all over the world, South Africa seems firmly committed to its racial policies. (UN votes on the subject are taken regularly. The General Assembly, for example, voted in late 1971—109 to 2—to condemn apartheid and to seek means of boycott. Only South Africa itself and Portugal voted against the motion, which expressed "grave indignation . . . over any and every act of maltreatment and torture of opponents of apartheid . . . and the increased prosecution of religious leaders opposed to that policy.") Government officials defend these policies by pointing out that black South Africans fare better than those of most Black African countries—as well they might in this, one of the richest lands in the world. But there have been some changes, chiefly in the form of blacks' increased awareness of their racial identity. Because of an economic boom there have been labor breakthroughs, with blacks filling jobs for which no whites were available, and improved salaries for some blacks.

Black students have demonstrated new pride in their race and more and more are calling themselves "black" instead of the pejorative "bantu." The new black consciousness, reflecting in part similar trends throughout the world, also has resulted in some improvement in conditions and salaries, although there has been little relaxation of strict segregation. The absurdity of the apartheid laws—and the way in which they are interpreted to favor whites—was illustrated in the 1972 appearance in Cape Town of dancer Margot Fonteyn, sadly not among the many distinguished performers who refuse to accept South African engagements. Nonwhites were not, of course, admitted to Miss Fonteyn's performances at a whites-only theater. But later, ballet-starved whites disguised as "coloreds" and Asians were admitted to the nonwhites theater, the police apparently turning their backs on this infringement of the law.

Alan Paton's beloved country is today probably the saddest land in the world with a government that is surely one of the most immoral. But it is, at the same time, one of the most fascinating and one of the most beautiful. One wonders how a population composed of antagonistic groups which expend great portions of time, effort, and money on fighting each other could have developed such a land. The Afrikaners and the English-speaking South Africans are kept busy enough hating each other, building separate schools and universities for each other, and at the same time establishing and maintaining separate facilities—housing, schools, transportation, etc.—for the Africans or "Bantu" (pure-blooded blacks), the "coloreds," (mixed-blood people), and the Indians for whom, incidentally, Mohandas Gandhi spent his early years fighting, one result of which was the implementation of his now world-renounced passive-resistance techniques.

But the country has managed to thrive and develop despite the hate that broods over it. Possibly because it is a land which has known much suffering, it has produced more internationally acclaimed writers than any other land that has ever been a part of the Commonwealth. These would include Alan Paton, Nadine Gordimer, Dan Jacobson, Peter Abrahams, William Plomer, Pauline Smith, Laurens van der Post—to name but a few. (Censorship, though, remains tight, of books of course, but of movies, too. Johannesburg film critics suspended their awards in 1971, explaining that the best of the year's movies, as rated by British and U.S. reviewers, were all banned in South Africa.) It is a rich land of gold, diamonds, and other precious natural resources. Its fertile farms and vineyards produce luscious fruits and grapes for South African-made wines and brandies. Its industry is advanced and money-making. Its cities' skyscrapers reach high into the sky. It is a land of strikingly handsome mountains; dramatic plains, known by the Afrikaans word "veld"; the unbelievably lovely Cape of Good Hope; the animal parks, among which is one of the biggest on the continent; seaside resorts on two oceans; one of the highest standards of living in the world for the ruling, selfish, and shockingly exploitive white minority, in contrast with abject poverty and police-state regimentation for the majority of nonwhites.

Is this a country to visit? The answer can only be a personal one. Actually to see an immoral authoritarian state—and South Africa is such a state—is to learn for oneself, to benefit from knowledge that can come only from firsthand experience. (Some visitors may, of course, wish they had never gone. Civil rights pioneer Roy Wilkins, executive director of the National Association for the Advancement of Colored People, made a 1972 trip, principally to address a conference on African education. But he made headlines around the world when the press reported his comments on American business in South Africa. Although it developed that he was urging U.S. firms in South Africa to improve the working conditions of their black employees and pay them the same as whites, his comments were at first reported as a defense of American business in South Africa, and he was publicly critized by both the American Committee on Africa and the Committee of Concerned Blacks. It should be noted that upon his departure he remarked that he found apartheid "appalling in the humiliation of the spirit of the people." It should be noted, too, that some three hundred U.S. firms operate in South Africa, and that a panel of specialists researching their policies and practices for the United Nations Association, in 1971 summed up: "With a few notable exceptions, they are not now in the forefront of the effort to improve the economic and social lot of their nonwhite South African workers. Indeed, there appears to be a tendency, dictated not locally but by parent companies at home, to lean over backwards not to offend the South African government.") But it is worth noting that in 1971 the Interamerican Travel Agents Society—a U.S. national organization of black travel agents—announced plans for a program that would convince the American travel trade to refrain from booking travel to South Africa. The decision came after the South African Embassy in Washington failed to reply to a society questionnaire on racial policies.

YOUR VISIT TO SOUTH AFRICA

Johannesburg: The biggest of South Africa's cities, Johannesburg serves as an introduction to the country for most visitors from abroad—at least for those arriving by air. Its wealth, of course, is based on the gold mined from beneath its streets, evidences of which are all about the town in the form of great refuse heaps. Along with these ubiquitous slag piles, Johannesburg's façade is one of soaring skyscrapers; it is the financial center, the industrial center, the mining center of the nation, and many of its white residents have become rich, as one can easily perceive by strolls through Commissioner Street and the other shop-lined main thoroughfares, or the handsome white residential sections. The "locations," or segregated housing quarters of the Africans, are a considerable way out of the city, and can be visited only with a special government permit, designed to prove that the law works both ways—Africans need passes to move about, and whites need special permission to visit African areas. Needless to say, the great majority of whites haven't the faintest interest in visiting African "locations," and whites are never stopped by the police for identity cards; Africans are—constantly.

A highlight of a Johannesburg visit is a trip through a gold mine.

Accompanied by guides, groups are taken 6000 feet below the surface to see how the valuable ore is extracted from the earth and, at the same time, under what conditions the lowly paid miners work. They are drawn not only from South Africa but from nearby countries, as well, housed and fed in special compounds resembling prisons, employed by contract for periods of many months, and given their quarters, food, medical care, and a pittance of a salary. On Sundays they are organized tribally for "recreational" dances—presumably voluntary—to which visitors are welcome. Dressed rather pitifully in costumes they've tried to piece together themselves, they do their best—obviously tired from a full week's work—to entertain. They might look a little livelier if their employers would at least provide them with attractive costumes. Drives about town? By all means take in the Zoological Gardens, the sweeping view of the wind-swept veld from Northcliff; the Wilds, a reserve devoted to South African flora, and, of course, the residential sections and the busy downtown area. *Night life* is varied and lively. There are several legitimate theaters, the plays being road-show productions from London's West End—at least, those whose companies are not boycotting the country, as a means of anti-apartheid protest—many concert halls, including the Great Hall of the English-language University of the Witwatersrand; drive-in restaurants patterned after those of California, with waffles, hamburgers, and hot dogs the featured fare; restaurants with South African dishes, all too many of which are English in origin; and a number of excellent continental European spots. *Tip*—Keep off side streets late at night, and if you are female, don't go out at all in the evening, unescorted. Johannesburg's crime rate is one of the highest of any city in the world. Unrest among exploited Africans is bound to make itself felt, and it is most apparent in this unhappy city—the only town in the world, except for Naples, for which I would offer such advice.

Pretoria: Just 40 miles from Johannesburg—and served by its airport—is Pretoria, the attractive administrative capital, and one of its most heavily Afrikaans-speaking cities. In the late spring (autumn to Northern Hemisphere visitors), thousands of purple jacaranda trees bloom on virtually all the city's streets. And the rest of the year, gardens and parks keep the town bright and colorful. Outstanding are the Union Buildings, the principal offices of the government; the house from which Sir Winston Churchill escaped during the Boer War; the magnificent palace of the prime minister (named, ironically, Libertas); the Voortrekker Monument, a bulky, graceless pile erected to honor the Boers who trekked north from the Cape and settled the Transvaal; and the home—now a museum—of the Transvaal's late president, Paul Kruger. Near Pretoria are the villages and farms of the handsome Ndebele people—Africans who have preserved traditional dress and ways of life. They ring their necks and ankles with thick beaded bracelets, and the women wear elaborate beaded aprons.

Kruger and other national parks: Three hundred miles from Johannesburg by car or tour bus is Kruger National Park, among the largest in Africa—a 200-mile-long rectangle, with a number of motel-like camps for visitors within its borders. No shooting allowed, of course, but photography takes its place, and visitors drive through the dirt roads of the park for close-up views of elephant, hippo, giraffe, kidu, impala, antelope, monkey, baboon, and—if one is lucky—lion and leopard. Parts of the park are open the year round, but the season for most areas is May 29 through October 15. The camps, where visitors stay in thatched-roof cabins known in Afrikaans as *rondavels*, and patterned on African huts, are booked months in advance, mainly by South Africans, so that reservations should be made as far ahead as possible. Kruger is a must for any visitor to Africa who will not have a chance to visit game reserves in other countries. It is more commercial than most others, overcrowded with busloads full of rubberneckers, and a little overcomfortable, with its luxurious dining pavilions and cabins. As a result of its constantly expanding human population, the animals (except for semitame baboons and monkeys that ride on car roofs) are making themselves scarcer and less visible, for which they can hardly be blamed. Less visited by far is the *Hluhluwe Reserve* (pronounced Shlo-shlo-wee) in Natal Province, which is one of the few areas in Africa where one can see the rare "white" rhino, as well as the more conventional "black" rhino. *The Royal Natal National Park* is a 20,000-acre reserve which specializes in superb scenery, swimming, riding, fishing—and animal viewing, to boot. It contains the Tugela River Falls, and towering Mount Aux-Sources.

Kimberley: World famous as a diamond-mining center, Kimberley lies between Johannesburg and Cape Town, in the midst of the harsh, barren veld. Its attractions are the modern miners' hostels of the De Beers mines, with a personnel policy fairly enlightened—for South Africa; the original, now abandoned, "Big Hole" mine, which is the world's largest man-made hole and still open to visitors, as are the old mine buildings near its edge; the now active mines, and the fascinating De Beers processing and sorting factories. In the town itself—still rather Wild West in *ambiance*—the chief landmarks of the old days are the unpretentious but charming Victorian-style office building which still serves as De Beers's headquarters and the history-filled Kimberley Club, of which Cecil Rhodes was a member.

Cape Town: Earliest of the European settlements, and known for centuries as the "Tavern of the Seas" because of its hospitality to mariners, Cape Town is one of the world's most spectacularly beautiful cities, and the only large South African town which approaches mellowness. Situated beneath the famed, flat Table Mountain, the city embraces a series of hills which lead down to the sea. To the west are the beaches of the Atlantic Ocean, and, to the east, those of the Indian Ocean. The cable-car ride up Table Mountain offers a fantastic view of the Cape Coast, and the visitor is advised to take in more of this region by means of a trip, by private car or excursion bus, to the Cape of Good Hope, which is a memorable half day's drive away. Cape Town blends the colonial period—both Dutch and British—with today. There are charming, narrow streets reminiscent of the early days; spanking new office buildings; the quiet and lovely Public Gardens around which the principal buildings are situated; the graceful Anglican cathedral (which for long displayed a huge poster board defiantly advising one and all that it was open to people of all races at all times); the

National Art Gallery; the Public Library. Elsewhere in the city are the impressive Rhodes Memorial, built somewhat along the lines of the one honoring Lincoln in Washington; Rhodes's home, which was the governor-general's Cape Town residence and is designed in the lovely Cape Dutch style which is typical of the region. Cape Town is the easiest of the country's cities in which to relax. One finds that more people seem less rigid, less biased, more cosmopolitan in their point of view than elsewhere. The non-white population is principally "Cape colored"—or mulatto. Along the Cape Coast, suburbs extend in both directions. There is the National Botanical Garden at *Kristenbosch*, and *Groot Constantia*, one of the few remaining old Cape Dutch houses, and now a museum; the *Marine Drive* runs for 100 miles around the Cape Peninsula to *Muizenberg*, a delightful resort. And the *Garden Route* extends along the Cape as far east as *Plettenberg Bay*—a stretch of 300 miles and one of the most exhilarating scenic drives in the world.

Durban: Durban, besides being a seaside resort on the Indian Ocean, is, as well, a major manufacturing center, a leading port, and the major English-speaking city of the country. Along its Marine Parade are dozens of resort hotels which run the gamut in luxury. There are amusements for children and mile after mile of beaches, swimming pools, and cafés. Most vacationers are South Africans or Rhodesians, for Durban offers year-round swimming weather, much like the resorts of Florida. Its African and Indian markets are interesting, and half a day's drive away are the mountain villages of *Zululand*, whose inhabitants—once-proud warriors—remain excellent dancers and craftsmen. Both north and south of Durban there are smaller resorts and more intimate resort towns, such as *Margate*. But Durban is the Queen City of the Natal coast, hardly elegant but with a distinction of its own—a blend perhaps of Asia, with a great Indian population (South African Indians are mostly restricted to Natal Province), Africa (the Zulu rickshaw drivers resplendent in brilliant costumes and great headdresses that must weigh fifty pounds, if the one I tried on is typical), and even America, if one can call American the hamburgers and hot dogs which waiters hawk on the sandy beaches. *Tip*—Swim only in protected, supervised beach areas, for there are hungry sharks about.

Other cities: If there's time on your itinerary, you might want to visit *Bloemfontein*, in the Orange Free State, another Afrikaner stronghold, and the judicial capital; *Stellenbosch*, an old Cape village with an Afrikaans-language university; *East London* and *Port Elizabeth*, both modern industrial cities, with few outstanding charms or inducements.

SHOPPING

The major cities are full of European-owned curio shops which pay little for African-made merchandise, and sell it at steep prices. I would recommend making purchases directly from Africans in the great markets of the major towns, or at roadside stands which they themselves operate. Worth looking for: earthenware bowls, simple and austere; beadwork—belts, covered gourds, etc.; woodcarving and basketry. Bargaining is the rule.

CREATURE COMFORTS

HOTELS—**Johannesburg:** Choose from the modern, six-hundred-room, full-facility Carlton (operated by Western International Hotels, the first U.S. luxury-hotel chain to acquiesce to the blandishments of the South Africans and operate a hotel in apartheid-land, for shame, for shame), President, Rand International, Langham, Balalaika, Moulin Rouge. **Pretoria:** Boulevard, Assembly, Culembourg. **Cape Town:** Mount Nelson (the traditional leader), Grand, Athurs Seat, President. **Durban:** Edward (the smart, old-school leader), Eden Roc, Four Season, Park View. **Bloemfontein:** Maitland. **Port Elizabeth:** Beach, Marine. **East London:** Deal's, King's; **Kimberley:** Savoy. RESTAURANTS AND NIGHTLIFE: **Johannesburg** restaurants include the Café Royal, Prospect, Chez André (French), and Franco's (Italian). There is dancing and entertainment at Ciro's, Greek Taverna, and Monk's Tavern.

Cape Town restaurants include Rossi's (Italian), Café Royal, and the grillrooms of the Mount Nelson and Grand hotels; the Mount Nelson Grillroom has dancing. Licensing hours, countrywide, are 10 A.M. to 11 P.M. daily except Sundays and religious holidays, when you may be served only at your hotel; women are still not allowed in bars, but may drink in hotel lounges. South African cuisine is generally dull with the exception of the fresh fish and seafood, and a few specialties: *sassaties*—curry-flavored kebabs; *bobotie*—a spiced meat favorite; and *braaivleis*—barbecue. *Biltong*, the dried meat, is easily skippable. Italian and Greek immigrants have taken to opening restaurants, for which be grateful. Wine-making is a fairly substantial industry and the wine is generally good, although by no means is every restaurant licensed to serve it; customers may, however, cart along their own.

NAMIBIA

Prior to World War I Namibia (South West Africa) had been a German territory. The League of Nations, after the war, mandated it to the Union of South Africa. After World War II, however, all mandates of the League became United Nations Trust Territories with the UN given the prerogative of placing them under the care of any power it chose to select. South Africa, however, would not give up Namibia; it ignored the UN's requests, and in recent years has administered it as a fifth province, even though it has not officially incorporated it into its own territory. It is in effect, a South African satellite—with a relationship not unlike that of the Soviet Union and the Baltic States.

In late 1971 and early 1972, Pretoria's arbitrary and repressive apartheid policy—extended to Namibia blacks as to those of the republic—began to backfire. More than thirteen thousand Ovambo workers in Namibia struck against a contract-labor system they specifically termed the equivalent of slavery. Their unprecedented action was so effective that work halted in the copper mines, commerce came almost to a complete halt, and public services were at a standstill. But the government's response was unprecedented, too. Since Ovambos total more than half of Namibia's population of about 650,000, the government knew it had to pay the strikers some heed. And it did, with an agreement giving them greater freedom of movement (they were allowed to change jobs, which had earlier been illegal), better pay and working conditions, and the possibility of living with their families—also heretofore illegal. There is no question but that the strike was a history-maker in southern Africa. What remained to be seen was whether one of its effects would be the transfer of Namibia from rule by Pretoria—with apartheid and Bantustans—to United Nations control, and the fresh start its overwhelmingly black populace has so long been denied. UN Secretary General Kurt Waldheim personally visited Namibia in 1972, and predicted that South Africa would grant it "self-determination and independence." He named no date.

Windhoek, the capital—a short flight from Johannesburg—is a small town with a still German atmosphere, at an altitude of 5000 feet. The leading hotel is the Continental. There is a substantial German community, the German language is still spoken along with Afrikaans and a little English, and there are even a few Rhine-type castles on the outlying hills. In Windhoek places of interest include the Old Fort Museum and the Administration Building, which has a colorful frieze that depicts the history of the area. *Walvis Bay* (leading hotels: Atlantic and Flamingo) is the chief port. The country is mostly plateau and desert, with diamonds and caracal the chief sources of income. There is a resort at *Swakopmund,* on the coast (leading hotels: Fuerst Bismarck and Panorama), and in the *Brandberg Mountain* is a Bushman rock painting called the *White Lady* and reputed to be thousands of years old. Besides the Bushmen of the Kalahari Desert, other interesting tribes include the tall, attractive Herreros whose women wear clothes modeled after those of Victorian missionaries' wives, and the Ovambos in the north. There is a huge game reserve at *Etosha,* with simple visitors' accommodations.

The issue of South Africa's mandate over South West Africa

was taken before the International Court of Justice by Liberia and Ethiopia in late 1960, and debated by the UN General Assembly's Trusteeship Committee—with South Africa (to no one's surprise) boycotting the debate. The Trusteeship Committee's resolution—which called on South Africa to end apartheid in South West Africa—was approved by the General Assembly, 78–0. Among the minority of abstainees in the vote was—and one is saddened to relate this—the United States. In 1966, the UN officially terminated South Africa's mandate over South West Africa, and the following year it appointed a council to administer the territory. In 1968 the name of the area was changed to Namibia, an alteration that South Africa for the most part chooses to ignore. In 1971, in an effort to ease the controversy and ill will surrounding the status of South West Africa, South Africa proposed to the World Court that a plebiscite be held to allow the people of the area to choose their own political status. At the same time South Africa asked for the opportunity to rebut the claims that the people of South West Africa are cruelly oppressed.

The World Court voted, in June 1971, overwhelmingly in favor of the UN resolution demanding that South Africa end its administration of South West Africa. And in October 1971, the UN Security Council strongly condemned South Africa's refusal to turn over control of Namibia to the UN—the United States voting with the majority of thirteen out of fifteen. The resolution stated that continued refusal to transfer the territory to UN administration, "could create" conditions detrimental to the maintenance of peace and security in the region.

THE SUDAN

Republic of the Sudan

Entry requirements: *A visa obtainable from Sudanese consulates, plus a health certificate (smallpox and yellow fever) and letters of reference.* **Best times for a visit:** *The Sudan is never what one might call air-conditioned. Winters, though, are considerably cooler than summers. There is very little rain—ever.* **Currency:** *The pound: 0.348 pounds=$1.* **Principal European language:** *English, with Arabic the official language.* **Domestic transport:** *Air service to major centers; Nile River steamer service; a fairly extensive rail network, much of it along the scenic Nile; and a poor-to-fair road system.* **Further information:** *Embassy of the Republic of the Sudan, Washington, D.C.; Government Information Service, Khartoum, Sudan.*

INTRODUCING THE SUDAN

The Republic of the Sudan is Africa's largest country. Here, after all, is a country with an area a third as big as that of the United States, and a population of some fifteen million. Until it gained independence in 1954, it had been a colony of one sort or another of one foreign power or another for several centuries; in its most recent pre-independence years, it had the dubious distinction of being occupied by *two* foreign governments simultaneously—one of the rare condominiums of modern times. Its people are hospitable, charming, and proud—and well they might be, for their country was the seat of the ancient civilization which experts now believe to have influenced the cultures of sub-Sahara Africa more than any other: the kingdom of Cush, which many archaeologists believe to have been the most African of the old societies. Beginning in 1000 B.C., its influence penetrated to the south and southwest of the great continent, and the developments which occurred, in fields such as agriculture, mining and work in metals, and community organization, have many of their origins in the forerunner of today's Sudan.

The best known of Cush's cities was *Meroë*, whose remains still stand, just 100 miles from the present Sudanese capital of Khartoum. Only a fraction of Meroë has as yet been explored by professional researchers, and many believe that what remains is the most important archaeological site in Africa, and one of the most important in the world.

Meroë and its environs flourished more than two thousand years ago. The pyramids, fortifications, temples, sphinxes, pottery bits, and other relics so far uncovered give evidence of a treasurehouse of art and architecture which the Sudan government's Antiquities Service hopes to unearth when more funds become available. Enough is known already, though, for it to have been concluded that Meroë, and other Cushite cities, were centers of the world of the period, receiving envoys and merchants from the north—throughout the then Mediterranean world—and from the African areas to the south. Meroë's culture was not Egyptian; much of it was considered indigenous, but there seems little doubt of Egyptian influence in certain spheres—authoritarian monarchies, elaborate caste systems, great monuments, a splendid architectural tradition utilizing iron, bronze, and stone.

Other Cushite cities were even closer to today's Khartoum—*Musawarat* and *Naga*, the latter the best preserved of all, with its imposing Lion Temple dominating all the ruins. It is a pity that more is not known of Cush. The temptations of ancient Egyptian relics have been more appealing to the diggers, and Cush is only beginning to have its day. Still, enough is known of its importance. This was the kingdom that for a brief period was Egypt's occupier—under King Piankhi—and that ruled from Egypt to Ethiopia, and possibly all the way into Uganda. Axum, Ethiopia's great ancient kingdom, was probably responsible for the downfall of Cush soon after A.D. 300. But Cush—unlike other vacuum-like ancient civilizations which made little impact on the rest of the world—left its imprint. Some believe it to have been responsible for bringing the Iron Age to sub-Sahara Africa—not only to the immediate south and east, but as far distant as West Africa, where Cushite culture and religion still remain a part of the fabric of life in certain regions.

The Sudan, in the sixth century A.D., was rapidly Christianized, and during the height of Coptic influence, churches dotted the banks of the Nile; during this period, the country was divided into two kingdoms, one in the north, the other in the south. But Christianity was not to last. In the thirteenth century, the Turkish rulers of Egypt moved south to Islamize the northern half of the Sudan, and its two kingdoms eventually disintegrated, to be replaced by a loose feudal confederation which lasted some three centuries. Then the Turks in Egypt again moved south, remaining in control until 1885, and employing, in the latter years, Europeans, including the famed General Gordon. But about 1880 the Mahdi, a politico-religious fanatic who called himself Messiah of Islam, initiated a revolt against the occupiers, established Omdurman as his capital, captured Khartoum, and killed General Gordon. The British advised the Turko-Egyptians to clear out, which they did, and the Sudan, under the Mahdi's successor—the Khalifa (Lieutenant) remained independent until 1898.

But sovereignty was not to last for long. Fearing that the French would come to dominate the region, the British got together with the Egyptians, and under the imperious Lord Kitchener returned with an expeditionary force which culminated in the Battle of Omdurman in 1898. The following year the Khalifa died in battle, and the Anglo-Egyptian Sudan came into existence as a condominium, with Britain supplying the great majority of the administrators and wielding the great bulk of power.

The British restored order and ruled—with the aid of a fantastically well-paid civil-service elite (the Sudan Service)—as well as an occupier could have, considering the current attitudes of the West toward underdeveloped peoples. Sudanese were gradually taken into administration, and education progressed. By 1944 they were sitting on provincial councils, and two Sudanese political parties developed—one favoring independence, the other union with Egypt. In 1948 a partly elected Legislature was established, and in 1953 the occupying powers agreed to grant independence, which was granted—completely and irrevocably, with no strings attached and without any violence—in January 1956. The new country chose not to affiliate with the British Commonwealth.

Sovereignty, despite the great enthusiasm of many Sudanese, has tough going. Corruption saturated the government; the major parties bickered more than major parties should; groups intrigued with Nasser and accepted great sums of money from his government, for which they were to have arranged a union with the new Egypt—which wanted more control over the all-important Nile waters than it was getting. In March 1958 the first elections since independence brought in a hard-working, conscientious Prime Minister, Abdullah Khalil, but he could not rout out corruption and intrigue as rapidly as he anticipated. Economic chaos—spurred by an Egyptian boycott of surplus cotton—ensued, and on November 17, in a bloodless *coup d'état*, the army quietly took over the government. Lieutenant General Ibrahim Abboud declared martial law, abrogated the constitution, dissolved political parties, banned public meetings, and suspended newspapers, with the aim of stopping "the bitter political strife between parties vying to secure personal gain." He banned further use of Old School titles such as "Pasha" and "Bey," hired a number of enlightened leaders to work in his government, and even got the rival parties' top brass to forget temporarily their rivalries.

However, in 1964 Abboud was overthrown and civil government was restored. During this time the long-standing conflict —it has, at times, amounted to civil war—between Christian and animist blacks in the south and the Moslem-controlled government of the north intensified, with widespread attacks against government forces. This conflict persisted until 1972, when the four million southerners were at long last accorded regional autonomy, and the Sudan established diplomatic relations with the Vatican, opening the door for the return of Christian missionaries to the south. In 1969, a military council, led by the Premier, Major General Gafaar al-Nimeiry, established a revolutionary council to govern the country. In 1970 he was elected President, formed a cabinet, and established a one-party system. The following year he was (a) deposed by a leftist coup on July 21 and (b) returned to power in a countercoup on July 24. It is no wonder that the Sudan asks visitors from abroad to go to the trouble of producing letters of reference before being issued visas.

YOUR VISIT TO THE SUDAN

Khartoum: The British, for reasons probably more political than social, never encouraged visitors to the Sudan and the Sudanese have never done so, either. Khartoum is, paradoxically, one of the most attractive cities the British built in Africa. Originally founded by occupying Egyptians in the early 1800s, it was destroyed by the Mahdi's ferocious dervishes, and rebuilt by the British under the direction of Lord Kitchener, who took over as chief architect. And who but such an egomaniacal chauvinist would lay out a town in the form of the British Union Jack? The great villas of the highly paid British civil servants occupied the most desirable location—along the banks of the Nile; they now serve adequately as government ministries and office buildings. But as pleasant as it is to walk along the river esplanade, there are other points of interest: the confluence of the White and Blue Niles at the White Nile Bridge; the delightful zoo at the river's edge; the University of Khartoum and its School of Medicine, founded by Kitchener and enriched by the British with a grant of two million pounds in appreciation of Sudanese World War II services; the National Museum, with its relics testifying to the country's rich ancient cultures; and the Republican Palace, formerly the headquarters of Lord Kitchener and his successors as governor-general.

Omdurman: In contrast to the capital—which after all is a European-designed city, still mainly an administrative center—is the much more Sudanese town of Omdurman, just a few miles distant. Though by no means ancient (it was built by the Mahdi's successor, the Khalifa, to replace battle-ravaged Khartoum), Omdurman embodies the Moslem flavor of the northern Sudan. During the years of the Mahdi and the Khalifa it was important not only as a capital but as a holy city as well. Pilgrimages to Mecca were replaced by treks to Omdurman, with its great Mosque Square (standing capacity: 100,000), which had served as the Court of Assembly of the Dervishes and is still the site of major gatherings, both religious and political. Bordering it is the tomb of the revered Mahdi, the immense silver-tinted Khalifa's Mosque, and that gentleman's residence, now a museum of Mahdi-Khalifiana—if it can be termed that—with a vast assortment of memorabilia, including a letter from the Khalifa to Queen Victoria, in which that lady was implored to join the ranks of Islam. Omdurman is a town of neat, square, mud-walled houses; long-robed people—the men in white, the women in black—camel caravans resting in the squares; basket-laden donkeys making their way slowly down the dusty streets; venerable barges, designed as they have been for centuries, in the Nile, along whose banks residents scrub both themselves and their animals.

Khartoum North: The third city in the Khartoum complex, Khartoum North is mainly industrial. It is of interest only in that it gives the visitor an idea of the extent to which the Sudan has come to grips with today's technology. Of the three towns, Omdurman has the biggest population—probably close to 200,000.

Wadi Seidna: A half day's drive from Khartoum, along the Nile, past the historic battlefield sites of pre-condominium days and through the tiny villages, one reaches the oasis-like center of Wadi Seidna, with a handsome swimming pool and luxuriant gardens.

Souba: This was the capital of the pre-Islamic Sudan during the days of the Christians. Its remains—what there are of them—are well worth a visit, which can be made in half a day's drive from the capital.

Wad Medani: This is the capital of the Blue Nile Province, and the center of the Gezira district—a triangle of a million acres between the White and Blue Niles, where, by means of irrigation, cotton and other crops are successfully cultivated. The area is a result of the construction of the Sennar Dam; it is a memorial to British administration at its best in the Sudan. By leaving early in the morning, one can visit Wad Medani and return to Khartoum late in the evening, precluding the need for overnight accommodation in the area. If the Sennar Dam itself is to be visited (and a dam is a dam is a dam—even in Africa), simple overnight accommodation can be had. But the day-long trip is recommended, insuring a glimpse of the countryside—cotton fields, ginning factories, open-air markets, Moslem mosques, and leaders' tombs.

Meroë, Musawarat, and Naga: These three centers of ancient Sudanese greatness (320–21) are still not developed as tourist centers, but it would be a pity not to visit at least one of them (Naga is the closest to Khartoum) and it would be worth making special arrangements for an excursion, upon arrival in Khartoum.

Port Sudan: Chief port of the republic, Port Sudan fronts the Red Sea and is a principal stopping-off point for African Moslems on pilgrimages to Mecca. It is not, in any other respect, a particularly interesting city, but it might be worth a day's visit while en route to Erkowit.

Erkowit: The Sudan's most-developed resort lies amid the Red Sea Hills, less than 30 miles by good road from Port Sudan, and a short flight from Khartoum. Formerly a sort of summer capital for British administrators, Erkowit has a simple but adequate resthouse, and is equipped with sightseeing facilities, not the least of which are camels, rented by their proprietors—the Fuzzy-Wuzzies, known before Kipling as the Hadendowa. The people of the area—Fuzzy-Wuzzies and others—are typical of the Hamitic-origin inhabitants of the northern Sudan. Though not exactly newcomers—they have been in the region a good four thousand years—they are considered descendants of Middle Eastern Hamitic peoples, in contrast to the southern Sudanese who are primarily indigenous black Africans.

The South: Treated as a separate entity during condominium days the South is largely undeveloped tribal, non-Moslem, and covered by great stretches of papyrus-producing *sudd* or swamp. Flights can be made to *Juba*, its principal town, for excursions into the countryside.

SHOPPING

Bargaining is the rule in the *souks*, or markets, but it is done with considerably more restraint than in neighboring Egypt, and neither merchant nor prospective buyer is unduly enervated. *Ideal sources:* Omdurman's souks with beautifully hand-carved ivory necklaces and bracelets; curved daggers lovingly fashioned of steel, orange-dyed leather and natural-colored snakeskin, and dark wood, tiny skullcaps, hand-crocheted before your eyes by Omdurman's talented lady artisans, and a great range of hammered copperware—trays, coffee servers, vases.

CREATURE COMFORTS

HOTELS—**Khartoum:** Old Sudan hands will remember that for many decades, the capital's principal hostelry was the venerable, once-grand Grand, perfectly situated overlooking the confluence of the two Niles. Sadly deteriorated during the early post-Independence period, the Grand has in recent years been updated with a good air-conditioned dining room, and air conditioning and private baths in some of the high-ceilinged rooms. But the Grand has competition. Indeed, it now takes second place, top honors in town going to its recent next-door neighbor, with an equally fine river-view situation: the Hotel Sudan; all the Sudan's bedrooms are with bath and air conditioning, and there is an air-conditioned restaurant, as well. There being no hotter capital in all Africa, Djibouti possibly excepted, note that air conditioning is nowhere more desirable. **Erkowit:** Government Rest House. **Port Sudan:** Red Sea. **Juba:** Juba. **Wadi Halfa:** Nile. **Wad Medani:** Gezira. Sudan's two national parks have a number of rest camps, but no food is available at them, and they are relatively inaccessible, in contrast with game reserves of neighboring countries.

SWAZILAND

Kingdom of Swaziland

Entry requirements: *No visa is required.* **Best times for a visit:** *The weather is generally temperate; rainfall occurs throughout the year, but May to October tend to be drier and pleasanter.* **Currency:** *South African rand: 0.714 rands=$1.* **Principal European language:** *English is the official language.* **Domestic transport:** *Limited roads and railway; internal air service.* **Further information:** *Embassy of the Kingdom of Swaziland, Washington, D.C.*

INTRODUCING SWAZILAND

Like Lesotho, Swaziland is a country of towering peaks, but it is considerably smaller—one of the smallest countries in Africa, for that matter. There are not more than 420,000 inhabitants in an area of 6000 square miles, but the white minority here—unlike Lesotho—hold a good two thirds of the land, with the rest reserved for the Swazi, most of whom are farmers. The country is almost surrounded by South Africa, except for the seventy miles of eastern border it shares with Mozambique. Swaziland was a British Protectorate from 1903, when the king of the time, Mbandzeni, sold part of his domain to the Transvaal Boers, and the remainder to Britain, which retained it after the formation of the Union. Though not as advanced politically as Lesotho, it made more progress economically, thanks to a number of British Colonial Development Corporation projects. In 1967 Swaziland became self-governing under the British and in 1968 it became an independent state, the last British territory in Africa to win its freedom.

Swaziland is a lush and beautiful land of rolling, fertile lowlands, rich plantations, and huge forests. Of the three former British protectorates in southern Africa Swaziland seems to have the best potential for economic development. With the aid of South African and British investment the country is exploiting its mineral and agricultural wealth—iron ore, asbestos, sugar cane, pineapples, citrus fruits, and timber are the main products—and exports are growing each year. Swaziland has been governed since 1921 by Kind Sobhuza II. Known to his people as Ngwenyama, or Lion, he is a colorful figure as apt to be found in formal Western clothes as in the national costume known as "mahia." He manages to preserve the traditions of the past while at the same time helping his country progress economically and socially. Swaziland's Hotel and Tourist Board is tremendously enthusiastic about the burgeoning tourist industry; most visitors are white South Africans.

YOUR VISIT TO SWAZILAND

Mbabane: The official capital and former seat of British officialdom is the most convenient headquarters for drives through the countryside, where the chief attraction—aside from the rugged mountains—is the population. The Swazi are handsome, superbly costumed people who retain many of their traditional customs. They are basically a rural people who live in villages of huts shaped like beehives. Mbabane itself, once a colonial town, is rapidly turning into a modern city.

Excursions from Mbabane: A few miles outside of the capital is the Mlilwane Game Sanctuary, well stocked with rhinoceros, giraffe, antelope, and a variety of birds. A drive across the country to Mozambique affords spectacular views, and visitors heading toward South Africa will enjoy traveling through the Edulweni and Malkerns valleys, backed by majestic mountains, toward the coastal route that leads to Durban. One of Swaziland's main attractions is the luxurious Royal Swazi Hotel and Casino, just seven miles east of Mbabane. Here one can enjoy golf, tennis, swimming, bowling, and—unique in all of southern Africa—gambling in the lavish casino. The hotel attracts an international clientele, and there is no color bar; the roulette tables, dance floors, and bars are crowded with white South Africans, black Swazi civil servants, Portuguese from Mozambique, Indians, and any other combination of nationalities and races. Worth visiting as well: the verdant forests surrounding the delightfully named town of *Piggs Peak*, the asbestos mines at *Emlembe*, and the rest resorts in the *Lebombo Mountains*.

SHOPPING

Grass skirts and mats, seed necklaces, oiled-wood utensils, and carvings can be bought in the market in Mbabane. Prices are reasonable, and bargaining is the rule.

CREATURE COMFORTS

HOTELS—**Mbabane:** The Royal Swazi—fully air-conditioned and with all recreational facilities, including gambling—is the leader. Others include the Holiday Inn, the Highland View, on the outskirts, the Swazi Inn, and the Tavern. **Manzini:** George Hotel.

TANZANIA

United Republic of Tanzania

Entry requirements: *A visa, obtainable from the Tanzanian Mission to the United Nations, 800 Second Avenue, New York; the Tanzanian Embassy, Washington, D.C., or other Tanzanian diplomatic or consular missions, plus a health certificate (smallpox, yellow fever). Although regulations may change, it is worth noting that visas are generally valid only for the mainland portion of Tanzania. Zanzibar is treated much like a country in its own right, insofar as foreign visitors are concerned. Separate Zanzibari visas are required for travelers arriving from mainland Tanzania; they may usually be obtained at the Zanzibar airport, after application forms are completed. These visas are primarily for Zanzibar Town. Special permission to tour rural areas is needed from the Zanzibar Friendship Tourist Bureau, which keeps a tight rein over all tourist activity. Additionally, visitors bound from the mainland for Zanzibar pay the republic's airport departure tax once upon departure from the mainland for Zanzibar; a second time when leaving Zanzibar, and—should there be a return to the mainland sector of the country, which is often the case—a third time, when exiting finally.*
Photographic restrictions: *The Tanzania National Tourist Board, in a document handed arriving visitors, requests that photographers ask permission before snapping pictures of individuals, the Swahili for this being,* Naweza kupiga picha? *If the reply is* hapana, *the pictures had best not be taken, for that is Swahili for* "No." *In Zanzibar, the authorities are probably more sensitive about picture-taking than anywhere else in Africa. The best rule is to take no pictures,*

even innocuous-seeming ones, without getting an okay of some sort or other from a local in the vicinity. **Currency:** *The shilling, of which there are about seven to the U.S. dollar, each shilling equaling about fourteen American cents. Regulations may change, but it is worth inquiring, before changing dollars into shillings, as to whether or not shillings may be reconverted to dollars upon departure. If such is the case, it is advisable to exchange dollars in small amounts, as needed.* **Principal European language:** *English, of which there is a good bit spoken in hotels, national parks, and transport terminals. However, Swahili is much more widely used and is the national* lingua franca. **Domestic transport:** *East African Airways flights connect major centers, and there are paved highways traversing some, but not all, important routes. There are two international airports. One is at Dar es Salaam, on the Indian Ocean coast. The other—built at a cost of ten million dollars to accommodate jumbo jets, and opened in late 1971—is Kilimanjaro International Airport. It is near the peak of that name between the towns of Arusha and Moshi, in the area of the major national parks.* **Further information:** *Tanzania National Tourist Board, P. O. Box 2485, Dar es Salaam, Tanzania; East African Airways, 576 Fifth Avenue, New York, and P. O. Box 543, Dar es Salaam, Tanzania; Zanzibar Friendship Tourist Bureau, P. O. Box 216, Zanzibar Town, Zanzibar, Tanzania.*

INTRODUCING TANZANIA

How big is Africa? It is, perhaps, easy to realize its vastness when one considers that the area of mainland Tanzania alone is equal to that of France and Germany combined. With its long Indian Ocean coastline, Tanzania has known the outside world for many centuries. Little has been known of its vast interior, but in recent years, archaeologists have uncovered evidence that leads them to believe that it has a history in which it can take pride, with a pre-European period during which an Iron Age culture thrived on its great plains. Indeed, it was in Tanzania's Olduvai Gorge, in 1959, that British anthropologist Louis S. B. Leakey excavated an almost completely intact skull of a man ascertained to be well over a million years old.

There have been elaborate civilizations along the coast. Until relatively recently, credit for their achievements has gone to Persians, Arabs, Indians, Europeans—everyone but the indigenous Africans. Lately, though, the anti-Africanists are being repudiated. Experts are convinced that the great merchant cities and trading kingdoms were predominantly African in their culture—and mainly black African, at that. Today's Tanzanians can hold up their heads as they look back upon a rich past, which was, it is true, a fusion of several cultures, but mainly their own.

This is not to say that the Africans—at least those of the coast—were always their own masters. Arabs of Oman and Zanzibar were the landlords for much of the coast for many centuries, with slaving one of their chief means of livelihood.

The Germans, beginning with missionary activity in 1848, were the first thorn in the Arabs' side. In that year Johannes Rebmann, while looking for converts, came upon Mount Kilimanjaro. Colonists and explorers—including the intrepid Stanley and Livingstone—were on the scene for the next four decades. (Stanley found Livingstone ["Dr. Livingstone, I presume?"] at Ujiji in 1871.) In 1885, the Kaiser granted a charter to the German Colonization Society, and later the Germans rented coastal areas from the Sultan of Zanzibar, who had considered them his own. German East Africa became an actual protectorate in 1889, but went out of existence after the First World War, when most of it went to the British to become Tanganyika Territory, parts to the Portuguese (which were added to Mozambique), and the kingdoms of Ruanda and Urundi to the Belgians, these last now the separate sovereign states of Rwanda and Burundi.

The Tanganyika Legislative Council first met in 1926, but it was only in 1958 that the territory had general elections. The

Tanganyika African Nationalist Union (TANU), led by a young, Edinburgh University-educated son of a tribal chief named Julius Nyerere, won hands down. Nyerere, who visited the United States in 1959, was elected Chief Minister—under the British—in 1960. The following year, the territory won complete independence from Britain, and Chief Minister Nyerere became Prime Minister Nyerere, only to have his title change once again the following year when Tanganyika changed its status to that of a republic, retaining Commonwealth membership, with Julius Nyerere its President.

Meanwhile, the Indian Ocean island that was to become a part of the still unborn United Republic of Tanzania was making political progress, as well. Zanzibar was evolving from the Arabian Nights into the latter part of the twentieth century. For a modest-sized island devoid of natural riches—it is just over fifty miles long—it had had anything but an immodest history. It would be difficult to find another area so small over which so much cloak-and-dagger intrigue had figured. Plotting, scheming, pirating, murdering, slaving, pillaging, lusting—name it and Zanzibar has had it. Heads were being chopped off at public executions as late as 1890, when, like proper Gilbert and Sullivan heroes, the British helped put a stop to the bloodshed after being called in as "protectors" by the reigning sultan. From then until independence came, the British remained on the scene in small numbers, the power behind the sultan's throne.

But they were not the first foreigners to occupy the island. The ancient Persians arrived about a thousand years back; their name—Zanzibar derives from the old Persian for "Land of the Blacks"—remains. Later, Arabs of Muscat and Oman began to cruise along the East African coast and grabbed up conveniently located Zanzibar, which they put to use for their operations as slave and ivory dealers. The Portuguese had their hands in the pie for a while, too, but control was eventually returned to Arab hands, and might have stayed that way had the Arabs been able to keep peace among themselves. But they were not so inclined. From the time of the protectorate agreement in

1890, the British Colonial Office ran the island reasonably well—introducing schools, hospitals, roads, and other modern appurtenances—under the sultan's name through the British Resident, a polite term for governor. (It used to take newcomers a while to learn which facets of Zanzibari life were the province of "H.H."—His Highness, the Sultan, or "H.E."—His Excellency, the Resident.)

I did not know the last Sultan of Zanzibar, Seyyid Abdulla bin Khalifa. But I remember his father. Seyyid Sir Khalifa bin Harub bin Thwain died in 1960 after a reign of nearly half a century. Short and slim, with a silky white beard, horn-rimmed spectacles, a friendly face, a passion for red automobiles (no one else on the island could have cars that color), and a modest manner, he had been one of Zanzibar's most beloved rulers. It is just as well that he died without having to witness the drastic changes that were to take place in his country. In 1962, Zanzibar achieved independence within the Commonwealth, and just two years later, the Afro-Shirazi party—representing the black majority of Zanzibar—overthrew the Arab-dominated government, forced the old sultan's son and successor into exile, and repressed the Arab and Asian minorities. Zanzibar, under Sheik Abeid Karume, the Afro-Shirazi leader, became a republic, with Abeid Karume the President, only to join forces shortly thereafter with Tanganyika, to become the United Republic of Tanzania. President Nyerere of Tanganyika became President of the united republic, with Abeid Karume of Zanzibar the first Vice President and the de facto, strongman ruler of Zanzibar. He was assassinated in April 1972 and succeeded by the more moderate Aboud Jumbe. The dominant trend in both areas of the republic has been socialism. Zanzibar shut itself off not only from the rest of the continent and the Western world but also from mainland Tanzania, discouraging visitors to its shores and requiring exit permits for its own people desiring to visit the mainland portion of the republic. It welcomed what is probably the largest proportion of Chinese planners and officials to be found anywhere in Africa, and brought in specialists from other Communist states (the police, for example, are East German-supervised). Communist influence or no, the American consulate, which opened its doors as long ago as 1837, is still operating. There being no other American enterprise on the island—commercial or otherwise—observers consider that the U.S. consulate's principal function is to watch the Chinese.

President Nyerere, in his own bailiwick on the mainland, has surprised those who observed him in the late fifties and early sixties, as his country went from colonial to independent status. In those days, Europeans on the scene considered him a pro-Western moderate. He has by no means turned his back on the West—far from it. But he has welcomed both help and ideas from the Communist world, and he has remained unpretentious, and less disposed toward the pomp and privilege that so many African leaders have borrowed from the Europeans they succeeded. (President Nyerere's trademark is the simple cotton or twill safari suit, with a collarless, short-sleeved jacket.)

Nyerere terms his philosophy "African democratic socialism." He has led the fight of black Africans against the white-dominated regimes of southern Africa—in Mozambique, Angola, Rhodesia, and South Africa, supporting the guerrilla movements against those governments. At the same time, Tanzania has worked closely with neighboring Kenya and Uganda since colonial days when the three territories shared a number of common services. When all became sovereign, they formed the East African Community, with headquarters in the Tanzanian city of Arusha. In 1971, the continued good work of the community was temporarily threatened when ousted President Obote of Uganda took refuge in Tanzania, at President Nyerere's invitation. The Tanzanian President has brought in a force of more than five thousand Chinese workers to construct the railroad between his country and copper-rich Zambia, so that nation will have an outlet to the sea through nonracist Tanzania instead of Portuguese Mozambique. He sent Tanzanian pilots and ground crews to train in China, and in 1972, his government revealed that it would be the first in Africa to receive Chinese-built MIG jet fighters. Nyerere has directed major attention to the plight of the mass of his country's peasants, with the most dramatic program in this regard the establishment of self-help villages known as *ujamaas*—share-the-wealth communes not unlike the *kibbutzim* of Israel. There are considerably more than a thousand *ujamaas*, and they are the kingpin of the policy of the one-party government that is based on agricultural development through hard work and self-initiative. Though hardly without detractors, the *ujamaa* community has been praised by the UN Economic Commission for Africa as the sole attempt on the continent to appreciably improve the ages-old pattern of farm life.

While concerning himself primarily with his people, President Nyerere and his government have not neglected the natural phenomenon that makes Tanzania unique in the world: the tremendous concentration of animal life. Tanzanian efforts at conservation and Tanzanian concern with ecological matters are probably surpassed by no country in Africa. An example of efforts in this direction is the Serengeti Research Institute, located in Serengeti National Park, founded in 1966 and with a core staff of a score of British, American, and European scientists who investigate the hows and whys of animal populations through research on animal behavior, migratory habits, vegetation, and other matters. The Institute works in close collaboration with the Tanzanian National Parks administration.

All along, the Tanzanians have been aware that despite their prowess in such areas as wildlife, cultural diversity (nowhere in East Africa is there a finer tradition of woodcarving, to cite but a single example), and scenic splendor, they have been taking a touristic back seat to neighboring Kenya. But with the emergence of the decade of the seventies, the government had begun a concerted effort to get its fair share of the tourist market. It retained a British hotel group for expert help on the construction of new hotels and national park lodges, and the operation thereof. It began to develop its Indian Ocean coast so that it could compete in the European—mainly West German—market with that of Kenya. In 1971, it opened a ten-million-dollar jumbo-jet-era airport in the northwest near its major national parks, so that visitors from abroad could gain access to the parks from a Tanzanian air gateway, rather than through the Kenyan capital of Nairobi, which is nearer and more convenient to the more noted parks than the Tanzanian capital of Dar es Salaam. Tanzania still is poor, still is beset by enormous problems, and it has occasionally, in its zeal for uplift solutions, come up with moralistic nonsense like bans on miniskirts—edicts that brought it no more credit than did the prohibition of long hair, to the colonels of the Greek junta, when they took over. But countries that have long been governing themselves make more than their share of mistakes; surely new lands like Tanzania must be allowed a few.

YOUR VISIT TO TANZANIA

Tanzania has tremendous diversity as well as great area. Most visitors find that they must be selective in their destinations. There are, of course, the globally famed national parks like Serengeti and Ngorongoro Crater. Too often, these constitute an entire Tanzanian itinerary. A great pity, this, for delimiting Tanzania in such a fashion excludes any more than a rudimentary acquaintance with the human population of the republic, as opposed to the animal. No, a Tanzania visit should include the capital, and samplings of other historic communities on the Indian Ocean coast—now opening up as a beach-resort area in its own right. And ideally, one should also become acquainted with at least one urban area other than Dar es Salaam. Arusha, near Mount Kilimanjaro and the major game parks, is a good bet in this area.

Dar es Salaam: Tanzania is a land of 120 tribal groups and a cosmopolitan population that includes Arabs, Asians, and Europeans, in addition to Africans. Representatives of all these groups help give Dar es Salaam, the capital, a great deal of its charm. Besides serving as the seat of government, "Dar"—as it is shortened locally and throughout East Africa—is an important Indian

Ocean port, and, for the visitor, a delightful bathing resort and good starting point for a tour of the territory. The city was little more than a fishing village as late as 1862, when an Arab sultan decided to make his headquarters there. Its exotic-sounding name means "Haven of Peace" in Arabic, and it is just that today—quiet and mellow, but at the same time, vibrant with color, and with a not unimpressive sprinkling of postindependence skyscrapers in its core area. When the Germans colonized East Africa, they took Dar over as an administrative center and developed it further; many of the substantial buildings they constructed still stand and remain in use—more picturesque than functional. The palm-fringed harbor, dotted with the pleasure craft of residents as well as commercial cargo liners, is one of the most perfect natural harbors in all of Africa. Visitors, with justification, often call it the prettiest, and are delighted to find that the beaches that flank it are of fine-grained white sand—perfect for swimming. (Convenient beaches include those at Oyster Bay—less than five miles from downtown—and Silver Sands, something more than twice that distance.)

Worth observing are the splendid, new-as-tomorrow campus of the University of Dar es Salaam on the outskirts, the twisting streets of the Arab-Asian sectors, where shops and minarets of white mosques vie with each other for pedestrians' attention; the National Museum of Tanzania, whose exhibits provide the visitor with a superb cultural introduction to the country and its peoples; the hand-carved heads of the Makonde people—unquestionably the finest in all of East Africa—in the curio shops and bazaars; and the tiny islands outside the harbor. Not open to the public but eminently worth an exterior glance is the long, low, neo-Moorish structure that had been known as Government House as the residence of the British governors, and now, as State House, is the home of the President.

Indian Ocean beach resorts: In an effort to compete with the resorts flanking Mombasa, Kenya's Indian Ocean port-metropolis, the Tanzanians have begun to develop the area around *Kunduchi*, about fifteen miles north of Dar es Salaam. Although intended primarily for the European market—brochures are printed in German as well as in English, to give you an idea—the hotels in the area are so attractive and luxurious, the facilities so extensive, and the beaches so lovely, that a day or two in the area might be just what the traveler on a hectic African schedule might need to break his journey.

Kilwa, some two hundred miles to the south of the capital, is rich in Afro-Arab-Persian and even European historical background. There are what remains of a venerable sultan's capital, of a Portuguese castle, and the Great Mosque is probably the finest on the Indian Ocean coast.

Bagamoyo, a onetime capital of German East Africa, a takeoff point for explorers as noted as Stanley, Speke, and Burton, and a slavers' terminus, is now quiet, but by no means without interest. Only forty miles north of Dar es Salaam, and with a harbor once full of dhows that sailed with slaves to Zanzibar and Aden, it is the site, as well, of stone corrals where the slaves were incarcerated, a chapel where Livingstone's body rested, and venerable Arab-built houses with elaborate doors not unlike those of Zanzibar.

Tanga is an old coastal town north of Dar es Salaam, and second only to it in size, among mainland communities. The sisal industry—Tanzania grows more of this fiber than any other country—is headquartered here, and nearby are such destinations as the old Arab port of *Pangani* and *Kigombe,* a village with murals on local themes covering the outer walls of its houses.

Lushoto, some hundred miles in the interior from Tanga, is a bracing holiday resort in the mountains, in a region of farms and coffee plantations. It is popular with locals because of its cool climate, well-stocked trout streams, forest-clad mountain summits.

Mount Kilimanjaro: Tanzania's most exciting landmark is Mount Kilimanjaro—Africa's highest peak, rising over nineteen thousand feet, and known to those who live within its shadows simply as "The Mountain." I have never observed a peak quite like it—flat-domed, the snows on its summit dripping down the sides like icing on a cake. It is surrounded by rich farmland and animal-filled plains, and it looks down, just across its northern base, on Kenya. For a visitor in East Africa to miss it—either from the air, from the Amboseli National Park across the frontier in Kenya, or from its own slopes—would be a great pity. Kilimanjaro casts a spell that takes effect from the instant one lays eyes on it. It can be viewed from *Marangu,* a base for those wanting to climb the peak, or for less strenuous walks along its lower regions, with their rain forests, waterfalls, and panoramic views—particularly that of Kibo, the senior of the two Kilimanjaro peaks. Tanzanians consider the ascent of Kibo more a stroll than a climb, but there are those who would consider a three-to-six-day hike to an elevation approaching twenty thousand feet as little more than that. *Moshi* and *Arusha* are the principal towns of the Kilimanjaro area, with the Mount Kilimanjaro International Airport lying between them. *Moshi* is Tanzania's Coffeeville—the core of the republic's coffee industry. Of special interest in this regard is the activity of the Chagga tribe, a group of some four hundred thousand industrious coffee growers who raise and market their crops through their own cooperatives, with headquarters in Moshi. Kilimanjaro's Kibo peak dominates the town, which has good accommodations and even a golf course among its amenities. *Arusha,* with the slopes of Mount Meru as a backdrop behind it, is at once the administrative seat for the northern region of the republic, the headquarters of the East African Community—the commendable economic union of Kenya, Tanzania, and Uganda that provides a number of joint services for all three countries, East African Airways being only one of these. This is a perky, good-looking German-founded town, with comfortable hotels, a superanimated public market (a good place to observe the tall, handsome Masai, in their finery and beaded ornaments, their long hair elaborately dressed with fat and red clay), interesting shops (after Nairobi, Arusha is East Africa's leading safari-outfitting center), golf and other sports facilities, and day-long treks to the top of Mount Meru (just short of fifteen thousand feet). Most important, though, is Arusha's pre-eminence as a departure point for both hunting and photographic safaris, and for tours of the national parks, one of which—again not unlike Nairobi—is its very own.

National parks: No African country surpasses Tanzania in this area. Tanzania offers quantity, quality, and geographic diversity within its parks. And it takes them very seriously. From the start of his administration, President Nyerere made crystal clear the high national priorities accorded to matters ecological. You will see why Tanzania wants to preserve its natural heritage and its great animal populace when you visit the parks. Here is a rundown. *Arusha National Park,* one of the country's newest, is not quite as close to town as Nairobi National Park is to the Kenyan capital. But it is still only forty-five minutes distant, and it is a half day of an Arusha visit very well spent indeed. The park embraces what had been the Momella and Mount Meru Crater game areas. The latter is noted for monkeys, but the park abounds in elephant, rhino, buffalo, hippo, a wide variety of antelope, and of course the giraffe, which is perhaps the landmark animal of the greater Kilimanjaro area. *Serengeti National Park* is one of the great ones of the planet, embracing some five thousand square miles. It quite literally *teems* with animals in a kind of profusion I have experienced nowhere else in Africa. The experts who know, claim that there are something like 1½ million animals in the area—thirty-five species of them, including lion, cheetah, and leopard. The May–June mass movement of zebras and wildebeeste over the plains, and their reversal of that operation, in the opposite direction, in November–December, is, quite literally, like nothing else on earth. But Serengeti at any time is a moving, memorable, and profound experience. *Ngorongoro Crater:* If the Serengeti plain is a profound experience, what with the prodigious quantities of animals, Ngorongoro Crater is unique, in large part because of the geography of the situation. The rim of the crater is at an elevation of some seventy-five hundred feet, and it is here—at either of a pair of comfortable lodges—that one headquarters. Come morning, the descent is made via Land-Rover-type vehicles that plunge down a rather pathetic excuse for a road that extends in an almost vertical direction, some two thousand feet in length. Horizontal once more, one is on a hundred-square-mile tableland in the company—at times intimate company—of countless members of the animal world. There are great herds of zebra and antelope of various species, not to mention the immense and ugly African buffalo. Rhino are in fair abundance, and so, for that matter, are elephants and hippo. A morning's drive is animal-filled enough for many a visitor. But some groups take a box lunch with them from the lodge and remain into the afternoon, before the miracle ascent upward. *Lake Manyara National Park* has nothing like the drama of either Serengeti or Ngorongoro. It is in the same general neighborhood, though, and its ace in the hole is a peculiar-type lion—found nowhere else in Africa so far as I know—that enjoys taking naps in the upper reaches of the park's acacia trees. The bird life is exceptional, too, particularly the brilliant hot-pink flamingos. But there are storks and egrets and many smaller birds, as well. And other animals besides lion, of course—elephant and rhino among them. What I like particularly is the park's hotel, atop a plateau, with its garden and swimming pool affording sublime views of the game-filled valley, and a rather historic plaque at the entrance commemorating the hotel's dedication by Sir Richard Turnbull, the last governor of Tanganyika Territory. Sir Richard was the colonial official whom I singled out in the first edition of this book as one of the ablest in Africa during the exciting transitional period when the continent was changing from one vast colony to a cluster of fledgling sovereign states. *Tarangire National Park,* not far south of Lake Manyara park, is particularly noted for its oryx, lesser kudu, and rhino. However, I mention it primarily because it has a tented camp rather than a hotel-like lodge, and for the visitor who may not have the experience of this kind of accommodation elsewhere in Africa, Tarangire might well be worth an overnight layover. Tented camps were the rule rather than the exception in African parks a decade or so back. Now the reverse is more often than not the case. And more's the pity, for such camps were the stuff of which safari life was all about. At their best, they are luxurious—with surprisingly modern toilet and shower facilities, delicious meals and good wines served in spacious dining tents, and comfortable cots in screened sleeping tents. And yet they are so inauspicious in appearance that animals not infrequently wander right through them come nightfall, rarely if ever disturbing occupants of the tents (guards are posted the night through), but conveying the romance of bush Africa that modern lodges are not always able to do. *Mikumi National Park* is one of the country's newest, with a lodge that is one of the handsomest in Africa, and a separate tented camp, as well. The park was created to offer a wildlife reserve to visitors headquartered in Dar es Salaam and the beach resorts nearby. There is a good deal of wildlife, although nothing like the quantities to be observed at Serengeti and Ngorongoro. Still, one sees elephant, hippo, lion, buffalo, giraffe, and antelope. When access to Mikumi includes plane service, it will be a real convenience. Driving, though, takes about five hours from the capital, over a dusty and difficult if not uninteresting route that takes one through villages and market towns that make for worthwhile rest/shopping/stopping points. *Gombe National Park* straddles the shore of immense *Lake Tanganyika* but is among the smallest in the country, and is unique in that it is one of the few in all Africa where one can see chimpanzees. *Kigoma* is the nearest town; it is the lake's chief settlement, a mecca for anglers, and just a few miles north of *Ujiji,* where Stanley met Livingstone at a spot marked by a plaque, on November 10, 1871.

Zanzibar Town: In no African city is a stroll more atmospheric than in Zanzibar Town. To walk its streets is to be part of a place where Asia, Europe, the Middle East, and Africa are fused. One sees long-robed, bearded, turbaned Arabs, Indian women in vivid, gold-flecked saris, the orthodox Moslems in heavy purdah. One sees Africans, the men often in Western shorts, their women in austere black. One sees neatly garbed Chinese and easy-to-detect East Germans; and during the winter months the streets are even more exotic, with the brawny crews of the ancient-design dhows, slowly sailed from Persian Gulf ports on the winds of the monsoon. The heart of the island, Zanzibar Town is old-appearing but not ancient; it dates back not more than two centuries. But its narrow, rough-cobbled streets; its high, whitewashed Arab houses, ex-palaces, and bazaars; its traditionally costumed people—all contribute to an atmosphere of great age and great charm. There is probably no single building which would stand out in the pages of a survey of world architecture. The distinguishing features, so far as building design goes, are the *doors of the Arab houses*. They are of heavy wood beams, studded, as ham might be with cloves, with shiny brass knobs, and framed by intricately carved teak doorways, their dark brown hues a perfect contrast to the whitewashed walls and the gleaming brass. Zanzibar Town has a smallish, intimate air, and one can walk about without difficulty. The harbor is small but uncommonly pretty, in part because the sea water is colored in varying shades of blue and green, thanks to the presence of coral reefs, and in part because the dominant landmark is the People's Palace, formerly the Sultan's Palace. This is a glistening white building, with all the essentials of a potentate's residence: a wall—not so high that it obstructs—around the grounds; a spacious balcony used in the old days for the not-infrequent appearances of the sultan and sultana; just next door to the palace is *Beit-el-Ajab* (The House of Wonders), a Victorian-type pile built for ceremonial purposes and now used as the government secretariat. Nearby is the Old Arab Fort, an eighteenth-century compound on the site of a ruined Portuguese church. It had been used as a prison by the Arabs and it was behind its massive towers that public executions took place. One of the old Arab houses served as the British Consulate from 1841 to 1874. Burton and Speke, the explorers, stayed there when fitting out their expedition to Central Africa in 1857, and it was there that Livingstone's body was taken on its arrival from Rhodesia. (Livingstone himself lived in still another Zanzibar palace—Livingstone House—where he prepared for his African trek in 1866; it is now rather unromantically used as a clove research laboratory.) The United States has had contact with Zanzibar for a surprisingly long period. The building which served as the first

American Consulate still stands. In 1861 the consul was blockaded there for a whole day by pirates from the Persian Gulf until they were bribed by the sultan with a thousand rupees to disperse. The island is not without other history-laden buildings. One is the House of Tipoo Tib, the Zanzibari who still is remembered as one of the most fantastically successful of the slave traders. The story goes that some forty slaves were buried alive in the foundations of his house, and it has credence because in those days the custom was to immure live slaves as a sacrifice when houses were erected. The price one paid for this rather ghoulish practice was an eternally haunted house—and there are many buildings on the island still said to be ghost-ridden. The Anglican Cathedral is not one of them, but even it is not without a singular background. Its foundations were laid in 1873 on the site of the last open slave market in the world. The main altar is just above where the whipping post once stood. All Zanzibar Town is a kind of museum, but there *is* a Zanzibar Museum—which is so designated. Its exhibits tell the story of the island's history and development.

Excursions out of Zanzibar Town: The rural regions of the island are lush, fragrant with the scent of cloves, and with a virtually unlimited coastline of swimmable beaches. In a single day, one can cover a great deal of territory, with *Mangapwani Beach* the destination. En route, the car will pass through clove plantations (cloves are hidden in the blossoms of flowering clove trees); neat African villages of thatched houses; the former country palace of the sultans; *Marahubi Palace,* now in ruins, built by a mid-nineteenth-century sultan for his harem, with unusual domed baths adjoining it; *Mtoni Palace,* still another ruin, dating to 1828, when it was put up as the home of the Arab reputed to have introduced the clove to Zanzibar; and remains of considerably more ancient Persian baths and venerable mosques. The island of *Pemba,* 30 miles northeast of Zanzibar, is without any actual towns, and is largely a maze of immense clove plantations, with no hotels, but with fine beaches and—a hangover from the Portuguese period several centuries back—bullfights—with (as in Portugal to this day) the bull not killed.

SHOPPING

Tanzania's great buy is the woodcarving of the Makonde people, the most talented carvers in East Africa. Indeed, not even in the territory to the south does one find anything approaching the beauty of the Makonde work: heads finely chiseled, sensitive, expressive, and mainly of men, but some of women as well. Because the Makonde are prolific, their work is relatively inexpensive, particularly if bought in Tanzania. (Prices are much higher when the stuff gets exported to the curio shops of Nairobi.) Makonde heads can be as small as a couple of inches in height. (I have one such piece, and it is one of the finest in a collection gathered from all parts of Africa.) Most are three or four times that big, though. In *Dar es Salaam,* the principal curio shops are good sources. I have found the most interesting pieces and the best prices in a shop simply called Novelties & Bookshop, at the corner of Independence Avenue and Mkwepu Street, near the Post Office. The Zanzibar Antiques Shop and Peera's, also both on Independence Avenue, also have good selections. Other good buys are Masai beaded jewelry—particularly the necklaces—elephant hair bracelets, and silver and jewelry articles, in such shops as Haji Brothers and the Silver Curio Shop. The woodcarvings sold on Dar street corners are mostly mass-produced trivia. *Arusha,* as mentioned earlier, follows Nairobi as a safari-outfitting center; there are a number of shops, including the Paris, with both ready-made and custom-made clothes and equipment. The public market is not to be missed for Masai and other handicrafts of the region, and the curio shops—including a branch of Peera's in the New Arusha Hotel, and Crafts and Curios, on Titi Road—are worth visiting. Public markets in the towns are invariably good for browsing if not for purchasing. So are the shops of hotels and the lodges of national parks. And occasionally, itinerant vendors have wares of some significance. The national parks shops also sell insignia of the parks in the form of pins and brooches. They also sell exceptionally well-prepared illustrated manuals describing the animal life of the parks in interesting detail. Bargaining is the rule everywhere except at national parks shops. English language newspapers—*The Standard of Tanzania*, and *The Nationalist* (the organ of the Tanganyika African Nationalist Union) keep one up to date on day-to-day activity. *Zanzibar:* Traditional Arab-design articles are Zanzibar's most interesting souvenirs—copper coffee pots and other copperware, silver pieces, and miniature *dhows*—the picturesque Arab sailing ships. Lightweight and authentic are the Zanzibari skullcaps, in white or beige, of finely embroidered cotton, and the also traditional pomander balls, clove-scented, of course, and cheap. A good source is the shop adjoining the Zanzibar Friendship Tourist Bureau, at the People's Gardens on the waterfront. Chances are, the Arab-style chests you see in the shops are imported from India.

CREATURE COMFORTS

HOTELS—Tanzania has made enormous strides in this area in recent years, in large part as a result of the government having called in Hallmark Hotels, an English firm, to provide technical and management assistance in a constantly expanding network of city hotels, beach resorts, and national park lodges. *Dar es Salaam*, which on the eve of Independence was without a first-class hotel, now boasts a pair of de luxe-category hostelries. The New Africa Hotel, which for years was the town joke, not having been "new" since the Germans built it before World War I, has been rebuilt to the point where it is among the handsomer urban hostelries in East Africa, with first-rate facilities, attractive air-conditioned rooms with bath, and a pleasant *ambiance*. The Kilimanjaro is no nearer the mountain of that name than is Bombay's Taj Mahal Hotel to the Taj itself in distant Agra. But the Kilimanjaro is a honey of a hotel—two hundred air-conditioned, good-looking rooms with bath, a swimming pool, and other amenities ranging from a swimming pool to a nightclub, and a splendid harbor-view situation. The Skyway, also new, modern and fully air-conditioned, is another good bet, and so are the Agip Motel and the Twiga Hotel, both fully air-conditioned. Dar es Salaam restaurants include the very good dining room of the New Africa Hotel; the several restaurants of the Kilimanjaro—Simba nightclub, Summit Steakhouse, Rombo dining room, and Bruncherie coffee shop; the rooftop, alfresco terrace of the Twiga Hotel, the Agip Motel Restaurant, and—away from the center—the dining room of the Palm Beach Hotel, once the town's finest inn, for seafood specialties. **Indian Ocean beach resorts:** The new hotels in and about Kunduchi are probably the most luxurious in Tanzania. They all offer complete resort facilities—both pools and beaches for sunning and swimming, facilities for snorkeling and deep-sea fishing, a variety of dine-drink dance spots, both indoor and out, and a heavily European clientele. They include the Kunduchi Beach Hotel, the Bahari Beach Hotel, and the Africana, with accommodation in the latter two in contemporary versions of the African thatched-roof *banda*. There is also the modern Mafia Fishermen's Lodge on *Mafia Island*. Excursions from these hotels are made to points throughout this region of the country, including Mikumi National Park. **Tanga:** The Planters Hotel is the old reliable in a region of a number of hostelries. **Lushoto:** The Oaklands. **Moshi and Arusha:** Moshi's best is undoubtedly the Livingstone, modern and capacious with vistas of Kilimanjaro. Arusha offers the atmospheric New Safari Hotel, deftly employing all manner of local Africana in its public-rooms *décor*, and the newer and bigger New Arusha, with a swimming pool, a number of shops, and other such amenities. **National Parks:** *Arusha National Park*, though less than an hour's drive from downtown Arusha, offers accommodation at modern, well-equipped Momella Lodge. *Serengeti National Park* offers several good choices. Seronera Lodge is the traditional favorite, with both thatched African-style cottages and tents, and a separate dining pavilion. More modern and luxurious are the Serenora Wildlife Lodge; the even newer Lobo Wildlife Lodge, built into the contours of a rock promontory in the north of the park; and the Fort Ikoma Lodge, on the site of a turn-of-the-century German outpost. At *Ngorongoro Crater* there is a pair of good choices, both on the very edge of the dramatic crater.

The elder of the two is Ngorongoro Crater Lodge, of rustic-log design, and the newer is good-looking, well-equipped Ngorongoro Wildlife Lodge. *Lake Manyara National Park's* accommodation is at the Lake Manyara Hotel, beautifully perched atop the Great Rift Wall overlooking Lake Manyara and the animal-filled Rift Valley. There's a pool in the garden, restaurant, lounge, bar, and most all rooms have bath. *Tarangire National Park:* A good place to live under canvas if you haven't done so elsewhere in Africa. The tented camp here has full restaurant/bar facilities. *Mikumi National Park:* Mikumi Lodge is one of the most imaginatively designed in Africa. All rooms have bath, the lounge areas are striking, and there are attractive restaurant and bar facilities. **Zanzibar:** Zanzibar Town offers the elderly Zanzibar Hotel, an ex-palace that is perhaps more atmospheric than comfortable, and with air conditioning and private baths in only some of its rooms. There is also the architecturally choice Afrika House, which I first knew in pre-independence days as the Zanzibar Club; it was, to its great discredit, one of the last remaining bastions of British Jim Crow in all Africa. Built originally as a rich Arab's townhouse, it remains very low on bathrooms, none of which is private. The modern Zanzibar Beach Hotel is a resort-type place some fifteen miles north of town, with full facilities.

TOGO

République du Togo

Entry requirements: *A visa, obtainable from French embassies and consulates where the Togolese have not yet established diplomatic missions, plus a health certificate (smallpox and yellow fever) and an onward ticket.* **Best times for a visit:** *The dry seasons—July through September, December through May—are preferable; April to June and October to November are the rainiest periods.* **Currency:** *The CFA franc: CFA 280=$1.* **Principal European language:** *French, with English spoken at air terminals and leading hotels.* **Domestic transport:** *Internal air service and good roads and railroads connect major towns.* **Further information:** *Service d'Information de la République du Togo, Lomé, Togo; Togo Mission to the United Nations, 801 Second Avenue, New York.*

INTRODUCING TOGO

Tiny Togo requires a hard search at a map of Africa. It is but 400 miles long, 90 miles wide at its thickest bulge, and with an Atlantic Ocean coastline of but 31 miles. Its nearly two million people are, however, citizens of a sovereign state.

Until it was granted independence on April 27, 1960, Togo had been known as French Togoland. It had been, with British Togoland, a German colony until the League of Nations, after World War I, arbitrarily divided it in half, mandating one portion to the British and the other to the French. Both became United Nations Trust Territories after World War II. The British region—after a plebiscite—was incorporated into Ghana when it became free in

1957. The French area was, meanwhile, progressing toward self-rule. Its own government, African-run, was set up under French auspices in 1956, and in 1960 the UN dissolved the trusteeship, upon France's request, and granted complete sovereignty.

Pre-European Togo abounds in legends of great kings, great battles, and Iron Age cultures. The first foreign traders were South Americans rather than Europeans—Brazilians, either of Portuguese descent or freed slaves returning to their native continent; many of the country's place names are derived from these settlers, most of whom were slave traders. In the mid-nineteenth century the Germans arrived on the scene, and although their rule was ruthless, rigid, and often cruel, the Togolese are not unmindful of some positive German contributions: a well-planned capital city, a small railroad network, a road system, an imposing cathedral, a telegraphic communications system, and modern piers. Togo, during the period of German eminence in Africa, was considered the model Teutonic colony.

France continued where Germany left off, but her contributions were primarily social and political. The best-liked of the French governors was Montagne, who brought about the establishment of the Togolese Unity Committee, which grouped together representatives from regions throughout the territory on a cultural basis and laid the spadework for national political activity. It was the Togolese Unity Committee that impelled the Togolese to strike out for independence. The committee's long-time leader was Sylvanus Olympio, who governed as Prime Minister after independence and gained a reputation as one of West Africa's outstanding politicians. Assassinated in 1963, he was replaced by Nicolas Grunitzky, who in turn was deposed in 1967 by a military coup headed by Lieutenant Colonel Étienne Eyadema. Eyadema, now a general, has headed the government since then, despite a number of plots to overthrow him.

Togo, a member of the five-nation Council of the Entente, is small and poor. Coffee makes up almost half its exports, and most of the people live by subsistence agriculture. Unofficially, however, a brisk trade in smuggling diamonds, cigarettes, whisky, and perfume may be the country's most profitable enterprise. The government is trying to attract foreign investment and aid and to exploit the country's mineral resources. They hope that Togo's compactness, its smallness, and the unity of the people will work in favor of its development and economic growth.

YOUR VISIT TO TOGO

Lomé: This is a small country, and a delightfully easy one to get about. Lomé, the capital, fronts the ocean, with a façade—over its African core—which is at once French and German. The major attractions within the town can be viewed within a day: the modern Chamber of Deputies building, the Cultural Center, newly named Independence Square, the Tokwa General Hospital, the German-built cathedral, the residential sections, and—of the most interest—the sights, smells and produce of the open-air market. An interesting aspect of Lomé's market is the preponderance of "market women," Togo's answer to Women's Liberation. As the wholesalers and retailers of textiles, food, and other consumer goods, these women—there are said to be more than five thousand in Lomé alone—have attained power and wealth, as well as a reputation for being the best traders in West Africa.

The Boulevard de la République hugs the sea, and on either side of the town one is confronted with wide stretches of sandy beach. Bathing is pleasant, although there is at times an undertow. Eighteen miles inland is *Lake Togo*, favorite retreat of Lomé residents, with a variety of recreational facilities and an excellent French restaurant and inn.

Coastal drives: The thirty-one-mile stretch of Atlantic Ocean coast is bordered by well-paved roads and ideal for day-long, half-day, and overnight excursions from Lomé. A small but adequate new hotel at *Atakpamé* makes it possible to spend a night there after exploring the surrounding countryside. All along the route are small fishing villages, whose residents are delighted to see visitors.

Up-country journeys: A trip into the interior, regarded as an offbeat adventure, can be a great success if it is understood in advance that there are only modest hotels and resthouses and no towns of any substance. Guides can be hired in Lomé through the hotels, and one should accompany the first-time visitor. He can also make arrangements for provisions—foodstuffs, camp beds, linens, mosquito netting, and the like. What to see? A great deal: this is a country of forty-four tribal peoples, each with its own language, customs, architecture, art forms, modes of dress. Highlights: The cocoa forests in the west, with Ewe villages concealed among them, many with great stone tombs of chiefs; the green-covered mountains around *Bassari;* the landscape of bold escarpments around *Lama-Kara;* the villages of the northeast, with houses resembling fairy castles—thatched turrets sheltering granaries and bedrooms, surrounding millet fields—inhabited by peoples whose dances, feasts, and religious ceremonials have changed little for many centuries.

SHOPPING

Carved wood sculpture, iron figurines, basketry, ceremonial masks (some cleverly fashioned of coconuts); ceramics, both bowls and decorative pieces, from Monsieur Boyer's shop at the Lake Togo Hotel; Monsieur Coustere, Boulevard Galliene, Lomé; and markets in towns and villages throughout the country. Except in the shops noted above, bargaining is the rule.

CREATURE COMFORTS

HOTELS—**Lomé** is unusually well equipped for visitors. The Hôtel Benin has 100 air-conditioned rooms, a fine French restaurant, a bar, lounges, and a sea view. Older but still good is the Hôtel du Golfe. Miramar follows. **Lake Togo's** Hôtel-Restaurant (fine French food) has a limited number of guest bedrooms. **Atakpamé** boasts the small Relais des Plateaux. **Palimé:** Concordia Hôtel; **Sokodé:** Hôtel du Centre.

TUNISIA

République Tunisienne

Entry requirements: *No visa is necessary for American tourists; happily, the only document required is a valid passport. Inoculations for the usual diseases are recommended, however.* **Best times for a visit:** *Spring and autumn are the ideal seasons for the northern regions, but the winter months—while cold in the north—are warm and sunny in the south. Summer is oppressively hot in the south, but about like New York or Washington in the north, with the added advantage of a string of Mediterranean beach resorts.* **Currency:** *The dinar, divided into 1000 millimes: 0.525 dinars=$1.* **Principal European languages:** *French, with some English in hotels, transport terminals, tourist offices and an interesting amount of German. Arabic is the official language.* **Domestic transport:** *Planes connect the major cities, and there is an excellent network of paved roads, as well as one of the best railroad systems in Africa.* **Further information:** *Office National du Tourisme en Tunisie, 47 Avenue Farhat Hached, Tunis, Tunisia; Embassy of Tunisia, Washington, D.C.*

INTRODUCING TUNISIA

Little Tunisia—and it *is* small in contrast with its North African neighbors—is well able to use its compactness as a lure for the traveler. It is one of the easiest of the African countries in which to get about, it is one of the most comfortable in which to stay, it offers more to see and do, per square foot, than almost any other country on the continent—and its welcome is hearty. Tourism is becoming an important industry. (Hotel beds jumped from 942 in

1961 to thirty-seven thousand in 1970—with an increase of six thousand beds per year, and proportionate quantities of tourists to sleep on them.) Frenchmen have been visitors, as well as residents, for many years, and of late other Europeans—Scandinavians and Germans, in particular—have followed in their footsteps. But Americans are only now beginning to realize what they've been missing: a lovely land, with a rich past dating to the days of the Phoenicians and the Romans; a landscape of mountain and desert, sandy beach, and blue sea, lush oasis and modern city; and a people more Western-oriented and modern-minded than any others in North Africa—predominantly Moslem in religion and culture, and often with a twentieth-century point of view and a bracing snap-to vitality which has helped gain their country international respect.

The Phoenicians conquered much of Tunisia some twelve hundred years before Christ, and dotted its coast with a series of towns, the most famous of which was Carthage, whose splendors came to rival those of Rome—to such an extent that the Romans destroyed it, and later built their own city over its ruins, as well as many others, not only on the coast, but in the desert of the interior as well. Tunisia was Rome's granary—much of it is still fertile—and was known as the Province of Africa, a name that came to be used for the entire continent.

Later the Vandals took over, and they were followed by the Byzantines. The militant armies of the Arabs occupied the country in the seventh century, bringing their Moslem faith with them, converting the indigenous Berber population, and constructing Kairouan, which is still one of the holiest cities of all Islam. From the thirteenth to the sixteenth centuries the country achieved power on its own steam by means of the Berber Hafsid dynasty, after which the Spaniards moved in, only to be ousted by the Turks, who allowed the Tunisians vitually to govern themselves for a brief period, when the Barbary pirates entered the scene, ruling the roost for some time. Another Tunisian dynasty—this one of hereditary beys—was set up in 1805, but the Europeans began wedging in—economically, at first—until in 1871 the French forced the reigning bey to sign the Treaty of Bardo. Tunisia became a "protectorate"—which meant that it was French-ruled, with figurehead beys nominally on the throne. The French period saw the construction of new European quarters tacked onto existing Tunisian cities, considerable work in public health, and some in education and transportation. Numbers of *colons* crossed the Mediterranean from the motherland, and it was not until after World War II—when Tunisia was a bloody battleground—that a nationalist movement in the form of the Neo Destaur ("New Constitution") party began agitating for independence. Premier Mendes-France granted home rule in 1954, and on March 20, 1956, the Paris government recognized Tunisia's sovereignty. Its first and only President—Habib Bourguiba—had been both educated and imprisoned by the French, as have so many African nationalists. He is Moslem, married to a Frenchwoman. And he is a pro-Western ball of fire—highly intelligent, a dynamic speaker, with a sense of humor, a devoted following, and little patience for those time-honored Moslem customs which he believes hinder progress. Bourguiba gently deposed the senile, illiterate bey, whom nobody has missed. He has made it possible for the first time for wives to divorce their husbands. He pleads with Tunisian women to unveil themselves and take part in the life of the community, and a surprising number are doing so. He wants—and is getting—more schools, factories, and hospitals. His aims are not unlike those of Atatürk in Turkey, except that he wants his Moslem revolution in Tunisia to be voluntary, whereas Atatürk's was compulsory. He can surely be ranked as one of the most outstanding leaders of any of the new post-World War II states, and when he retires—he has said he wants to bow out in 1974—his successor will have a tough act to follow. Two groups appear to covet the Presidency. Bourguiba himself has suggested that his own Premier, Hedi Nouira, follow him. But there is, as well, a group favoring a democratic, multiparty state, under lawyer Ahmed Mestiri.

YOUR VISIT TO TUNISIA

Tunis and environs: Some three-quarters of a million of Tunisia's citizens live in Tunis, the capital, from which it is easy to depart on excursions, not only to the immediate area, but throughout the country—which is no bigger than the state of New York. Tunis itself is like no other North African capital. It does not have the gleaming white quality of Rabat, in the interior of Morocco. It does not directly front on the Mediterranean, as does Tripoli, in Libya. It is much smaller than Algiers. And it does not have the Nile, or the Pyramids, as has Cairo. Built on the Lake of Tunis and connected with the port of *La Goulette*, on the Mediterranean, by a channel, Tunis is really two towns: a charming, modern, French-built quarter with fine hotels, sidewalk cafés, excellent restaurants, and Paris-type boutiques; and the Old City, which preceded the Gallic occupation by many centuries, and which is the site of what many travelers—this one included—consider the finest *souks*, or bazaars, in North Africa, along with those of Marrakesh, Morocco. Here, along winding, whitewashed, arcaded streets—cool, clean, and running the gamut in odors and scents—are the *souks* of the perfumers (Attarine), of fruits (El Fakha), of wool and weaving (El Leffa), of shoes (Balghajii) of goldsmiths, silversmiths, leatherworkers, carpet weavers, copper, and more—an endless maze of streets where one can lose oneself easily—but never for very long. A permanent exhibition of Tunisian crafts, ideal as an introductory course for the shopper, is located near the Dar (Gate) Ben Abdullah. Old Tunis is a city of mosques—many of them with delicate octagonal, Turkish-type minarets, in contrast with the square towers of the North African Arabs. It is the city of the Palace of Le Bardo—the former beylical residence, rich in mosaics, carved-plaster wall *décor*, elegant columns and arches, shimmering pools in quiet courtyards, and glittering reception rooms. And it is the city, too, of the Bardo Museum, which ranks with the finest in North Africa—and that is saying a great deal. A visit to its four sections—Punic, Roman, Byzantine-Christian, and Arab—provides a graphic picture of the glory that was (and to many extents, still is) Tunisia. Near the city—just a 7-mile drive—is *Carthage* (named *Kart Haddacht*—New Town—when it *was* new in 814 B.C.), overlooking the blue Mediterranean and now, of course, but a shadow of what it was.

Still, bits and pieces of the earlier Punic Carthage and the later Roman Carthage remain: baths, temples, columns, amphitheaters, harbor installations. And the Lavigerie Museum, atop Byrsa Hill, exhibits relics from the ruins and affords a fine perspective of the town's layout. Only a mile or two away is the *American Military Cemetery*, where thousands of veterans of the North African campaign are buried at a handsome site, overlooking the sea, with the Stars and Stripes flying alongside an attractive interdenominational chapel and reception room, where the American attendants welcome visitors. I am not generally a sightseer of cemeteries, but I was very moved by my visit to this one. One is advised to stop at Carthage *before* going to *Sidi-Bou-Saïd*, where, with no difficulty, it would be easy to retire for life. This is a tiny village—almost purely Tunisian—atop an inspired hill, from which one has an overpowering view of the unbelievably lovely Gulf of Tunis. Sidi-Bou-Saïd's compact streets house tiny open-air cafés, a graceful mosque with a minaret of perfect proportions, chalk-white stucco houses accented with blue doors, shutters, and grillwork the color of the Mediterranean, minuscule shops, and always—from yards and gardens and side alleys and dead-end streets—that fantastic, overpowering view of the gulf. (Yes, there *is* a little hotel, if you'd like to stay overnight!) Even farther north is *Bizerte*, famous as a World War II military center, and until 1963 the site of a great French naval base, as well as bathing beaches.

Other beaches: Take your choice—*Gamarth, Hamman-Plage-les-Pins, Amilcar, Le Kram, La Goulette, Radès, Hammam Lif*. And on the other side of Tunis, on the Gulf of Hammamet, is a land of orchards, oranges, and lemons, plus hot springs, jasmine, and roses (*Korbous*, the main resort), and still more beach towns and fishing villages, culminating at the town for which the gulf is named—*Hammamet*, with seafront hotels running the gamut in luxury, and fronting the handsomest stretches of sand on the Mediterranean.

South of Tunis: With a week or ten days to spare, the visitor can take in the principal attractions of the south; this time can, of course, be lengthened or shortened. *The Medjerda Valley* is a striking example—particularly for the American visitor—of how U.S. aid, combined with private initiative, can transform a 168,000-acre area, once menaced by erosion and flood waters, into a teeming agricultural area. The Medjerda project was administered by a team of agricultural experts of the United States Operations Mission, in conjunction with Tunisian technicians, some of whom were U.S.-trained. Tunisian, United Nations, and United States officials consider it a model in land use for other African areas. Other southern highlights are of a different vein. *Sousse,* actually more central than southern, is built on the site of the ancient Roman town of *Hadrumetum.* Somewhat newer Arab ramparts are still part of its façade, as is an eighth-century fortified *ribat,* or Moslem convent, and a maze of early Christian catacombs not unlike those of Rome. The Sousse Museum is a storehouse of mosaics, both Roman and Christian. Nearby is *Mahdia,* which was the capital of the descendants of Fatima, daughter of the Prophet Mohammed. Its port, lying between the crumbling walls of two venerable forts, is believed to be the oldest in existence in a state of preservation little changed from the original. It is close to *Monastir,* named for an early Christian monastery, and located on a little peninsula jutting into the sea, with still strong Arab walls, a splendid gate, and slender, square-towered mosques. To the south is the *Coliseum of El Djem,* rising like a mirage from dusty, desert-like plains, and even more elegant than its counterpart in Rome: 488 feet long, 390 feet wide, 130 feet high, dating back to A.D. 238, and with an outside wall of three superimposed series of 64 arcades, an underground maze of stables, chambers, and corridors, and a seating capacity of 60,000. Still, continuing south, is Tunisia's second city (over 200,000 population), *Sfax,* on the outskirts of which is the Forest of Olive Trees—eight million of them, covering one and a half million acres and providing olives for the modern oil factories of the Sfax region. Sfax itself—at least the Old Town—is enclosed by the remains of crenelated Arab ramparts, accentuated by massive square towers. Within, in the Great Mosque, are the vibrant *souks,* not as well kept as those of Tunis, but equally as lively. The harbor is frenetic with the activity of

Sicilian sailboats, little Greek vessels, old-style Tunisian barges, and modern cargo liners. And on the outskirts are acres of gardens —ranging from cactus to pomegranate, pistachio to eucalyptus, almond to banana. *Kairouan,* in the interior—not far from Sousse—remains one of the most sacred cities of Islam. A town of pale pink towers and richly embellished gates, its Arab founders built it in the desert over a thousand years ago, as the capital of Ifriquia—the Arabic for Africa. It did not retain that honor for long, but it has never lost its religious prestige, nor, indeed, its skilled artisans. Kairouan carpets—as the visitor can see in a walk through the centuries-old *souks*—remain soft-shaded masterpieces today. But Kairouan's chief attractions are its mosques—the Great Mosque of Sidi Okba, with it crescent-topped minaret towering 130 feet in the air, is one of the finest in the world. Others include the Saouïa and Sidi Sabab mosques. But the true jewel is the first-named, and a climb up the steps of its minaret on a moonlit night is a memorable experience. These are the only Tunisian mosques open to non-Moslems, and for those of us who can never go to Mecca, this city is the perfect substitute. It ranks as the fourth holiest town of Islam; only Mecca, Medina, and Jerusalem precede it. *Gabès* is literally an oasis in the desert, alongside the sea, on a gulf bearing its name. Still small, palm-fringed, and deliciously green, its charm becomes apparent when one walks from the palms and banana trees of the oasis right up the sandy beach for a dip in the ocean. From Gabès one can make trips to other oases towns, such as *Tozeur*—lying amid seven hundred thousand palms, and *Matmata,* a town of four thousand cave-dwelling troglodytes. Gabès is on the route to the *Island of Djerba,* at once a bathing resort and a living museum, with warm sunny winters and always cool summers, the terrain of an oasis—palm and olive trees and orange orchards—and good hotels. This is the very same Djerba of Ulysses and the Legend of the Lotus. It is, too, the home of a "Protestant" Moslem sect—the Wahabites—who live in the little town of *Houmt Souk,* and whose little houses are of white or blue, with open terraces. These people are Africa's leading spice growers, and fine weavers as well. They share the island with a unique Jewish community with a truly ancient synagogue and a way of life little changed from pre-Christian times. Jews from Central Europe, the Near East, and all over Africa come to Djerba just to visit the synagogue—which is claimed to date back to the period when Nebuchadnezzar destroyed Solomon's Temple. The main Jewish communities, *Hara Kebira* and *Hara Shgira*, are sites of frequent religious processions, during which the Torahs, or scrolls—among the world's oldest and most valuable—are carried by the long-gowned rabbis.

SHOPPING

What *not* to buy can be a problem in Tunisia. The *souks* of Tunis—and indeed of all the cities, as well as the small towns and villages—are chock-full of beautifully handcrafted carpets (Kairouan, Gabès, and Gafsa are the best), gold and silver jewelry, beaten copper trays and bowls, djellaba robes, babouches, leather slippers in white and yellow, ceramics (jugs and vases and bowls), leatherwork (which is generally inferior to that of Morocco), blankets, embroidered linens, rattan matting, lace, wrought-iron grillwork. There are rug shops in Tunis outside the *souks*, in the Rue de l'Église (which specialize in shipping purchases abroad), and in every major town there is a Handicraft Center where regional products are on display and information available which will be helpful to the shopper. Bargain everywhere.

CREATURE COMFORTS

One can count on being comfortable in Tunisia—and on eating well, even in most of the towns and resorts away from the capital. New hotels are being constructed all over the country, and older hotels are being modernized, some under private auspices, others through the enterprising Society of Tourist Hotels, which is government-aided.

HOTELS—**Tunis:** The delightful Tunis Hilton is set in the Belvédère Park section of the city and has excellent food and service, luxury accommodations, and a swimming pool. The Africa is downtown's modern, luxury leader—a part of Air France's Meridien chain. First-class hotels include the Tunisia Palace and Claridge. Others: Majestic, Carlton, Maison-Dorée. **Carthage:** Amilcar. **Bizerte:** Corniche, Jalta, Nadour. **Sousse:** Hana, Hill Diar, Ksar, Marhaba. **Sfax:** Des Oliviers, Mabrouk Palace. **Gabès:** Oasis. **Hammanet:** The modern Sheraton is a lovely, low-slung cluster of five two-story pavilions, embracing 105 rooms, set in forty-five acres of gardens and lemon groves, fronting a seven-hundred-foot beach. *Décor* is smart neo-Moorish, and facilities range from heated pool and tennis to a wide range of wine-dine-dance spots. Other leaders include: Miramar, Parc-Plage, Yasmina. **Djerba:** Ulyssée, Sirènes, Bousten. **Kairouan:** Aghlabites. **Monastir:** Skanès Palace, Esplanade, Palmiers.

Food and Drink—Most hotels serve excellent French cuisine. The most noted food specialty is *couscous* (semolina sprinkled with water and oil, sifted and rolled into small grains and steam-cooked twice over the pot of vegetable soup that will later be served with it, along with boiled meat, and sometimes meat balls, sausage, chick-peas, or kidney beans). Other Tunisian treats: doughnuts, Tunisian-style, chick-pea soup, hero sandwiches, again Tunisian-style, with stuffings of olives, pickles, and tuna fish; *mechoui* of lamb—roasted on a spit, well spiced. There are grill rooms on the Avenue de Londres and in the Medina that serve sausages, liver, and chops broiled over coals *en plein air*. Delicious! Tunisian wines, while often without the delicacy of those of France, can often be very good. A few in the "Vins Supérieurs de Tunisie" class worth remembering: Bonne Bouteille (red), Clos des Arcades (red, white, rosé), Khalifa (red, white, and rosé). Tunis's European sector has a dozen-odd sidewalk cafés, many pastry shops. The Tunis Municipal Theater has programs of ballet and symphonic music.

UGANDA

Republic of Uganda

Entry requirements: *A visa, obtainable from the Uganda Mission to the United Nations, 801 Second Avenue, New York; the Uganda Embassy, Washington, D.C., or other Uganda diplomatic or consular missions; plus a health certificate (smallpox, yellow fever). The Ugandans, at their New York office, pass out an instruction sheet on entry requirements, as do many countries. Theirs is the only one, though, of any nation I know of, which, after listing the dreary specifics of visa-issuance, concludes with this cheery admonition: "Do have a good time in Uganda." All is not lost; some diplomats have a heart.* **Best times for a visit:** *The least pleasant months are during the rainy season—March to May, September to November. Otherwise, Uganda, despite its equatorial position, is surprisingly comfortable, thanks to altitudes averaging four thousand feet.* **Currency:** *The shilling, of which there are about seven to the U.S. dollar.* **Principal European language:** *English, which is the official language. However, Swahili, the* lingua franca *of East Africa, is widely spoken. And there are, of course, a number of local languages.* **Domestic transport:** *One of the best African road networks—more than eight thousand miles in length, with major arteries paved; East African Airways connections to major towns, with the international airport at Entebbe the principal terminus.* **Further information:** *Uganda Tourist Board, P. O. Box 4251, Kampala, Uganda; United Touring Company, P. O. Box 167, Kampala, Uganda; East African Airways, P. O. Box 523, Kampala, Uganda, and 576 Fifth Avenue, New York.*

INTRODUCING UGANDA

Uganda has no fewer problems than any other emerging state. It is small in area, particularly when contrasted with its neighbors. It is landlocked, and a considerable distance from the sea. Its politics, thanks to an oddball categorization of its peoples that is at once monarchial and republican, are as complex as you'll find in Africa. Withal, Uganda is an extraordinary gem of an emerald-green land with which the visitor invariably falls in love at first sight, thanks not only to the physical beauty of the place, but to the Ugandans themselves. They are East Africa's charmers.

This country, about the size of Oregon, is acknowledged by Europeans to have been the site of highly advanced African cultures long before the arrival of the white man in the latter part of the nineteenth century. But, as is often the case when Europeans judge cultures in Africa, the indigenous Africans have not always been given the credit for their achievements.

Until recently, the high state of development in pre-European Uganda was thought possible only because of the migration of Hamitic peoples with a Middle Eastern origin, who brought with them remnants of the late, great Egyptian civilization. Now, archaeologists know that the reverse was the case. The peoples living in the Uganda area were a part of the Azanian civilization, which flourished from A.D. 500 to 1500. They were black Africans, and they themselves built up a quite respectable Iron Age civilization, which did not subside until they were conquered by the less developed—but physically powerful—Bahima, who were (and still are) tall, handsome, agricultural people who had migrated from the northeast. They conquered the settled, more advanced craftsmen of the area, who were made to consider them "protectors," much like the semi-serf relationship of many medieval European peoples, and their rulers.

The descendants of the ancient Hamitic conquerors still remain the aristocrats of modern Uganda's most important region—the province of Buganda, which all through the British period, remained an African kingdom within the larger territory.

It is this strange structure which has made modern Uganda history unique in Africa. J. H. Speke and J. A. Grant—two Britons—were the first Europeans to visit Uganda. They were on a search for the source of the Nile, and they found it, in 1862, at Lake Victoria's Ripon Falls. So began British interest in this territory. In 1875 King Mutesa of Buganda welcomed Protestant, Roman Catholic, and Moslem missionaries from abroad, but his compulsively anticlerical son, after ascending the throne, was responsible for many of their successors' being murdered. In 1894 Great Britain interfered, in an attempt to bring peace to the region, and in that year all of Uganda—the kingdom of Buganda included—became a British protectorate. The king of Buganda—or kabaka, as he was called—was designated the paramount chief of the entire country. Indeed, the relationship of the kabaka—particularly the last reigning kabaka, the late Sir Edward Mutesa II, known as "King Freddie"—to his own people (they are known as the B*a*ganda, in contrast to their kingdom which is B*u*ganda, in further contrast to the whole country which is, of course, *U*ganda) and to the nationwide political leadership, has been the thorn in Uganda's side, and quite possibly the major impediment to its political maturity.

Under the British—who nowhere in their colonial history are known to have eschewed the divide-and-conquer maxim—Uganda embraced a quartet of kingdoms, all subservient to the colonial administrators, with the Baganda by far the largest and most powerful. When independence came to Uganda's East African neighbors in the early 1960s, Uganda latched onto the freedom bandwagon, too. Although it had no leader with the international stature of Kenya's late Tom Mboya or Tanzania's President Julius Nyerere, it became a sovereign state in 1962 with Milton Obote—a non-Baganda—emerging as its first Prime Minister, but with a hard-to-define bit of local autonomy remaining for Buganda, whose kabaka, King Freddie, was named the national President, an office largely ceremonial, but still not without significance.

Mr. Obote and King Freddie did not hit it off, each resenting the influence of the other. Mr. Obote, having a nationwide constituency behind him, deposed the kabaka in 1966, arbitrarily scrapping the Constitution, creating a new one and having himself installed as President of Uganda. King Freddie escaped by climbing over a twelve-foot-high wall of his palace and grabbing a cruising taxi. He turned up some weeks later, ill with malaria, in Bujumbura, Burundi, where he was granted asylum, eventually finding his way to London. The thirty-sixth ruler of his people, with a three-century-old family tree and a Cambridge education, King Freddie was found dead in 1969 in the simple London rooming house that had been his home in exile. He was forty-five, and a coroner's inquest determined the cause of death to be acute alcohol poisoning. Meanwhile, President Obote abolished the monarchy, propped up his power with the aid of a secret police corps, survived the wounds of a would-be assassin, and began to move his country to the political left, under the aegis of a loudly proclaimed "Common Man's Charter." Government became more arbitrary. Opposition parties were banned. Moves were made for the nationalization of industry, and President Obote appeared to be making as many enemies as friends. Indeed, in retrospect, the brightest spot of his Presidency was the 1969 visit to Uganda of Pope Paul VI—the first ever of a reigning Pontiff to Africa. The Pope dedicated a shrine to the earlier-mentioned religious martyrs of the late nineteenth century, consecrated African bishops, made strong antiracism, anticolonialism statements, and conferred with both Nigerian and Biafran leaders in an attempt to bring those then-warring factions together.

The year 1970 saw Obote successful in obtaining parliamentary okay for his nationalization policies. And as that year came to a close, he appeared to have been feeling secure enough to have announced that the people would soon be naming their own chief executive. *The Uganda Argus* for December 15, 1970, carried this bold, eight-column banner: "This Is Dr. Obote's Proposal—The People to Elect President." Well, less than seven weeks thereafter, on January 25, 1971, while President Obote was on his way home from the Commonwealth Prime Ministers' Conference in Singapore, an up-from-the-ranks army officer who was commander of both the army and air force and an ex-boxing champion, staged a coup and took over as Uganda's President. He was Major General Idi Amin. Although his takeover displeased Tanzanian President Nyerere (in whose country Mr. Obote took up residence in exile) and threatened to impede the tripartite cooperation of Uganda, Kenya, and Tanzania in the commendable East African Community, the Uganda of Amin, bloodlessly and without panic, resumed business as usual. And toward the end of 1971, Uganda and Tanzania agreed to keep their economic union alive.

The new President found himself popular with conservative business and industrial interests, those Western governments who were apprehensive of the Obote brand of socialism, and, interestingly enough, the Baganda people, many of whom continue to miss their kabaka and their special monarchial status. President Amin, though a non-Baganda himself, pleased the two-million-plus Baganda (they constitute a fifth of the total population) when he returned King Freddie's body to Kambala for a state burial, and publicly considered the possibility of restoration of the kabakaship. Were monarchy to return, King Freddie's son, Prince Ronald Mutebi, would be his father's successor as kabaka.

YOUR VISIT TO UGANDA

Uganda's chief touristic competitor is Kenya. But the Ugandans know this and they have not been idle. Indeed, they are building up one of the finest tourist plants of any African nation. They have not only increased accommodations in their pair of globally famous national parks, they have also established a new park of consequence. And they operate one of Africa's largest chains of hotels and lodges, with a commendable executive-training program that sees young Ugandans sent to Europe to learn the tricks of the trade, thence to return to their homelands and management in their own enterprises. Uganda deserves time on African itineraries—the pair of urban centers, of course, coupled with Murchison Falls National Park as a minimum, with the other two major national parks ideally fitted into the picture, as well.

Kampala and Entebbe: Uganda's two principal cities are within commuting distance of each other. Entebbe is a small, British-built town on the shores of Lake Victoria, Africa's second largest fresh-water lake. It is just twenty miles by expressway from Kampala, by far the larger of the two, and the political-commercial-cultural center of the republic.

The visitor arriving by air will begin his tour in Entebbe. Even before alighting—while the plane flies low over the blue waters of the immense inland sea that is Lake Victoria—it is possible to appreciate what Sir Winston Churchill wrote when he visited the country near the turn of the century. "Uganda," he said, "is a fairy tale. You climb up a railway instead of a beanstalk, and at the end is a wonderful new world." Except that one now generally flies, what he wrote obtains today. This little land is one of startling beauty. Entebbe—quiet, small, completely lacking in bustle—is vivid with flowering trees and green parklands bordering the azure lake. The President's Residence—Government House in British days—is high on a hill, overlooking the neat white buildings of the town and the great lawns that separate them from the water's edge. Besides offering good accommodations, there are facilities for yachting, tennis, and fishing. The thickly foliaged Botanical Gardens are so dense and jungle-like that they have been used as the setting for Tarzan films, authentic jungle being much more difficult to come by in many parts of Africa than most moviegoers realize. And there are half-day launch cruises departing Entebbe Pier every morning for the Equator.

The drive to Kampala is through lush Buganda countryside, past neat villages and pleasant farms. Built on a series of seven hills—much greener, it must be said, than Rome's—Kampala lacks both the mellowness of Dar es Salaam and the vibrance of Nairobi. There is a whole slew of modern buildings, skyscraper office blocks, and public architecture, as well. In this latter group, the worth-visiting structures are the Parliament, with its splendidly decorated foyer—the treasure is an immense carved wooden mural; the National Theatre and Cultural Centre (watch the papers for programs), the Uganda Museum (where the specialty is African musical instruments—the attendants will play them for you), and the handsome campus of Makerere University. Makerere, during the pre-independence period, served as the university for all of British East Africa. Now the Ugandan national university, it retains an enviable academic reputation and attracts an international student body. Noteworthy are the library (for its bronzes and murals), the School of Fine Art (ceramics, sculpture, graphics, painting), and the unusual "apocalypse" ceiling of St. Francis's Chapel. Principal shops are in and about downtown's Kampala Road, and each of Kampala's hills is crowned by a major building. The most imposing are the principal mosque of the town, and the Anglican and Roman Catholic cathedrals (something like half of Uganda being Christian). The traditional-design Tombs of the Kabakas of Buganda are open to the public, with knowledgeable young guides to show visitors about. The center-of-town Independence Statue of mother and child is exemplary. The city market is the essence of Kampala—joyful, noisy, and with wares including ceramics and crafts.

The national parks: Uganda's hold their own with any country on the continent, and that is saying a great deal, as any Africa traveler knows. *Queen Elizabeth National Park* is framed by the Ruwenzori peaks, shares a border with that of Zaïre's Albert National Park, is flanked by Lakes Edward and George, and is also a neighbor of Rwanda's Kagera National Park. One interesting section of the park is known as the "Explosion Area" and is pockmarked with giant craters of extinct volcanoes. But it is the animals that are the park's outstanding assets. Road markers read "Elephants Have Right of Way"—and while there is no doubt that they are amusing to photograph, they are to be taken seriously. Besides the elephant that wander about, there are hippo, pelicans, buffalo in immense herds, waterbuck, warthog, and even lion, leopard, and cheetah. Visitors stay in attractive safari lodges, and within a couple of days much of the park's area can be traversed by Land-Rover, and a great deal of game seen and photographed—often at closer range than one might imagine possible.

Even more spectacular is *Murchison Falls National Park.* (One should not be deceived by the Anglo-Saxon place names that remain in what was British Africa; they were originally chosen by the colonial authorities to make Britons feel at home in the tropics, and some of the newer African states—Uganda in particular—have been most generous in retaining them.) Murchison Falls National Park, to continue, is the site of one of the world's marvels—the tumultuous falls where the waters of the Nile are forced through a rock cleft only twenty feet wide, and then plunge in foaming, roaring cascades to a gigantic river pool 160 feet below. The best way to have a look at the park's animal population is to take a launch trip along the Nile, from Lake Albert to the foot of the falls. En route, the attractions are absolutely unbelievable quantities of deceptively sleepy looking crocodiles (nowhere in all Africa are crocodiles to be seen in greater numbers) on the banks, schools of placid-appearing hippo plunging about in the shallow waters, elephant in the swamps flapping their ears to cool themselves, and probably occasional buffalo and antelope. Lion, baboon, and rhinoceros are seen in other areas of the park, as is a fantastic variety of birdlife. The photographer would do well to have twice as much film on hand as he anticipates using; locales such as this are not the place to worry about making the Kodak people rich. *Kidepo Valley National Park* embraces a unique five-hundred-square-mile area, way in the northeast, directly on the border with the Sudan. It takes its name from the Kidepo River and is at an elevation of between three hundred and four thousand feet, with mountains in the six-thousand-to-nine-thousand-foot category as a backdrop. The Uganda government made the area into a park because it contains species that are not seen in either the Queen Elizabeth or Murchison Falls parks. Indeed, some buffs term Kidepo Uganda's answer to Tanzania's Serengeti. At any rate, the attractions include such antelope as eland, greater and lesser kudus, klipspringers, the tiny dik-dik Bright's Gazelle, Chanler's Mountain reedbuck, and the roan antelope. There are, as well, herds of zebra, giraffe, ostriches, both leopard and cheetah, hyena, buffalo in large herds, and elephant.

Other points of interest: A half day's drive from the sister cities —through lush, thickly foliaged countryside—is *Jinja,* a rapidly growing industrial town whose chief landmark is a Hindu temple, designed in traditional Indian style. Nearby is *Ripon Falls,* on Lake Victoria, discovered by Speke in 1862 as the source of the Nile, and so designated now by a plaque. The energy of the waters was harnessed by the construction of *Owens Falls Dam,* which Queen (then Princess) Elizabeth dedicated in 1954. Interesting, too, is Jinja's golf course, which has one unusual rule of procedure: any player may lift his ball out of a hippopotamus footprint without penalty. *Kabale* is the highest of Uganda's towns (6200 feet), on the watershed between Lakes Edward and Victoria, in the highlands of Kigezi. It is near the *Kanaba Gap,* reached by a winding drive leading to an escarpment overlooking a panorama of the misted blue cones of the *Mufumbiro Volcanoes,* or "Cooking Pot" mountains, two of which are still active. The highest peak, Karisimbi, is often snow-covered, and the slopes are covered with bamboo and primeval forest, and contain a gorilla sanctuary which you may, or may not, care to inspect. At the foot of the legendary *"Mountains of the Moon"*—the Ruwenzori Range—is *Fort Portal,* the Western Province's chief administrative center and a perfect base for climbers headed for the Ruwenzori, less energetic tourists who would simply like to relax and enjoy the views, and travelers en route to the *Ituri Forest,* where the pygmies live mainly by hunting game with their own spears, the blades of which are considerably bigger than their hands. They are pleased to receive visitors, dance for them, and pose for photographs with them, but they expect to be remunerated in cash or cigarettes, or a combination of the two.

SHOPPING

Long outshadowed by its East African neighbor, Tanzania, as a source for handicrafts, Uganda has made marked improvements in this respect. It has never, of course, been without good traditional craftsmen. The problem has been one of marketing—getting the product from the artisans to retail sources convenient for the visitor. What happened was that the government stepped into the picture and established the National Handicraft Center. It has quite obviously retained pros to run its shops. They know their Africana, and just how and where to obtain it. Quality is high, designs are authentic. Prices are fair. Range is wide. The principal outlet is the center's big shop on Kampala Road, downtown in the capital, but there are branches, a particularly noteworthy one—small but with an exceptionally choice stock—off the lobby of the Kampala International Hotel. Outstanding are the carved ivory (women's heads, whimsical crocodiles, elephants, other subjects both large and small), the basketry (note especially the very finely woven pieces; these are from the western part of the country on the Rwanda border, and are outstanding in a continent noted for its basketry), traditional fly whisks with handles of fine beadwork (those in the national colors—black, red, and gold—are very good-looking), hand-blocked cottons by the yard that make up well as dresses, blouses, shirts, draperies, or what you will; and a good deal else. Export licenses are needed for larger pieces of carved ivory and other "game trophies." These cost something like half a dollar and are obtainable at National Handicraft Center shops. Uganda is proud of its contemporary artists and with justification. There are usually exhibits of current work, all of it for sale, of course, at the Nommo Gallery, on Victoria Avenue, next to the Uganda Club, in Kampala. The Pottery, just outside of Kampala, on the road to Jinja, sells ceramics that are hand-made on the spot. The noisy, vibrant public markets, in Kampala of course, but in all the towns, are invariably worthy of exploration. And all about the country, in and near hotels and lodges, one finds curio sellers, some of whose merchandise is worthwhile. There are small souvenir shops in hotels and national park lodges the country over. Uganda Waragi is a liqueur-like spirit used as the basis for mixed drinks and cocktails, and sold by the bottle everywhere, should you want to be the first on your block to serve, say, a Uganda Glory, or an African Heartbeat or even a Hippo's Dream (this last consists of Waragi, Cointreau, dry vermouth, and lemon juice) at a party.

CREATURE COMFORTS

HOTELS—I mentioned earlier that the Ugandans are East Africa's charmers, and you'll see what I mean when it comes to creature comforts. They appear to have an innate knack of making guests feel at home. And they have some excellent facilities. I lead off with **Entebbe** because it is at once the site of the republic's international airport, and of a hotel that is quite as pleasant as it was in pre-Independence days. On the shores of Lake Victoria and only a mile and a half from the airport, the Lake Victoria Hotel is a sprawling white structure—elderly, gracious, with spotless rooms (all with bath, many air-conditioned), a lovely dining room, a cocktail lounge whose bar is upholstered in zebraskin, and a capacious swimming pool with umbrella-covered tables on the lawn surrounding it. **Kampala's** leader is the Kampala International—fourteen stories, three hundred rooms, each with bath and terrace; swimming pool, restaurant, and Leopard's Lair rooftop nightclub, and shops (see Shopping). You may know this one by its original name, Apolo. Trouble was that it was called not after the Greek god (spelled Apollo), but after Milton Apolo Obote, who was deposed as Uganda's President in 1971, with the name change following. Equally luxurious is the even newer, but smaller, Nile Hotel, with more than forty three-room suites among its facilities, and a location adjacent to the Uganda Conference Center building. Old, or at least elderly Africa hands, might remember a hotel named the Imperial in Kampala. Its designation, understandably enough, was considered inappropriate after independence, and it is now the Grand, close by the International, overlooking Jubilee Park, with its Baraza Café the town's leading informal gathering place, a fancier, air-conditioned Grill Room, guest rooms all with bath but with or without air conditioning, and a pool around which drinks are served. Also vintage, but still good, is the Speke. In the same quarter as the International and the Grand, it features private baths and balconies in all rooms, Italian specialties in its coffee shop/terrace, and an international menu in its patio-centered Hacienda Grill. **Murchison Falls National Park** has two comfortable lodges. Paraa is smack in the center of the park, overlooking the Nile, with the launch-boat pier just below it. Guest rooms are spacious and all with bath, lounges are spacious, congenial bar, bright dining room, and you have not lived until, at dusk, while you are sitting on the completely open, Nile-view terrace enjoying a drink, the neighborhood elephants slowly gallumph by to look you over, and pass right along. Chobe Lodge overlooks the Goragung Rapids, and every one of its rooms (all have bath) overlooks the river that is jampacked with hippo and crocodiles. There are full facilities, of course, including a swimming pool and a cocktail terrace, directly below which the elephants and hippos do their thing. A third lodge is scheduled for 1973. **Queen Elizabeth National Park** visitor headquarters is at Mweya Safari Lodge—modern, good-looking, with a swimming pool, pleasant rooms with their own terraces and baths, and a super situation overlooking Lake Edwards, with the Mountains of the Moon as a backdrop. The 250-bed Ishasha Safari Lodge is scheduled for 1973. **Kidepo Valley National Park's** modern katarum Safari Lodge is a beautifully designed cluster of bungalows surrounding a principal pavilion, on an eminence offering a superb panorama of the game-filled valley; all facilities. **Elsewhere in Uganda:** I know of no country in Black Africa with a higher proportion of good hotels dotted throughout the countryside. This is a situation for which we must thank an enterprise known as Uganda Hotels Limited; a subsidiary of the government's Uganda Development Corporation, it operates all of the foregoing hotels and safari lodges, and its properties are to be found in less celebrated but strategically located locales, as well, including *Jinja* (Crested Crane Hotel), *Tororo* (Rock Hotel), *Mbale* (Mount Elgon Hotel), *Gulu* (Acholi Inn), *Masindi* (Masindi Hotel), *Kabale* (White Horse Inn), *Masaka* (Tropic Inn), *Kasese* (Margherita Hotel), *Soroti* (Soroti Hotel), and *Lira* (Lira Hotel). The last two of this group were Danish-designed, built with the aid of a Danish government loan, and are to be followed by others of similar origin, in other small provincial centers.

Restaurants and Nightlife—In *Entebbe,* the Lake Victoria Hotel, with its pleasant restaurant, cocktail lounge, and pool. In *Kampala,* the leading hotels double as the best eating places. These include the International, Nile, Grand, and Speke; at all of these there are bar-lounges and informal cafés as well as proper restaurants, some with dancing. Chez Joseph is a commendable restaurant featuring French-style cuisine. Aside from the hotel dine-dance rooms, there are nightclubs like the Florida (on the road to Entebbe), the Susana, and the New Life, at which there's lots of music, lots of noise, and lots of fun, Kampala style. The Jambo Gardens of the Silver Springs Hotel is worth remembering on Sunday evenings, when an African dance troupe provides the entertainment. Watch the papers for performances—of plays, dancing or of the National choir, at the Uganda National Theatre in Kampala, and bear in mind that the capital has four cinemas, one of which is a drive-in.

UPPER VOLTA

République de la Haute-Volta

Entry requirements: *A visa, obtainable from French consulates, where Upper Volta has no diplomatic representation, plus a health certificate (yellow fever and smallpox).* **Best times for a visit:** *The dry months—January through April—are ideal; rain, however, is not incessant during the remainder of the year and need not deter visitors in Africa at the time.* **Currency:** *The CFA franc: CFA 280=$1.* **Principal European language:** *French, with English spoken in leading hotels and transport centers.* **Domestic transport:** *Roads and plane service link the two major towns.* **Further information:** *Service d'Information de la République de la Haute-Volta, Ouagadougou, Upper Volta.*

INTRODUCING UPPER VOLTA

Upper what? Upper Volta is the name. It is derived from the Volta River system, which includes three Voltas—Red, White, and Black. And it is one of the world's least-visited republics, with tongue-twisting names for its two chief cities—and a Champs-Elysées and Bois de Boulogne to placate those of its French residents who long for Paris.

Upper Volta's peoples include one of Africa's oldest still functioning kingdoms, whose traditions have changed little, despite the country's rapid changeover to the twentieth-century world. Europeans did not penetrate this landlocked region until the eighteenth century, and it did not officially become a French colony until 1919. The French split up its territory among that of several adjoining French West African provinces for a few years prior to World War II, but after the war, restored its identity to it. In 1958 it chose to become a semi-autonomous republic of the French Community, and in 1960 its leaders advised General de Gaulle that it wanted complete independence, which was granted in August. Upper Volta is one of the five states of the Council of the Entente, which was formed primarily to conduct joint independent negotiations with the French. It coninues to receive economic and technical aid from the Paris government. And is governed by the increasingly less-austere military regime of Gen. Sangoule Lamizana, which succeeded an earlier, unhappy, and corrupt period, under President Maurice Yameogo. An outspoken opponent of the Yameogo regime was the then Roman Catholic archbishop of Ouagadougou, a member of the Mossi tribe named Paul Zoungrana. Five years later, he became the second African cardinal in the history of the Church.

Voltaic peoples had known imperialism long before the French subdued them in the past century. Their most important group—the Mossi—created an empire in the fourteenth century. Believed to have come to the Volta region from Nigeria or Dahomey, the Mossi subjugated indigenous tribes to their will, fought battles with the ancients of Timbuktu and of Gao—to name but two of their most distinguished adversaries. Their ruler, the Moro Naba, is hereditary, and controls a traditional council of ministers, beneath whom there is a rigidly defined hierarchy, an intricate series of ceremonials, a fine arts-and-crafts tradition, and a justifiable pride in a great and vivid history, which if not entirely peaceful was no more warlike than that of the Christian West.

Tucked away in the forests and savannas of the interior, Upper Volta, one of the poorest of African states, has known relatively few visitors in recent years, other than French administrators and businessmen. It has never been a popular tourist country. There is, however, just enough of the twentieth century—comfortable hotels, decent roads, good French food, rapid air service—to make the visitor comfortable. What are the lures? This chapter highlights just a few.

YOUR VISIT TO UPPER VOLTA

Bobo-Dioulasso: Though not the capital, Bobo-Dioulasso (familiarly known as Bobo) is the larger of the republic's two cities, with a population of more than seventy thousand. Those sections of it developed by the French are pleasant and spacious. Wide boulevards are bordered by gardens and dominated by a huge modern market. The African sectors, both new and old, are good walking territory, for this is, after all, an ancient African-established town, thriving long before Europeans came upon it, and founded—so the legend goes—by a hunter who was so impressed by good hunting in the area that he and his tribe—the Bobo—settled the region. Still, from the banks of the now dry stream—the Marigot Oué—which the Old Town borders, one has a splendid view, not only of teeming streets, but of the women of the town washing brilliant-hued clothing, which is spread out on the riverbanks to dry in the sun. Excursions from the town? There are as many as the visitor has time for. These would include the *Dinderésso Forest,* at the source of the Kou River—the favorite promenade spot for the town's residents; the *Cliffs of Borodougou,* affording a magnificent view of wide plains, as well as ancient grottoes with decorated interior walls, still used as headquarters for the animist religious groups of the region, with workshops for the design of superb ceremonial masks; and two *waterfalls—Koro,* near a village nearby built among a formation of rock, and *Takalédougou,* not far from *Touziana,* site of an interesting-to-visit missionary training school. *Boromo,* for those driving from Bobo to *Ouagadougou,* the capital, might be an interesting stopover point. It is amid a forested region alive with game: hunting is forbidden, but the cameraman is afforded a field day, with subject matter running the gamut from panthers to buffalo.

Ouagadougou: Quieter, less commercial, and smaller than Bobo-Dioulasso, Ouagadougou (pronounced *Waa-ga-doo-goo*) is the capital of the republic. Its major monuments are the modern government buildings and the immense Catholic Cathedral, in many ways as Romanesque as one would find in France, and quite the most imposing of any in French-settled Africa. Adjoining it is a craft school operated by the White Sisters, to help keep alive the folk arts of the country. The concentration is on beautiful hand-woven rugs, which can be shipped abroad without difficulty. Ouagadougou's principal attraction, at least for the visitor not on business with the government or the shopper anxious to embellish the floors of his home, is the *Palace of the Moro Naba*, hereditary king of the Mossi people. The building is surprisingly modern and Western in basic design, and it is by no means as elaborate as one might expect for so ancient a monarchy. But the ceremonials and the structure of the Mossi come alive with a visit, and if one is lucky enough to be present on a Friday morning (at seven A.M.!) he can witness the weekly ritual on the palace grounds. The entire African community assembles to pay tribute to its leader. The Moro Naba's authority was limited by the French during their occupation, and the responsibilities of his five ministers increased. The current government has done little to change the situation, so that even though the Moro Naba is now without great temporal powers, his spiritual eminence is little diminished—as one can easily see at the Friday-morning ceremonies. Despite its African name and its overwhelmingly African personality, the capital is not without remaining traces of *la présence française*, the chief among them being its chief thoroughfare, the boulevard-like, palm-lined *Champs Elysées*, and—just outside of town—the *Bois de Boulogne*, a vast, verdant park which the capital's residents consider their promenade favorite. Besides the *Bois*, there are other excursion destinations: *Pabre Dam*, near a tiny Mossi village and Black Sisters' mission; the *Po and Leo* region, a wonderfully well-populated game reserve, running the gamut from elephants to tiny antelope; and *Koudougou*, home of the *Sukomsé* sect, unusual in that it does not practice circumcision and has what might be called an Afro-Puritan outlook on sexual matters, and an elaborately rigid set of rituals and prohibitive regulations—as well as a culture whose dances and sculpture are distinctive enough to warrant investigation. An interesting day trip from Ouagadougou can be made to the village of *Sabou,* about sixty miles from the capital, famous for its *Pool of Sacred Crocodiles.* The crocodiles are worshiped by the local residents, who fish and boat freely among the dangerous beasts.

SHOPPING

Hand-woven rugs at the Catholic Mission in Ouagadougou; *objets d'art* in wood, ivory, and iron, as well as leatherwork and hand-woven cloth at markets in the principal towns and villages. Bargaining in the markets is the rule. And don't overlook shopping possibilities in tiny villages traversed in the course of excursions into the countryside.

CREATURE COMFORTS

HOTELS—**Bobo-Dioulasso:** Royal Hotel—all rooms air-conditioned, swimming pool; Buffet Hotel. **Ouagadougou:** Independence Hotel—all rooms air-conditioned, swimming pool, tennis court, restaurant, and nightclub; Central Hotel; Buffet Hotel, centrally located. **Arly:** Upper Volta is justifiably proud of the new encampment at Arly, the point of departure for a tour of the Arly Reserve. It has twenty comfortable rooms and a swimming pool. **Other centers:** Simple but usually adequate rest camps, accommodation for which should be booked in advance from one of the major cities. INDEPENDENT RESTAURANTS—*Bobo-Dioulasso*—Le Perroquet; *Ouagadougou*—L'Eau Vive, L'Oasis.

WEST AFRICA: OFF THE BEATEN PATH

Guinea-Bissau
São Tomé and Príncipe
Equatorial Guinea
Spanish Sahara
Cape Verde Islands

These areas are, for the most part, without modern hotels, and their capitals are not on the main air routes. Visas are needed for all, and health certificates (yellow fever, smallpox) are required. For the traveler who would have a look for himself, here is the line-up.

Guinea-Bissau: Officially designated as an "overseas province" of Portugal, this territory—fighting for its independence—has but a minimum of the continental charm so often brought abroad to their possessions by the Portuguese. Don't expect anything like Angola's Luanda or Mozambique's Lourenço Marques in *Bissau,* this colony's capital, or *Bolama,* its second city. There is a population of about half a million, mainly agricultural. Much of the countryside is low and swampy, and aside from hotels at the two coastal cities (Grande, Avenida, and Portugal in Bissau, Pensão and Turismo in Bolama), there are few facilities for visitors. Nor is the colony's atmosphere conducive to tourism. Guinea-Bissau has what is probably Africa's most successful guerrilla movement. Guerrillas reportedly control at least half the country, despite relatively large—constantly replenished—forces of troops from Lisbon.

Sao Tomé and Príncipe: These two islands and a handful of smaller islands adjacent to them constitute what the Portuguese call the "Overseas Province" of São Tomé and Príncipe. The total population is less than seventy thousand in an area of some four hundred square miles. São Tomé island lives on its extensive cocoa crop, cultivated ever since it was settled in the sixteenth century by Portuguese Jews who were exported there from the mother country after refusing to become Christians. Its capital city bears the name of the island—São Tomé. The *pousadas* (state-operated tourist inns) of San Jeronimo and Miramar are comfortable, as is the Pousada Salazar, located in the mountains fifteen minutes from the capital.

Equatorial Guinea: Once known collectively as Spanish Guinea, and then separated into two territories, the island of Fernando Po and the mainland enclave of Río Muni became the independent republic of Equatorial Guinea in 1968. Río Muni, the mainland area, is the more populous and less developed part of the country. Largely forest and mountains, it is wedged between the Cameroon and Gabon republics. The island of Fernando Po, just a few miles from the coast of Cameroon, is more developed and prosperous. It has a modern jetstrip, from which relief flights were flown to Biafra during the Nigerian civil war, as well as modern roads and schools. It surprises visitors with its great forest-covered peaks, two of which exceed nine thousand feet. Cocoa is the main crop, with many of the plantation workers imported from Nigeria. The top hotel in Fernando Po is the Monterrey in the capital, Santa Isabel. In Río Muni, there is the Gurea, in the city of Bata. Before gaining independence from Spain, Equatorial Guinea was a prosperous cocoa exporter and popular with visitors seeking a sleepy tropical setting. Now, however, the country has become notorious for the harsh, repressive government of President Francisco Macias Nguema, which has resulted in a mass exodus of frightened Spaniards, Portuguese, and Nigerian plantation workers. The Europeans were largely responsible for the country's economic progress, and their departure has caused the abandonment of stores and plantations and has led to economic chaos. The country still receives aid from Spain, despite disputes with the former mother country, but she has also established ties with the Soviet Union and China, both of which maintain large embassies.

Spanish Sahara: Stretched along the Atlantic Coast between Morocco and Mauritania, Spanish Sahara (known also as Spanish West Africa and Rio de Oro) is an immense patch (over one hundred thousand square miles) of desert, with less than a handful of rather pathetic settlements which pass as towns, a tiny population (probably less than 50,000) and an airport at *Villa Cisneros.* The peoples of the interior are pastoral Moslem nomads, and those on the coast live by fishing. The one hotel of the colony is the Ipasa in Villa Cisneros. Sound inviting?

Cape Verde Islands: Another of Portugal's "overseas provinces," these islands are a little more than 300 miles off the Senegal coast, and are home to less than 200,000 people—mostly African coffee farmers. Santiago, the largest of the ten main islands, is the site of *Praia,* the capital. The islands are mostly mountainous, with a number of volcanoes, one of which—9200-foot Pico de Cano—is active. Transatlantic ships sometimes stop at *Pôrto Grande* to refuel. Air and ship service to the islands is mostly from Lisbon. In Praia there is the Pousada Praia-Mar, and on Sal Island, the Estalagem Morabeza.

ZAÏRE

République du Zaïre

Entry requirements: *A visa, a health certificate (yellow fever and smallpox), a police certificate, bank letter, and an onward ticket.* **Best times for a visit:** *The dry periods—June through August, November through March—are ideal; other months are intermittently rainy, but, on the other hand, fresher and greener.* **Currency:** *the zaïre, which is the equivalent of $2 U.S.* **Principal European languages:** *French, Flemish, and English—with more of the last-named than you might imagine. Swahili is spoken by many Africans and Europeans.* **Domestic transport:** *Air Zaïre connects the major centers, many minor points as well, and flies to a number of neighboring lands, and to Europe, too. Many good roads, and steamer services on the Zaïre River and on the large lakes.* **Further information:** *Ambassade de la République du Zaïre, Washington, D.C.; Commissariat Général au Tourisme, Boîte Postale 9502, Kinshasa, Zaïre.*

INTRODUCING ZAÏRE

Think of sub-Sahara Africa and, chances are, you think of the Zaïre Republic, which was the Democratic Republic of the Congo until it changed its name in October 1971. The new name is taken from the original name of the Congo River—which in Zaïre is now known as the Zaïre River. The pronunciation is "*Zay-air.*" This is the region of thick tropical forests, of wild animals on the plains, of Stanley and Livingstone, of ivory and of slavery, of white-robed missionaries and pith-helmeted colonists, of drumbeats and dances, masks and carvings—all the images that the word "Africa" evokes.

Zaïre has been, in this century, the most romanticized of the African territories. It is an African state with many riches and many problems.

Zaïre is almost as big in area as Western Europe, or India. It is eighty times the size of its former occupier, Belgium. The famous river which runs through it is the second longest on the continent and one of the longest in the world. The population, when one considers this immensity of area, is small: about twenty-two million people. Much of the country is covered by forest, but it is rich in natural resources—copper, uranium, and industrial diamonds, of which it produces almost three-quarters of the world's supply.

Before the Europeans began carving up Africa into colonies for themselves, the entire lower Zaïre River area was an ethnologically united African empire. As long ago as the sixteenth century, European traders found an Iron Age society in the lower Congo region, with a feudal organization similar enough to those in Europe so that African chiefs were offered—and accepted—European-type titles. They became dukes and barons, as well as Christians. One studied theology in Portugal and was made a bishop to Pope Leo X—the first black bishop of the Catholic Church. Later emissaries were sent to the Vatican for many years. They had a highly organized social and religious structure, with ultimate belief in a Supreme Being. They smelted and forged iron and other metals; they carried on extensive trade with neighboring peoples. Their society was tightly knit, with working patterns adaptable to the environment.

But the slave trade—at first engaged in by Arabs from the East and later by Europeans as well—decimated their populations, demoralized their communities, and brought havoc to many facets of their culture. They were not strong enough to resist the colonizing Europeans of the nineteenth century, and the ancient Kongo Kingdom found itself part Belgian, part French, and part

Portuguese. Much of it—the Portuguese region excepted—is free again, but along the lines of the arbitrary European frontiers.

From the time that the first Portuguese—Diogo Cão—and his successors visited the Congo basin in the late fifteenth century, there was little penetration into the interior, until Arab slavers, coming from the East, began their trade in "black ivory" about 1820. It was not until several decades later that Livingstone—the first of the Europeans—explored the region; his next major follower was Stanley, who discovered the course of the Congo River on a long trip lasting from 1874 through 1877. News of his exploits reached the King of the Belgians, Leopold II—an ambitious man, not satisfied to rule over a country as small as Belgium, and no doubt anxious for extracurricular activity which would distract public attention from his notoriously dissolute personal life. He sent for Stanley, learned of the untapped potential region, set up something called the International Association for Exploration and Civilization in Central Africa—ostensibly to abolish slavery—and dispatched his man Stanley to the scene. Stanley set about signing treaties with chiefs, and acquiring more and more land for Leopold—who never visited Africa. Later, in 1885, at the Berlin Conference, the European powers split up Africa among themselves, and Leopold asked for—and received from the other conferees—*personal* title to the area. He set it up as the Congo Free State—*not* as a Belgian colony—and ruled it singlehandedly until 1908. By that time he had become immensely wealthy on rubber and ivory. He had also incurred the wrath of the Western world, which had come to learn of the atrocities his subordinates had used to "develop" the country.

Leopold's men forced African workers to fill quotas; those who did not were either killed or horribly mutilated—the amputation of feet or hands was the usual punishment—and one which was a European innovation in Africa. The slaughter was so widespread that the population is today some 7,000,000 fewer than estimated at the turn of the century.

Taking over from their king—who died a year after the Belgian government assumed control of his personal "Free State"—the

Belgians set about to make amends for the atrocities of their late sovereign. The Belgian government retained interest in the huge business monopolies—copper, diamonds, etc.—and they did not at once abolish forced labor. But they evolved a policy of benevolent paternalism. The races were separated, the only exceptions to the rule being *évolués*, an African elite whom they gave some education.

For the masses, decent urban housing was constructed, basic education (mainly undertaken by government-subsidized Catholic missions) became fairly widespread, and there was training for skilled and semiskilled occupations. But no political activity was permitted—even for the tightly controlled white-settler minority, and no Africans were allowed to study for any profession except the Catholic clergy; nor were they permitted to go abroad to universities, as was the case with Africans in French and British territories. (In 1960 there were fewer than twenty college graduates in the country; today more than ten thousand are reported to attend a college or university.)

The idea, of course, was to satisfy the Africans by allowing them to develop occupationally, to see to it that they had decent homes in which to live and—by colonial standards—decent salaries and medical care. But the word got around that other African peoples were getting their freedom, and that Asian territories were becoming sovereign. In 1958, after a tragic uprising in Kinshasa, the government began to see the handwriting on the wall. "Eventual" independence was promised; the color bar was made less rigid; settlers were implored by administrators to treat Africans like human beings—which was difficult for many of the whites to do.

But this was not enough. Agitation increased from the political parties which had recently been formed to elect town councilors in the major cities. And in December 1959—to the surprise of the world—Belgium announced that its immense colony would become independent within five months, that economic aid would continue to be provided, and that Belgian technicians and civil servants would stay on the scene where wanted. Conferences lasted all winter in Brussels and Leopoldville, and there were intertribal skirmishes up to the very day of independence.

Patrice Lumumba, a dynamic ex-postal clerk, leader of the only country-wide political party, and the only politician with a national following, received enough pledged support from the other parties to form a government; he was elected Prime Minister as an advocate of a strong, centralized government, with tribalism de-emphasized. Joseph Kasavubu, a mild-mannered school-teacher and head of the populous Lower Congo peoples, was named President—the less powerful of the two top posts.

Of all the African colonies gaining nationhood, none was prevented from political development so much as the then-Congo. The only political experience of the people had been two local-council elections in the towns. Virtually no African had served in the civil service, and only one member of the original cabinet was a university graduate.

Shortly after independence came in June 1960, the army mutinied, and some of its members attacked civilians. The army, before independence, had been called the Force Publique; it was actually a police militia—Belgian-officered, rough, ruthless, with its chief function that of keeping the masses quiet and obedient. It was hardly fastidious in its methods. And it is worth noting that the attacks on Belgians came only from members of this Belgian-trained goon-squad-type police force—*not* from the local civilians.

Nonetheless, Belgian settlers, administrators, and technicians panicked and fled to the motherland, while at the same time the Brussels government sent troops—to fight. Premier Lumumba asked the UN to intervene, and Secretary General Dag Hammarskjold—within what seemed like minutes—organized with ingenious agility an international force of soldiers (mostly Africans) and technicians.

Lumumba, meanwhile, kept appealing to the UN to expel the Belgian troops, and after two Security Council directives, they finally began to leave. Meanwhile, Moise Tshombe, a rich tribal chief backed by the powerful Belgian mining company in the rich Katanga Province (now renamed Shaba), declared that his province (with its Belgian advisers and Belgian-led army) was seceding; Tshombe formed a first-rate fighting force headed and trained by British and Rhodesian mercenaries. Albert Kalonji, Baluba tribal leader whose people had long been at odds with supporters of Lumumba, announced the secession of *his* region of Kasai Province.

Kasavubu, as chief of state, then proclaimed that Lumumba was no longer Prime Minister, and named Joseph Ileo to the post. Ileo never had a chance to take over. Lumumba continued to claim that his ouster was illegal (it all depended upon one's interpretation of the country's new constitution), and in the meantime, a young army colonel, Joseph Mobutu, stepped in as strong man and appointed a group of educated young Congolese to run the country as the College of Commissioners. With his consent, Belgians began to return, confusing the operation of the UN mission.

Lumumba, who had fled to Stanleyville (now Kisangani) upon being ousted by Kasavubu, was murdered in 1961, under mysterious circumstances. He promptly became a martyr, canonized by radical leaders around the world as a symbol of the Africans' fight against neocolonialism. The Katanga secession, which involved heavy fighting between Tshombe forces and those of the UN, ended in 1963, and the following year Tshombe was made the country's new Premier. When a new revolt broke out—staged by a group of peasant rebels calling themselves *simbas* (the Swahili for lion)—Tshombe again used mercenaries, quelling the revolt after six months of bloody fighting. In 1965 Mobutu again seized power and gradually gained control of the government. Today he runs the country with a firm hand, but despite authoritarian rule, Zaïre's economic picture is improving rapidly after a decade of so much turbulence. Rich mineral and agricultural resources are being exploited vigorously, foreign trade and investment are growing, and plans are being made for badly needed modernization of transportation facilities, and for the revival of what had been a considerable tourist industry. Mobutu's government is not without its excesses, but it has helped to unify the country, re-establish world confidence in it, and attract substantial foreign investment. President Mobutu made news around the world in late 1971 and early 1972 when he announced new names not only for the country itself, for copper-rich Katanga Province (now Shaba, which means copper in Swahili), for the Stanley Pool (Malebo Pool), for Mount Stanley (Mount Ngaliema), but also for Mr. Mobutu himself. He replaced his Christian names, Joseph Désiré, with African ones, styling himself Mobutu Sese Seko, and setting a precedent for other Zaïreans to follow; all Zaïreans were required to drop baptismal names and adopt African ones, and Roman Catholic priests who refused to give children African names at baptism were made liable to prosecution. (Earlier post-Independence years saw Léopoldville become Kinshasa, Stanleyville changed to Kisangani, Elisabethville renamed Lubumbashi, and Albertville named Kalemie.) Even the names of the newspapers—mostly French—were Africanized. (*Le Progrès*, for example, became *Salongo*—meaning "return to work.") But surely the most euphonious change was that of the national airline: Air Congo became Air Zaïre.

YOUR VISIT TO ZAÏRE

The Zaïre Republic can easily keep a visitor fascinated for many weeks. The highlights? Here they are, briefly.

Kinshasa: Just across the Zaïre River from Brazzaville, capital of the Congo Republic, Kinshasa (formerly Leopoldville) is quite as twentieth-century modern as one could imagine: solid, substantial, functional, comfortable, and virtually devoid of the style or charm evident just across the river in Gallic-accented Brazzaville. Its attractions, other than the white skyscrapers, massive government buildings, wealthy diplomatic quarters and poorer, but still modern, African housing projects, are few but not to be minimized: the impassable Zaïre River Rapids—the river is unnavigable from Matadi to Kinshasa, from there inward it *is* navigable to Kisangani (formerly Stanleyville), and beyond, in other detached stretches—the excellent National Museum, which is a prerequisite for any visitor not familiar with African art and collections of it in other museums, and Lovanium University, found in 1954 by priest-teachers from Belgium's venerable Louvain University, with an integrated student body, and modern facilities. Faculty members and students are happy to show visitors about—to the labs, to the dormitories and dining halls, to the atomic reactor (yes—an atomic reactor!) and to the classroom and recreation buildings. Lovanium, like the other universities of Black Africa, is among its most reassuring institutions.

Kisangani: originally called Stanleyville, Kisangani is the chief town of Orientale (Eastern) Province. It is the kind of town one imagines in the African tropics. It was there that the film *The Nun's Story* was filmed (the entire community was in love with Audrey Hepburn for many years), and just outside the city is the picturesque Malebo Pool with the fishing villages of the Wagenia tribe. They make their catches in immense nets which they ingeniously hoist over the rapids on poles, and nearby are the Lokele people, who make their homes in immense dugout canoes, carved from single pieces of timber. Boat rides along the river—with muscular oarsmen providing the power—can easily be arranged.

Every African community has an open-air market, but if I could visit only one, it would be that of Kisangani. Here, in well-defined sections, are on sale all the commodities used by the people of the region—gay *batik* cloth worn by the women in wrap-around style; cooking implements, some European, some African-wrought; home furnishings—stools, chairs, tables—monkey-meat steaks; whole, fresh-killed monkeys, monkey fur, neat white pyramids of ground manioc, dried whole tobacco leaves; mounds of rice, stem after stem of bananas, which are boiled, fried, roasted, and of course eaten from the skin. Look carefully, and you'll find masks, woodcarvings, hand-forged iron spears, and drums of varying shapes and sizes.

Kisangani's European community is small, but it lives well. There are several good hotels, a surprising number of nightclubs—some with musical entertainment—and a thoroughly delightful alfresco zoo and café high on the banks of the river, where many locals congregate for a cool drink at the end of day, in time to see the sun set over the river and watch the zoo's elephants being led into the water for an evening bath. The country's youngest university, Free University of Zaïre, is located in Kisangani.

Kivu Province: If Kisangani is typically tropical-African, Kivu Province is just the opposite—at least on first meeting. It has, in the first place, a heavenly year-round climate which, if not quite temperate, comes close. It is mountain country, with many of the mountains still active volcanoes. It is lake country—indeed, it is named for the body of water which was the last of the great African lakes to be discovered by Europeans. It is farm country—crops are terraced on the sides of great hills. It is, as well, animal country—wild as they come and lots of them. It is a region of fascinating tribal peoples. And it is, too, resort country.

Most of the Belgian settlers in Zaïre made their homes in Kivu Province. They developed a number of pretty towns along the lake's edge, and it is doubtful if most of them could have lived nearly as comfortably in crowded Belgium. The capital of the province is *Bukavu,* handsomely situated on a series of five green, hilly peninsulas jutting into the blue waters of Lake Kivu. The houses are graceless but substantial, the gardens are lovely, the view of the lake superb.

Also suitable as a headquarters for the visitor is smaller *Goma,* not far away, also on the water's edge, and in the vicinity of a row of eight volcanoes in an area of terraced plantations, groves of coffee trees, fields of wild flowers, clumps of bamboo and even gardens of raspberries and strawberries, with red jasmine scenting the air. Only two miles away is *Kisenyi,* just over the frontier in Rwanda (page 280). The two towns are twin resorts with good accommodations, cafés, and shops, and a nearby village where Watusi dancers traditionally perform.

Virunga National Park lies along the western shores of *Lake Edward,* stretching northward to the Kivu volcanoes, including the most famous of the active ones: Nyamlagira and Nyiragongo. One can get a good view of these craters through the veils of sulfur gases and molten lava—if one really cares about such natural phenomena. Myself, I prefer the park's wildlife: elephants, hippos, lions, leopards, buffalos (the greatest hams of all—they love to stand still for full-face photos), antelopes in great variety, and thousands upon thousands of aquatic birds. The Ruindi Camp is the park's principal lodge, and from it visitors in their own cars, accompanied by African game wardens, make forays through the park on narrow dirt roads. The rule of the park, as in that of every game reserve in Africa: stay in the car, except when escorted about on foot by the wardens. A full day of viewing—or, better yet, a day and a half, including an early-morning pre-breakfast trek—gives one views (and photographs) of virtually every type of animal, the elusive lion possibly excepted. En route back to Goma, make a stop at the completely isolated falls of the Rutshuru River, which flows into Lake Kivu. Or, if there's time, go north from Ruindi to still another lodge, for a cliff's-eye view of *Lake Edward* and its teeming bird population.

Continue on (your excursion from Goma can be arranged for any number of days you prefer—four should be the minimum) over the roller-coaster-like Escarpment de Kabasha, passing the Equator marker, through thick forests and friendly villages with conical-roofed thatched huts, and make a stop in the *Ituri Forest*, home of the pygmies, who remain the hunters they have been for more centuries than man knows. These are presumed to be Zaïre's original inhabitants. They have never integrated into the life of the normal-sized community. They wear very few clothes, hunt with magnificent spears considerably taller than they themselves, and are delighted to pose for photographs and dance (rather pitifully) for visitors. Their fee is a combination of cigarettes and money—a few dollars' worth (in total) is usually acceptable.

Farther along the route are the *"Mountains of the Moon"*—the fabled Ruwenzori range, hovering over the Zaïre-Uganda border, eternally snow-capped, and dazzlingly impressive. A not-too-hot hotel is located at their base, with its situation better than its accommodations. Stay overnight, though, for a sunrise view of the mountains, which, like all famous peaks, are covered by mist more often than they have any right to be.

Virunga Park adjoins Uganda's Queen Elizabeth National Park (page 370). Animals need no passports to cross from one to the other, and from it, one may either go into the Ugandan preserve or return to Goma.

Lubumbashi and Shaba Province: Formerly called Elisabethville, Lubumbashi is the capital of the copper-rich Shaba (ex-Katanga) Province, which borders Zambia, itself a land with extensive deposits of that ore. Lubumbashi's wealth has helped make it an imposing city. Its pride and joy, a new civic auditorium-theater, is one of the few truly handsome examples of Belgian tropical architecture in the country, and its museum of African arts ranks with that of Kinshasa. The altitude—over 4000 feet—makes for a pleasant climate, but there is little else to see in the town, aside from its modern shops, office buildings, and public facilities. The visitor who is fascinated with mining operations might want to make excursions to the copper mines outside the city. For others, trips might be made to other attractions of Shaba Province—*Kalemie* (formerly Albertville), on the shores of Lake Tanganyika; the *Upemba National Park*, near *Lake Kisale*, and the villages of the principal tribal groups: the Baluba, with their superb sculpture; the Balunda, whose village fortifications can still be seen; the Batshioko, talented carvers in wood—tables, taborets, masks, and drums—and great dancers as well. Shaba Province crafts typify those to be found throughout the country—dramatic, inventive, wonderfully decorative, and, as is the case throughout Africa, irrevocably interwoven with the people's religion.

Other areas: If you've time to spare, consider visits to these centers: *Bunia*—where the last of the duck-billed women live, disks having stretched their lips grotesquely; *Epulu*—with its elephant training station (unique in Africa) and its okapi capture station, where these rare animals, found only in Zaïre, are rounded up for distribution to zoos throughout the world; *Luluabourg*, site of an interesting museum of art and folklore, and headquarters for excursions to *Mushenge*, seat of the important Bakuba Chieftaincy, with the home of the Bakuba king (or *nyimi*), and center for these people's hand-woven cloth, wood, and wrought-iron crafts.

SHOPPING

This country's craft traditions are among the finest in all Africa: masks, drums, spears, elephant-hair bracelets, ivory (carvings, bracelets, necklaces, brooches), dramatic wood sculpture. Try the open markets of the major towns, as well as those of the villages which you drive through. Bargaining is the general rule.

CREATURE COMFORTS

HOTELS—Zaïre is serious about wanting to develop a modern tourist industry—as well it might be, with all it has to offer. Two modern hotels in **Kinshasa,** the capital, are manifestations of this aim. One, the Inter•Continental Kinshasa, cost close to eight million dollars and was jointly financed by the government of Zaïre, the Agency for International Development, and Inter•Continental, which is a global subsidiary of Pan American World Airways and has hotels in a number of other African countries. IHC's Kinshasa hostelry is a ten-story, 260-room, river-view, fully air-conditioned structure in the Kalina residential section, convenient both to downtown and N'Djili International Airport. Facilities include a capacious swimming pool, cocktail lounge, coffee shop, and smart rooftop restaurant-*boîte*. Also modern, and in downtown Kinshasa, is the luxury-class Okapi, named for the animal unique to Zaïre, and overlooking the river, with swimming pool, restaurant-*boîte*, coffee shop, and air conditioning throughout. Older favorites include the Regina, the Memling, and the Guesthouse Sabena. Worthwhile Kinshasa restaurants include Le Pergola and Le Zoo—both with gardens, and La

Devinière, Brussels, Mini-Club, and Gourmet. **Matadi:** Metropole, Guesthouse Sabena. **Kisangani:** Hotel Zaïre Palace, Résidence Équateur. **Bukavu:** Riviera, overlooking the lake; Résidence. **Kalemie:** Metropole, Des Touristes, Palace. **Lubumbashi:** Leopold II—attractive, central; Ambassador; Guesthouse Sabena, Elizabeth, du Katanga. **Luluabourg:** Pax, L'Oasis. **Boma:** Guesthouse. **Goma:** Des Grands Lacs—very attractive. **Ruindi** (Virunga National Park): Ruindi Camp.

ZAMBIA

Republic of Zambia

Entry requirements: *Valid passport, of course, and for U.S. citizens, a visa, obtainable at the Zambian Embassy, Washington, D.C., or the Zambian Mission to the United Nations, 150 East 58th Street, New York. A return or onward transportation ticket is also required.* **Best times for a visit:** *Much of Zambia is elevated—on a plateau ranging from thirty-five hundred to seven thousand feet, with a remarkably comfortable climate—considering the nearness to the Equator—as a happy consequence. The nicest months are May–August, when it is coolish and dry, temperatures ranging from sixty to eighty degrees. The months of September, October, and November constitute a hot, dry season (eighty to ninety degrees). And the rainy part of the year is between December and April, again with eighty- to ninety-degree temperatures.* **Currency:** *The unit of exchange is the kwacha, K1.00 equaling about $1.40 U.S. Now if the kwacha is not exotic-sounding enough for you, consider the ngwee, of which there are one hundred to the kwacha, each worth about 1.25 American cents.* **Principal European language:** *English is the official language. The daily newspapers are English-language, the government conducts its business in English, and all educated Zambians speak it. But there are half a dozen principal African languages, as well, Bemba and Nyanja the chief among these.* **Domestic transport:** *Zambia Airways, operated with management and technical assistance provided by Alitalia, connects Lusaka, the capital, with Livingstone (site of Victoria Falls), the Copper Belt, and game reserves. It flies also to such neighboring countries as Malawi, Zaïre, Kenya, Tan-*

zania, and Mauritius, as well as to Rome and London. Several air charter services fly between Lusaka and Livingstone and the game reserves. The Zambia National Tourist Bureau has a spiffy fleet of air-conditioned buses and safari wagons for sightseeing and transfers in major areas, and for scheduled service between Lusaka and Livingstone. Self-drive cars may be rented in Lusaka and Livingstone, and chauffeur-driven cars in Lusaka. The road network continues to improve, the government policy being to pave all roads from key provincial centers to the capital. The Lusaka–Livingstone drive, via the Mundli Hills, takes about six hours, but the most noted highway is the Great North Road, linking Lusaka, Ndola, and the Tanzanian capital of Dar es Salaam, on the Indian Ocean. The railway linking landlocked Zambia and Tanzania (estimated completion date: 1975) is perhaps the most publicized of modern times. It is a joint Zambian-Tanzanian venture, with the bill—some three hundred million dollars—being paid by the People's Republic of China. **Further information:** *The Zambia National Tourist Bureau's American office is at 150 East 58th Street, New York, other branches are in London, Frankfurt, and Livingstone, with the headquarters (P. O. Box 17) in Lusaka.*

INTRODUCING ZAMBIA

Of the modern African states, Zambia is surely among the most remarkable. There seems no middle ground for its assets and liabilities; they run to extremes. Of the assets the top three are a vein of copper that makes Zambia the world's principal exporter of that metal; a first President—Kenneth Kaunda—who is one of the brightest young leaders on the continent; and a natural marvel—Victoria Falls—which is one of the wonders of the world and places Zambia in Africa's top touristic rank.

The minus side is quite as formidable. Zambia is landlocked, with no seacoast—and therefore no harbors—of its own. And

Zambia is southern, the sole nation with an enlightened, progressive policy in all of southern Africa. Its immediate neighbor, the Republic of Rhodesia, is ex-Southern Rhodesia (Zambia, before it became sovereign, was the British protectorate of Northern Rhodesia), which is outdone in the realm of white supremacy only by the Republic of South Africa, a land so rich and powerful that it figures excessively heavily on the southern Africa scene. Still another neighbor of Zambia is the Portuguese colony of Mozambique. Little Malawi—ex-Nyasaland—is sovereign, to be sure, but with an Uncle Tom kind of policy, *vis-à-vis* its relations with giant South Africa. Botswana (ex-Bechuanaland) is independent, too, but still too new a nation to have achieved any kind of stature for itself. And even newer are the little black-enclave states of Swaziland and Lesotho (ex-Basutoland), still so poor that they dare not make themselves appreciably offensive to the lily-white government of South Africa.

The result is that Zambia, since it became independent in 1964, has oriented itself to the north. It found that it had much more in common with the Kenya of Kenyatta, the Tanzania of Nyerere, the Zaïre of Mobutu, even the Ethiopia of Haile Selassie, than with the Rhodesia of Ian Smith, the Malawi of Dr. Banda, the African colonies of fascist Portugal, let alone the Big Brother apartheid of South Africa.

Independence for Zambia has, therefore, meant considerably more of an adjustment than has been the case in most African countries. There were, to begin with, the powerful, foreign-owned companies that controlled the copper mines, leaving little of their wealth within the country. Over a period of a half decade, the government exercised more control in this area, becoming majority shareholder in the two companies by 1969, and later also assuming controlling interest of banks, insurance companies, major department stores, and other business firms of substance.

Communications with the outer world became a major problem, too, for as a British territory, before and during the short-lived, unhappy period of the Federation of Rhodesia and Nyasaland, Zambia had been linked with the south. When Rhodesia went off on its own in 1965, Zambia at once decided to improve the five-hundred-mile highway connecting Lusaka and Ndola with the Tanzanian port-capital of Dar es Salaam on the Indian Ocean. And to replace use of the Portuguese port of Beira in Mozambique, efforts were directed at the creation of a railroad to link Zambia with Tanzania and the sea. When none of Zambia's Western friends would help in this respect, Zambia and its neighbor, Tanzania, turned to the Chinese, who are providing not only capital (some three hundred million dollars) but technical know-how and labor—some thirteen thousand "advisers"—as well. The first 313-mile stretch of the 1162-mile railroad was completed in late 1971; the project is scheduled to be finished in 1974.

Independence meant a new national airline, too. The old Central African Airways of the Federation period went its way, with each of the three ex-Federation partners starting its own. Zambia, knowing it needed management assistance to run an international, intercontinental airline, turned not to its old colonial master, Britain, but to Italy's Alitalia for help, quite possibly remembering not only the expertise of the Italian technicians who built the Kariba Dam on the Zambezi River in the years just before independence, but recalling their affability, as well, and the refreshingly unpatronizing way in which they collaborated with their African coworkers on that monumental project.

With its copper revenues, Zambia has been able to spend money for the long and sadly neglected education of its people, and not only in elementary schools. There has been a high-school building program, and the new University of Zambia in Lusaka has one of the handsomest and best-equipped campuses on the continent. Housing, particularly in the towns, has had priority, too (Lusaka is a model African city in this respect). And power is foremost in government planning, for although the earlier-mentioned Kariba Dam is now jointly owned by Rhodesia and Zambia, it is the Zambians' bad luck that the dam's generating plant is on the Rhodesian bank of the Zambezi. The Zambians now want to build a dam and hydroelectric station on the Kafue

River, entirely within their territory. Concurrently, the development of rural Zambia continues, with modernization of agriculture and village life the goals, difficult as they are. President Kenneth Kaunda was re-elected to his second term in 1968. His longtime Vice President, Simon M. Kapwepwe, broke with him in 1971 to form his own opposition party. He was arrested by the government in 1972, and his party banned.

Their big, Texas-sized plateau of a land, though inhabited by early Iron Age farmers a thousand years ago, was to know invasions in later centuries by blacks from Zaïre and, more recently, Arab slave traders and Europeans. Dr. Livingstone discovered Victoria Falls in 1855. In 1891, the area became a kind of company colony, administered by the copper barons of the British South Africa Company. The British government took over the reins in 1924, creating the Protectorate of Northern Rhodesia. The thirties saw the arrival on the scene of slews of get-rich-quick Britons come to cash in on the really big copper boom. With their counterparts in Southern Rhodesia, they gradually got London to let them become domestically self-governing, as the Federation of Rhodesia and Nyasaland. That lasted from 1953 until 1964, by which time the Africans in all three territories—the two Rhodesias and Nyasaland—came to realize that they had been had: their Federation was a racist South Africa-in-the-making. There were inquiries and commissions and debates *ad infinitum.* And then the Federation dissolved. Southern Rhodesia became the Republic of Rhodesia, breaking away from the mother country when it would not condone its racist politics. Nyasaland became Malawi, black in government and populace but a rather pathetic patsy for its white South African neighbors. And Northern Rhodesia became sovereign—but with no messing around. Its new name derives from the African name of the Zambezi River. (One country named for Cecil Rhodes seems quite sufficient.)

With all of its problems and projects and growing pains, and with so many hostile neighbors furious that its copper is under black control, Zambia comes up with another surprise: tourism.

One would think it might conclude that its collective hands were full enough. But President Kaunda is a well-traveled man. (I first heard him speak in 1959 in New York's Carnegie Hall, and I was embarrassed for my country when, a little over a decade later, he returned here, not only as President of his own country, but as chairman of the Organization of African Unity, only to have President Nixon reportedly cancel a pre-arranged White House meeting, and to reschedule it at a time when President Kaunda was scheduled to address the United Nations General Assembly in New York, thus making the Nixon meeting impossible. A year later, after offending not only Zambia but all of the African countries who are members of the OAU, Mr. Nixon had the courtesy to receive in Washington Mr. Kaunda's successor as head of the OAU, President Moktar Ould Daddah of Mauritania.) The Kaunda government not only welcomes tourists from friendly countries (it justifies its visa rigmarole because of the proximity of Rhodesian, South African, and Portuguese neighbors of whom it is understandably wary). But it operates a professionally staffed tourist bureau that actively and skillfully solicits tourism through its offices both at home and in Britain, continental Europe, and America. I suggest you go. Aside from Victoria Falls and the modern cities and the game parks and the good facilities (Inter•Continental Hotels, with its American know-how, is on the scene in two cities, to give you an idea), Zambia typifies the kind of modern African state that we want to see more of. Because, unlike so many others, it has that copper money to invest in its future, it is busy, up and at 'em, doing things, experimenting, not always succeeding, making mistakes, but busy. Trying. Out to seek its own destiny.

YOUR VISIT TO ZAMBIA

The trick about Zambia, the touristic trick, that is, is to stay long enough to see more than Victoria Falls. Even the Zambians themselves tend to sell their capital short as a visitor destination. And they shouldn't. Include Lusaka. Of course, visit the Falls and Livingstone. Arrange, as well, for an excursion to at least one of the major national parks, Kafue or Luangwa Valley, staying a night or two, for the accommodations are good. Compared to such heavily traveled parts of the continent as Egypt or Morocco or Kenya, Zambia is relatively virgin tourist territory. The visitor from abroad still is regarded as an individual—and an interesting individual, at that. This is a situation to be savored for as long as it lasts.

Lusaka: The republic's capital is everything that the seat of government of a young African state should be: modern and still-a-building, spotlessly clean and handsome, at once a governmental-cultural-commercial melting pot. Lusaka is not now, and will not be for many years to come, a southern counterpart of Nairobi. It is much lower-key, considerably quieter, and no question about it, without the diversion to detain one for an overlong introductory period. Withal, it is agreeable. If you stay at the Lusaka Inter•Continental, you find yourself in the very center of the city's social/diplomatic life. You cool off with dips at the pool. And you take in the sights. The Parliament, housing the unicameral national legislature, is a honey of a modern-design structure, with a visitors' gallery from which you may watch the members debate bills, and a splendid copper dome. The late Princess Royal, aunt of Queen Elizabeth II, laid the cornerstone in 1964. The Anglican Cathedral of the Holy Cross, built before independence, is one of the loveliest modern churches in Africa (its cornerstone was laid by Queen Mother Elizabeth in 1957). There is a new-as-tomorrow Hospital Center, a zippy Public Library (within: the city's information center, with maps, brochures, and the like), middle, low, and low-low housing projects, some of them very well done indeed. (One of the older projects is the site of the birthplace of President Kaunda, a simple little house that is now a national historic site), rather striking office buildings (the one to pause at is the Anglo American Building, housing the Lusaka branch of the Zambian National Museum in Livingstone, which shows the work—much of it excellent—of contemporary Zambian painters and sculptors.)

Main Street is Cairo Road—so named years ago when Lusaka was a pioneer outpost on the Cape-to-Cairo route. It is a wide, wide boulevard in the center of which ambulatory curio sellers vend their very ordinary woodcarvings. There are several massive department stores that are interesting for browsing, with wares ranging from Polish china and Bulgarian *feta*-type cheese to Gilbey's gin and Indonesian batiks, from which Zambian women fashion *chitenge*, the national dress.

Lusaka's open-air market is vast and well-kept, with vendors selling everything from chickens to chairs, including millet, from which the locals make their own beer, dried tobacco that smells good, and dried fish that doesn't. Woodland, in contrast, is the posh residential area—worth driving through—with its showplace the imposing mansion that had been home to governors of Northern Rhodesia—as Government House—and now, renamed State House, is the President's residence. Just outside of town is the fourteen-million-dollar conference center that was built for a meeting of the heads of state of Third World nations in 1970—to so much criticism that it may still not be open to the public at the time of your visit; the beautiful campus of the University of Zambia, which you do well to inspect (note the gardens) and an unusual Botanical Garden.

Livingstone and Victoria Falls: The town of Livingstone, touristic capital of the republic, still has about it the quietly inviting *ambiance* that typified it before independence. There are differences, though, important differences. Before Northern Rhodesia became Zambia and Southern Rhodesia, Rhodesia, Livingstone straddled both sides of the Zambezi. And one crossed the river-spanning bridge as one would a fairly wide boulevard. Today, though, things are different. The Livingstone—or northern—side of the Zambezi is Zambia. Across the bridge is the town of Victoria Falls, Rhodesia. Regulations may change, of course, but the way things stand currently, at least in the case of American citizens, one may cross from Zambia to Rhodesia on the bridge, and either stay in Rhodesia (no visa is needed for Americans) or return to Zambia. But one may not cross over to Zambia from Rhodesia without a Zambian visa affixed to one's passport.

As in Lusaka, Inter•Continental is the key hotel word. IHC's Livingstone outpost is the Musi-o-Tunya Inter•Continental. Musi-o-Tunya means "The Smoke that Thunders" in the local language and that is what, quite aptly, the people have called Victoria Falls from time immemorial. As well they might. The falls are 326 feet at their highest, with the Zambezi 1850 yards wide at the point of the falls. The normal dry-season annual flow of water over the falls is 150 million gallons per minute, and the spray, which rises hundreds of feet into the air, can be seen as far as twenty miles away. You can easily spend half a day looking at the falls from the various bridges, walks, paths and belvederes.

But Livingstone has other lures. Most important, beyond doubt, is the National Museum of Zambia, which has a first-rate collection of the art—masks, carvings, other artifacts—of the various regions of the republic. There are, as well, an easily driven through game park (the animals have been especially imported for the purpose of being viewed), a dance troupe that performs traditional dances on a regular schedule, and sundowner (cocktail-hour) cruises, with drinks and dancing, along the Zambezi on luxury launches.

Kafue National Park: two hundred miles west of Lusaka, is billed by the Zambians as "the largest game sanctuary in Africa." With an area equaling that of Wales, this is a fair description. There is no question but that it is big, nor that it offers the visitor a superb opportunity to observe a variety of wildlife. Species seen at Kafue include elephant, lion, leopard, buffalo, hippo, crocodile, waterbuck, and other antelope. Unique to Kafue are night game-viewing tours, for viewing nocturnal prowlers such as leopard, cheetah, and hyena. One may go on one's own for a day or two, or on longer, all-inclusive camera safaris. Most comfortable accommodation is at the modern Ngoma Lodge, with its own swimming pool; or at the more rugged Safari Village. The season: May through December.

Luangwa Valley National Park: 340 miles east of Lusaka, embraces six thousand square miles, is open from May to November, and has quite as diverse an animal population as Kafue. Animal-viewing treks—by foot, with experienced guards accompanying—are a feature at Luangwa. The park's principal lodge is Mfuwe, but there are a number of other simpler camps.

Other national parks: Modernized lodges are to be found at two areas on Lake Tanganyika—Kasaba Bay and Nkamba Bay. And, toward the end of 1971, President Kaunda signed an agreement with a conservation group called Wildlife Conservation International, headed by American businessman A. H. Stange, to create a twenty-four-hundred-square-mile wildlife refuge, on the banks of the Zambezi in the southeastern section of the country. The area is one where poaching by hunters had almost wiped out vast numbers of animals, including the red lechwe, which once numbered in the hundreds of thousands but has been reduced to some eighty thousand. The new refuge is to include visitor-viewing facilities and a center for the study of the ecology of the area. The tentative name of the new park is Zambia International Wildlife Park No. 1. Zambia is renting it to the conservation group for a twenty-five-year period for a "peppercorn" rent of a dollar a year.

The Copper Belt is much more frequently the destination of business rather than pleasure visitors to Zambia. Still, for the tourist interested in copper mining, it is by no means without interest. The hub of the area is the wealthy town of *Ndola*, where the lures are modern hotels (one has a casino), good restaurants, well-stocked shops full of imported luxury goods for the well-to-do mining families, the interesting Monkey Fountain Zoo, and a number of private clubs abounding in sports facilities and usually offering temporary memberships to visitors. Source of all the riches are the mines at nearby Kwana Mkubwa. *Kitwe*, some forty miles west of Ndola, has a pair of copper mines, and an affluent populace with all of the expected amenities. *Chingola*, some thirty miles west of Kitwe, boasts the richest copper lode in the country at its Nchanga mine. It is likewise proud of an eighteen-hole golf course, one of the best in southern Africa. The Copper Belt, with its excessive concentration of European mining personnel and their families, has clung much longer than it should have to the kind of racist attitudes that continue to prevail among whites in Rhodesia and South Africa. Prejudice can no longer be as overt, in this black republic, as it once was. But it has not yet disappeared.

SHOPPING

Take a look at the superb carvings, masks, basketry, and pottery, and weapons in the National Museum of Zambia at Livingstone, and then take a look at what the curio vendors are hawking along Cairo Road in Lusaka, and you wonder if you're in the same country. There are, of course, some better-quality things than the Cairo Road stuff, but not, when all is said and done, a great many. Zambia, like so many African countries, is losing touch with its rich traditional culture. At any rate, here are some sources, for browsing if not for buying. In *Lusaka*, the gift shop of the Lusaka Inter•Continental Hotel offers a sampling of what is currently available. But don't stop there. Much more fun are the big department stores of Cairo Road, particularly Mwaiseni and ZCBC. In both of these, there are departments vending locally produced copperware—bowls, vases, ashtrays, cigarette boxes, trays, and the like. There are exceptions to the rule, of course, but by and large, the designs of this excellent-quality copper are sadly tacky. The situation is not unlike that of another great copper-producing country, Chile, whose locally made wares are of a similarly low artistic level. One would hope that the copper producers, with their foreign contacts, might get a designer or two to come up with some good ideas. Also available in the department stores are charming Zambian-designed Christmas cards (particularly at Mwaiseni), the all-ocasion, short-sleeved safari suits popularized by President Kaunda and wearable everywhere in tropical Africa; bolts of Indonesian *batik* cloth, the printed cotton goods Zambian women use to fashion their national costume, the *chitenge;* locally produced industrial products, including good-looking china, and other wares from food to furniture, from points throughout both capitalist and Communist worlds. In *Livingstone,* the National Museum of Zambia operates a shop of its own that is probably the best single source of authentic handicrafts, with the carved ivory particularly outstanding, and the annual museum calendar a noteworthy souvenir. Figures of better-known woodcarvers like Sililo and Brown are to be found in the Curio Shop, and zebraskins are available at the Zambezi Game Skin and Curio Company. *Elsewhere,* there are curio shops in the leading hotels and the game park lodges, as well as itinerant curio sellers. Additional purchases might include the English-language newspapers, the *Times* of Zambia, the Zambia *Sunday News,* and the Zambia *Mail;* they provide a lively picture of day-to-day Zambian affairs. Zambian magazines, also valuable for background, include *New Writing from Zambia* and *University,* a publication of the University of Zambia.

CREATURE COMFORTS

HOTELS—Standards are high, both in the towns and at the national parks. You will be very comfortable. In **Lusaka,** the Lusaka Inter•Continental leads among the hotels. Guest rooms are tastefully decorated, all with bath, of course, as well as air conditioning. Additionally, there are a rooftop restaurant-*boîte* that is the smartest in town, a good-looking, well-operated lobby-floor coffee shop, a cocktail lounge that is a principal Lusaka congregating place, and a honey of a pool. Highly recommended. No. 2—and I can remember it from the time I researched the first edition of this book, when Zambia was still Northern Rhodesia—is the Ridgeway. It remains attractive and well-operated, with its ace-in-the-hole a restaurant-café flanking the reflecting pool (for looks, not for swimming, more's the pity) of its inner court. Many, but not all rooms, have bath and air conditioning. The Lusaka Hotel, off Cairo Road downtown, is essentially a commercial hotel—clean, modern, and offering private bath with many, but not all, of its rooms. Out of town are the modern Andrews Motel—all of its thirty rooms have bath and there's a pool, and the smaller Copper Chalice; all of its eight rooms have baths, and there is a pool. But this place is best known for its restaurant and nightly dancing. Which leads us to dining in Lusaka. The in-town leader is the Inter•Continental; there is dinner-dancing and entertainment nightly on the roof, as well as the coffee shop and the pool-café. The Ridgeway Hotel offers both its Ambassador and Pool Terrace restaurants, with dancing in the former. There is Italian food at the Rosi, Chinese cuisine at the Lotus Inn, steaks and dinner-dancing at the Carlton Café, African music at the Tambalala, and rock/soul music at the Rockwood Pleasure Resort. **Livingstone's** leader is still another Inter•Continental, this one called Musi-o-Tunya. The M.O.T. Inter•Continental has the falls as its front yard, with a swimming pool, as well. Within, in the main pavilion, are a congenial cocktail lounge, a neat little coffee shop, and the handsome main dining room. The big, air-conditioned bedrooms, all with bath, of course, are in a pair of separate buildings. This one-hundred-room hostelry is the smallest in the global Inter•Continental chain, and, at the same time, the most intimate, with a delightful, relaxing *ambiance*. No. 2 is the elderly North Western Hotel, well operated, with private bath in its better rooms, and a restaurant. **Kafue National Park:** Ngoma Lodge features a cluster of two-room chalets around a central building at which is located a swimming pool, with the restaurant and bar-lounge within. Each chalet has its own bath. Safari Village, seventeen miles northeast of Ngoma Lodge, comprises eight thatched-roof shelters each accommodating two persons, with showers and toilets in a separate building. Food and supplies are brought from Ngoma, and meals are prepared over open fires. Half a dozen simple camps are to be found elsewhere at Kafue. **Luangwa Valley National Park:** Mfuwe Lodge is Luangwa Valley's principal shelter. It offers comfortable accommodation (some units have private facilities), air conditioning, a swimming pool, restaurant, and bar-lounge. On the drawing boards are plans for an additional 120-bed lodge in this park. **Kasaba Bay, Lake Tanganyika:** Kasaba Bay Lodge, modernized and expanded, with a group of self-contained chalets its chief pride; restaurant, bar, lounge. **Nkamba Bay, Lake Tanganyika:** Nkamba Bay Lodge, though smaller than Kasaba Bay Lodge, is quite as modern; it too has had recent improvements, including self-contained chalets with private facilities, and there are a restaurant and bar-lounge. **Ndola's** Savoy Hotel bespeaks the wealth of this Copper Belt headquarters city. Modern, attractively decorated, and with seventy-eight rooms, all with bath. There are first-rate dine-dance-drink facilities, as well, and a special attraction is the casino—Zambia's first. The Elephant and Castle Hotel follows; about half of its rooms have baths; restaurant and bars. In **Kitwe** one's choice should be the Edinburgh. All fifty-nine of its good-looking rooms and suites have baths. The restaurant is one of the most inviting in Zambia, and there are a trio of bars. **Government rest houses**—simple but clean and inexpensive—are to be found in rural areas throughout the country.

INDEX

O4